CHARLIE VS GARRET

CHARLIE VS GARRET

The rivalry that shaped modern Ireland

EOIN O'MALLEY

First published in the UK in 2025 by Eriu
An imprint of Bonnier Books UK
5th Floor, HYLO, 105 Bunhill Row,
London, EC1Y 8LZ

Copyright © Eoin O'Malley, 2025

All rights reserved.
No part of this publication may be reproduced, stored or transmitted in any form or by any means, electronic, mechanical, photocopying or otherwise, without the prior written permission of the publisher.

The right of Eoin O'Malley to be identified as Author of this work has been asserted by him in accordance with the Copyright, Designs and Patents Act, 1988.

A CIP catalogue record for this book is available from the British Library.

Hardback ISBN: 978-1-80444-268-5

Also available as an ebook

3 5 7 9 10 8 6 4 2

Typeset by IDSUK (Data Connection) Ltd
Printed and bound by CPI (UK) Ltd, Croydon CR0 4YY

Every reasonable effort has been made to trace copyright holders of material reproduced in this book, but if any have been inadvertently overlooked the publishers would be glad to hear from them.

This book is a work of Non-Fiction. Some names may have been changed to respect the privacy of those mentioned.

The authorised representative in the EEA is
Bonnier Books UK (Ireland) Limited.
Registered office address: Block B, The Crescent Building,
Northwood, Santry,
Dublin 9, D09 C6X8, Ireland
compliance@bonnierbooks.ie
www.bonnierbooks.co.uk

En memoria de mis padres

Contents

Chronology of Key Political Events	ix
Preface	xiii
1. Flawed Pedigree	1
2. Children of Men	15
3. Young Turks	31
4. Arms and the Man	49
5. Trading Places	71
6. Let's Sack Jack	89
7. Taking Control	103
8. Revolving Doors	119
9. The Survivor	133
10. Garret the Good, the Bad and the Ugly	151
11. The Northern Line	167
12. Drifters	181
13. Top Boy	195
14. The Bonfire of the Vanities	213
15. Long Shadows	233
Acknowledgements	247
Endnotes	251
Glossary	289
Biographies	293
Index	323

Chronology of key political events

1951   General election. Éamon de Valera becomes Taoiseach of a minority government dependent on support of independent TDs.
Charles Haughey's first election in Dublin North-East. He fails to get elected.

1954   General election. Second inter-party government formed between Fine Gael, the Labour Party and Clann na Talmhan, with John A. Costello as Taoiseach.
Haughey again fails to get elected in Dublin North-East.

1956   Haughey loses the Dublin North-East by-election.

1957   General election. Fianna Fáil win an overall majority. De Valera is Taoiseach.
Haughey is elected in Dublin North-East edging out his Fianna Fáil running mate Harry Colley by fewer than 100 votes.

1959   Presidential election. De Valera elected President. Seán Lemass becomes Taoiseach.

1960   Haughey appointed parliamentary secretary to the Minister for Justice.

1961	General election sees Lemass elected Taoiseach in a Fianna Fáil minority government. Haughey appointed Minister for Justice.
1964	Haughey appointed Minister for Agriculture.
1965	Liam Cosgrave becomes leader of Fine Gael. FitzGerald elected to Seanad Éireann for Fine Gael.
1966	Lemass retires. Jack Lynch becomes Taoiseach. Haughey becomes Minister for Finance.
1968	Referendum to change electoral system is defeated.
1969	Outbreak of the Troubles. General Election sees Fianna Fáil government returned with Lynch as Taoiseach. FitzGerald elected to the Dáil in Dublin South-East. Haughey re-appointed as Minister for Finance.
1970	Haughey sacked as a result of the Arms Crisis, and later acquitted in arms trial.
1972	Ireland votes to join the EEC.
1973	General election. National Coalition formed, with Liam Cosgrave as Taoiseach. Garret FitzGerald becomes Minister for Foreign Affairs.
1974	Stormont executive in Northern Ireland collapses.
1975	Haughey returns to Fianna Fáil front bench.
1977	Election sees Fianna Fáil landslide. Jack Lynch returned as Taoiseach.

FitzGerald becomes leader of Fine Gael. Frank Cluskey becomes leader of the Labour Party. Haughey appointed Minister for Health and Social Welfare.

1979 European and local elections.
Jack Lynch retires as Taoiseach and leader of Fianna Fáil.
Haughey elected Fianna Fáil leader and appointed Taoiseach.

1980 First hunger strikes begin in Northern Ireland.

1981 Second hunger strikes begin. General election in June sees minority Fine Gael-Labour coalition take power with FitzGerald as Taoiseach. Michael O'Leary becomes leader of the Labour Party.

1982 General election in February. Minority Fianna Fáil government elected, Haughey becomes Taoiseach.
Dick Spring becomes leader of the Labour Party.
General election in November. Fine Gael-Labour coalition formed with FitzGerald as Taoiseach.

1983 Phone tapping of journalists revealed. Haughey survives no-confidence motion.
George Colley dies.

1984 New Ireland Forum reports.

1985 Des O'Malley expelled from Fianna Fáil.
Anglo-Irish Agreement signed.
Progressive Democrats founded.

1987 General election sees Fianna Fáil minority government elected with Haughey as Taoiseach.

FitzGerald steps down as leader of Fine Gael.
New Fine Gael leader, Alan Dukes, announces Tallaght Strategy.

1989 General election is inconclusive. Fianna Fáil-PD coalition formed. Haughey becomes Taoiseach for the fourth time.

1990 Ireland hosts EC presidency.
Mary Robinson elected President of Ireland.

1991 Challenge to Haughey's leadership. Albert Reynolds resigns from cabinet.

1992 Haughey steps down as Taoiseach and leader of Fianna Fáil.
Albert Reynolds wins Fianna Fáil leadership and becomes Taoiseach.
PDs leave government.
General election in November sees Fianna Fáil-Labour coalition formed with Albert Reynolds as Taoiseach.

PREFACE

This book is both a long time coming and put together very quickly. I am (still) writing a book on the performance of Taoisigh from 1979 on, with a view to charting both how the men holding the office (there have only been men thus far) operated and how the office has changed. I picked 1979 as a starting point because it was then you could see a centralisation of power into the office of the Taoiseach. Charles J. Haughey expanded the Department of the Taoiseach both in terms of numbers of staff, but also in roles. What had been a 'post office' – an administrative office designed to circulate government decisions and ensure correct protocols were adhered to – became a centre of power. Haughey changed the Department into a powerhouse, driving policy change. It set the government's agenda rather than facilitating the government's decisions. In the old phrase 'chairman or chief?', Haughey looked like a chief. His successor, Garret FitzGerald, looked the same. Both were energetic, hugely ambitious and intent on change. They were going to use the office to deliver that change. That book would then look at how these two men and their successors used the office of Taoiseach.

I wrote half a book on that, and then stopped. After a hiatus, I went back to the book and realised it was too long. Much of what I had written was off the argument of the book I had in mind. Around the same time I listened to an *Irish Times* podcast on Haughey and FitzGerald. While what Pat Leahy and Hugh Linehan said on the podcast was not wrong, their description of the Charlie/ Garret-dominated 1980s suggested that the two men had parallel careers, and sequential premierships. One took over and ruled, and then the other took over and ruled. What was missing was how the two men (and how democratic leaders in general) interacted. Leaders don't just say what they want and attempt to sell it to the public and then deliver it within the political system; leaders operate under constraints, and part of the constraining environment under which they operate is a sort of strategic game with the opposition leader, where one leader tries to back the other into a corner.

With Haughey and FitzGerald this happened a lot.

So I decided to write this book instead, one that looks at each of them and how they performed, but also emphasises the extent to which they influenced each other.

Growing up in Ireland in the 1980s you could not help but be aware of Charles Haughey and Garret FitzGerald. They dominated the news, their images were on our TV screens, we heard their distinctive voices on the radio and we saw them on posters on billboards and lampposts. It was the Garret and Charlie Show. Not only were they everywhere, they mattered. The decisions they took impacted our lives. Oddly, however, the differences in policy were not that great.

The two men, Charles Haughey and Garret FitzGerald, were the Big Beasts of the political jungle, but there were other significant political figures in the 1980s. People such as Ray MacSharry, Des O'Malley and Dick Spring also mattered. Des O'Malley was my father, and so I saw these events and these men with a particular and a peculiar view. In the 1981 election, as a good little Fianna Fáiler, I proudly displayed an election poster of Charlie Haughey from my bedroom window. At this time it was becoming clearer to me that the view of Haughey in my house was less than positive. By contrast, there was a respect for Garret FitzGerald that one normally doesn't have for people from the other side.

Des O'Malley was engaged in a battle for control of Fianna Fáil with Charles Haughey and over that decade I saw that battle just behind the front line. I heard conversations at home and keenly felt the tension in the house. I also heard it played out on *Morning Ireland* each morning, read it in the paper each day and watched it on *Today Tonight* at night. It was a time of turmoil. There were a lot of elections; there was a lot of other politics, the daily reports of bombing and murders in the North, the hunger strikes, the efforts at peace. The economy was in poor shape and domestic politics struggled to react.

This book is not a work of history; I am not a historian. I am a political scientist. There is an argument running through this book that competing political leaders influence each other. They do not run on parallel tracks, each taking over and running a country for a time, with opposition making no impact. Rather, they try to trap each other, and push the other to do things they would not otherwise have done. Haughey and FitzGerald were conscious of each other and acted differently in government and opposition because of the other. In a way, the electoral competition prevented them from dealing with the problems the country faced.

For this ongoing work I have interviewed about a hundred former ministers, TDs, senators, advisers and civil servants. I did long interviews with both Charles Haughey and Garret FitzGerald in the mid-2000s on how they constructed and ran their governments. They were both fascinating, gracious and charming. I was very grateful for their time. I am also grateful for their work.

The 1980s was a depressing time in Ireland. But from that crisis the seeds of a new, radically different country were planted. Even though they did not like one another and spent much of their careers working against each other, they complemented one another. Both had serious flaws, which will be interrogated in the course of the book. The Ireland that we see today is imperfect, but in most ways it is substantially better than it was. Credit and blame for both the improvements and imperfections cannot be laid solely at the feet of these two men, but they, their rivalry and how they interacted, significantly shaped modern Ireland.

Eoin O'Malley
Cádiz, April 2025

1.

Flawed Pedigree

In the summer of 1979 Pat Kerrigan, a Labour TD from Cork City, and Seán Brosnan, a Fianna Fáil TD representing Cork North-East, died. Their deaths necessitated two by-elections, which traditionally the party of the deceased member 'moves the writ' to call. With Fianna Fáil's large majority there was no threat to the sitting government from the results of these by-elections. As the Taoiseach, Jack Lynch, was from Cork, Fianna Fáil was expected to win both seats. It expected it itself. Despite the party's poor result in that June's local elections, a review of the two constituencies just before polling concluded that 'only apathy would worry Fianna Fáil in Cork'.[1] But this level of expectation was misplaced. There was a sense that Lynch's government lacked the energy or ideas to deal with the mounting economic and security problems facing the state. In March 1979 over 150,000 PAYE workers marched in Dublin to protest against tax inequality. It was the largest gathering since Jim Larkin led the protests against the lock-out of workers in 1913.

If the 1960s had been a time of optimism in Ireland, the 1970s saw that optimism give way to despair. The oil crises of the 1970s meant that long queues at petrol stations were normal. The Fine Gael–Labour coalition that took power in 1973 was both radical and conservative. The conservative instinct was to insist on balanced budgets; the radical one wanted to reform the Irish tax system with new taxes on wealth, capital gains and inheritance. But that government had limited room to manoeuvre. Inflation reached 21 per cent in 1975 and unemployment crept higher than it had been in the grim 1950s. In this context Fianna Fáil won an unprecedented majority in the 1977 election on the promise that tax cuts and spending would kick-start the economy. Initially popular, these policies failed to deliver on their promise.

In 1979, the Fianna Fáil government introduced a 2 per cent 'turnover tax' on farmers, a group who had been barely subject to any taxes. In a country that still had a sizeable and important agricultural base this was politically unpopular. High inflation led to strikes as workers demanded pay rises to make up for increasing prices. The year 1979 saw the highest number of days lost to industrial action since the late 1930s – about 1.5 million days.[2] A postal strike lasted 19 weeks, from February to June, making it one of the longest and most bitter strikes in the history of the public service. It included telephone operators and others employed by the Department of Posts and Telegraphs. At a time when business depended on a postal system, the strike severely damaged the economy. During the strike telephones were not repaired, and the dispute exposed a creaking telecom system in which customers could wait years to get a new phone connection.

Though the government stood firm and eventually conceded just a modest pay increase – much less than was demanded by the strikers – the strike was used by some within the party to destabilise the government. In fact, Fianna Fáil's large majority masked a deep split within a party that was once a monolith. The Arms Crisis in 1970 exposed divisions in Fianna Fáil over its policy on Northern Ireland. Fianna Fáil had a mix of 'Keep the Peace' pragmatists and 'Brits Out' nationalists, which varied in strength depending on what was happening in the North. The Troubles that dominated the 1970s had by 1979 taken almost two thousand lives. That year, 1979, was quieter, at least until August. Late that month the Provisional IRA assassinated Lord Mountbatten, a British war hero, confidant and relation of Queen Elizabeth and mentor to her son, Prince Charles, blowing up his boat off Mullaghmore in County Sligo. Later that day the IRA killed 18 British soldiers when a bomb went off under a travelling convoy near Warrenpoint, County Down. Lynch's response was inept and would get him into trouble. On 9 September Síle de Valera, a young Fianna Fáil backbencher, but one with a famous name, criticised her party leader for having abandoned republicanism.[3] Times were tough for Jack Lynch, and for the Irish people.

Yet 1979 was also a time of some optimism in Ireland. In late September Pope John Paul II visited Ireland. He said Mass in Dublin's Phoenix Park to over a million people. In all, over 2.5 million people attended some part of the papal visit. The country was delirious when John Paul II kissed the ground at Dublin Airport, and later, in Galway, when he told the 'Young people of Ireland, I love you', the crowd was in raptures. The Church seemed in its pomp. A traditional Irish music revival occurred alongside the emerging rock and punk scenes, with bands like Thin Lizzy, The Undertones and The Boomtown Rats attracting international attention. There was a new decade to come. Could the 1980s be Ireland's decade?

※ ※ ※

The by-elections were set for 7 November 1979. Garret FitzGerald, the leader of the opposition Fine Gael party, saw them as the first tests of the changes he had brought about in Fine Gael since taking over the party two years earlier. Fine Gael poured significant resources into the by-election campaigns, and FitzGerald himself featured prominently. Garret was the product it was selling.

FitzGerald was a conundrum. He was *Doctor* Garret FitzGerald, an academic prone to speaking in statistics rather than plain English. His hair was chaotic. He spoke at such speed that few could follow. He was too busy with ideas to concern himself with the aesthetics of politics. He didn't dress smartly. He looked and sounded otherworldly, and certainly not a smooth salesman for his party. Yet people admired his command of policy and his ability to rattle off relevant facts. Perhaps even more, they admired his integrity. Garret stood for something.

Traditionally Fine Gael was a part-time party that mainly stood for its opposition to Fianna Fáil. It wasn't a case of what Fine Gael *was* but what it *wasn't* . . . and it wasn't Fianna Fáil. FitzGerald had been one of the leaders of a group who had tried to impose an ideology on the party in the 1960s. When he took over as leader in 1977 FitzGerald professionalised the party, creating some enemies along the way. He also set out a vision of a more modern, secular Ireland that made Fine Gael look different, and attracted many women and young people to the party – and politics – for the first time. If the 1980s could be Ireland's decade, Garret could be the man to deliver that.

Fianna Fáil too put time and energy into winning these by-elections, with all senior cabinet ministers travelling to Cork to canvass. Despite these efforts and the expectations of observers, Fine Gael won both seats. There was elation for Garret. His reforms were working and Fine Gael could now take on Fianna Fáil in its leader's backyard. The defeats spelled significant trouble for Lynch, who was under mounting pressure within the party for his government's moderate stance on Northern Ireland. Fine Gael's victory in both by-elections had the effect of speeding up the departure of Jack Lynch, who had been planning to retire in early 1980. On 5 December 1979, Lynch announced his immediate retirement.

The contest for the leadership of Fianna Fáil was one Charles J. Haughey had waited over 13 years for. He was meant to contest it in 1966. Jack Lynch's 'interim' leadership lasted much longer than people had expected. Although it was meant to help him, the sudden leadership contest caught George Colley, the leading candidate for the Fianna Fáil leadership, off guard. Colley's people had assured Lynch that their man was safe. Now they weren't so sure.

There were no speeches allowed in Room 560 of Leinster House, where the Fianna Fáil party's 82 TDs assembled on 7 December 1979 to choose Lynch's replacement. It was a straight fight: Colley versus Haughey. Though they were the same age and had been to the same school, they were very different men. George Colley was 'straight, too damned straight' according to one ally, steeped in Fianna Fáil, a fluent Irish speaker, almost a clone of the ascetic men who had led the struggle for independence. But he was politically naive. Haughey was smart, possibly too smart. He was not born into Fianna Fáil, but had worked hard to cultivate grassroots support within the party. Though they were not fully aware of it, many suspected he had used his political positions to enrich himself, displaying a lifestyle that many of the old guard found vulgar. But Haughey was almost preternaturally conscious of power and how it worked.

Just to get to here was a remarkable achievement. In 1970 Haughey's political career appeared to be over. A modernising cabinet minister in the 1960s, he considered contesting the party leadership in 1966, but instead was appointed Minister for Finance. He was dashing and well dressed, and with his country house and his hunting he looked like an aristocrat. Haughey had never publicly expressed strong republican views, which made his involvement in a plot to import arms to help the nascent Provisional IRA so confounding. When the arms plot was revealed, Jack Lynch sacked Haughey, but Haughey was acquitted in a subsequent trial and remained in the party. Haughey used his time to travel the country to party meetings, building relationships with younger, ambitious would-be Fianna Fáil candidates, many of whom admired his association with the Arms Crisis. Charlie's popularity in the party made it hard for Lynch to resist bringing him back into the tent. Lynch returned him to the Fianna Fáil front bench in 1975 following his sort of exile. Back in government in 1977, Lynch brought Haughey into his cabinet. Many of the new intake in the Fianna Fáil landslide of 1977 were Haughey supporters, and he used his departments, Social Welfare and Health, to ensure that backbench TDs were supported for any constituency needs.

When Willie Kenneally, the parliamentary party chairman, announced the result of the leadership contest – 38 votes for Colley, 44 for Haughey – there was applause, but no cheering. It was immediately followed by the burning of the ballots, which briefly set off a fire alarm in the party room on the fifth floor of Leinster House. Habemus 'The Boss'. Ray MacSharry, the junior minister in George Colley's own department who had nominated Haughey, went out to tell supporters at the entrance of Leinster House. Then there was cheering. Though Haughey's campaign team had expected him to win, it still came as a relief. Haughey had maintained a very low profile in the short leadership campaign, and was thought by some of his team to be too confident. But Haughey had plotted his victory expertly. He won because he had put in years of work courting backbenchers.

In the party room Haughey spoke, expressing his great honour and humility at achieving the office of leader of Fianna Fáil, and soon-to-be Taoiseach. He thanked George Colley, his 'old school pal', for his offer of loyalty and support. Colley, though obviously shaken, praised Haughey's 'ability, capacity and flair', in turn pledging his full co-operation with the new leader.[4] Just after midday Haughey went down to give a press conference in the Seanad antechamber, flanked by the government chief whip, Michael Woods, and PJ Mara, Haughey's close adviser. They were accompanied by cheering supporters from the back benches of the parliamentary party pushing to get behind him. It was chiefly the backbenchers who had elected him, judging that Haughey offered the best chance to save their seats.[5]

Haughey fielded press questions deftly, provoking ironic cheers when he pronounced, 'I condemn the Provisional IRA and all their activities.' He set out 'the peaceful unification of Ireland as my primary political priority', but said that while there would be a shift in emphasis there would be no change in Fianna Fáil's 'northern policy', referencing the Fianna Fáil policy from October 1975, which called for a British statement of its intention to withdraw from Northern Ireland. Moving on to the economy, he made some uncontroversial comments about the economic development of the country, but did say that he would give a very high priority to developing a successful climate of industrial relations.

Haughey then went back to his large home, Abbeville, in Kinsealy, north County Dublin, where he received guests. One was Fianna Fáil TD Seán Doherty, one of his most enthusiastic supporters, who had earlier laughed when he heard Haughey's prediction of the result:

'Do you know, you're the worst fucking judge of people I ever met.'[6] But it didn't matter. He was the leader now. Some who had voted for Colley made the trip out, anxious to show that their loyalty was with the new man.[7] The party would row in behind him.

But not all were happy to declare their loyalty. George Colley met with his supporters at his home in Dartry on the southside of Dublin, where they discussed whether to serve in a Haughey cabinet if asked. They agreed it would be better to stay in to keep an eye on him.[8] Colley, who became Tánaiste, extracted extraordinary concessions; a veto over appointments to Justice and Defence. A few weeks later he would make a speech saying that he had never offered unconditional loyalty to Haughey.[9] Haughey demanded loyalty. According to some of those who worked closely with him, Haughey was an alpha male, who needed to be in control, and be seen to be in control. It angered him that he did not get the loyalty that he felt his predecessors had been given. This refusal would cause rancour within the party, which would rise and fall intermittently over the next five years.

※ ※ ※

While they did not like each other, there was never any personal rancour between Charles Haughey and Garret FitzGerald. They had known each other for decades, having been to college together in the intimate atmosphere of UCD's Earlsfort Terrace in the 1940s. Though they had never been close and were on different sides of a party divide, there was mutual respect for each other's ability. Haughey, the more senior of the two in the 1960s, had offered FitzGerald work. FitzGerald was accused of 'going easy' on Haughey in the inquiry in the aftermath of the arms trials because of their long relationship – something FitzGerald rejected.[10] FitzGerald did not fully trust Haughey, but Haughey was rarely anything other than charming. It was 'a relationship [that] was never intimate, but never hostile'.[11]

So it came as a surprise that in the debate on Haughey's election as Taoiseach, a moment usually reserved for polite well-wishing, that Garret FitzGerald took the unusual step of making a personal speech.

He actively tried to convince those Fianna Fáil TDs who had voted for Colley to vote against Haughey in the Dáil. Haughey, FitzGerald said, was unsuited to the office of Taoiseach because unlike his six predecessors, Haughey was not motivated by public service:

> Deputy Haughey presents himself here, seeking to be invested in office as the seventh in this line, but he comes with a flawed pedigree. His motives can be judged ultimately only by God but we cannot ignore the fact that he differs from his predecessors in that these motives have been and are widely impugned, most notably but by no means exclusively, by people within his own party, people close to him who have observed his actions for many years and who have made their human, interim judgement on him.[12]

FitzGerald was attacked for using the phrase 'flawed pedigree' to describe Haughey. This was no off-the-cuff comment. The speech was planned and written the night before with some advisers at his home in Rathmines. He later acknowledged that the phrase – immediately seized upon by Haughey's supporters – was a mistake. He blamed the hour of the night that it had been finished – 4.30 a.m. – and that he had not consulted with his wife, Joan, on the speech.[13] FitzGerald referred to Haughey's motives rather than his class, but as a comment from someone born into comfort among the Irish political elite to the son of a soldier raised in a lower-middle-class part of Dublin, it was interpreted differently. FitzGerald was certainly an intellectual snob, but probably not a class snob. The rest of FitzGerald's speech lost its impact.[14]

One of the primary reasons for FitzGerald's concern and distrust was Northern Ireland. Haughey rhetorically adopted a more Irish-republican approach to Northern Ireland than the rest of his senior party colleagues, but it was an approach that was popular among the Fianna Fáil grassroots. But Haughey's involvement in the Arms Crisis made him suspect. He was conspicuously wealthy, which led many to speculate about the source of his wealth. Haughey's election was expected to boost Fine Gael because it gave the party a clearer foil to market FitzGerald against – 'an uncovenanted bonus to Fine Gael' was how FitzGerald put it.[15] That didn't quite play out.

FitzGerald was obsessed with Haughey. Fine Gael went so far as to hire psychologists to prepare a report on Haughey that concluded that he was indecisive, not a trait Haughey ever displayed as a minister. Throughout the 1980s Fine Gael focused on Haughey as leader. FitzGerald seemed in fear of him, or at least in fear of what he might do. Haughey did not fear FitzGerald. He nearly always looked relaxed in debates, and remained more controlled than FitzGerald in communicating with the public. Yet there were times when FitzGerald cornered Haughey – not least when he accused Haughey of having 'fiddled the books' during a debate in the February 1982 election campaign. Haughey responded, 'That is not so. This is all fiction. Garret FitzGerald is making all this up out of his head. He can't substantiate a word of this.'[16] But the press didn't agree.

FitzGerald was a media darling, and the media rarely missed the chance to praise him. They created an image of him, encouraged by FitzGerald himself, as a sage-like figure. One contemporary journalist said of him, 'his knowledge [of foreign affairs] was awe-inspiring ... the brilliant intellect, the man with the total grasp of figures and economic factors and above all, the man of integrity.'[17] Haughey too cultivated a media following. He could be immense fun to be around and exuded a star quality that few others could match. When he first entered the Dáil he engaged a public relations consultant, something unheard of at the time. Journalists such as John Healy, a colourful if partisan *Irish Times* columnist, were courted to ensure his message would be delivered. However much they enjoyed him, many of the senior political correspondents increasingly viewed Haughey as a malevolent force. As a result he sometimes lost his temper with journalists. One recalled the reaction when he pushed Haughey on a particular point. Haughey ripped off the microphone and stormed out, shouting, 'I don't have to take this from a fucking RTÉ party political fucking hack like you – you can fuck off with your interview!' While stories such as these would do the rounds among journalists and politicians, amazingly such outbursts were never reported or broadcast.[18]

Though he had a healthy majority when he was elected Taoiseach in December 1979, Haughey's weakness within his own party meant that he would seek to get his own mandate, and so election preparations were stepped up in both Fianna Fáil and Fine Gael. But if FitzGerald was a hero in the country, his parliamentary party remained to be convinced. What mattered to the party was that he yielded it votes.[19] He was a vote-winner in the Cork by-elections, but he was also capable of basic political errors. When the party contested a by-election in Donegal in late 1980, FitzGerald failed to manage expectations in the party. He used the by-election as a plebiscite between Haughey and himself. Given it was Donegal, Fianna Fáil was always the likely winner, and so it transpired. According to one contemporary, FitzGerald became depressed by the result and stayed at home for ten days.[20]

❊ ❊ ❊

Over the course of the 1980s Garret FitzGerald and Charles J. Haughey would dominate Irish politics. They would face each other in four elections, and one or other of these two men would lead Irish governments until 1992. Though they governed Ireland for the whole of the 1980s, neither had stable majorities. FitzGerald governed only with the support of a divided Labour Party latterly led by an inexperienced though dogged Dick Spring. Haughey lost the majority he inherited in 1979 and it was never recovered. He struggled with party infighting, and in 1989 was forced to bring Fianna Fáil into a coalition government with a long-time rival, Des O'Malley.

It was a decade of remarkable change in Ireland. In the 1977 election Fianna Fáil and Fine Gael received over 80 per cent of the votes – the two parties dominated Irish politics. When Haughey assumed power in December 1979 the country was economically backward. One observer at the time noted that 'Despondency seems to be on the increase, as though the intractability of our problems has at last sapped our will to solve them'.[21] The Catholic Church appeared to be at the height of its powers. Bishop Eamonn Casey was the warm-up act for the Papal Mass at Galway racecourse dedicated to the youth of Ireland. It was attended by up to 300,000 people. Bishop Casey sang to the crowd alongside another well-known priest, Fr Michael Cleary, and welcomed the Pope when he arrived. In Northern Ireland violence had become depressingly normal. Each evening reports of bombs and shootings barely registered shock anymore, so common were they. Things were set to get even worse.

Just a few months after Haughey left office in early 1992, it was revealed that Éamonn Casey had fathered a child with an American woman, Annie Murphy. Her revelations on national television rocked the nation, and a few months later, after Fr Cleary's death, similar revelations were made about him. These were the start of a scandal that would destabilise the Catholic Church and eventually see it lose its considerable power in Irish society.

Haughey left office in February 1992 at a time of economic growth. Although unemployment was still high, it was falling, and there was a genuine sense that the country had moved on from the depression of the 1980s. Within two years the term 'Celtic Tiger' would be coined, and in retrospect it is clear that Ireland was at the start of a long period of unprecedented growth.

By 1992 there was the sense that there was a chance at peace in Northern Ireland, if not yet a permanent settlement. It was built on efforts by FitzGerald and Haughey to engage both the British government and violent nationalism. FitzGerald succeeded in getting an agreement that would transform the relationship with London, though Haughey opposed it and generally tried to prevent this success. Less than two years after Haughey's retirement, his and the UK prime minister Margaret Thatcher's successors, Albert Reynolds and John Major, would agree the Downing Street Declaration, which would set in motion a process on which their work would be built. That would lead their successors, Bertie Ahern and Tony Blair, to negotiate the signing of the Belfast or Good Friday Agreement, which would largely end a decades-long civil war.

In the election that took place some months after Haughey stood down in 1992, Fianna Fáil and Fine Gael's combined support was less than 65 per cent of the vote. The Dáil included three parties that had not existed in 1979 – the Green Party, the Progressive Democrats (PDs) and Democratic Left. The Labour Party had made its long-promised breakthrough. Coalition government, once an aberration, was now the norm, with Haughey having agreed to govern with the PDs in 1989. Ireland had a new president, Mary Robinson, who was unusual in more ways than simply being the first woman to hold that office.

These remarkable changes happened because of and at times despite political decisions and non-decisions mainly by these two men. Haughey is widely credited with Ireland turning the corner from 1987, but was enabled by and indeed this was planned by FitzGerald, who, before he retired from frontline politics, promised to support a minority Fianna Fáil government that would be fiscally responsible. How Garret FitzGerald and Charles Haughey interacted changed Ireland. Each looked over their shoulder to anticipate how the other might react. Throughout the decade both men made decisions that would change Ireland, but they also didn't make decisions or were less decisive than their personalities would have suggested, in part because of the other. When they each took control of Ireland both were confident and bursting with ideas. Haughey soon became concerned about his power within his party. That power had to be gained by a slow process of attrition, and it was only later that the confident, decisive figure would reemerge. FitzGerald took the opposite trajectory. He was initially full of confidence, but a weak coalition and a fear of Haughey made him hesitant and ineffectual.

This was in part a result of the type of politician each was. Neither Haughey nor FitzGerald wanted power as an end in itself. Both were progressive modernisers and intent on using their power and the state for positive social change. We can observe that in Haughey's early ministerial career and in the many initiatives FitzGerald started as Taoiseach. But they each took different approaches to politics.

Haughey was a pragmatist. He was aware of what could be achieved. He could be impatient with protocols and procedures, and was willing to ignore them if doing so could help him achieve his goal. But he rarely took on issues that looked doomed to fail. Haughey was rarely guilty of overreach, proposing large, expensive or polarising agendas. Many of the initiatives he was famous for in his ministerial career were discrete schemes, more easily deliverable, such as free travel or the Succession Act. Even when he took on a big project – social partnership, for example – he laid the groundwork to ensure that it could be delivered. Or he was cautious; for instance, in his early contacts with Sinn Féin/IRA, any actions were secret and deniable.

FitzGerald was an optimist. He would propose changes, in the expectation that he could convince others of their worth. FitzGerald struggled when people did not come around to his way of thinking. In his 'constitutional crusade' he castigated Irish society and the Irish state, and was shocked when people got defensive. He misunderstood the nature of political power. FitzGerald had done limited preparatory work, little work with Church leaders or outreach to the unionist community. He had not really prepared the Irish people. Nor had he thought to start with smaller, less divisive initiatives first. He had not even considered whether it would work – would secularising the Irish state make a blind bit of difference to unionist attitudes to a united Ireland? In suggesting an ambitious polarising agenda before the time was right, FitzGerald was guilty of strategic naivety. This overreach meant it inevitably failed.

FitzGerald did succeed as a sort of 'influencer'. He could not directly achieve goals, but he enabled them. First by normalising them, but also by allowing Haughey to eventually do things that Haughey was reluctant to try in his earlier periods as Taoiseach.

Both FitzGerald and Haughey set their governments' agendas, and their time in the office of Taoiseach was decisive for the direction of the country, good and bad. People's assessments of both men often depends on where they come from. When they died the reactions reflected their careers. Haughey passed away at home in Kinsealy on 13 June 2006, aged 80, having been treated for prostate cancer for several years. Garret FitzGerald died in the Mater Hospital on 19 May 2011 following a short illness, aged 85. Haughey's death caused many to reflect on the recently revealed controversies of his financial affairs. Garret FitzGerald was lauded, particularly in the letters pages of the *Irish Times*, the paper for which he had written for fifty years. For some, Haughey was brilliant but corrupt, with character flaws that prevented him succeeding, whereas FitzGerald was honest, a Taoiseach who did much to modernise Ireland and restore integrity to the body politic. For others Haughey was an effective leader who started Ireland on the road to what was to become the Celtic Tiger, whereas FitzGerald's flaws as a manager, and inability to delegate, prevented him from dealing with the faltering economy. Neither view is wholly accurate. Neither was the comic book hero nor the cartoon villain that is often portrayed. And whatever one's view of either man, their relationship and rivalry made them do things they would not have otherwise done, and had a lasting impact on Ireland well beyond the decade during which the two men dominated.

2.

CHILDREN OF MEN

Born months apart in the mid-1920s, Charles J. Haughey and Garret FitzGerald were both children of the new Irish Free State. Both sets of parents were deeply political. Both sets of parents were part of the Irish revolution, and their fathers both supported Michael Collins, the Treaty and the Free State. FitzGerald and Haughey had peripatetic early lives, and neither were 'from' where they eventually grew up. But Garret and Charlie came from very different backgrounds and would take very different routes to the top of Irish politics. They seemed to come from opposite ends of the social scale. FitzGerald was the son of a cabinet minister, living in large homes and going to elite schools. Haughey was the son of a soldier, who in the 1930s settled eventually in Donnycarney, an area predominantly made up of public housing schemes in the expanding suburbs on the northside of Dublin. He was educated in the local national school, and depended on a scholarship to go to the local Christian Brothers School.

These differences tend to be overemphasised, often to create myths. FitzGerald was not from as wealthy a background as is often suggested, though he was exceptionally well connected. Haughey did not come from poverty, though both his supporters and detractors sometimes found it useful to play that up. What is true is that they were both exceptionally talented and rose easily in their worlds, coming to occupy the same political offices. Moreover, that talent was obvious from early on.

Even at a young age Garret FitzGerald knew he was destined for greatness – he admitted to keeping all his letters from the age of six so that future historians could use them.[1] His early interest in politics was clear, but it was when he was 15 that a teacher in Belvedere College, Ronnie Burke-Savage SJ, planted the idea that he might aspire to become Taoiseach. His family background was in politics. Desmond FitzGerald was a London-Irish would-be poet, the son of Irish immigrants from southwest Tipperary or north Cork and Kerry. He was born Thomas Fitzgerald in London in 1888. Though Tommy's father, Patrick, was a blocklayer, Tommy was able to gain access to a Catholic boys' school in east London. He developed literary aspirations at school, and on leaving school wrote poetry and did some journalism while working as a junior civil servant. He was serious enough about it to be in a poetry circle that included the American modernist poet Ezra Pound. Thomas Fitzgerald adopted the name Desmond, because it was the anglicisation of the Irish for South Munster, where the FitzGeralds (a Norman family) had ruled. He probably also added the capitalisation of Gerald in his surname, as most Irish Fitzgeralds had lost it over the centuries.

Desmond's attraction to Gaelic culture drew him to Ireland and Irish nationalist circles. It was in Irish language classes in London run by the Gaelic League that he met his future wife, the Belfast-born Mabel McConnell, who was four years his senior, and working in London as a teacher. She was also a secretary to the Anglo-Irish socialist writer George Bernard Shaw. On paper she was an unlikely Irish nationalist. Her father, John McConnell, an Ulster-Scots Presbyterian unionist, was the managing director of the Royal Irish Distillery in Belfast. McConnell was a close friend of Sir James Craig, the first prime minister of Northern Ireland. Mabel became a revolutionary Irish republican, who for a time adopted a new name, Meadhbh ní Chonaill, to indicate her Irishness. An unexpected pregnancy in 1911 meant they married quickly in Brittany, France, against her parents' wishes and without much money. They moved to the Dingle peninsula in 1913 to take part in a movement for Irish independence through Irish, where Desmond's 'intuitive conviction [was] that [they] were on the eve of a national revival'.[2] Desmond was an organiser for the Irish Volunteers and a member of the Irish Republican Brotherhood. He was banished from Kerry and certain parts of the country by British authorities for these activities, and the family moved to Bray, where he continued to organise for the Irish Volunteers. He was much less radical than his wife, in fact he was 'a very conservative Catholic', but they were both in the GPO for the Easter Rising, even though he opposed it. Desmond was imprisoned in England for his part in the Rising, and was an aide to Éamon de Valera, by then the leader of Irish nationalism. FitzGerald was elected as a Sinn Féin abstentionist MP in the 1918 election, becoming the director of publicity for the Dáil government, and was on the pro-Treaty side, eventually becoming Minister for External Affairs. Mabel, however, was sympathetic to the anti-Treaty side, and it was only loyalty to her husband that kept her on the pro-Treaty side, though it seems to have put some pressure on their marriage. She later accepted that the pro-Treaty side was right.[3]

Garret Desmond FitzGerald, born in February 1926, was a 'child of reconciliation'. The youngest of four boys, his household was at the centre of Irish political and intellectual life. His upbringing was comfortably upper middle class in the elite of Irish society. Writers, academics and lawyers were entertained in the family homes, first in Wicklow, then in Blackrock, south County Dublin and finally in a large, detached villa on Temple Road in Dartry. The prominent writers Seán Ó Faoláin and W.B. Yeats, for instance, were guests in the FitzGerald's house when Garret was growing up. Desmond's innate conservatism meant he was attracted to fascism; and, disgusted by the anti-clerical atrocities of the republican government, he sided with the nationalists in the Spanish Civil War – a position his youngest son copied. That position in the elite of Irish society might not have been as comfortable financially as it appeared, as the family was renting for some of his upbringing, and the frequent moves were a result of that. Perhaps supported with an annuity from Mabel's father, they could afford to holiday in France, from which Garret would develop a love of France and French culture.[4]

FitzGerald's mother's Protestantism would have a deep impact him, not least from when she scolded him as a child for making an anti-Protestant remark – 'You know that I am a Protestant, Garret?' It was this realisation that he was the product of the different traditions on the island that led to his sense of responsibility to consider the views of the northern unionists. Young Garret was sent to Ring in west Waterford to learn Irish, and then to Belvedere College, the elite Jesuit school in Dublin city centre. FitzGerald seems to have found school easy; in Belvedere he was placed in a class two years ahead of his contemporaries. He was a precocious youth who engaged in theological debates with his Jesuit teachers. Being younger than his classmates, he remained an extra year in Belvedere to study philosophy before going to university. Following his brothers, FitzGerald joined the Local Defence Force during the Emergency, which he found a 'broadening experience', being exposed to 'foul language' for the first time.[5] Having no interest in sport put him at a disadvantage in making friends at school, as surely did his not being in class with boys his own age. In any case he preferred the company of women, something he would finally be able to enjoy when he went to UCD.

❖ ❖ ❖

Charles Haughey's parents were also involved in the struggle for Irish independence, but never reached Garret FitzGerald's parents' heights in the movement. Charlie's father, Johnnie Haughey, born in 1899, was a decade younger than Garret's. He had been one of the commanders in the 2nd Northern Division of the IRA during the War of Independence. Johnny Haughey was a republican from Swatragh, in east County Derry, a predominantly Catholic village separated from Derry City by the Sperrin Mountains. Johnnie took part in raids on the Ulster Volunteer Force and retired army officers. As part of an underground guerrilla force, he was often on the run as a young man, sleeping in outbuildings and reliant on sympathetic families for food. One of those he would depend on was Sarah McWilliams. Charlie's mother was born in 1901 to a farming family near Swatragh. She was in Cumann na mBan, the women's section of the Irish Volunteers during the War of Independence, though she saw no military action. Her job was primarily to serve the male volunteers, including Johnnie. The two were married in August 1922 in Donegal. It was at this time that the Treaty was splitting the country in more ways than one. Though it brought about the formal partition of Ireland later that year, the Haugheys sided with Michael Collins in viewing the Treaty as a means to secure independence, and Johnnie took an officer post in the newly formed Free State army. He moved south in the newly partitioned country for military training in the Curragh to serve in a rapidly expanding army. But immediately Johnnie Haughey found himself involved in a civil war against his republican comrades, though there are no records of his involvement in that war. He was 'ordered to remain' in the Curragh at its outbreak, which suggests he might have been seen as sympathetic to the other side.[6]

Cathal James Haughey was born in Castlebar, County Mayo, where Haughey's father was stationed at the time, in September 1925, a few months before FitzGerald. He was the third child of a growing family, which would reach seven children. Johnnie Haughey was stationed in various parts of the country, but his health declined as he developed multiple sclerosis. The family moved to a farm in County Meath, soon after Seán, as Johnnie was also known, retired his army commission in March 1928, having reached the rank of commandant (a rank just above captain). He probably took one of the inducements the state was offering in an effort to scale back the size of the army.[7] Haughey's declining health made farming impossible and in the early 1930s the family bought a modest but comfortable new home in a privately built development in Donnycarney on the north side of Dublin. There Sarah struggled to raise a large family, with an infirm husband, supported only by a small army pension and a deep faith.

Cathal Haughey went to school at the Christian Brothers national schools in Marino, Scoil Mhuire and Scoil Iosaf. As with FitzGerald, things came easy to the young Haughey. He was a confident, even a cocky, boy. At school he excelled, both academically and in sport. In

1936 he won the Dublin primary hurling championship with his school, where Cathal was known as a tough, physical player. He could master subjects faster than any of his contemporaries. But entry to secondary school was not guaranteed. In 1938, aged 12, Cathal won a Dublin Corporation Scholarship, coming first in the city, to gain entrance to St Joseph's CBS – Joeys – in Fairview. Haughey spent some of his summers in Swatragh, where his family remained active in republican circles; his uncle Pat McWilliams was interned during the Second World War.[8] Somewhat like FitzGerald's Protestant heritage, Haughey's family roots and experiences in Swatragh influenced the formation of his political views. Like FitzGerald, when he was 15 Haughey joined the Local Defence Force, and later the army reserve, An Fórsa Cosanta Áitiúil (FCA), where he became an officer. It was clear that he was a natural leader of the platoon known as 'Haughey's Fusiliers'.

It was Haughey's closest friend in school, Harry Boland, the son of a Fianna Fáil minister and nephew of the revolutionary of the same name, who fired Haughey's interest in politics, though Boland was initially much closer to George Colley, another son of a Fianna Fáil grandee also in Haughey's class in Joeys.[9] Haughey became involved in Fianna Fáil through these two friends, helping in election campaigns. His father had been a supporter of Collins, whose portrait hung on the wall of the family home in Donnycarney, and, as Haughey admitted, his father was 'a committed supporter of Cumann na nGaedheal'.[10] Though we might now have a sense of a deep divide between the eventual supporters of Fianna Fáil and Fine Gael, it was not unusual for people who took a pro-Treaty position to switch sides later, often attracted by Éamon de Valera's new nation-building movement. Haughey considered a career in the army, but from Joeys he would win another scholarship, to UCD, where on Harry Boland's suggestion he studied commerce from 1943 to 1946. The state was important in giving him opportunities to realise his potential, something he remained conscious of throughout his life.

✽ ✽ ✽

Although they went to secondary schools about a mile apart, it was only at university that FitzGerald and Haughey's paths crossed for the first time. University College Dublin was a small place whose campus was at Earlsfort Terrace, just off St Stephen's Green in Dublin city centre. If Dublin had once been one of the great European cities, in the 1940s the capital of the still young Irish state was decidedly provincial, and most UCD students would have known each other. The atmosphere at UCD was rather conservative; the clerical students stood out for their dark robes and not being allowed to mix with the 'ordinary' students. Drinking happened in the city centre, and it was common to see writers such as Patrick Kavanagh or Brendan Behan in the bars. Though they would have known one another, and even shared some lectures, Garret and Charlie did not mix socially. They were in different university societies, Haughey in the Commerce Society and FitzGerald in the Literary and Historical. Haughey, FitzGerald observed, tended to socialise with the sons of prominent Fianna Fáil ministers. FitzGerald said he preferred the company of women. Indeed, from their early schooldays each socialised in quite different ways: Haughey was one of the lads, whereas FitzGerald was more aloof from male company. He was, and would remain, less adept at managing other people.

FitzGerald, as the son of a prominent Fine Gael former minister, and living in a large house in a Protestant enclave in upper Rathmines, was socially Haughey's superior, though Desmond FitzGerald was down on his luck since the party lost power. Desmond FitzGerald had lost his seat, and was by this time a senator with a waning interest in politics. He lectured for a time in Notre Dame in the United States to supplement his income. Garret studied languages and history, and claimed that he found it all very easy and enjoyable.[11] Haughey too excelled academically, became involved in debating, and, closer to home, kept up his sporting activities. He won a Dublin Club Championship in 1945 with Parnells, where he was known as an aggressive player who would talk back to referees.[12] The major political event at the time was the Second World War.

Ireland, under Éamon de Valera, adopted a policy of neutrality, from which Ireland developed its sense of itself as a neutral country. That policy was predominantly pragmatic – devised as a way to save Ireland from the terrible aerial bombing that destroyed many UK and German cities. But the policy was not without its critics. One senior Fine Gael politician, James Dillon, resigned from the party in opposition to its support for neutrality. Dillon felt there should be no neutrality in a war between parliamentary democracy and fascism.

FitzGerald supported the Allies during the Second World War, a time when many in Ireland, perhaps including Haughey, had a sneaking regard for the Germans, if only because they were fighting the British. It was an early example of Garret's iconoclasm. Though he was from the mainstream, Garret was willing to take positions that were not in the mainstream of Irish society. Haughey's republicanism was on show when, in reaction to Trinity College students burning an Irish tricolour on VE Day, he and a friend tore down a Union Jack hanging from a lamppost on College Green and burned it, apparently causing a small riot, something FitzGerald witnessed. It was an incident that Haughey later admitted he had 'been dining out on – suitably embellished of course'.[13]

Haughey formally joined Fianna Fáil in 1948, campaigning in that year's election, though his attachment to the party was observed well before then, not least by Garret in Earlsfort Terrace. Much later, when suggestions were made that Haughey had once held Fine Gael sympathies, he wrote to the *Irish Times* 'to catch up with a lie'.[14] Even a cabinet colleague, Kevin Boland, the brother of his friend Harry, would later refer to him as 'that bloody little Blueshirt', being suspect in part due to his father's position in the army.[15] Garret canvassed for Fine Gael in the 1948 election, though he did not formally join the party until much later. He signed up to the party's position on its continued membership of the Commonwealth, something it would abandon the following year, under pressure from within the new inter-party government[16] and the opposition Fianna Fáil party.

CHARLIE VS GARRET

Both Charlie and Garret met their wives at UCD. After a series of relationships, FitzGerald met his future wife at a French Society meeting in November 1942, and showed characteristic impatience in his decision to get married. The marriage to Joan O'Farrell, when he was just 21, was a success, even if his father disapproved of his son's haste. Joan was at least his intellectual equal and would become his most trusted adviser. She was born in England in 1923 to a middle-class Irish family that was in financially straitened circumstances. Her father had suffered a mental breakdown, and was committed to an asylum, and Joan, her mother and sister returned to Ireland in 1933. The wedding in 1947 was a small affair, mainly due to Joan's mother's limited means.

Maureen or Máirín Lemass was in the UCD Commerce class with Haughey at that time. The various stories of their meeting include one that he spotted her on Grafton Street, and on finding out that she was the daughter of the then Minister for Industry and Commerce, Seán Lemass, he was reported to have said 'I'm going to marry her.'[17] She was shocked when she visited his home in Donnycarney to see the portrait of Michael Collins on the wall, though her father was less perturbed – 'didn't he fight for him?' She and her sister, Peggy, were mourners when Haughey's father died of multiple sclerosis in early 1947 aged just 48, only a few months before FitzGerald's father would die.[18] Maureen Lemass and Charles Haughey were married in 1951 – the Taoiseach, Éamon de Valera, attended the wedding – and the newly married couple lived at 332 Howth Road, Raheny, a middle-class suburb on the northside of Dublin, but by no means a house of luxury.

Though both FitzGerald and Haughey had an interest in politics, their foremost concern was to earn a living to support their new families. Haughey joined Harry Boland's brother's accountancy firm after graduation, and he qualified as a chartered accountant in 1950, also becoming a barrister, but he never practised. The pair set up their own accountancy firm, Haughey Boland, as soon as they qualified.

Haughey ran as one of four candidates in the 1951 general election, on the ballot with Oscar Traynor and Harry Colley, George's father. Haughey polled very poorly, but was co-opted onto Dublin Corporation in 1953. He was a candidate again in the 1954 general election, but again failed to win a seat, and he lost his Dublin Corporation seat in the local elections in 1955. Haughey was beginning to look like a serial election loser, something that deeply concerned both him and his father-in-law.

Haughey had been handpicked by Lemass to join a committee on the reorganisation of Fianna Fáil after the party's defeat in 1954,[19] which entailed travelling the country and submitting reports to Lemass.[20] Haughey was co-opted to the Fianna Fáil National Executive in December 1955,[21] and then selected for Fianna Fáil in the 1956 by-election caused by the death of the independent TD Alfie Byrne. Byrne's son won a 'quiet election'[22] easily, while Haughey was 'the local man' who promised to 'stop the drift to disaster' under the inter-party government; but the election significantly raised Haughey's profile, in which the election literature acknowledged he was 'not as well known on the field as his brother, Paddy or "Jock" Haughey'.[23] He eventually won election to the Dáil in the 1957 general election, taking the fourth seat, and unseating Harry Colley, who was never a big vote-getter. Haughey would never struggle to get elected again.

Haughey's financial fortunes had changed as well. Though Boland would say that they earned little enough from the accountancy firm,[24] and a TD's salary was about IR£1,500 (equivalent to about €48,000 in 2023), by the late 1950s Haughey was able to buy Grangemore, a large house with 45 acres of land in Raheny, for IR£10,000, where he kept horses, enjoyed fox hunting and started farming.[25] Boland said that Haughey used to come into the office grumbling that it was 'terrible weather for us farmers', even though, according to Boland, he had 'started growing lettuce ... we'd walk out in disgust when he started saying that.' The 1950s was a time of grinding poverty, unemployment and high emigration, so the source of Haughey's financial advancement was unclear at the time, but it did coincide with his move into politics. Though the claim was always made that he was making shrewd investments, what we later found out about his association with businessmen at the time, particularly in property development, make it more likely that he was facilitating them with political access. His father-in-law having just become Taoiseach would have made Haughey a valuable ally. Haughey was friendly with Matt Gallagher, a property developer, whose son Patrick claimed that his father had advised Haughey to buy the Grangemore property.[26] It might well have been good advice, but it does not explain where Haughey had found the money to buy it in the first place. If, on their arrival at UCD, FitzGerald was very much the social superior of the two, Haughey now looked to have overtaken him.

※ ※ ※

FitzGerald also had his eyes firmly fixed on a political career, but he would take a more circuitous route, both professionally and politically. In 1951 he was 'deeply conservative', siding with the country's Catholic bishops in opposition to the Mother and Child Scheme, and going so far as to heckle Noël Browne, the Minister for Health at the time.[27] On graduation FitzGerald took a job in Aer Lingus, where he was a research analyst – a new job that allowed him to invent a role. He did a review of timetables and by reducing the turnaround times for Aer Lingus planes FitzGerald sometimes claimed that he introduced the model that would later make Ryanair so profitable. Much later in life he would impress people with his ability to find the cheapest flight connections, even if they were not always the fastest. While working at Aer Lingus he developed an interest in business management and economics and also started writing, becoming a freelance journalist as an Irish correspondent to various international newspapers, a role that made him well known in Irish political circles. He eventually wrote for the *Irish Times* on economics, after which 'within a couple of years I came to be regarded as an economist', even though he had no formal training or any real knowledge of economic theory.[28]

On leaving Aer Lingus in 1958, FitzGerald needed to find suitable employment that would give him the freedom to write and involve himself in political debates. In what he described as a 'preparation for politics', he negotiated a full-time job in UCD, specialising in industrial economics, where he continued to have a wide engagement in Irish policy debates though various forums, including the European Movement, a group promoting Irish membership of the European Economic Community (EEC).[29] In the European Movement he became friendly with George Colley and Fianna Fáil senator, Eoin Ryan, whose fathers had also fought in the GPO in 1916. He also took on consultancy work, sat on state boards and was a correspondent for *The Economist*. All these more than made up for his giving up secure employment in Aer Lingus. His mother's death in 1958 led to an inheritance that enabled him to buy a large house, 75 Eglinton Road in Donnybrook, an upmarket suburb of Dublin.

Charlie's and Garret's comfortable financial situations were not matched in the country. In the 1950s the Irish economy was still predominantly agricultural. Growth was anaemic and emigration had soared. On almost any measure of social progress Ireland was a poor country and getting worse. Left-wing economics was winning the public debates internationally on state intervention, but it would not work for a small economy that was a 'free rider on Britain's decline'.[30] Yet Fine Gael's attachment to orthodox economics also appeared to have failed, putting pressure on the second inter-party government, which lost power in 1957. FitzGerald was somewhat removed from Fine Gael at the time.

After Éamon de Valera's election to the presidency in 1959, Haughey's father-in-law, Seán Lemass, became Taoiseach, starting a process of modernisation and opening up the Irish economy through a Programme for Economic Expansion. At this time FitzGerald shifted politically, moving away from his father's conservatism. He became more liberal on social issues and moved to the left economically, adopting something akin to social democracy, mainly, he claimed, as a result of his conservatism being unable to stand up to the scrutiny of his students and his children.[31] FitzGerald admitted to voting for Fianna Fáil in 1961, attracted by Lemass's modernising instincts. Haughey asked FitzGerald to do some work for the Fianna Fáil party, an offer FitzGerald effectively turned down by quoting Haughey his fee for the work. FitzGerald thought it an attempt to draw him 'into the maw of the party'.[32] He may have been right – Haughey was unusual in being interested in policy, and Haughey would have seen in FitzGerald someone who was also unusually policy-focused and full of ideas. It says something about FitzGerald's relationship with both Haughey and Fine Gael that the approach was made at all. Clearly FitzGerald was not seen as a gut Fine Gaeler and their personal relationship must have been passable. For FitzGerald there might have been some attraction to Lemass's Fianna Fáil. At that time Fine Gael was led by James Dillon, someone whose approach to politics looked more suited to the nineteenth century. It was a deeply conservative party but, more than that, it was an amateur party. Its leadership approached politics almost as an extra-curricular activity. Labour was another option for FitzGerald, though its opposition to Ireland's membership of the EEC would have made him very wary. On being asked why he chose Fine Gael over Labour, he cited his problem with Labour's policy on the EEC and its relationship with the unions. FitzGerald claimed he felt he could shift Fine Gael thinking from its conservative position,[33] which showed significant ambition and self-belief. His self-belief was matched by his energy: getting involved in debates related to the economy, planning, transport, Church doctrine, public administration, electoral reform, the EEC and Northern Ireland. One friend observed that he 'displayed an inexhaustible energy and an apparently unlimited capacity for work'.[34]

FitzGerald was unusual in his policy approach. A 1964 *Studies* article set out the political thinking that was to define his life, setting out his support for the concept of consent as a precondition for unity with Northern Ireland, his support for a social welfare system, and a check on private property rights that was unusual for his party.[35] Though FitzGerald did not formally join Fine Gael until 1966, he was by this time very much part of Fine Gael. In 1964 a Fine Gael TD, Declan Costello, wrote the policy document *Towards a Just Society*, which also reflected FitzGerald's social democratic thinking. FitzGerald's contribution was a paper on a wealth tax – something that would have been anathema to many solid Fine Gaelers. The party accepted the *Just Society* document without any enthusiasm. One senior party figure called it a 'traumatic amalgamation ... that would have outraged even the most radical members of rural and traditional Ireland'.[36] In part because the party had nothing else to offer the electorate it became its manifesto in the 1965 general election. But at its launch the party leader James Dillon contradicted the main tenets of *Towards a Just Society*, with the reassurance that Fine Gael 'shall rely on private enterprise. We are a private enterprise party.'[37] Costello and FitzGerald were disappointed that it was not embraced by the party. The two men might have helped shift the party somewhat, but they had certainly not yet won over hearts or minds.[38] There was an emerging divide within Fine Gael.

FitzGerald came close to running in the 1965 general election. He was offered a nomination in Dublin South-East, but after initially accepting, he turned it down. Election to the Dáil was far from a certainty as Fine Gael was also running John A. Costello, Declan's father, a long-time sitting TD and former Taoiseach. The other two seats had been occupied by outgoing TDs Seán McEntee and Noël Browne. Instead, FitzGerald successfully ran for the Seanad (on the Industrial and Commercial panel), in those days very much a part-time occupation.

FitzGerald was a rising star in Fine Gael. He was assisted in canvassing for the election by his colleagues from the emerging social democratic wing of Fine Gael, Alexis FitzGerald and Jim Dooge, two men FitzGerald would lean on throughout his political career. Dooge was a sitting senator and candidate on a different panel, so sharing a car for the arduous Seanad campaign made sense. The Seanad election took him out of Dublin and gave him an opportunity to meet people across the party for the first time. Being a senator would also allow him to continue his journalism, consultancy and activism, as well as teaching in UCD. FitzGerald wrote to Haughey during this election campaign seeking, if not a high preference, at least a preference: 'you will at least consider me less undesirable than some of the other Fine Gael candidates!' In response, Haughey expressed his regret that FitzGerald was 'going over to the enemy'.[39] They were still friendly enough. Indeed, FitzGerald might have regarded Haughey with some admiration, as part of a reforming government. For by this time Haughey was not just a rising star, he was a star.

3.

YOUNG TURKS

While Garret FitzGerald was establishing his reputation as a public intellectual, Charles Haughey quickly became a major public figure. For one who had had such a tortuous entry to the Dáil, Haughey's subsequent rise was impressive. While his father-in-law becoming Taoiseach in 1959, soon after Haughey's election, hardly harmed his prospects, he in any case stood out from many other TDs. He was obviously exceptionally talented. His exceptional ambition was also clear. Unlike FitzGerald, who was a professional journalist, Haughey needed to learn the then modern idea of public relations. Haughey engaged an *Irish Times* journalist, Tony Gray, to advise him on communications, something unheard of in those times.[1] He regularly featured in profiles in the national newspapers. Even before he was elected Haughey was effectively a full-time politician, active throughout the country as an unpaid party organiser. Haughey allied himself enthusiastically to Lemass and his Programme for Economic Expansion. He had earlier pressed for his addition to the Fianna Fáil ticket in Dublin North-East on the basis that he could 'speak with authority and accuracy on any conceivable subject'.[2] Haughey's maiden speech on the 1958 budget emphasised helping industrialists to make profits: 'I should like to put forward the proposition that the trouble with this country is that too many people are making insufficient profits.'[3] He spoke frequently in the Dáil on economic development, and differed from many of his contemporaries in being unusually well informed in budget debates.[4] At the end of 1960 Haughey came third in an election to the Fianna Fáil national executive.[5]

In 1960 Haughey's constituency colleague, Oscar Traynor, the oldest minister in Lemass's cabinet, was struggling with the workload in the Department of Justice. Seán Lemass decided that he would need some help to ease the burden and after some debate offered Haughey the job of parliamentary secretary to the minister, today a minister of state.[6] Haughey said Lemass told him 'As Taoiseach I am offering you this appointment on behalf of the government, but as your father-in-law I am advising you not to take it,' though Lemass would have known there was no chance that his advice, if serious, would be heeded.[7] Haughey took the job, and immediately showed the flair, attention to detail and administrative skills that would characterise him throughout his career. He tended to identify discrete reforms that he could deliver, and which would be associated with him. Haughey engaged in a programme of law reform Lemass had requested.

Though the 1958 Programme for Economic Development had yet to yield much fruit in terms of economic growth, there was a sense that Lemass was on course to modernise the Irish economy. The 1961 election was the first without de Valera as leader, so it was natural that there was some nervousness within Fianna Fáil. The party was helped by the lack of a credible alternative government. Fine Gael leader James Dillon was even more orthodox in his economics than his predecessors, John A. Costello and Richard Mulcahy.[8] Labour had yet to recover from the experience in government with Fine Gael, and was opposed to coalition. The new Labour leader, Brendan Corish, was unable to get the full use of the party leader's office, which his predecessor, William Norton, refused to vacate. Even if it gained Garret FitzGerald's vote, in 1961 Fianna Fáil lost eight seats from the total seats it had won in 1957, and now had 70 seats in the 144-seat Dáil. The division in the opposition meant that Lemass could rely on two of the six independent TDs to either support him or abstain, which would enable Fianna Fáil to introduce its programme.

Both Harry Colley and Oscar Traynor retired at that election, and Haughey comfortably topped the poll, with a surplus of about 1,500 votes, which helped to bring in two party colleagues, including George Colley, his old schoolmate and son of Harry Colley, whom Haughey had edged out in 1957. Haughey hosted a dinner for Traynor and Colley on their retirement, which was attended by all senior Fianna Fáil figures – a sign of Haughey's willingness to build good relations in the party.

In forming his government in 1961 Lemass made more significant changes to the cabinet than he had when taking over from de Valera in 1959. Though he kept many of the old guard, such as Frank Aiken and Seán MacEntee, he started to promote a new generation of Fianna Fáil TDs, including his son-in-law, who became Minister for Justice. Lemass was already 60 years old and was impatient for reform. He brought in Donogh O'Malley and Brian Lenihan as parliamentary secretaries, both of whom would in time be seen as reforming ministers. He told Lenihan to study the EEC, in what would be a preparation for membership.[9] Lemass spoke with Brian Walsh, a Supreme Court judge, suggesting that the Supreme Court should be 'flexible and creative in its interpretation of the constitution'.[10] This would have a major impact on Ireland: over the coming decades the courts would assert themselves as essentially political actors.

Those appointments would be important for Haughey as the three – himself, Lenihan and O'Malley – would become close allies in what would become Haughey's first attempt at the party leadership. In Justice his secretary was Peter Berry, who had worked with ministers since the 1920s. Berry observed of Haughey, 'he was a joy to work with and the longer he stayed the better he got' and he possessed a 'first-class intelligence with initiative, application and tenacity'. Berry did, however, take note of Haughey's temper when Berry refused to sign off on the appointment of a political friend.[11] Haughey's abrasiveness was as clear as his intelligence. A memorandum submitted by a civil servant was returned with a single word written in the margin: 'Balls'. The civil servant later conceded that 'The minister's verdict was probably right.'[12]

Even though he was now a minister, he did not limit himself to his brief. Like FitzGerald, Haughey involved himself in all aspects of policy and took views on many topics. But his main job was to make advances in Justice. Haughey became a reforming minister, introducing the Succession Act; though his successor Brian Lenihan was minister when it passed, Haughey did the bulk of the work. The purpose of the Act was to deal with the large number of people dying intestate – with no will. The tradition since the Famine had been for farms to be passed down to the eldest son, and this was reflected in law, which at times led to many widows in rural Ireland being left destitute. The Act was a socially reforming measure that also had the advantage that it replaced a practice that had predated independence; Haughey told one audience it was a law 'the Irish people will have given to themselves, not something handed to us by an alien jurisdiction'.[13] The law would entitle a spouse to two-thirds of any estate, regardless of what the will said. For Haughey it was a proposal that 'aroused terrific hostility', though not from the Church, which encouraged the change.[14] Though Haughey would regard it as a major life achievement, there was some opposition from Fine Gael, including Garret FitzGerald, who, with Declan Costello, took the very conventional view that the state should not 'dictate how every Irish man and woman shall leave any property they possess as between members of their family . . . Fine Gael has always stood for individual liberties.'[15]

There were some progressive reforms from Haughey which would get FitzGerald's approval. For example, he expanded the provision of free legal aid,[16] which would open up the legal system to those of more limited means, and extended it to appeals as well as courts of first instance. Haughey curtailed the application of the death penalty through the Criminal Justice Act, which retained capital punishment only for some political offences and the murder of gardaí. Haughey also significantly expanded the Department of Justice, securing extra funds for it.[17]

That antipathy to an 'alien jurisdiction' was by no means indicative of support for the then active IRA. The IRA border campaign, which had commenced in 1956, saw in the late 1950s its first attacks on British targets for decades, mainly aimed at army barracks and police stations around the border. By the time Haughey became minister in 1961 it was coming to an end, but Haughey's reintroduction of the Special Criminal Court and the 'most intensive drive against illegal organisations since the early war years'[18] probably hastened its end. His departmental secretary, Peter Berry, claimed Haughey 'broke the back of the Organisation'.[19] This tough line against the IRA was almost certainly pre-approved by Lemass, but Haughey pragmatically enabled it with an arms amnesty for the IRA.

His pragmatism was also evident during the 1961 Macushla Revolt, when gardaí went on a go-slow to highlight issues of pay and conditions among younger officers. While dismissal was sought (and granted by the government) of 11 of the protesting officers, Haughey secured an agreement to reinstate the officers, consenting to look at the issues they had raised.[20] He introduced the Intoxicating Liquor Bill, which regulated opening hours and licences for pubs and restaurants. He also introduced the Official Secrets Act, which was mainly a measure that consolidated existing practice. Haughey's overall approach in Justice suggested that he was a liberal, interested in progressive law and penal reform, and along with Brian Lenihan, Donogh O'Malley and Paddy Hillery, he was one of a new generation of Fianna Fáil ministers whose instincts were reforming, activist and progressive.

The resignation of Paddy Smith as Minister for Agriculture in October 1964 opened up a position in what was then both an important and sensitive department. Smith's resignation was ostensibly over the government's economic policy, which he felt favoured urban areas. The immediate appointment of Haughey, a Dublin TD, to Agriculture might have been politically risky, but it showed Lemass's trust in his son-in-law's abilities and his disregard for the concerns of rural Ireland. Haughey played up his landholding in Raheny, which was at the time being used for farming: 'Sure, am I not a farmer myself?' he claimed. His 'farm' was sometimes disparaged by Dáil opponents as 'henhouses'.[21] Haughey hoped to increase productivity in agriculture, commercialising it in part through the amalgamation of small farms, but also through subsidies for beef factories.[22] If he had hoped to be as reforming a Minister for Agriculture as he had been in Justice, he would not have the chance. Most of his time in Agriculture was spent firefighting. Farmers were concerned about milk and beef prices. They were well organised, and started a series of blockades in Dublin in 1966, which caused traffic problems in the capital. It was a time of some tension for Haughey, though he appears to have had the support of his cabinet colleagues and parliamentary party. He would not have been completely wrong in assuming that the National Farmers' Association (NFA) was a Fine Gael-dominated organisation. Haughey initially refused to increase the price of milk and beef on the basis that it was unaffordable. He also refused to speak with the NFA while the blockades continued, which made him appear high-handed. It took Seán Lemass's intervention to resolve the situation; his promise to open talks to end the pickets in Dublin helped Haughey back down without losing face.[23] If he had been progressive and dynamic in Justice, he was reactive and at times appeared petty in Agriculture.

By this stage both Haughey and FitzGerald could be thought of as politicians with a strong social conscience. Though not yet elected, FitzGerald was on a mission to change Fine Gael. He would make statements that would have been mainstream in a socialist party, not one that was traditionally seen as a party for conservative professionals and big farmers. FitzGerald spoke frequently in favour of social democracy, or indeed 'modern socialist thought'. He told one audience, ironically in the upmarket Shelbourne Hotel, of the 'evils of social neglect ... many groups in society lack even the basic essentials of life – adequate nutrition, warm clothing, a sound dwelling with sufficient rooms for all to live in decency.' He advocated for what were seen as radical ideas, such as profit-sharing in companies and a wealth tax. Though FitzGerald was clearly on the left of Fine Gael, he was opposed to the 'authoritarian socialism of the centrally planned economies'.[24]

Haughey was a prominent member of a modernising government with a desire to 'rise the tide' in the expectation that it would lift all boats. Haughey was genuinely interested in the plight of the poor, likely in part inspired by the poverty he would have seen growing up. Haughey spoke of Fianna Fáil as a 'progressive political party ... with an enlightened social conscience', and he could point to the party's practical achievements in social programmes.[25]

One of the most important of those social programmes was the introduction of free secondary education, often regarded as one of the most important and far-reaching policy decisions of any Irish government. It was famously, and unconventionally, announced on 10 September 1966 by Haughey's friend, Donogh O'Malley, Minister for Education, at a National Union of Journalists conference in Dún Laoghaire:

> I propose from the coming school year, beginning in September of next year, to introduce a scheme whereby, up to the completion of the Intermediate Certificate course, the opportunity for free post-primary education will be available to all families.

The free education policy had a longer gestation than just an off-the-cuff announcement. Paddy Hillery, one of O'Malley's predecessors in the Department of Education, had worked on a proposal to introduce it, including costing it. It did not seem to cost that much. O'Malley discussed it with his friends, Haughey and Lenihan, over lunches. They would be allies when it went to cabinet. What happened next is uncertain. According to John Healy, the journalist Haughey cultivated, Haughey possibly sounded out his father-in-law, 'the Boss' Seán Lemass, who seemed interested. This was exactly the sort of radical proposal Lemass had encouraged from his younger ministers. According to Healy, who may not have been the most reliable witness, there was some concern that 'Some hoor is going to leak it to Garret FitzGerald'.[26] A similar if opposite case was made by FitzGerald, who would later claim that the only reason O'Malley made the announcement before receiving cabinet approval was because he had heard Fine Gael was planning to make a similar announcement. O'Malley was, even by his own admission, a 'wild one'. He and Haughey enjoyed drinking together, the fallout of which sometimes got O'Malley into trouble with his Taoiseach. Professionally O'Malley was disinclined to follow convention. Lemass might have encouraged O'Malley to announce the free education scheme as a kite-flying exercise, and one that might make formal cabinet approval easier to acquire. O'Malley drafted a speech, and seems to have shared it with Lemass, though Lemass denied it,[27] that indicated the plan was agreed and in train, which it was not.

When O'Malley made the announcement on that Saturday evening the response was enthusiastic. By Monday there was more enthusiasm. Fine Gael's opposition was muted. Lemass nonetheless wrote to O'Malley to remind him of the normal government procedures. The following cabinet was tense, but Haughey and Lenihan supported the proposal, and O'Malley pointed to the popular response. Though Jack Lynch, as Minister for Finance, was angry that the convention of collective cabinet responsibility had not been observed, public, media and political support was so great that it would have been electorally impossible for the cabinet to withdraw the announcement.

✽ ✽ ✽

In the mid-1960s both Fine Gael's and Fianna Fáil's leaders would stand down. For Fine Gael James Dillon decided to go immediately after the 1965 general election, at which Fianna Fáil won an overall majority. Dillon announced his resignation at the Fine Gael parliamentary party meeting following the first meeting of the new Dáil. By this stage the new Seanad had not been elected, so Garret FitzGerald would not have a vote in a leadership contest. Yet he did expect some discussion in the wider party, and that Declan Costello would be the candidate for the social democratic wing of the party. That did not happen. Liam Cosgrave was nominated at that parliamentary party meeting. Cosgrave, whose instincts were not liberal, was seen as a moderate who had been supportive of *Towards a Just Society* – the document that had signalled Fine Gael's shift to the left – and indeed had chaired the committee that produced it, though he did not contribute to writing it.[28] The social democratic side of the party did not have time to organise themselves and nominate someone from that side of Fine Gael, and Liam Cosgrave was made leader by acclamation. The nature of Cosgrave's victory caused suspicions in the party – it seemed like a stitch-up by the conservative wing. As a disillusioned Declan Costello withdrew, Garret FitzGerald emerged as the most prominent voice from the social democratic wing of the party.

Haughey was still Minister for Agriculture and dealing with the farmers' protests when Seán Lemass announced his intention to retire in late October 1966 – his health having become an issue – with the intention that a younger man take over. Lemass had forewarned Jack Lynch of his plans, leaving him in no doubt of his desire for Lynch to take over.[29] Lynch was an experienced minister, who had risen to Minister for Finance after the 1965 election, but he had none of Haughey's or O'Malley's dynamism. Despite his understated nature, he was well known and popular throughout the country. Jack Lynch was a sporting legend, having won many All-Ireland titles for Cork, in both football and hurling. The problem for Lemass was that Lynch did not want the job. Lemass also tried Paddy Hillery, and may have preferred him, but Hillery did not want the job either.[30] There was a growing sense that Fianna Fáil would have a formal contest for the leadership and that George Colley and Charles Haughey would be the candidates.

Haughey was on business in London when Lemass announced his retirement. His constituency supporters arranged to greet him at Dublin Airport with placards that declared 'Charlie is our Darling' and 'Charlie is the Greatest'. This latter phrase led one wag in Leinster House to wonder aloud how the sentence was to be finished.[31] This was a planned campaign that succeeded getting Haughey on the front pages of newspapers the following day. Even to be a candidate demonstrated remarkable ambition, given that he had only been in the Dáil for nine years, and a minister for just five. But he had been the party's director of elections for the successful 1965 election, and the party expected a generational change. He was by then the most senior Fianna Fáil man in Dublin. He was one of the most prominent ministers, gaining a reputation not just as an effective minister, but also a stylish man about town. One problem was his age. He was barely 41, so any colleagues with ambitions for the leadership would have known that his leadership could last so long that it might end their chances. According to Maureen Haughey, Lemass's daughter, Lemass advised him that it was too early for his elevation to Taoiseach.[32] The other problem was that Haughey may have overestimated his popularity. Donogh O'Malley, who later canvassed TDs for Haughey, was probably only exaggerating a bit when he told Haughey that his chances of success in a leadership election were lower than he thought: 'Charlie, if there was a vote on it in the party tomorrow morning, you'd get three votes. Your own, mine and Lenihan's. [And] I'm not sure Ollie here [a nickname for Lenihan] wouldn't welsh on you at the last minute.'[33] Lenihan too did not think Haughey was all that popular in the parliamentary party.[34]

If Haughey represented the pro-business, Lemassian tradition in the party, George Colley was the man who represented traditional Fianna Fáil values. He also had to return home from official business on hearing of Lemass's retirement, and at the airport Colley indicated that his 'hat is in the ring'.[35] Remarkably, as a TD for just five years, Colley was considered more likely to win. He was thought at the time to have the support of Lemass if Lynch did not stand, though if Lemass thought it too early for Haughey, he surely must have felt the same of Colley.[36] Colley was well regarded by the older generation, many of whom felt Haughey too showy. He was a fluent Irish speaker, and represented that tradition in the party, but his record as minister was hardly stellar.

Of the other names spoken of at the time, one caused more fear among senior people in Fianna Fáil. Neil Blaney, a TD since 1948, an experienced minister with a deep knowledge of the party grassroots and machine politics, would be the candidate to represent the nationalist wing.[37] He was a single-issue candidate, but his candidacy made the race 'dangerously unpredictable'.[38] The party elders did not like these choices, or at least they did not like the prospect of a split party. With Colley and Haughey in attendance in early November, Lemass again tried to persuade Jack Lynch to run. Lynch again refused, although less emphatically. Under significant pressure from various people within the party, not least Lemass, on 3 November Lynch eventually agreed to run.[39] Haughey recognised the need for a tactical retreat, immediately withdrawing his name, as did Blaney, and Lynch easily defeated Colley in a vote of Fianna Fáil TDs on 9 November 1966.

This was immediately framed by Haughey's supporters as a leadership 'decision deferred'.[40] Lynch promoted Haughey to Finance and Blaney to Agriculture, but Lynch was described as a 'reluctant Taoiseach'.[41] Jack Lynch added to the impression that he was an interim leader by talking of himself as a compromise candidate.[42] Lynch was right to feel that he would have beaten any of the candidates in a full contest. As with Fine Gael, the shift to a new generation of leaders would have some impact on the operation of the party. Whether Fine Gael chose Cosgrave or Costello, or Fianna Fáil chose Lynch, Colley, Blaney or Haughey, was in one sense immaterial. The factions that these parties had suppressed by personal loyalties or force of personality were now more likely to express themselves openly.

It reveals something of the thinking in Fianna Fáil that there was such opposition to Haughey's candidacy among the old guard. This was in part distaste at the younger man's increasingly lavish lifestyle. At the time he was seen as 'a bit of a wide boy with a terrible reputation as a womaniser'.[43] While still just a parliamentary secretary he had insisted on being accommodated in the fashionable George V hotel in Paris, and was able to get a booking there when even the Department of Foreign Affairs failed.[44] He was conscious of his place in history, even at an early stage in his career. Civil servants would routinely correct factual errors said by ministers in the record of the Dáil; Haughey insisted that they also 'polish up the text'.[45] Haughey used the media skilfully to bolster this image. The *Irish Times* columnist John Healy became a propagandist for Haughey and would remain so throughout his career. But it was also an aversion among the more conservative party elders to the direction Fianna Fáil was going under Lemass, with its greater association with business.

The Lemass-inspired and Haughey-run TACA was an organisation set up after the 1965 general election to pay for the party's election expenses. It offered membership for IR£100 a year (about €2,500 in 2023) to get Fianna Fáil-supporting businessmen to donate to the party in return for access to ministers.[46] Many on the committee that ran TACA were in the property industry and close to Haughey. Haughey had become friendly with prominent businessmen such as property developers Matt Gallagher and John Byrne, and hotelier P.V. Doyle. TACA was run out of the Burlington Hotel and treated separately from Fianna Fáil's other fundraising activities.

Haughey was an enthusiastic supporter of the development of Dublin city, which usually meant the destruction of derelict Georgian houses and their replacement with incongruous modern office blocks – which were often rented to the state. At the unveiling of one such building he said, 'I for one have never believed that all architectural taste and building excellence ceased automatically with the passing of the eighteenth century.'[47] His enthusiasm for modern buildings may not have been just a reflection of his desire to see Ireland enter the twentieth century. Developers were making a lot of money, and according to one who was close to Haughey, 'Fianna Fáil was good for builders, and builders were good for Fianna Fáil, and there was nothing wrong with that.'[48] It was known that councillors were now willing to deliver rezoning of land for developers in exchange for what were effectively bribes. Haughey's closeness to developers led many to assume that he might be involved in assisting them in ways that used public influence for private profit. It was thought that he was a 'sleeping partner' in John Byrne's property business.[49] A comment by George Colley in 1967 that 'people in high places appear to have low standards' was interpreted as a reference to Haughey and corruption.[50] The 1969 sale of his house and land in Raheny for about IR£200,000 (about €4.5m in 2023 prices) to a company controlled by Gallagher at a large profit caused more comment and speculation. The sale enabled him to buy Abbeville, a large house and extensive estate in Kinsealy, near Malahide. He also bought 127 acres in Ashbourne, County Meath for IR£30,000 (€680,000 in 2023), without a mortgage, to be used as a stud farm.[51] He was involved in hunting, sometimes wearing a bowler hat, which caused comment from some in politics; he seemed to have completed his transition to country squire. Haughey actively courted positive media attention, which he received in a series of profiles for newspapers.[52] Haughey never had a problem getting positive publicity from a largely acquiescent media.

There were allegations from the opposition, including constituency rival Conor Cruise O'Brien, that Haughey would gain personally from a decision he made in avoiding tax on the profits of the sale of his land in Raheny. Haughey received strident defence for his avoidance of tax in a series of *Irish Times* editorials that accused O'Brien of 'the politics of envy', and in a statement during the 1969 election campaign Haughey even claimed that he was selling his Raheny house and lands as an act of charity, to help provide much-needed housing.[53] The Revenue Commissioners denied the allegations, issuing a statement to indicate that Haughey would not have been liable under the older tax rules.[54]

If there were concerns about Haughey's lifestyle and behaviour at the time, clearly the new Taoiseach did not share them; he promoted Haughey to Finance, the most important job in government after Taoiseach. Though this promotion may have been as much to get him out of Agriculture, where he had failed to appease the farmers, he could easily have been given another senior role.[55] Again Haughey applied himself, becoming the 'dominant personality' in that government,[56] while Lynch at the time 'was a bit dreamy'.[57]

In Finance Haughey again showed flair, imagination and efficiency. He was also lucky as Ireland was going through a small boom when he took over. One of his more high-profile ideas was a tax exemption for artists, which was hardly a big vote winner, but helped develop the arts in Ireland, and encouraged many world-famous writers and artists to move to Ireland. It made the country a much more sympathetic place for artists and seemed to stem from his genuine interest in the arts. More popular was his introduction of the free travel pass for old-age pensioners, free radio and television licences for the elderly. This was a measure that would yield Haughey favourable attention for decades to come. He increased the amount of money given to sporting and artistic organisations. He introduced tax exemptions on horse breeding, which would help make Ireland a centre for that industry. His secretary, T.K. Whitaker, thought that Haughey had a penchant for the spectacular, that he would take all the praise for any popular measure, and that he used the position 'to promote himself'. Whitaker was also concerned that Haughey's expansionary policies – in response to Costello and FitzGerald's *Just Society* document – created inflationary pressures that needed to be tamed.[58] Haughey recognised that ministers would work best when they took on discrete issues that were deliverable in the short period a minister had.[59]

Haughey was in awe of Lemass, and in ways tried to continue his work, both in style and substance. Even Haughey's voice bore remarkable similarities to Lemass's. Whether intentional or not, Haughey's intonation and emphasis in speech were the same as his father-in-law's. Lemass had said that he 'acted on the principle that the only way to avert mistakes was to do nothing. As I did not intend to do nothing, I discounted mistakes in advance.'[60] Haughey saw things similarly; he freed many of the semi-state companies under his control from parliamentary oversight, in the expectation that they would take more calculated risks.

In 1968 two things happened that would have an impact on Haughey. Donogh O'Malley, Haughey's best friend in politics died aged 47, and Haughey was injured in a serious road crash. Paddy Hillery thought Donogh's death had a major political influence on Haughey's career because 'he'd listen to Donogh. After Malley [sic] was gone there was no one he'd listen to.'[61] For Haughey the impact was as personal as it was political: 'to a large extent, the fun went out of politics the day Donogh died.'[62] His death had another implication: the election of Donogh's nephew, Desmond O'Malley, who would later become a rival. Haughey's car accident was so serious that he was out of the office for a number of months. One contemporary associate of Haughey said of his car crash that it was as if he 'had undergone some kind of mental plastic surgery'.[63]

Haughey's interest in a pact between government, employers and unions became evident at this time. Haughey revived the dormant National Industrial and Economic Council, which was designed to provide guidelines on wages, an early attempt at corporatism.[64] Like Lemass, he hated strikes, and thought that businesses were too willing to give in to striking workers.[65] In 1969, when inflation was becoming a problem, Haughey proposed a pay/incomes policy at an 'unprecedented' pre-budget meeting between the Irish Congress of Trade Unions (ICTU) and the economic ministers. The now reconstituted and renamed National Economic Council convened a meeting of government, unions and the Federated Union of Employers in April 1970, with what seemed to be the basis for what would much later become 'social partnership'.[66]

If Haughey was keen to promote harmonious industrial relations, it was in part because he saw in a newly invigorated Labour Party a more full-blooded socialism than Ireland had ever seen. The party had moved to the left, joining the Socialist International in 1967. Although led by the mild-mannered and moderate Brendan Corish, the Labour Party was now full of emerging stars who were more intellectual and thrusting in their approach. People such as David Thornley, Conor Cruise O'Brien and Justin Keating gave the party a greater confidence and when the 1969 election was called, Labour boldly declared 'The seventies will be socialist', though its election slogan was the more banal 'The New Republic'.

While still a senator, FitzGerald had hoped to use a 1968 referendum on changing the electoral system as a means of increasing collaboration between Fine Gael and Labour. Both parties knew that if the referendum had succeeded in replacing the proportional representation system with first past the post, the two parties would have to co-operate to avoid massive Fianna Fáil majorities. There were even some who thought they should consider a merger. FitzGerald's position on this referendum was unclear. He was opposed to the Irish electoral system, and Cosgrave asked him to sound out the Fine Gael front bench on the issue. He is said to have reported back that ten were in favour of retaining the system, and eight wished to replace it. It is odd then that Cosgrave pushed so hard for the party to support the Fianna Fáil position, and failed, weakening his leadership ahead of the 1969 election.[67]

Haughey was appointed the national director of elections for Fianna Fáil in 1969 and it was his budget, as Finance Minister, that the party could lean on. That budget increased social welfare payments and pensions, and was criticised as an election budget. Haughey's reaction to the emergence of the left in Labour was more interesting, however. He would use the Labour slogan to warn against the dangers of socialism, and few opportunities were lost on Haughey to bring up 'Cuban Socialism', referencing the call by Conor Cruise O'Brien to open an Irish embassy in Havana. Fianna Fáil used the slogan 'Let's back Jack' to build on Lynch's popularity in the country. While Jack Lynch travelled around the country in what for some seemed like a tour of convents and meetings with nuns, much of the Fianna Fáil campaign was in effect a 'red scare' against Labour, which, he said, preached 'an alien gospel of class warfare, envy and strife'.[68] Haughey told the large crowd outside the GPO at the party's final rally the night before polling that Labour would nationalise key Irish industries, including Guinness, though this was not official Labour Party policy. The presence of people such as Noël Browne in the Labour Party – who Haughey would describe as an 'extreme left wing social theorist' – allowed him to claim at a public meeting that 'the extreme policies of the left-wing intellectuals of the Labour Party' would have a devastating effect on employment.[69] Fianna Fáil did not have a manifesto, in part because it had never seen the need for such a thing, but also because Haughey claimed that 'Manifestos have a Marxist ring about them.'[70]

Fine Gael's 1969 campaign was more muted than Labour's, despite that in Cosgrave it now had a leader from the twentieth century. The party had formally adopted the *Just Society* as its manifesto and 'Winning through a Just Society' as its election slogan, but as in 1965, it did so with little enthusiasm, and the divisions within the party remained. An attempt by FitzGerald and Costello to change the party name to Fine Gael – Social Democratic Party was blocked by the chairmanship of the conservative Gerard Sweetman. FitzGerald was disappointed with his party's engagement with the *Just Society* approach – in 1969 it was little more than an election slogan. Being well known from his contributions to the media and in politics, FitzGerald was the natural candidate to stand for the party in Dublin South-East when John A. Costello stood down in 1969. FitzGerald was easily elected, comfortably topping the poll. FitzGerald was also a national figure, and one on whom Liam Cosgrave would lean for both his expertise on economics and also his media skills. FitzGerald was comfortable on both radio and the now important medium of television. But as well as its party divisions, Fine Gael's other problem was that it had no plausible route to government. Labour had ruled out coalition with Fine Gael, as it felt the necessary compromises of coalition stopped the party developing a working-class base. Most working-class people at the time voted for Fianna Fáil, and it would be harder to win them over if Labour was in power with Fine Gael, usually seen as the party of business, professions and big farmers.

Though Fianna Fáil was expected to lose the election in 1969, and despite a two percentage-point drop in support, it picked up seats and returned to government with a comfortable majority. This was partly due to the lack of transfers between Labour and Fine Gael, but also because constituency boundaries had been redrawn, reducing the size of constituencies, which helped Fianna Fáil where it was strongest.[71] Labour did well in Dublin, overtaking Fine Gael, but lost seats overall. The two parties took up the opposition benches again. The result confirmed Lynch's position as Taoiseach and party leader. Haughey was rewarded for his work as director of elections with the retention of the Finance portfolio after the election. If Haughey was still annoyed at Jack Lynch's assumption of the leadership he did not show it. Paddy Hillery observed of Haughey's relationship with Lynch: 'Haughey did an enormous amount of work, and made it successful. Charlie was totally devoted to success, and Charlie had the power. He was doing things *for* Jack, not through him.'[72]

Garret FitzGerald meanwhile, newly elected to the Dáil, would become a dynamo, one of the most productive and prolific members of the opposition, though in ways that would not always endear him to Cosgrave. These troubles would be minor compared to what was about to happen to Charles Haughey.

4.

ARMS AND THE MAN

Though it did not feature in the campaign, the 1969 election took place at a time of growing unrest in Northern Ireland. In 1968 civil rights protests and an increasingly militant nationalist leadership were making demands to end the discrimination against Catholics in the North. A few weeks after the June 1969 election, the first death took place in what would become known as the Troubles. There was growing tension in Derry, and in August rioting reached a climax during the Battle of the Bogside. On 12 August 1969 an Apprentice Boys parade led to a confrontation in which nationalist residents of the Bogside, armed with stones and petrol bombs, attempted to prevent the march going through their area. They then had to defend themselves against a loyalist mob, and to prevent the security forces, the RUC and B-Specials entering the Bogside. It was clear that policing was not impartial, and that the security forces were facilitating attacks on Catholic areas.

The crisis demanded a response from the Irish government. Paddy Harte, a Fine Gael TD for Donegal, contacted Jack Lynch to report what was happening and recommended that pressure should be put on the British government to intervene.[1] But there were divisions in the Irish cabinet, with some of the more hawkish or anti-British, led by Neil Blaney, urging that the Irish army make incursions into Northern Ireland. Jack Lynch spoke to the nation on 13 August, indicating that 'the Irish government can no longer stand by and see innocent people injured and perhaps worse.'[2] Worse soon happened. The following nights saw more violence, with seven people killed in disturbances in Belfast.

Lynch's statement was misheard, misremembered and misreported as him saying that the government could no longer stand *idly* by, implying that the Irish government would make a more active intervention. The government put the military on 'a state of immediate readiness', leave was cancelled and field hospitals were quickly set up at points along the border to assist refugees escaping violence in the North.[3] Headlines in the South screamed 'NORTH AFLAME' and 'BELFAST ABLAZE'. Lynch called for a United Nations (UN) peace force to intervene. He was hoping to get the UK government more interested and involved, encouraging the introduction of British troops in the hope it would ease the situation. Those troops were introduced, to the immediate relief of northern Catholics, but eventually they too would be seen as part of the problem in what would become a three-decade-long conflict that would claim over three and a half thousand lives.

Despite political rhetoric on partition, Northern Ireland had not been an issue of great interest to many in southern Irish politics. To a large extent the southern political establishment had turned its back on the North as a problem. One exception was Garret FitzGerald. Partially because of his mother's Ulster Protestant and grandfather's unionist heritage, FitzGerald was unusually thoughtful about what approach should be taken. He was in favour of unity by consent, by which he meant that any attempt at unity should proceed only if the position of the Protestant majority in Northern Ireland, and what would be the Protestant minority in a unified Ireland, was respected. In 1964 FitzGerald had written that 'Relations between North and South would be based on wholehearted acceptance of the principle that political unity must be preceded by a unity of hearts.'[4]

FitzGerald was not the first or the most prominent person in Irish public life to acknowledge this issue. Lemass had made an important speech at the Oxford Union in 1959 in which he said, 'Our goal is the unity of Ireland by agreement and we cannot expect speedy results.'[5] He moved symbolically as well, beginning to use the term 'Northern Ireland' instead of 'the six counties'.[6] Seán Lemass had

had two historic meetings with Captain Terence O'Neill, the prime minister of Northern Ireland, in early 1965, which were intended to start a normalisation of relations with Northern Ireland. In 1965, in response to Vatican II, Lemass wrote to Justice Minister Brian Lenihan to consider any changes that the Irish state might wish to consider. He highlighted in particular the issue of divorce, which might be reasonably interpreted as being motivated by a desire to make concessions to unionist opposition to a united Ireland.[7] Lemass had formed an informal All-Party Oireachtas committee on the constitution, with a view to its modernisation. On retirement he joined the committee and became an important voice on it, the person who 'drove the deliberations', according to one Fianna Fáil member of the committee. It advocated for a position on national unity that would be 'less offensive to the North', and in particular it unanimously agreed to recommend a rewriting of Article 3 of the constitution, which claimed a right over the territory of the whole island, to: 'The Irish nation hereby proclaims its firm will that its territory be re-united in harmony and brotherly affection between all Irishmen.'[8]

This approach was a rejection of the traditional nationalist approach of blaming British involvement for the divisions on the island and within Northern Ireland. Fianna Fáil policy under its founder, Éamon de Valera, was that partition was a crime imposed by Britain and could only be undone by Britain.[9] It was significant that Lemass, one of the leaders of the nationalist movement in the revolutionary period, was not just willing to sign up to this new proposal, but was presumably one of the drivers of it. But 'unity by consent' was not yet government policy, and the committee report, and the spirit of cross-party co-operation that it had been written with, disappeared in 1968 when the Lynch government introduced the second referendum to change the electoral system to first past the post, even though the committee had unanimously decided against that proposal.[10]

The 'unity by consent' approach became official government policy when Jack Lynch made the Irish government's position clear at the outset of the Troubles. Lynch's thinking was heavily influenced by Ken Whitaker, by this time the new Governor of the Central Bank. In a speech made in Tralee, County Kerry a month after his television address, Lynch said:

> It was and has been the Government's policy to seek the reunification of the country by peaceful means. The unity we seek is not something forced but a free and genuine union of those living in Ireland based on mutual respect and tolerance and guaranteed by a form or forms of government authority in Ireland . . . Of its nature this policy – of seeking unity through agreement in Ireland between Irishmen – is a long-term one . . . Perseverance in winning the respect and confidence of those now opposed to unity must be sustained by good-will, patience, understanding and, at times, forbearance.[11]

This speech was printed and circulated in the UN, designed to put pressure on the British government to intervene in Northern Ireland, and to gain support from the United States and countries in Europe. But the attempts to involve the UN were also a means to give Lynch some breathing space.[12]

※ ※ ※

The strife in the North was an emotive issue, provoking disturbances in Dublin, and Lynch was expected to act on the implications of his broadcast. Lynch was lucky in that the leaders of the opposition, Liam Cosgrave and Brendan Corish, did nothing to inflame or exploit the situation. There were splits in Fianna Fáil, however. In cabinet these splits were between pragmatists such as Lynch and Paddy Hillery, and more fundamentalist nationalists such as Blaney and Kevin Boland, who were calling for a limited military intervention *in* Northern Ireland with a view to somehow forcing UN involvement. Haughey was not clearly on one side or the other; he kept his counsel and made any contributions 'in a calm, logical manner'.[13] Garret FitzGerald was at the time engaged in a letter-writing campaign to get media and government ministers to end the media practice of saying 'the six counties', and to instead use the official term 'Northern Ireland'. Haughey generally referred to it as Northern Ireland, rather than the 'north of Ireland' or 'the six counties', suggesting he was one of the pragmatists. His role in defeating the IRA when he was Minister for Justice also pointed that way. In Agriculture Haughey had followed his father-in-law in inviting the Northern Ireland Minister for Agriculture for a private lunch at his home when he was in Dublin for a rugby international (Haughey himself refused to attend rugby matches).[14] And in a debate at Queen's University Belfast in 1962 Haughey made a conciliatory speech toward unionists, while arguing for unity, indicating that he was open to seeing 'whether a political and constitutional structure could be devised, which would ensure, no matter what happened, that the interests of those minority groups would be adequately safeguarded and protected.'[15] In 1969 Haughey wrote to Lynch to outline practical problems that would have to be overcome 'in any moves to evolve a new constitutional relationship between North and South.'[16] None of these few interventions on the issue indicated a republican zealot. Add to this his tendency to be led by Lemass, who himself had clearly shifted to a more pragmatic position. But Haughey was the son of an old IRA man, albeit one who had joined the Free State army, and his roots in Swatragh may have given him a natural antipathy to unionists.

Earlier, in 1955, his local cumann produced 'a six-page typed document, [which] offered an aggressive case as to why Fianna Fáil should use physical force to secure Irish unity',[17] which it is likely that Haughey wrote with George Colley. This was not the work of very young men filled with youthful exuberance. Haughey was almost 30 and already an (unsuccessful) election candidate several times over. Later, in an exchange with his Secretary, Ken Whitaker, he differed from Whitaker's support for the proposed changes to Article 3 of the constitution, that 'we would never abandon the moral right to use force. We have the right to use force to defend the national territory.'[18] In these discussions Haughey shows a more irredentist nationalism aimed at ending partition than he had as yet publicly displayed.

Though the new cabinet decided against military intervention, it did agree to build field hospitals on the border and to move troops close to the border to facilitate the escape of refugees. The troop movement was seen as being for a doomsday scenario in which there were attacks on the Catholic population and no protection from the British.[19] On 16 August the government agreed a fund of IR£100,000 (€2.1m in 2023 figures) 'to provide aid for the victims of the current unrest in the Six Counties'.[20] Haughey, as Minister for Finance, had the role of arranging disbursement of the monies with a minimum of bureaucracy to persons or groups that 'could be vouched for as responsible and trustworthy'.[21] These included the Irish Red Cross and similar organisations.[22] Haughey immediately arranged to meet with representatives of the Red Cross.

A cabinet sub-committee was set up to keep abreast of the situation in the North, with three ministers from border counties, including Blaney, and Haughey as the finance minister. Tellingly, it did not include the Minister for Defence, Jim Gibbons. This was not set up to plan for military activity. According to one member, Pádraig Faulkner, the sub-committee met once and did not agree anything of substance. A second meeting was arranged, but neither Blaney nor Haughey showed up and as far as Faulkner was concerned the sub-committee 'ceased to exist'.[23] What happened with that money would be a source of controversy that would have implications for Irish politics through generations.

What happened then is disputed. According to Garda intelligence, in August 1969 Haughey seems to have met with Cathal Goulding, the chief of staff of the IRA. But when this was raised in cabinet, Haughey dismissed it as inconsequential. That alone was an extraordinary admission: a cabinet minister meeting with the leader of an illegal organisation that he had a few years earlier tried to dismantle. It might have been his brother Jock Haughey who had met with Goulding.[24] The fact that he could wave it away like that might have meant Lynch thought Haughey was denying that it had happened; that Lynch was unaware but saw no great harm when he found out; that Lynch was aware of it and approved; or he was aware of it and could do little to control Haughey. Whatever it was, it seemed that Lynch was not fully in control.

There are enough reports from ministers normally regarded as reliable who were at the cabinet table to confirm that the Irish government had decided on a diplomatic approach and its interventions were to be aimed at relief. Blaney, one member of the cabinet sub-committee, who was then Minister for Agriculture, met with Captain James Kelly, an army intelligence officer with strong nationalist leanings. Though Blaney was Kelly's main contact, with whom he claimed to have been meeting weekly in autumn 1969, Kelly also met with Haughey. Haughey gave him a cheque from the money allocated for relief to cover his expenses. Kelly did not meet with the Minister for Defence, Jim Gibbons, before March 1970.

The Special Branch reported that Haughey met with the Officer Commanding of the Dublin Brigade of the IRA in September 'in which a deal was made that the IRA would be facilitated with the movement of arms to Northern Ireland, and in return would call off the burning and destruction of property of foreign wealthy residents.'[25] There followed attempts by Captain Kelly to source and import arms for use in the North, which were expected to be delivered to Northern Ireland for use by informal 'Citizens' Defence Committees'. These committees became the nucleus of the Provisional IRA. Those who engaged in this activity claimed that it was authorised by the Irish government, and that they were working with authority from Blaney and Haughey. Weapons training was given to six civilians, authorised by the Minister for Defence, but cancelled by Lynch as soon as he found out.

Captain Kelly and his superior officer, Colonel Michael Hefferon, met with Haughey in his Kinsealy home, Abbeville, on 2 October 1969 in preparation for a meeting with the Citizens' Defence

Committees. Haughey arranged for Kelly to be paid IR£500 for expenses (equivalent to about €10,000 in 2023). That meeting with Citizens' Defence Committees in Bailieborough, County Cavan on 4–5 October 1969 was, according to Kelly, the 'genesis of the plan to import arms'.[26] Kelly had indicated to these committees that money would be available from the Dublin government.[27] This money would be from the accounts Haughey controlled.

Over the following months plans were put in place to import arms, with Blaney acting as the political lead and Captain Kelly the conduit to the Defence Committees that were soon becoming indistinguishable from the IRA. The IRA itself was on the verge of a split between the Officials, under a left-wing leadership, and the more sectarian Provisionals, who were more concerned with setting themselves up as 'defenders' of nationalist areas. The arms, if imported, would go to the emerging Provisional IRA.

Peter Berry was told of the Baileborough meeting and sought to alert his minister and the Taoiseach, both of whom were unavailable. He spoke to Haughey, who reassured him, but when Berry received more reports he decided he needed to speak to the Taoiseach. Lynch visited Berry, who was ill in hospital, and according to Berry (who was on heavy medication) he thought he informed the Taoiseach of Captain Kelly's part in Baileborough. The conversation was interrupted several times by nursing staff, and Lynch was reported to have said to Berry, 'This is hopeless, I will get in touch with you again.'[28] Lynch denied that Berry told him about Captain Kelly's involvement in the Bailieborough meeting, but according to Colonel Hefferon, Jim Gibbons, the Minister for Defence, made a complaint on behalf of the Taoiseach about Captain Kelly's activities. This was disputed by Gibbons. By early December there was an awareness in the security services that Haughey's brother Jock was involved in the attempt to import arms. Berry noted that his sense at the time was that he hoped 'that the police information was not true in relation to Mr [Charles] Haughey, or that at least whatever he was doing was government policy'.[29] Berry's view that it was unlikely that

Haughey would do anything illegal might have been shared more generally. However, when a number of men carrying arms were arrested in Donegal, and Lynch wanted them charged, Haughey rang Berry angrily wondering who would make such a 'stupid decision to arrest these men'.[30]

Much of the confusion around the Arms Crisis centres on what Lynch knew and when. Lynch's cabinet was split. There was a sense that Lynch did not know what to do; he told Paddy Hillery, 'I don't know which way to turn and what will I do tomorrow?' Hillery knew that with trouble in Northern Ireland 'all the hawks [in the cabinet] would want to invade the North with a force that wasn't capable of doing so.'[31] Blaney was increasingly making the hardline case for the use of force in public. Adding the 'idly' to Lynch's earlier 'we will not stand by' statement, he told a crowd of supporters in Letterkenny, County Donegal on 8 December 1969 that 'The Fianna Fáil party has never taken a decision to rule out the use of force.'[32] When it was put to Lynch that he should do something about his minister, Lynch replied meekly, 'Has he said something?'[33] At the Fianna Fáil Árd Fheis in January 1970 a clear Blaney faction put pressure on Lynch and the government's stated position. But it was seen as a Blaney problem. The position of Haughey was less clear. At that Árd Fheis Lynch appointed Haughey as one of his nominees to the Fianna Fáil national executive, suggesting that in early 1970 Lynch still trusted Haughey.[34]

All the while Blaney, Haughey, Captain Kelly and others[35] were involved in securing arms. Jock Haughey tried to purchase arms in London, but it was cancelled when it was realised they were under surveillance. Routing arms from the US was ruled out by Blaney, because he felt that the Continent could be quicker. They got the help of Albert Luykx, a businessman originally from Belgium with whom Blaney was acquainted.[36] In the army there was suspicion of Captain Kelly's activities and a sense that he was a rogue operator, and a feeling that Colonel Hefferon tacitly endorsed what was going on.[37] But in the army, there was no certainty whether Kelly was working with government authority. And we have to assume that Hefferon thought, as he claimed, that given the involvement of government ministers there was government authority for these activities. Certainly his minister, James Gibbons, seemed to be aware of the arms importation, even if the arms smugglers were not reporting to Gibbons directly.

A government decision made on 6 February 1970 has been used to argue that the arms importation was part of a government plan. It seems to have been based on a discussion in cabinet that the country should prepare for a 'doomsday' scenario in the North. An oral, rather than written, directive given by Jim Gibbons to the army was originally conveyed as 'prepare and train the Army for incursions into Northern Ireland'. The lack of clarity caused some confusion in the army. General Seán MacEoin, the Chief of Staff of the Irish army, sought clarification from the minister. In an addendum to the directive, Gibbons appears to have told the army that 'demands were made for respirators, weapons and ammunition, the provision of which the government agreed.' When Hefferon was later asked by Garret FitzGerald whether the directive gave authority to import arms, Hefferon replied, 'No, it didn't.'[38] For a later movement of arms that Gibbons ordered, MacEoin reported that Gibbons told him 'he was acting under pressure from Mr Blaney'. That might have been the case more generally. MacEoin's impression was that this was a preparatory move for a 'doomsday situation', and that there was no sense that the government knew even under what circumstances troops might cross the border. In any case, this directive suggests an army operation, which could have used normal channels to procure arms, not one that was covert and being conducted by members of the IRA. The directive, such as it was – 'very brief and in the most general of terms' – certainly cannot be used as evidence for the authorisation of the earlier attempts to import arms.[39]

❊ ❊ ❊

On 3 April 1970 Garda Richard 'Dick' Fallon was shot dead attempting to arrest one of three people robbing the Royal Bank of Ireland on Arran Quay in Dublin. The robbery was one of a series undertaken by Saor Éire, a small Trotskyite offshoot of the IRA. The armed gang escaped with IR£2,000 (€40,000 in 2023), thought to be used to buy arms. The Garda Siochána were deeply shocked by Garda Fallon's murder. It was the first murder of a garda in decades. Over 1,000 members of the force attended the funeral, and senior gardaí were incensed because they suspected that government ministers had been involved in the importation of the pistol used to kill Garda Fallon. Garret FitzGerald later repeated in the Dáil an allegation made by Peter Berry, 'that the gun that shot Garda Fallon was imported through Dublin Airport in September 1969 with the knowledge of a member of the then Government.'[40] It seems that by this stage Peter Berry knew that something needed to be done.

Meanwhile, the attempt to source arms from Europe was progressing. By early April arms had been sourced from Otto Schlüter, a German arms dealer based in Hamburg, who was paid IR£22,000 (about €430,000 in 2023) from the money allocated to Haughey for 'relief' in Northern Ireland. Now it was a matter of importing them into the state. John Kelly, the IRA man, was in Dublin airport attempting to facilitate that, claiming he was 'an assistant to Mr Haughey's assistant'.[41] But Schlüter made no attempt to conceal the arms. There were customs issues as well as problems with using a passenger plane to transport arms. The Department of Transport asked Justice whether the cargo of arms due in on a plane from Vienna should be allowed in. Berry realised that the arms were associated with a 'J. Kelly', who had the same address as Captain James Kelly. Berry told the Minister of Justice, Micheál Ó Móráin, that Captain Kelly's activities were known about, and that they should indicate that the arms would be allowed in; they could then seize the arms when they arrived in Dublin.[42]

Quite how Haughey found out about this is unknown, but Haughey's private secretary, Anthony Fagan, claimed that Blaney contacted Haughey at this time. On Saturday 18 April Haughey called Peter Berry to ask if he knew that a certain consignment was due to arrive at Dublin airport the following day.

>Berry replied, 'Yes, Minister.'
>
>Mr Haughey then asked, 'Can it be let through on a guarantee that it will go direct to the North?'
>
>Berry replied, 'No.'
>
>Haughey's response was, 'I think that is a bad decision', to which Berry did not respond.
>
>'Does the man from Mayo know about this?' asked Haughey, referring to Ó Móráin.
>
>'Yes.'
>
>'What will happen when it arrives?' asked Haughey.
>
>'It will be grabbed.'
>
>To which Haughey is said to have responded, 'I had better have it called off.'[43]

It was called off, but it is not clear exactly how. At midday on Monday 20 April Haughey's private secretary telephoned Captain Kelly in Vienna to tell him that Haughey and Gibbons had discussed the matter and the importation was to be called off. Gibbons claimed that Haughey said it should merely be postponed.[44] Haughey and Gibbons met later that afternoon, so the discrepancy may have been the result of more than one conversation between the ministers.[45] Berry then bypassed his minister, Micheál Ó Móráin, and went to Lynch. He had earlier asked President de Valera whether his duty was to his minister or to the state; de Valera told Berry that it was to the state, and his duty was to inform the Taoiseach.

Lynch claimed to have discovered on 20 April 1970 that his Minister for Justice, Micheál Ó Móráin, was not keeping him informed that Haughey and Blaney appeared to be involved in a conspiracy to import arms using money from the Northern relief fund. There is great disagreement as to what Lynch knew and when. It seemed many of his ministers knew about the unconventional arms importation, and so it seems unlikely that he had no knowledge of it. It was entirely plausible that Ó Móráin was not keeping him informed, however. Ó Móráin was suffering from alcoholism, for which he was hospitalised, and missing work frequently. Gibbons was also not keeping the Taoiseach informed, and his claims of what happened and what he knew were inconsistent. So it may have been that Lynch was not receiving reliable information. He might also simply have forgotten. It was an exceptionally busy and stressful time, during which Lynch was prone to rely on Paddy whiskey to keep himself calm. He was able to function on prodigious amounts, a bottle of whiskey a day, sometimes more. However, as was later shown in the Littlejohn affair, Lynch's memory sometimes let him down. Still, an allegation that a number of your ministers are engaged in a plot to import arms for an illegal organisation hardly seems like something one would easily forget.

But on 20 and 21 April Lynch received reports from the Gardaí on the arms importation. Lynch did not appear to act swiftly or decisively in response to the information. His apparent inaction over the following days is the subject of speculation. Did he hope that the attempted importation had now been stopped and that the issue would go away? Or was he working out how to act? Some senior army officers who had been suspicious of the activities of James Kelly briefed Lynch at his home in Rathgar and reported that he seemed genuinely shocked.[46] Colonel Hefferon had recently retired and his replacement, Colonel P.J. Delaney, was suspicious of Captain Kelly's activities and ordered Kelly to cease all contact with the North. Kelly decided he needed to retire quickly, which took effect on 1 May.[47]

At a time when each actor was operating in a fog, and no one quite knew who to trust or who else was involved, Lynch, it seems, did not trust even Peter Berry, whom he regarded with some suspicion.[48]

Possibly Lynch used this time to establish the facts. Lynch tried to contact Haughey, but was unable to speak to him because he was hospitalised with a fractured skull and other severe injuries sustained in what was reported as a riding accident, though even that was questioned, with rumours circulating that Haughey had been beaten up following a sexual tryst in a pub in County Meath. On 29 April Lynch interviewed both Haughey, who was still in hospital, and Blaney, and they denied any knowledge of the arms plot, a position Haughey was to maintain throughout. Lynch requested the two ministers' resignations but they asked for time, which, remarkably, Lynch granted them. Lynch told his cabinet of the allegations on 1 May, though Blaney, who was present, appeared to ignore it, and the meeting moved on to another matter.[49] Paddy Hillery recorded at the time that 'the meeting ended with everyone thinking that the case was closed as far as the Blaney Haughey episode ... It seemed to be something with which [the Taoiseach] had dealt and did not want to happen again.'[50]

Captain Kelly was arrested and taken to the Bridewell on 1 May 1970. He admitted he was a military intelligence officer operating on both sides of the border and claimed his activities were part of a government-authorised operation, but said little else. He said he would speak to the Taoiseach. He was then taken to Government Buildings. Lynch instructed Kelly to tell him all he knew. Kelly refused, saying 'it's not my business to name people in this situation ... I'm not going to act as accuser.' He told the Taoiseach to ask his ministers, and the Taoiseach said he had, but that they would not talk to him.[51] He was returned to the Bridewell. If Kelly had really felt he was operating a covert but government-authorised operation, he would surely have been happy to talk openly to the Taoiseach. If Berry had realised he had to act in the aftermath of the Garda Fallon murder, it seems Lynch now realised action was necessary.

Lynch sacked Ó Móráin on 4 May 1970, in what seems to have been an attempt to clear the way to deal with the issue. On 5 May the leader of the opposition, Liam Cosgrave, probably having been informed by Phil McMahon, a retired Garda Special Branch officer familiar with Garda intelligence, reacted to the announcement of Ó Moráin's resignation by asking, 'Is it only the tip of the iceberg?', hinting that he knew more of what was going on.[52] The note that Cosgrave had received on Garda notepaper mentioned Blaney, Haughey and Gibbons, as well as Captain Kelly and Colonel Hefferon. It said, 'See that the scandal is not hushed up.' This was likely a direct result of the Fallon murder.

Cosgrave assembled his closest colleagues. These did not include Garret FitzGerald, whom Cosgrave did not trust sufficiently. That evening, 5 May, Cosgrave privately informed Lynch what he knew. Cosgrave returned to his party colleagues and said that Lynch had confirmed the allegations were true. It would seem that Cosgrave accepted Lynch's assurances that the Minister for Defence, Jim Gibbons, was not involved in the plot, and that Hefferon too was not involved.[53] Just before 3 a.m. on 6 May, Lynch's press secretary telephoned a statement to newspapers to announce that Lynch had sacked Blaney and Haughey. The statement did not say why they were sacked and in that information vacuum rumours began to circulate. Soon journalists started to reveal that Haughey and Blaney had been sacked for a conspiracy to import arms. No one was surprised by Blaney's alleged involvement, but many well-informed journalists were shocked that Haughey could be associated with such an activity and assumed that some mistake had been made.[54]

The following few days were a period of extreme tumult and tension in the country. Kevin Boland immediately resigned from cabinet in protest, as did another parliamentary secretary with nationalist leanings, Paudge Brennan, and rumours circulated about army involvement. The Dáil resumed at 10 p.m. on 6 May, on the nomination of a new Minister for Justice, Desmond O'Malley. The debate, which began with the Taoiseach outlining what he knew, focused on the arms plot. The Dáil sat again the following morning to react to the crisis and RTÉ set up a live outside broadcast from Leinster House for the first time. No one was quite sure what would happen or be revealed next, and there was a real sense that Fianna Fáil might split. The debate nominating Blaney, Boland and Haughey's replacements was the longest continuous Dáil session in the history of the state, from 10.30 a.m. on Friday 8 May to 11 p.m. on Saturday 9 May. Four cabinet ministers had now been replaced in as many days.

On 28 May Blaney, Haughey and three other alleged co-conspirators were arrested and charged with attempting to illegally import arms.[55] Haughey was home from hospital by this stage, but still recovering from his injuries. When he was arrested at his home in Kinsealy, Haughey was consulting with a Supreme Court judge, Brian Walsh, who was found by gardaí fleeing from the back of Haughey's house.[56] This was exceptionally unusual and highly suspect behaviour for a judge, particularly one so senior. In response to rumours, Walsh later claimed to colleagues that he was just returning a book he had borrowed.[57]

Blaney disputed the charges and they were dismissed in the District Court for a lack of evidence.[58] The others did not use this challenge and so were sent for trial. The first trial collapsed when the judge recused himself, having been accused of bias.[59] The defence of three of the accused was that they had understood that their activities were sanctioned by an official government decision, which appeared reasonable, given that they were liaising with senior government ministers. When the second trial started the main evidence against Haughey centred on the phone call he made to Peter Berry on 18 April, a statement by Jim Gibbons that he had not authorised any importation and statements by Haughey's private secretary, Anthony Fagan.

The testimonies of Berry and Gibbons were disputed by Haughey. Specifically, Haughey disagreed with a part of Berry's testimony denying he knew what was in the consignment. He claimed that he had said, '*whatever it was* it will have to be called off'.[60] Haughey also claimed that his involvement was only because he was the most senior minister in Dublin, and so 'on duty' for any decisions that needed to be taken.[61] He denied telling Gibbons that he would call it off for a month. Gibbons said he responded that Haughey should call it off for good.[62] Haughey claimed that he had nothing to do with a conspiracy, if one existed. He was facilitating a consignment at the request of an army intelligence officer. In his evidence Haughey painted himself as a mere apparatchik, which, given that he was a dominant force in that government, is implausible.

Giving evidence against Haughey, Gibbons 'was given a rough time in the witness-box and he performed miserably.'[63] Conor Cruise O'Brien observed of Gibbons on the stand that 'he revealed himself as a martyr to amnesia and ellipsis.'[64] The evidence of the former director of military intelligence, Colonel Michael Hefferon, was that the Minister for Defence had been aware of the activities of Captain Kelly, which contradicted Gibbons. Gibbons admitted that Kelly had informed him of an operation, but claimed that his non-response was to indicate his disapproval, which seemed an unusual interpretation. However, Captain Kelly later admitted that he was reporting directly to Blaney, which was itself unusual and outside his chain of command.[65] In much of the debate about the plot people have pointed to a government decision to store surplus army weapons for use in the event of a complete breakdown of law and order,[66] and – possibly because of some ambiguity in the language Gibbons used – have conflated this with the a decision to import arms for Defence Committees. However, the army movements to the border were understood by ministers at the time to be for a 'doomsday situation', not to supply 'defenders' protecting Catholics from loyalist attacks.[67] In queries from army officers as to under what circumstances these arms might be distributed, Gibbons struggled to adequately explain what the weapons were for or how they might be distributed. In similar questioning in court, Gibbons still struggled.

The judge put it to the jury that they had to decide who was telling the truth, between Berry and Gibbons on one side and Haughey on the other.[68] Gibbons's performance as a witness was so bad in other areas that his credibility was likely damaged in the conflict over the Haughey–Gibbons conversations. The jury wasted no time in accepting Haughey's co-defendants' version of events – that it was a government-authorised operation – and because of that the jurors acquitted Haughey.[69] The judge might have asked the jury to decide between Haughey's contentions and those of his co-defendants. Haughey's defence contradicted the other three defendants, who said they had been working to import arms but assumed it was legal. In saying he had no knowledge, Haughey was clearly lying. But it did not matter that he was lying, because once the jury felt it was a government-authorised operation, he could not be found guilty of a conspiracy.

When the verdict was handed down, Haughey in as many words called for Lynch's resignation: 'those responsible for the debacle have no alternative but to take the honourable course open to them.' He made plain his ambition to lead Fianna Fáil, which was 'part of my life', and was highly critical of Lynch's Northern Ireland policy that unity could only be achieved by consent. He went so far as to praise one of his co-defendants, John Kelly, a founder member of the Provisional IRA, as a 'fellow patriot'.[70] Haughey was thinking of his next move, 'acting as a man who felt that the next few days and weeks . . . were more important' than the result of the trial.[71] If he was testing the water to see what support he would get, he soon found out. Fianna Fáil circled the wagons around the leader. Lynch was in the US on government business when news of the acquittal came through. Returning home three days later on 26 October 1970 Lynch was met by a large number of Fianna Fáil TDs and ministers at Dublin airport, which demonstrated his strength within the party. Haughey, whose career would have been ended had he been convicted, was still in a desperately weak position. He judged it prudent to retreat.

※ ※ ※

One thing Haughey had was public popularity, and now he had a myth. As he left the court, crowds outside chanted 'We want Charlie!' From the trial Haughey developed a reputation as 'a good republican' without having ever admitted to being involved in any activities.[72] He clearly emerged as the leader of the more republican wing of Fianna Fáil. His one real rival for that mantle, Neil Blaney, was soon to be out of the party. Haughey received enormous amounts of correspondence in support of him. He began to display a style he would retain through his life: 'Not one to shake hands readily – a bow suffices. The vanity is near the centre all right – but beneath the patrician hauteur for mass consumption, that he is one of the boys – maybe.'[73] When his co-defendants were carried shoulder-high, he 'remained aloof from the excessive exuberance'.[74] Haughey was no longer the brash, thrusting young minister. He held himself as a national statesman. He walked more slowly, almost gliding. He perfected the use of his hands as a means of communication. A flick of the wrist could indicate whether who he was speaking to should continue or stop.

While Haughey now started to use more old-fashioned nationalist rhetoric, he was careful not to directly criticise government policy and did nothing to risk expulsion from the party. Voting confidence in Jim Gibbons as minister a few days after the verdict was handed down must have grated. Having taken extreme risks with his career, in considering his political future Haughey was not going to take rash action now.

The uncertainties of the Arms Crisis have thrown up some theories about what really happened, who was involved and why. First, it is clear that Haughey was involved. Too many of the protagonists place him at the heart of the arms importation. Haughey literally controlled the chequebook. Add to this that his brother was involved in the operation. If Lynch was an accomplice, as some suggest, why did Haughey not testify to that effect? Haughey was fighting for his political life and his liberty. It seems the most obvious way out of the problem, if, as some now allege, this was a government conspiracy and not one conducted by rogue ministers. If Lynch was only forced to countermand the order by the Special Branch and Berry's uncovering of the plot, why would Lynch have had to involve himself at all? He could have made a legal, if secret, government decision.

Nothing in Lynch's make-up suggests he would have wished to do such a thing. His policy was to move away from confrontation, and he was hardly trying to hedge his bets. Lynch's position at the head of the party had been secure since the election in 1969. Any time we know of when he found out about an activity that might support armed rebellion in the North, such as the army training of civilians in County Donegal, he put a stop to it. Paddy Hillery, who was a disinterested observer, said: 'There was no winking or anything like that. Jack wouldn't do that.'[75]

Briefings to journalists at the time suggested that Haughey and Blaney were victims of Lynch's 'felon setting'. This was later taken up by a journalist who argued that Lynch at best let things proceed, or at worst actively directed charges be taken against his ministers for involvement in a government-authorised operation.[76] Michael Heney believes that Haughey might have been the victim of a political trial. He claims that there was no arms plot as such, as it was a government-authorised operation, but when it was discovered by the Gardaí, Lynch acted against Haughey and Blaney. Except that the plot was never 'uncovered'. A query from Aer Lingus to the Department of Transport could easily have been dealt with, had it been a government operation. A problem with Heney's contention that it was a government operation is that it relies heavily on one conversation – between Gibbons and Lieutenant General Seán MacEoin – which was brief and general, and that conflated two operations, one to make existing arms available, and one to import arms through an unconventional route, for a destination that had no government decision to support it. Even Haughey's sympathetic official biographer, Gary Murphy, is sceptical of Heney's interpretation.

An alternative theory is that Lynch had not authorised anything, but when he discovered what was happening, he allowed it to continue in order to 'gut Haughey', as one observer of the trials put it. Why did Lynch not seek and secure (as he undoubtedly could have) Haughey's removal from the party immediately after the trial, and why did he later bring Haughey back in? There is no evidence that Lynch was antipathetic to Haughey before the Arms Crisis, nor that Lynch was power-crazed enough to engage in such a ludicrous plot. Lynch was reported to have been genuinely concerned when Haughey was involved in a serious car accident in 1968, and Haughey was regarded by the pragmatists in the party as an effective and rational minister, even if they did question his lifestyle.[77]

It has been suggested that ambition might have been Haughey's motivation for his involvement in the arms plot, as it offered a way to unseat Lynch.[78] Certainly, immediately after his acquittal he did challenge Lynch's leadership. He got the support of Blaney and Boland, but not many more. If he really thought that Lynch's leadership was temporary he might have seen this as a route to power, but it was hardly clear how, and it would have been exceptionally risky. Another explanation is that he was unwilling to allow Blaney to gain advantage from his involvement. Haughey may have thought he could control Blaney. But even if the plot had not been discovered by Berry, what would it have achieved for Haughey? Perhaps if events got out of control in the North, he would have been in a position to claim he was opposed to the government's policy. But he could have done that without involving himself, as Boland had. Haughey was already emerging as the natural successor to Lynch. It could be that Haughey's involvement was a mix of sincere concern for the position of nationalists in the North, and a more fundamentalist anti-partitionism than he had ever shown. One of those closest to him says that he was a 'gut republican'.[79]

Exactly why Haughey would involve himself in this activity will never be definitively known. Haughey did not speak of it to family or friends, and his private papers do not reveal anything that gives any insight into his motivations. What we know of Haughey from his earlier career, and later, is that he was willing to cut through red tape and disliked bureaucracy, so it is hardly unusual that he would go outside normal procedures to achieve what he wanted. In October 1970, despite his acquittal, Haughey was now at a crossroads. His political career and reputation appeared in tatters. But he wasn't finished. Leaving the Department of Finance when he was sacked in May, he had told civil servants, 'I'll be back again.'[80]

The Arms Crisis had an impact beyond Fianna Fáil. The convulsions in the party had convinced Brendan Corish, the Labour leader, that it was his duty to offer voters an alternative to a Fianna Fáil government. That meant coalition with Fine Gael. In 1971 informal contacts were made between the two parties, with Garret FitzGerald leading them for the Fine Gael side. FitzGerald would use these contacts to make a play for his party's leadership.[81] Just as Haughey found himself sidelined, Garret FitzGerald was moving centre stage.

5.

TRADING PLACES

At 43 Garret FitzGerald was a relatively old first-time TD in 1969, but his experience in public affairs and as a legislator in the Seanad meant he was unusually active for a new TD. On his first day in the Dáil chamber he did not give a normal maiden speech but put an array of questions to the Taoiseach, Jack Lynch, about government policy and the Taoiseach's approach in a host of areas. Lynch responded that 'The Deputy should slow down a little bit'.[1] But FitzGerald was not one for slowing down. There was simply too much to do.

FitzGerald had opinions about almost everything, not least the emerging situation in Northern Ireland, something no one at the time knew would last so long and take so many lives. FitzGerald differed somewhat from the traditional view, which was to blame the problem on partition and assume that if partition were ended the problem would be solved. He drafted a policy document in which he set out his clear preference for change in the status of Northern Ireland to come about 'with the consent of a majority of the people in Northern Ireland'.[2] This was written at a time when Protestants were the clear majority, so he certainly meant with the consent of the two communities. He developed a relationship with John Hume, who was becoming the leader of Northern nationalism.

FitzGerald's instincts were iconoclastic. He was at odds with the mainstream position of his party on the compulsory teaching of Irish, the clerical management of schools, inheritance tax and the legalisation of contraceptives. Despite this he quickly rose within Fine Gael and was appointed to the front bench immediately on his election, first as spokesman for education. One correspondent welcomed his rapid elevation but noted, 'it is difficult to imagine him constrained within any strait-jacket.'[3] He spoke on many issues, in the process annoying many of his front-bench colleagues. FitzGerald and party leader Liam Cosgrave initially got on well enough; they were dubbed 'FitzCosgrave' by journalist John Healy, who suggested that Cosgrave was a puppet of FitzGerald. This was untrue, but it managed to annoy Cosgrave.[4] In fact, FitzGerald frequently clashed with Cosgrave, who 'could not conceal his dislike of Garret'.[5] FitzGerald canvassed as early as 1970 for Cosgrave's removal, and according to his increasingly conservative colleague Dick Burke, he saw himself as the likely victor. He failed at that time, but it was clear to Burke that 'from day one Garret wanted to be leader of the party.'[6] Cosgrave had given the impression that he was surrounding himself with a loyal clique, to the annoyance of the liberals, and was increasingly isolated within Fine Gael, as his conservative approach was repulsive to many on its liberal wing.[7] In 1971 FitzGerald put together a private list as to how the party might vote in the event of a challenge to Cosgrave's leadership. In it there were three candidates: Cosgrave, Tom O'Higgins and FitzGerald. According to Richie Ryan, FitzGerald accidentally left the list behind as he left a meeting; the list showed FitzGerald's expectation that he would come second in the first round, and then win in the second round.[8]

Though he was a leading liberal in Irish society, FitzGerald remained a devout Catholic, and was quite patrician in his approach. In 1971 a young liberal senator representing Trinity College, Mary Robinson, tried to introduce a bill that would permit the importation and sale of contraceptives. The first reading of a bill is usually a formality that takes place without debate. Unusually, this bill was blocked at this stage. There was a sense that the political system was not going to be a route to progress in this area. In May of that year an organised protest against the ban on sale of contraceptives took place. The protesters very publicly brought contraceptives on the train from Belfast, where they could be legally bought. There was a half-hearted attempt to stop the protestors at Connolly Station in Dublin, but the main aim – to get society to discuss these issues – was achieved. In late 1973 the issue was subject of a High Court and then Supreme Court challenge, in which a married woman, Mary McGee, who after several difficult pregnancies was told her life would be in danger if she became pregnant again, claimed the right to import contraceptives for her private use. In a landmark judgment, Mr Justice Brian Walsh invoked US Supreme Court decisions in the McGee case. It introduced a right to marital privacy and showed that the courts could from then on be a much more active policy-making institution in Irish society. The political system was now required to legislate for this right.

FitzGerald was capable of annoying even those he might have more naturally sided with, such as the campaigners for women's rights. On watching *The Late Late Show* one evening, which that night was dedicated to feminism, he became so incensed by the suggestion that TDs did not care about the plight of women that he made the short trip from his home on Eglinton Road to RTÉ's studios, where, demonstrating his closeness to the Irish media, he was allowed on to the show to tell the women how much he cared. This had the predictable effect of annoying feminists even further.[9]

FitzGerald tended not to be 'clubbable' within his party and was often willing to pick fights not worth having. He upset many of his colleagues, some of whom felt he did not make any effort to sugar-coat his opinions to make them more acceptable to the intended audience. It was a feature he recognised in himself: 'I am basically a very combative person, and always have been. I have always involved myself in controversy, argument and debate ... and am really much more of an activist and troublemaker.'[10]

Within Fine Gael, FitzGerald was seen as a troublemaker whose talents needed to be managed. Cosgrave agreed with Tom O'Higgins that FitzGerald's talents were underused in Education and promoted him to Finance spokesman in April 1972, something that seemed natural given his status as a celebrity economist – he was described as 'the brilliant and eloquent economics expert' by the UK ambassador at the time.¹¹ But FitzGerald continued to speak on issues well beyond his brief, including on Northern Ireland, which irritated Richie Ryan, the party's spokesman on the North. If promotion to Finance was to settle differences between FitzGerald and Cosgrave, it was not immediately clear. At the party's fiftieth Árd Fheis in Cork on 20 May 1972, Cosgrave made a fiery speech ostensibly criticising 'commentators and critics' – but really taking aim at some of the critics within his own party – as 'mongrel foxes, they are gone to ground and I'll dig them out and the pack will chop them'.¹² FitzGerald knew he was one of the targets of the jibe, and he briefly considered walking off. Cosgrave, a very partisan politician, had been reticent about co-operation with Labour, and Garret FitzGerald took a leadership role, asking the parliamentary party to open discussions about coalition in advance of the 1973 election.¹³ He used the co-operation between Labour and Fine Gael to push for Liam Cosgrave's removal, suggesting that Cosgrave might be a barrier to coalition.

FitzGerald was active on a Public Accounts Committee (PAC) inquiry into the Haughey-controlled relief funds allocated to Northern Ireland. The government and opposition effectively put Charles Haughey on trial again. FitzGerald had already grown deeply suspicious of Haughey, and it was here that he would be able to express it. The arms trial had seen strong evidence that the arms shipment was paid for using the money that Haughey controlled as Minister for Finance. Most of that money was unaccounted for, and the PAC inquiry of 1971 sought to uncover where it went. Blaney said that it was channelled to Citizens' Defence Committees in the North, 'many of which fused into the nucleus of the Provisional IRA'.¹⁴ Haughey pleaded ignorance; he suggested that he controlled broad policy but had little to do with the day-to-day management of the funds.¹⁵

When Haughey's brother 'Jock' Haughey was called to give evidence to the PAC inquiry in February 1971 he refused to answer questions, successfully challenging the proceedings in court, which found that the inquiry resembled a criminal trial.¹⁶ It could still report, but the inquiry lost much of its potency. FitzGerald was told by some that he went soft on Haughey in PAC. In the Dáil and in PAC, most of FitzGerald's energy was directed at the Taoiseach, Jack Lynch. It might be that FitzGerald felt Haughey's career was essentially over. Haughey was determined that it was not over. Haughey knew Fianna Fáil was the only plausible vehicle for his ambition to become Taoiseach. To do that Haughey would vote dutifully with his government, including on the Offences Against the State Bill of 1972.

This bill would allow a senior garda's opinion to be taken as evidence of membership of certain proscribed organisations, such as the Provisional IRA. FitzGerald was one of the many in Fine Gael who opposed the bill on civil liberties grounds. The split in Fine Gael almost ended Liam Cosgrave's leadership, who after some consideration favoured supporting the government proposal. Cosgrave called a parliamentary party meeting, which did not heal those differences. Paddy Cooney, the Fine Gael spokesman on justice, criticised the government for not using the powers already available to it. The party tabled an amendment, which might have defeated the government. It was known that the Taoiseach, Jack Lynch, was prepared to call an election on this issue, against what would have been a divided Fine Gael party.[17] Cosgrave did little to bridge relations within his party or with Labour with a speech in the Dáil that referred to 'Communists and their fellow-travellers and soft-headed liberals ... always talking about repression.'[18] Yet Cosgrave was in a clear minority within his parliamentary party.

It was a bomb exploding in Dublin on the night of 1 December 1972 that saved Cosgrave's leadership. The debate on the bill was taking place when two bombs detonated in Dublin city centre, killing two men and injuring over a hundred people. The bombs were probably planted by loyalist paramilitaries (though there remains suspicion of British collusion), but it was initially assumed that this was the work of the Provisional IRA.[19] The Dáil was suspended for an hour, and by the time the vote was to take place the Fine Gael party had rowed in behind Cosgrave. The Fine Gael amendment was withdrawn, and Cosgrave's confident appearance on television that night won him more support. FitzGerald later admitted that Cosgrave was right both on the substance and the politics of the issue, but that was not how he felt at the time.[20] FitzGerald still pushed for Cosgrave's removal at a subsequent parliamentary party meeting, claiming that Cosgrave 'neither led nor followed', but Cosgrave won the vote easily.[21]

Jack Lynch could see that Cosgrave was not leading a unified party and would have called an election immediately, except that Christmas intervened and he was wary of being seen to make political capital of the tragic bombing. He instead chose to wait until early in the new year, calling an election for 28 February 1973.[22] It was a surprise to most observers. The timing was controversial because it denied those aged over 18 but under 21 the recently acquired right to vote – the new legislation had not yet come into effect. The day after the election was called, on 6 February, Cosgrave and Tom O'Higgins met Brendan Corish and James Tully from Labour and after just a few hours they agreed in principle to form a coalition government if the results allowed. It helped that Cosgrave and Corish liked each other and had worked together in the second inter-party government. A day later, the two parties issued a joint manifesto under the title *There is an Alternative*, which was a 14-point programme for government that hoped to transform Ireland into a 'modern progressive society based on social justice'.[23] This was exactly the sort of plan FitzGerald was looking for.

Ireland had recently joined the EEC, and though Labour had opposed membership, the issue was now off the table, so the two parties could agree to 'pledge [themselves] to maximising Ireland's influence within the European Community'. Differences within Labour on Northern Ireland were buried in an anodyne pledge to find a 'peaceful solution in the North'. There was a promise to declare 'a housing emergency', and Garret FitzGerald inserted a commitment to a wealth tax.[24] The agreement completely changed the nature of the campaign, because now, as the slogan indicated, there was an alternative to Fianna Fáil, which had been in power for the previous 16 years.

It might have been expected that security issues or Northern Ireland would dominate the 1973 election campaign, but in fact the economy featured most, and specifically it was prices or cost of living issues that emerged as the most important issue in an opinion poll.[25] Both sides made significant promises to increase social welfare payments and reduce taxes, such as VAT on food. Fianna Fáil tried to emphasise the differences between Fine Gael and Labour, the proposed coalition parties and differences within them, especially on security issues, highlighted in that Offences against the State Act episode. But Fine Gael's election ad, 'Don't blame the government. Change it' might have resonated most with the mood in the country.

As Finance spokesman, FitzGerald frequently clashed with George Colley, the Minister for Finance, and FitzGerald's combative nature was welcomed within Fine Gael, even if some of his unorthodox views were not. His willingness to take on Fianna Fáil ministers contrasted with the more laid-back, even lazy approach of others on the Fine Gael front bench. In the 1973 campaign FitzGerald was thought to have easily beaten Colley in a TV debate, in which he 'conveyed the impression of being better informed and more sure of his arguments'.[26]

Haughey kept a low profile in the 1973 election, although he comfortably topped the poll in his Dublin North-East constituency. His candidacy saw some annoyance in Fianna Fáil, with the Fianna Fáil elder statesman Frank Aiken refusing to stand in protest.

Despite Fianna Fáil gaining votes in 1973, the transfer pact between Fine Gael and Labour gave the parties a seat bonus, which allowed Liam Cosgrave to become Taoiseach of a 'National Coalition'. Its 14-point plan, *There is an Alternative*, was Ireland's first programme for government. This was going to be the 'government of all the talents'. FitzGerald assumed he would get the job of Minister for Finance. It was the job he wanted. He had already started to consult with civil servants and likely coalition colleagues, and between the election and the formation of the government he had made a speech setting out his economic approach.[27] But Cosgrave was unwilling to give a portfolio such as Finance to FitzGerald, someone he did not trust, though he said it was because FitzGerald lacked Dáil experience.[28] Corish was offered Finance, but he knew better than to accept. So instead Richie Ryan was offered and accepted it.

Cosgrave was curt when offering FitzGerald Foreign Affairs. FitzGerald might have been disappointed with not getting Finance, but as Minister for Foreign Affairs he was central to government policy on two issues he was deeply interested in, Northern Ireland and the EEC, of which Ireland had just become a member. For Cosgrave, having FitzGerald in Foreign Affairs had two advantages. It was a policy area on which they did not diverge greatly, though while it was said of Cosgrave that his 'views on relations with Britain are indistinguishable from those traditionally held by Fianna Fáil', FitzGerald's views were by this time mainstream.[29] The main 'foreign' policy area that would take up government time would be Northern Ireland, and it was one which the Department of the Taoiseach still formally controlled. Since FitzGerald would be attending EEC meetings, it also meant that he would spend quite a lot of time out of the country.

FitzGerald was typically energetic in Iveagh House, the home of the Department of Foreign Affairs. Despite the fact that his wife's fear of flying meant that he too was initially reluctant to fly, he took to diplomatic travel with alacrity. Well versed in world affairs, he fitted in with foreign ministers and world leaders. Much of his foreign work was with the EEC Council of Ministers. He was an enthusiastic integrationist, which was in tune with the mood of the time. He was a natural at conversing with other foreign ministers, and enjoyed the task of hosting the Presidency of the Council of Ministers in the first half of 1975, which meant that he represented the EEC in relation to its foreign policy. In his autobiography he reveals himself as a patrician who clearly enjoyed rubbing shoulders with other world leaders, and in a different time he might have been happy to redraw maps of distant lands like a European statesman. FitzGerald regarded Foreign Affairs as the high point of his career.[30]

At home he had more deadly issues to deal with. FitzGerald expanded the Northern Ireland unit in the Department of Foreign Affairs, making it a well-resourced section. He immediately tasked the diplomat Seán Donlon with the role of opening up channels of communications with political and religious leaders in Northern Ireland. This also had the effect of bringing in many new people to the Department who identified with FitzGerald, and felt some intrinsic loyalty to him later when he became Taoiseach.[31] The Northern Ireland issue was to see more progress than perhaps expected, as the government helped shape the Sunningdale Agreement, a peace accord that saw power-sharing in Northern Ireland, including a role for Dublin through a Council of Ireland. (The Good Friday/Belfast Agreement was later referred to as 'Sunningdale for slow learners'.) While this was led from the Department of the Taoiseach, the Department of Foreign Affairs was actively involved at all stages.

The Stormont parliament – Northern Ireland's seat of self-government since the 1920s – had been suspended and direct rule from London had been imposed by the British in March 1972, a time when violence in Northern Ireland was near its height. The British government under Ted Heath was interested in seeking long-term solutions to the communal violence, and held a plebiscite on Irish unity shortly after the 1973 election. It was boycotted by nationalists, and so the 99 per cent vote in favour of maintaining the union was not meaningful. The British published a White Paper on *Northern Ireland Constitutional Proposals* soon after FitzGerald was appointed to Foreign Affairs in 1973. The proposals provided for an assembly elected by proportional representation, an executive drawn from both communities and 'institutional arrangements for consultation and co-operation between Northern Ireland and the Republic of Ireland'.[32] These were very much along the lines of the solution preferred by the SDLP, a party increasingly dominated by John Hume.

FitzGerald had become close to Hume, whose analysis of the problem was that the relationship between the two communities was damaged and only political institutions that enabled power sharing would be able to fix them. That relationship caused some irritation in the government, particularly with Conor Cruise O'Brien, who remained the Labour Party spokesman on Northern Ireland, even if he did not always actually speak for his party.

The UK government's Constitutional Proposals caused deep divisions in the Ulster Unionist Party (UUP), which itself was no longer the monolith that had once represented all of unionism. The British pushed ahead with these plans nonetheless and an election took place for a Northern Ireland Assembly in June 1973. That election exposed the splits in unionism, with a breakaway Vanguard party and the Democratic Unionist Party (DUP) under Rev. Ian Paisley polling well. The election saw the SDLP established as the main voice of nationalism. In holding an election, the British had done the easy part first; now it needed an agreement for what shape that executive would take.

The UUP narrowly agreed in October 1973 to enter a power-sharing executive. Under the Constitutional Proposals it was expected that an executive coalition of the UUP, SDLP and the cross-community Alliance Party would be formed by 1 January 1974. That was agreed on 21 November, but issues remained. Despite the divisions within unionism, the British went ahead with a proposed conference to agree the details of the Constitutional Proposals document. That took place over a weekend in early December in Sunningdale, in the south of England. Two key components caused difficulty. One was an insistence that Ireland change its Articles 2 and 3 – which claimed sovereignty over the six counties of Northern Ireland; the other a proposed Council of Ireland – a North–South ministerial body that would at least give ministers from Dublin some input in the running of Northern Ireland. There was an acceptance that a referendum to remove or amend Articles 2 and 3 would most likely be defeated, so that was not pushed. The National Coalition of Fine Gael and Labour did, however, accept that 'there could be no change in the status of Northern

Ireland until a majority of the people of Northern Ireland desired a change in their status.' It was Ireland's most formal recognition of Northern Ireland's status, but the Ulster unionists found the Council of Ireland objectionable and it was watered down somewhat; but even then it seemed to be a concession too far for many unionists. In the Irish government, Conor Cruise O'Brien was sensitive to unionist concerns, and felt that this clause could lead to the collapse of the agreement, but FitzGerald felt 'that *exclusive* attention to legitimate unionist concerns may dangerously exacerbate tensions on the nationalist side, thus abandoning mainstream moderate nationalism to the IRA'.[33] The two men were, at that stage, probably as close to each other on Northern Ireland as any others in government. They both rejected the myths of romantic Irish nationalism. But they did not get on personally, and O'Brien would become a fierce critic of what he would see as FitzGerald's attachment to Hume. It must have hurt, though, because FitzGerald always saw his sensitivity to unionism as peculiar to him. FitzGerald assumed joint chairmanship, but his style irritated some, which one British diplomat described as 'a bee . . . buzzing in Dr FitzGerald's bonnet (very excitedly, as his always do).'[34]

In any case the British and one part of the unionist leadership was willing to accept the Council of Ireland. How could the Irish government reject that? When an agreement was reached at Sunningdale on 9 December 1973 FitzGerald admitted to feeling that 'we had arrived. The whole [conflict] was settled . . . the IRA were not involved, and we were obviously thinking about the parties, but it seemed that if we got an agreement, we thought the IRA would be almost made irrelevant.'[35] This was FitzGerald's great goal – to wipe out the IRA, for he saw it as the source of much of the problem in Northern Ireland.

And so, on 1 January 1974 many executive powers were transferred to the Northern Ireland executive and assembly. But O'Brien was right, and FitzGerald was proved wrong; the Ulster Unionist leader and chief minister Brian Faulkner was too weak to bring a majority of unionists with him.³⁶ Almost immediately Faulkner indicated a problem. A speech by Cosgrave, designed to reassure a southern audience, was taken up by unionists to indicate a lack of good faith. O'Brien claimed that the Irish government oversold this idea of the Council of Ireland.³⁷ Most Protestants opposed it as a slippery slope, and the Provisional IRA saw it as selling the Catholic population short of its stated goal of unity. Sunningdale was also problematic in that it deferred many of the trickier decisions, such as the operation of the Council of Ireland. Faulkner was forced to resign as party leader when he lost a party vote on the Council of Ireland, though he remained in the executive. A campaign led by loyalists was started to bring down the new Stormont executive, with the slogan 'Dublin is just a Sunningdale away' used to appeal to unionist fears of a united Ireland.³⁸

A UK general election at the end of February caused the two communities to polarise, as elections there usually do. Anti-agreement unionists won more seats in Northern Ireland, and the British government changed, with Harold Wilson's Labour Party coming to power. Wilson had less interest in Northern Ireland than Heath, and he used the term 'spongers' to refer to loyalist strikers.³⁹ Many in British Labour had sympathy for the idea of Irish unity, and found dealing with loyalist intransigence frustrating. The Wilson government actively considered a unilateral withdrawal from Northern Ireland. This private proposal scared the Irish government; Garret FitzGerald warned the British that it was likely to lead to all-out war.⁴⁰ If political leadership is about making a difference, it is interesting to consider what another leader would have done in the same situation. A Lynch government would have certainly tried to dissuade the British from a disorganised withdrawal. A Blaney government would have almost certainly encouraged it. What a Haughey government in the mid-1970s would have done is much less certain.

Wilson was disinclined to defend the Sunningdale Agreement. He had not signed it, and anyway, 1974 was a year of significant upheaval in Britain – he had enough to be doing. When an Ulster Workers' Council strike was called, starting on 14 May, blockading roads, closing factories and restricting electricity, the London government did very little to break it. On 17 May bombs in Dublin and Monaghan killed 32 people. This horrific event, with no warnings, reminded the South that it did not want to import the Troubles. Ten days later the always precarious power-sharing executive in Northern Ireland collapsed. After this the UK Labour Party viewed Northern Ireland primarily as a security concern and as an internal problem, and tried to bring the two communities together, but excluding Dublin. FitzGerald's involvement was reduced, though he tried to maintain contacts with the British. Security concerns were ever present in the South. As well as the Dublin and Monaghan bombings, the IRA murdered a Fine Gael senator in March 1974, and in 1975 a Dutch businessman was kidnapped by the IRA. In 1976 the newly appointed UK ambassador to Dublin was murdered by the IRA near his official residence in south County Dublin, on his way to his first official meeting with FitzGerald. This led to an amendment to the Offences Against the State Act, which Fianna Fáil cynically opposed. The episode eventually led to the resignation of President Cearbhall Ó Dálaigh.

After the failure of the Sunningdale Agreement, FitzGerald was even more heavily influenced by Hume, even though, as Conor Cruise O'Brien pointed out, he had been badly misled by Hume as to what would be acceptable or not to Northern unionists. It was odd that FitzGerald did not have a better sense of this himself, given his mother's background. Indeed his only close relations on the island were Belfast Protestants. One of FitzGerald's senior officials, Seán Donlon, observed that 'the relationship with the SDLP was very close, to the point of intimacy before, during and after' Sunningdale.[41] In this FitzGerald would differ from Haughey who was more sceptical of Hume, and who viewed the Northern Ireland problem in a different way – as a problem that the British and Irish governments need to solve.

FitzGerald did, however, continue an initiative started by Jack Lynch, which aimed to change attitudes in the US to the nature of the conflict in Northern Ireland. Irish-Americans 'had inherited parental or grandparental memories of a colonial war and . . . with their curious frozen-in-aspic concept of Irish nationalism, saw democratically elected Irish governments, whatever their composition, as quislings'.[42] The concerted effort to change US opinion was to yield benefits later in his career.

FitzGerald, meanwhile, was a very effective media performer, and used his contacts to push his image as an activist, if somewhat unkempt, minister. Ted Nealon, later a government press secretary and Fine Gael TD, but then an RTÉ journalist, made a piece for RTÉ's *7 Days* programme that looked like a PR shoot for FitzGerald, with him making a virtue of his ruffled appearance as not being that important compared to high politics: He was shown as someone who was always on the go; he revealed that there was no time in his busy schedule to even get his hair cut, so he had his wife, Joan, do it. 'You can try what you like with my hair, it always stands up. It's just made like that.'[43] In that report the *Irish Press* political correspondent Michael Mills speculated that FitzGerald's impatience might be a problem for him if he wanted the leadership of his party. He continued to involve himself broadly in cabinet discussions, having engaged an economist as a special adviser, even going so far as to produce proposals for Finance, in clear breach of government procedure.[44] He frequently leaked and lobbied against his Taoiseach, Liam Cosgrave.[45] He continued to split opinion within his own party, with many remaining mistrustful of him.

※ ※ ※

While the National Coalition of Fine Gael and Labour could claim some reforms in its favour, it faced economic headwinds. There was a recession, caused by the first oil shock, in 1973–74. The government initially borrowed heavily to maintain public services, but then tried to scale these back. It could never get a handle on inflation, and no jobs were created. Farmers were being brought into the tax net. The Minister for Finance, Richie Ryan, got the epithet 'Red Richie' and 'Richie Ruin' from a popular TV show, *Hall's Pictorial Weekly*. Late in the government it introduced a wealth tax – FitzGerald's idea – that upset many of Fine Gael's natural supporters. In an address to the nation in late 1975 Liam Cosgrave told the people, 'Next year is going to be tough. There is no point in putting a gloss on that hard economic reality.'[46] Though the Irish economy was starting to improve in 1976, it was not going to make up for the fact that prices had doubled since the start of that government.[47]

Neither was the government internally coherent. Each party tended to be accused of simply implementing the other's policies. Cosgrave had surprised most of his colleagues by voting against a bill that would legalise contraceptives, helping to defeat it. For the Labour Minister for Industry and Commerce, Justin Keating, 'there were three parties in Government, Fine Gael, Labour and the FitzGerald–Keating grouping'.[48] Within the parties, especially Labour, there were tensions between pragmatists and ideologues, with a young senator and academic from Galway, Michael D. Higgins, leading the ideologues who opposed Labour's involvement in coalition or indeed any compromise.[49]

The Fine Gael party organisation had also not received any renewal in the years that the party had been in government. Most senior members concentrated on policy issues, so while Fianna Fáil engaged in an organisational overhaul, policy development and regular polling of voters, Fine Gael remained an 'amateurish and authoritarian' political organisation.[50]

On 21 May 1977 Liam Cosgrave addressed the Fine Gael Árd Fheis in bullish fashion when he complained about media enquiries into the 'Heavy Gang' – allegations of systematic Garda beatings of terrorist suspects. Cosgrave took an orthodox law-and-order approach to police brutality – very different from how Garret FitzGerald viewed it. Cosgrave said of those making enquiries, 'some of them are blow-ins. Now as far as we're concerned they can blow out or blow up'.[51] The following morning's *Sunday Independent* reported rumours that an election was on the way – 'All Set for June 15'. The date was wrong, but only by a day.

When Cosgrave called the election, he did so without knowing the popularity of Fianna Fáil. Only an opinion poll published during the election campaign showed that Fianna Fáil was likely to achieve an overall majority, leading FitzGerald to wonder aloud whether a Taoiseach could 'undissolve the Dáil?' The timing of the election was one thing, but the government seemed to go into the election without an obvious strategy. Fianna Fáil focused on the economy, with a manifesto that promised to cut taxes and increase spending, in the hope that the economy would pick up enough that no new borrowing would be needed. Even at the time commentators warned that Fianna Fáil's proposals were potentially dangerous, but they offered them with a self-confidence that voters bought. A new style of campaigning imported from the US appealed to the younger voters who had recently been enfranchised, as T-shirts and stickers emblazoned with 'Bring back Jack' emphasised Lynch's proven popularity over the dour Cosgrave. Conor Cruise O'Brien tried to emphasise Charles Haughey's presence on the Fianna Fáil ticket as a negative. But it was used against O'Brien, who was criticised as 'anti-national' for making his attack via the BBC. Cosgrave too liked to speak on security matters, suggesting that Fianna Fáil could not be trusted. But voters were interested in the economy, not Northern Ireland, and Garret FitzGerald rejected O'Brien's plea to focus on Haughey.[52]

When the votes were counted it showed the polls were broadly right. The result for Fine Gael and Labour was made worse by an earlier gerrymandering of the constituencies designed to ensure a majority for the outgoing coalition. It increased the number of three-seat constituencies, on the assumption that Fine Gael and Labour would together outpoll Fianna Fáil, giving the government parties a seat bonus. It backfired spectacularly, delivering a huge majority for Fianna Fáil, and putting Jack Lynch back in as Taoiseach.

Cosgrave resigned his leadership immediately, pre-empting an inevitable leadership challenge. A survey by NOP for the *Irish Times* in advance of the election showed that after Cosgrave, Garret FitzGerald was Fine Gael's best-known minister, and most favoured to succeed him. In the event, 49 per cent chose him, and he was also the only cabinet member to come close to Cosgrave in terms of popularity.[53] Though it was not his intention, Cosgrave's decision to put FitzGerald in Foreign Affairs possibly helped FitzGerald because it meant that FitzGerald had been away for many government meetings during the coalition's lifetime. This was a distinct advantage for FitzGerald when it came to the allocation of blame for what were seen as austerity measures. The deputy leader, Tom O'Higgins, had been chosen as the party's candidate for the presidential election due to take place in 1973. So O'Higgins chose not to run for the Dáil in 1973, effectively ruling himself out of cabinet and politics. As a moderate, in between Cosgrave and FitzGerald, O'Higgins might have been a natural candidate to succeed Cosgrave.

FitzGerald's team was quick to canvass support and he was immediately confident of victory. Foreign Affairs had been a happy time for FitzGerald, who had enjoyed the foreign travel and had established a reputation as a statesman. With O'Higgins and Declan Costello gone, and Richie Ryan – the favourite in the conservative wing of the party – choosing not to run, probably hurt by his time in Finance, and Paddy Cooney having lost his seat, there were not many rivals left for FitzGerald. Then Peter Barry decided to run. Barry, a solid if unexceptional performer in government, ran with the presumed backing of the more traditional members of the party leadership, including Cosgrave. Barry canvassed support, and was confident of 25 of the 62 votes in the Fine Gael parliamentary party – just seven votes short of the number needed for victory. Barry and FitzGerald arranged a meeting and compared notes. Garret thought he had 43 votes and Barry just 19. Instead of assuming that this was mind games on FitzGerald's part, or using this information to redouble his efforts, Barry conceded defeat. Peter Barry was not as hungry as FitzGerald was for the job. Barry probably fairly assessed that much of his support was to 'stop Garret', rather than reflecting any active support for himself. After a decisive defeat the party was in the mood for change. Peter Barry felt that 'The humour of the grassroots was that they were so shocked by the defeat in the election that they could only see knights on white horses and Garret appeared to be that.'[54]

And so, on 1 July 1977, Garret FitzGerald was unanimously chosen to lead Fine Gael.

6.

LET'S SACK JACK

When he became leader of Fine Gael, Garret FitzGerald's goal was to replace Jack Lynch, the most popular politician in Ireland. In 1977 Charles Haughey's ambition was the same – to replace Jack Lynch. For FitzGerald the 1970s were years when he eased his way to the party leadership. For Haughey the decade was much more difficult. At the start of the decade his career appeared over. Many assumed it was. But Haughey had not given up. He was back in cabinet following the 1977 election. But Haughey had had to work hard to get to that position, and that opinion poll that had given Fine Gael such as shock at the start of the 1977 election campaign contained bad news for Haughey. Although he was a distant second after Lynch in terms of popularity among Fianna Fáil supporters to become Taoiseach, he was also the least popular of the options given them. Haughey was still a polarising figure.[1]

It was hardly a surprise. In 1970 Haughey was out of cabinet, and *persona non grata* for most senior members of Fianna Fáil. For his old friend Brian Lenihan, visits to Haughey in Abbeville were necessarily surreptitious – he would not risk visiting him in his own state car.[2] His attempt to topple Jack Lynch immediately after the arms trial failed miserably, but so did the PAC inquiry into the funds that Haughey controlled, which some at the time saw as a political trial designed to end Haughey's career, a view Haughey shared.[3] He was still popular among many of the elite in Irish society, according to Muiris Mac Conghail, who marvelled at the attendance at one of Haughey's parties in Abbeville.[4] Haughey's wilderness years were not a desert crossing. He did not retire, or even re-evaluate his life. Haughey just started again from where he was.

To beat Lynch he was forced to take a longer view. In 1971 Lynch was in complete control of the party – Seán Lemass observed as much to Paddy Hillery.[5] Haughey sought to rebuild himself within the party with a view to taking over the leadership of the party from the bottom up.[6] Though he was then on the back benches, much of Fianna Fáil politics in the early 1970s centred on Haughey and what to do with him. Unlike Blaney, who openly defied the party leadership, Haughey did nothing that would cause censure. He took no part in the semi-rebellion against Lynch that Kevin Boland fomented at the 1971 Fianna Fáil Árd Fheis. Haughey shook Lynch's hand on the stage and told Hillery, 'I've nothing to do with this.' Hillery believed him.[7] Haughey used his time to get to know the grassroots and the organisation of the party. He accepted any invitation to a Fianna Fáil event around the country. Those invitations might have been in contravention of an informal 'Shun Haughey' directive. Haughey engaged in what became known as the 'rubber chicken' circuit, 'half pilgrimage and half recruitment drive' funded by business friends.[8] Aided by a small group of supporters, including PJ Mara and Liam Lawlor, he spent three or four evenings a week travelling around Ireland to cumainn and Comhairle Ceanntar meetings. As ministers contended with the worsening crisis in the North in the early 1970s, the local Fianna Fáil organisations were delighted to get a person of Haughey's stature to speak to them. His speeches were uncontroversial, never risking anything overtly critical of the party leadership. These trips built connections and popularity with the party's grassroots, 'manipulating the vanity of those on the lower rungs of the party'.[9]

Haughey worked his way back into the party organisation. He got on the party's trade union committee, and was elected one of the party's vice-presidents in 1972, which gave him a position on the National Executive.[10] There were only five nominees for five positions, but it is revealing that the leadership did not seek to exclude him. Lynch seemed to welcome his co-operation, whereas the old guard, Frank Aiken, Seán MacEntee and Erskine Childers were all deeply opposed to Haughey. Aiken urged that Haughey not be allowed to stand as a party candidate in the 1973 election, going through with his threat not to run himself when Haughey was a party candidate.[11] Lynch and Haughey's only interaction in that election was 'an embarrassing handshake' at Ballymun shopping centre during an election walkabout.[12] Haughey had built up a formidable local party organisation that offered services to constituents that went well beyond what was normal, including gifting Christmas turkeys and helping to cover the cost of funerals. It was a very expensive operation. Haughey was returned in that election with an increased vote. His main rival for the still not vacant leadership, George Colley, had performed poorly as the economics spokesman in that election, especially in a television debate with Garret FitzGerald, and his political capital in the party was significantly reduced. In the aftermath of the 1973 election, in which Fianna Fáil lost power, Haughey told one journalist, 'If the Taoiseach resigns, I will definitely be in the market [for the Fianna Fáil leadership]. But I have many important soundings to make before the party meeting.'[13]

If Haughey had ever seriously considered leaving politics or Fianna Fáil after the Arms Crisis, his financial affairs might have made him reconsider. Haughey's lifestyle and his constituency operation required heavy funding that relied on borrowing from banks and gifts from friends. Since those loans or donations would create expectations for future preferment, he had to keep going.

His personal life was also complicated. In 1972 Haughey commenced a long-term love affair with Terry Keane, the journalist and wife of a High Court judge. The affair was conducted in expensive restaurants – the Tandoori Rooms and especially Dublin's Le Coq Hardi, where he spent up to IR£1,000 a week – and on weekends away in luxury hotels in Paris and in friends' flats.[14] While the relationship was initially secret and furtive, as it continued there was no attempt to conceal the relationship from Keane's family; Haughey became a somewhat normal and regular part of family life for Terry Keane's children. It was behaviour that was anathema to the social mores of the time, that would have ended a political career in the US or the UK, and surely in Ireland, and it is evidence that Haughey remained a risk taker. It seems he was not even faithful to Keane – there were many rumours of other affairs. Haughey's lifestyle represented a complete rejection of the austere approach of the revolutionary generation of his parents and father-in-law.

Broadcaster Gerry Ryan, a frequent visitor to Abbeville, was struck at how it 'exuded wealth and privilege', noting the number of staff who were employed in the estate.[15] In 1974 Haughey bought Inishvickillane, an island off the Kerry coast, for IR£25,000 (€260,000 in 2023). While his property purchases were self-financed by profits from previous property sales, Haughey's expensive lifestyle at this time was largely financed by loans. A later tribunal that looked into his finances shows that in the 1970s he was writing cheques for IR£12,000 (about €125,000 in 2023) a month and that his bank was increasingly concerned at the size of his overdraft.[16] This was managed by his business partner, Des Traynor, who had been a partner in the Haughey Boland accountancy firm, but was now managing director of Guinness Mahon, a small merchant bank. There was a 'unique' level of secrecy in Haughey's finances, on which he failed to pay tax.[17] In 1976 he sold for a huge profit the stud farm in Ashbourne, County Meath he had bought in 1968. What had been a rural village was becoming a satellite town and the IR£350,000 (€3.6 million in 2023) he made from the sale was used to pay down some of his debts.[18] There were rumours of corruption, and that the missing money from the Northern 'relief' fund might have been spent by Haughey on his own lifestyle. Later disclosures suggest that as well as borrowing heavily, he was dependent on donations from wealthy businessmen.

Garret FitzGerald's finances were also a cause of concern for him in the mid-1970s, though his problems were on a different scale.

On becoming Minister for Foreign Affairs in 1973 FitzGerald had to give up many of his other roles, including consultancy and work in UCD. These losses were not made up for by his ministerial salary, which was not generous in the 1970s. He observed that his outgoings greatly exceeded his income and his overdraft rose. He sold his large house on Eglinton Road, settling eventually in a house in Palmerston Road, also a very comfortable house, but a smaller one, shared with his by now married daughter.

✳ ✳ ✳

Tired after an intense period in government, many of the Fianna Fáil front bench took a relaxed, almost amateur, approach to its period of opposition starting in 1973. By contrast Haughey worked hard in the Dáil, speaking extensively on many bills, especially on the arts and the economy. He was pro-business, while maintaining strong links with the trade union movement.[19] On the 1974 budget statements, he gave a forensic critique of the National Coalition government's proposals. He criticised the government for failing 'to resist the temptation to curry favour on the basis of a soak-the-rich campaign', complaining that they might oversee the end of private property in the country.[20] Haughey was no free market zealot however. He advocated economic planning where government was an equal partner with the trade union movement and employers.[21] He became a joint secretary of the party, along with his friend Brian Lenihan. Lynch believed that bringing Haughey back onto the front bench would unify, or at least pacify, the party, and so in January 1975 Haughey was made Fianna Fáil spokesman on Health and Social Welfare, often regarded as a mid-ranking position. Lynch did not consult with Des O'Malley, one of his closest confidants, who would have advised against it. It was all the more surprising given that O'Malley had told Lynch in January 1972 that Haughey had met with senior IRA figures after the arms trials in 1970 and shared some intelligence about a possible informer within the IRA.[22]

Though he was back on the front bench, Haughey was not in the inner circle of the party. But Haughey understood power better than any of his rivals, including the importance of party institutions. That explains his decision to tour the party's grassroots meetings, which selected candidates who would become TDs and senators, who would elect the leader.[23] He joined policy committees, which could set party policy. Senior party members had often ignored these, because the party was so frequently in government, and government set policy. Haughey worked diligently at his brief in opposition, and was certainly involved in pushing for a significant shift in Fianna Fáil policy on Northern Ireland, which sought for Britain to declare its 'commitment to implement an ordered withdrawal from her involvement in the Six Counties of Northern Ireland'.[24] Though it was claimed as having been adopted unanimously by the front bench, it was not. Lynch and his allies opposed the new policy, introduced by Michael O'Kennedy, later a Haughey ally.[25] It was at odds with Lynch's earlier Tralee speech, which aimed at assuaging unionist fears. The new policy was criticised by the SDLP and by unionists, though welcomed by Sinn Féin, which, referring to the splits in Fianna Fáil, asked publicly whether the party's policy represented 'the political opportunism of O'Kennedy and Haughey or the weak-kneed subservience to Britain of [Ruairí] Brugha and Lynch'?[26]

Haughey's approach to Northern Ireland was different from Lynch's and Garret FitzGerald's. If they wanted to build for unity through engagement with unionism, Haughey rejected this approach. He preferred to go over the heads of unionism and engage the British directly. It was also an approach that was much more popular in the Fianna Fáil grassroots, which he continued to cultivate, though it was not yet a view shared by the general public.[27] The Fianna Fáil party was being modernised, and it was ready for the coming 1977 election campaign. Haughey knew that a poor result for Fianna Fáil in this election would likely lead to a leadership competition. The oil crisis, the unpopularity of the National Coalition, a professional election campaign by Fianna Fáil and a manifesto that promised to pump-prime the economy would help secure victory. The manifesto was largely the work of Martin O'Donoghue, an economist and close adviser to Jack Lynch, but Haughey was said to have been privately scathing about it.[28]

The 1977 election delivered Fianna Fáil its biggest ever majority. That did not seem like good news for Haughey. His rival's popularity had delivered the victory. But at the count in Dublin he looked delighted. When the journalist Geraldine Kennedy asked why he was so pleased with himself – it was a Lynch majority – Haughey replied, 'Yes, but they're all my people. Now I know I'll be leader.'[29] By contrast, Lynch made little effort to cultivate his new TDs; one of that cohort, Bertie Ahern, wondered if Lynch even knew who he was.[30]

Haughey was appointed Minister for Health and Social Welfare, not a senior ministry, but one that Haughey could see advantages to having. He would use it to seek the party leadership. In June 1977 his team thought Haughey would only be certain of 12 or 13 votes out of the 84 available.[31] He could do something about that. He set up a large private office headed by Brendan O'Donnell, Haughey's private secretary from Agriculture, to help deal with the many queries from the party's backbench TDs that the Health and Social Welfare portfolios generate, which became a recruiting office for Haughey's leadership ambitions. O'Donnell and PJ Mara kept lists of TDs, their interests and likely leanings in the inevitable contest between Colley and Haughey. As Séamus Brennan put it, they would 'find out where people itched so that Haughey could scratch'.[32]

There was another possible candidate for the leadership of Fianna Fáil. Paddy Hillery was by then President of Ireland, but it was known in political circles he was not enjoying the job. Was there a possibility that Hillery would quit the presidency to contest the Fianna Fáil leadership? It was very unlikely that Hillery would do such a thing, not least because he had agreed to take the job in order to give some continuity to the office. It would be difficult for him to find the vacant seat he would need to be eligible to stand for the leadership. Still, Hillery remained convinced that in autumn 1979 Haughey had spread rumours that President Hillery was on the verge of resigning because his marriage was about to end as a result of an extramarital affair. There was no truth in the rumours, but they became so endemic that Hillery was forced to formally deny them in a press conference. Hillery's certainty that Haughey was the source of the rumours was based on a comment Haughey later made to Hillery – 'It is all over now' – and also from some information he received from friends. The rumours abated some months later when Haughey achieved his goal.[33] If Haughey was responsible for the rumours it shows the extent of his strategic thinking in closing off any other paths to defeat.

In the Department of Health Haughey brought in regulations to restrict tobacco advertising, including that they must display health warnings, making Ireland the first country in the world to do so. He banned smoking at his press conferences and on the platform of the Fianna Fáil Árd Fheis. This was the sort of bold yet simple measure that had marked him as different in his earlier ministerial career. But Haughey had a more difficult problem to deal with. The McGee decision on the right to buy contraceptives required a political response. The failure of the National Coalition to legislate meant it was now on Haughey's desk. It is hard to overstate how sensitive the issue of contraceptives was at the time. Many in Fianna Fáil were uncomfortable with any liberalisation. There were demands from feminists to legalise some form of birth control or family planning. Haughey risked a conservative backlash if he was too liberal, but neither could he do nothing. His 'Irish solution to an Irish problem' was hardly liberal, and some saw it as cynical: married couples could be prescribed contraceptives by their GP. However, it was a pragmatic solution to a political problem. It passed, despite significant opposition within the party, and it did not cause major problems from the Church. Jim Gibbons refused to vote in favour of it, which would normally have led to disciplinary procedures – he could have lost his seat in cabinet, or been temporarily expelled from the parliamentary party – but Lynch did nothing, which raised questions again about favouritism and their relationship in the Arms Crisis.

The government also annoyed many backbenchers who were sent out to defend a farmers' levy. Taxing farmers was a big issue, and unpopular in rural areas. Colley, who was in Finance, announced the introduction of the levy, and negotiated some amendments to the measure, but the government backed down, annoying urban and PAYE workers, as well as those TDs who had spent their time defending it.[34] There were PAYE protests and pay strikes in key public services. With the second oil crisis the economy also started to falter, and the results of the 1979 local and European elections were very bad for Fianna Fáil. Many of the Fianna Fáil TDs elected in 1977 were now concerned for their seats. It was acknowledged that Lynch would not lead the party into the next election, so they started to think about who might. Haughey was unaffected by the government's worsening image. An opinion poll in May 1979 showed Haughey to be the most popular politician in the country, with an approval rating ahead of Lynch and his main rival for the succession of Fianna Fáil, George Colley.[35]

❖ ❖ ❖

The other man out to remove Lynch was also working hard. The task facing Garret FitzGerald in 1977 was not easy. The party he took over was catatonic, moved to action only at elections, but even then its electoral performance was determined mainly by whether Irish voters were sufficiently tired of Fianna Fáil. FitzGerald had 'not so much to rouse Fine Gael as to create it'.[36] He saw Fine Gael as an essentially amateur political organisation split between party elites who governed or aspired to government, and local activists with little interest in policy.[37] While in opposition many Fine Gael TDs worked other jobs, with some travelling from the Law Library to spend evenings in Leinster House. The party was badly exposed by Fianna Fáil, which by 1977 had introduced a more professional organisation and political communications strategy than had ever been seen before.

Fine Gael had an inferiority complex and struggled to show itself as a distinct political movement beyond its not being Fianna Fáil. Despite this, expectations were high, and FitzGerald took on the challenge with enthusiasm and characteristic energy. In his favour, Fine Gael's poor electoral showing in 1977 meant that the likelihood of a Fine Gael comeback, regardless of any activity, was high, and Jack Lynch, though popular, was coming to the end of his political career.

One of Fine Gael's challenges was 'quota squatting'. Fine Gael was nearly always assured a seat in every constituency, and once a TD was elected, the party candidate selection rules made it easy for that TD to hold that seat by preventing good candidates from running on the same ticket. While it suited the 'squatters', it damaged party morale and put a limit on the party's electoral performance. FitzGerald quickly came to an arrangement to replace the party's general secretary with a young but widely experienced marketing executive, Peter Prendergast, and the former journalist and head of the Government Information Service, Ted Nealon, became Fine Gael's director of Press and Information. In September 1977 the three men started a nationwide tour, spending a day in each constituency over the next six months.[38]

FitzGerald inherited a parliamentary party that was stronger in rural areas than urban ones. In choosing his front bench he removed several older, more conservative people, such as Paddy Donegan, who had caused the resignation of President Ó Dálaigh during Cosgrave's government. FitzGerald took the decision to promote young TDs and candidates, and Prendergast encouraged young people to get involved in the party. They drafted a new party constitution which was designed to diminish the power of sitting TDs, remove 'paper branches' – local party branches that did not really exist but gave a TD some voting power – and to give more power to ordinary members. The 1978 Árd Fheis endorsed these proposals with enthusiasm, and Prendergast started to fill positions of constituency organisers who would liaise with party headquarters independently of the local TD. The Árd Fheis was a success also in that having moved to the RDS, where Fianna Fáil had started to hold its Árd Fheis, the party managed to fill the main hall with over four thousand delegates for the party leader's address.[39] FitzGerald set up a youth section, and encouraged dissent and criticism of his leadership.

This was genuine – he loved debate. He encouraged more women to get involved in politics, many of whom would later serve in cabinet well after FitzGerald had left office.

FitzGerald's liberal policies, in particular in relation to Northern Ireland, contraception and divorce, attracted many new members to the party. Despite his bedraggled appearance, for Prendergast the product to be marketed was Garret – 'people liked Garret, they trusted him and they wanted him to succeed because he was somehow removed from the usual run of politicians.'[40] Under Garret, Fine Gael was different – it stood for something. In spite of this progress, and FitzGerald's significant efforts, there was little reward at the European and local elections in 1979. Though Fianna Fáil, as the governing party, was punished, Fine Gael's vote share barely rose from the 1977 general election result, by less than three points to 33.1 per cent. Rather than questioning their strategy, this gave added impetus to Prendergast and FitzGerald to keep up pressure for party reform.[41] FitzGerald's relationship with the parliamentary party remained rocky, but he used the election of some older TDs to the European Parliament to remove them from the front bench.[42] The local elections did at least bring in a swathe of new councillors, who could form the basis of a new intake of candidates at the subsequent general election.

Meanwhile in Fianna Fáil the pressure on Lynch was coming to a head. Those poor European and local election in the summer of 1979 results worried many of the backbench TDs that their seats were in danger. A 'Gang of Five' backbench TDs from rural constituencies started to canvass support for Haughey without his overt direction, but undoubtedly with his tacit approval. Jackie Fahey, a long-standing conservative TD who represented Waterford, Tom McEllistrim, a Kerry TD from a republican family, Seán Doherty from Roscommon, Mark Killilea, a TD from Tuam, Co. Galway, and Albert Reynolds differed as to why they wanted Haughey, but all saw him as the best man to lead the party in the 1980s. Many of them were men who had met Haughey over the previous ten years when he toured the country. For instance, Albert Reynolds, a new

TD from Longford, had sat through the arms trials and had grown to admire Haughey.

They did not have to try hard to foment discontent within Fianna Fáil. The economic miracle promised by the 1977 manifesto remained undelivered, as prices and unemployment both rose. The bitter strike by postal workers further damaged the economy, and Haughey as Minister for Social Welfare facilitated the striking workers by giving them social welfare payments immediately. He also covered a large bar tab for the workers in some pubs in Dublin. All this had the effect of prolonging the strike and further destabilising the Lynch government.[43] The Gang of Five had gathered signatures for a leadership challenge. They were ready to go when the Boss said so.

And Lynch struggled to keep a lid on the anti-British sympathies many in the parliamentary party held. Síle de Valera, a new TD but with a symbolically important surname, made a speech in Fermoy on 9 September 1979 that was critical of government policy. In the aftermath of the murder that August of Lord Mountbatten in County Sligo, Lynch secretly conceded to the UK government that UK helicopters could enter Irish airspace in 'hot pursuit'. The two Cork by-election defeats on 9 November added to the sense that Fianna Fáil needed a new leader soon. Garret FitzGerald's Fine Gael was now able to beat the Taoiseach in his own bailiwick. Lynch seemed listless during the by-election campaigns and was ashen-faced after the results.

An *Irish Press* story on the UK helicopters in Irish airspace was denied, but Lynch let slip in the US that it was actually true. One Fianna Fáil backbencher, Dr Bill Loughnane, called Lynch a 'liar', which sparked outrage among senior people in Fianna Fáil. A disciplinary motion against Loughnane was proposed, but the leadership had to back down in the face of a likely loss in the parliamentary party. Lynch returned from the US and was met at Dublin airport by Fianna Fáil TDs and senators. But this 'show of force' was more muted than had been seen ten years earlier in the aftermath of Haughey's arms trial acquittal. The fight had gone. And so without Haughey having to pull the trigger of a leadership confidence motion,

Lynch bowed out on 5 December 1979, earlier than he had planned to. Lynch had wanted Des O'Malley to be a candidate, but O'Malley was reluctant. Lynch was assured that Colley had the numbers.[44] But Haughey was much better prepared than his rival.

Colley and his supporters, such as O'Malley, had had little contact with the backbenches, nor were they popular with them. Colley himself seemed to believe that canvassing for the support of the Fianna Fáil TDs who made up the electorate for the leadership contest was beneath someone who aspired to the office of Taoiseach. He assumed it would come to him.[45] Colley represented continuity, but if seats were going to be saved, the Fianna Fáil backbenches decided Fianna Fáil needed change. Most of the cabinet stuck with Colley, not out of loyalty or any devotion to him, but because they felt it was what they were expected to do. Even Haughey's old friend Brian Lenihan was assumed to be voting for Colley. The only member of cabinet to publicly support Haughey was Michael O'Kennedy, who contacted Haughey to let him know he was voting for him. This was a gamble by O'Kennedy, but a calculated one. Haughey felt he had 52 votes; his supporters thought it was closer to 42, still, a bare majority. The word went around that O'Kennedy was voting for Haughey, which would reassure some of the more uncertain TDs.

Even if Colley had canvassed effectively, the two-day campaign was probably not long enough to overhaul Haughey's initial lead. Haughey had already done his work over the previous decade. There were allegations of bribery and intimidation, although these have been denied.[46] If indeed jobs were promised or people leaned on, that would hardly be unusual or immoral in a political contest. Indeed, others have said that Colley's side made promises and threats. Most backbench TDs did not need to be promised ministerial jobs. They were voting for Haughey to save their seats.[47]

On 7 December 1979, Haughey won the leadership of Fianna Fáil by 44 votes to 38.

7.

Taking Control

Haughey might have won the Fianna Fáil leadership on 7 December 1979, but Garret FitzGerald was determined to stop him from becoming Taoiseach the following week. FitzGerald's fear of a Haughey government was genuine. He thought Haughey treacherous. His involvement in the Arms Crisis no doubt partially explains FitzGerald's position, but so too did Haughey's unexplained wealth, and the sense that Haughey's interests were not for the country, but for himself. The opposition parties still harboured naive hope that some Fianna Fáil TDs would not vote to elect Haughey Taoiseach. The debate on his nomination was unusual in the enmity. Frank Cluskey, the Labour leader, appealed to the Fianna Fáil TDs in the Dáil:

> I speak as an Irishman to fellow Irish men and women: in the name of Ireland, in the name of Irish society, in the name of the Irish nation – [Ceann Comhairle: SIT DOWN] – think very hard indeed before walking through those lobbies today – [Interruptions] – and voting for Charles J. Haughey as Taoiseach, a man whom you know more than I is totally unfit for that position.

Garret FitzGerald made a speech in which he spoke of Haughey's 'flawed pedigree', again stating that unlike the previous Fianna Fáil holders of the office of Taoiseach, Haughey was not fit for office, and he named Fianna Fáil TDs who he knew were fearful of Haughey as Taoiseach. That only served to annoy those Fianna Fáil TDs, who in any case hardly considered that not voting for Haughey as Taoiseach was a realistic option. But FitzGerald believed that his friend, George Colley, could be persuaded, otherwise he would not have made the speech.[1]

On 11 December 1979 Haughey won the vote comfortably. He was Taoiseach. He had the large majority in the Dáil that he inherited from Lynch in 1977. Garret FitzGerald appeared petty and bitter.[2] But FitzGerald recognised that having Charles Haughey as his opponent would benefit Fine Gael electorally – 'an uncovenanted bonus to Fine Gael' was how he described it in that Dáil debate. Many people in the country simply did not trust Haughey. Where Lynch could appeal to the greater part of the Irish public, Haughey's appeal, though more intense, was narrower.

Having reached the top, Haughey had little time to enjoy it. Despite his huge majority in the Dáil, he led a divided Fianna Fáil party. George Colley and Des O'Malley were shocked and distressed at Colley's loss in the leadership contest, but Haughey knew he could not leave them out of cabinet if he wanted to keep the party together. Haughey's position was weak enough that Colley remained as Tánaiste. It indicates the level of suspicion in Haughey, and Haughey's weakness, that Colley was able to secure from him a veto on the appointment of the key security ministries, Justice and Defence. Just nine days after Haughey becoming Taoiseach, George Colley gave a speech in Baldoyle disputing Haughey's claim to have Colley's unconditional loyalty.[3] Immediately there were suggestions that Colley would be sacked, a course of action Colley later agreed would be expected in the normal course of events, but Colley knew Haughey was still too weak.[4] The two met a day later and a crisis was averted, but it affected Haughey more deeply than his opponents might have realised. There was an insecurity in his position that was intolerable. His desire to be the top man was not satisfied by just being the nominal top man, and Haughey found Colley's behaviour humiliating.[5]

Haughey was cautious in picking his first government – he would be cautious in this respect throughout his career. He kept many existing ministers in place, many of whom were loyal to Lynch. He brought in some new faces, including those who had been instrumental in his achieving office. Michael O'Kennedy was rewarded for his support with appointment as Minister for Finance. Two of his most capable supporters, Albert Reynolds and Ray MacSharry, were brought to cabinet. He appointed Máire Geoghegan-Quinn as Minister for the Gaeltacht, even though she had voted for Colley, making her the first female cabinet minister since the foundation of the state. In so doing he was aware of the symbolism, telling her, 'We're going to make history.'[6] He made Brian Lenihan Minister for Foreign Affairs, suggesting he knew that Lenihan had in fact voted for him in the leadership contest. Haughey increased the number of ministers of state (junior ministers) from 10 to 15, allowing him to reward many more of his supporters, some beyond the level their talents would warrant.

Haughey immediately rearranged the government departments and expanded his own Department of the Taoiseach. He closed down the short-lived Department of Economic Planning and Development, bringing some of its senior staff into his department, which he reorganised, appointing two secretaries (one to the department, one to the government), and created discrete sections within the department to reflect his priorities. He brought the National Economic and Social Council (NESC) under the aegis of the department's new Economic and Social Policy Section,[7] under Pádraig Ó hUiginn. The expanded department now had three deputy secretaries and five assistant secretaries, and this was regarded at the time as the start of a 'presidential'-style government.[8]

These changes represented the most radical reorganisation of government since the foundation of the state, and Haughey tried to dominate his governments. While he was good at spotting talent, in those early ministries he sought to take control of key departments by placing yes-men in them. Gene Fitzgerald was appointed to the Department of Finance in December 1980 – O'Kennedy having become Ireland's EEC Commissioner – which was effectively under Haughey's control; he ran the estimates negotiations with ministers himself from inside

Fitzgerald's office, while the Minister for Finance sat in the corner reading the paper.[9] This level of control was not just for those ministers who might have been regarded as incompetent – even in Foreign Affairs, a post held by Brian Lenihan, it had become 'notorious far outside the corridors of Iveagh House that the Taoiseach handles the Department over the head of [the] Minister'.[10] Sometimes departmental briefs were sent directly to Haughey without being seen by the relevant line minister. His opponents were suspicious of the way he took control of ministries and expanded the Department of the Taoiseach. One civil servant later observed that Haughey 'liked to contact middle-ranking civil servants . . . getting them to do things, sometimes without the knowledge of their superiors or ministers . . . if they weren't prepared to do the things he wanted . . . they were effectively sidelined.'[11] This was a view supported by a later tribunal, which found Haughey had a propensity 'to involve himself in the affairs of individual Government departments, without any, or any proper reference to the responsible Ministers, and in so doing to deal inappropriately with individual Civil Servants.'[12]

Haughey was a very effective chair of government and an efficient administrator. His cabinet meetings were short and decision-focused. He would question ministers' proposals, and could be cutting if he felt a minister was not on top of their brief. He was much more interventionist than Jack Lynch had been, contacting less experienced ministers to see how they were addressing particular issues, and leading some to wish he would leave them alone.[13]

Haughey would work from his home in Kinsealy for a few hours in the early morning. Then from about 10 a.m. he would meet with key advisers in Government Buildings, principally his unofficial chief of staff, Pádraig Ó hAnnracháin, but also Brendan O'Donnell, Frank Dunlop and later Pádraig Ó hUiginn, PJ Mara and Martin Mansergh. They would 'shoot the breeze, exchange opinions on whatever had been happening, and look at the agenda for the day.'[14] Haughey would have a sort of shopping list for the day and would issue instructions on what he wanted done. Abbeville became an informal

Taoiseach's office. An earlier plan to build an official Taoiseach's residence in the Phoenix Park, put in train by Jack Lynch, was abandoned, in large part because of the cost but also because Haughey felt no need for one – he had his own large residence suitable for holding meetings. At the weekends, especially Sundays, he would bring in civil servants, and had clerical staff to hand to keep working. His meticulousness and attention to detail forced those working for him to work harder.[15] For them he was often charming, with an irreverent sense of humour, though he also had a volcanic temper, which at times he would let loose at his closest confidants, particularly Mara.[16] Haughey acquired the sobriquet 'the Boss', probably chosen because that was what his father-in-law, Seán Lemass, was called when he was Taoiseach.

Haughey wanted to be like Lemass: decisive and effective. But this was a miserable period in Irish history, with frequent strikes and shortages of some goods. Haughey had an immediate problem. The country was broke. Haughey went on air to give a broadcast to the nation on 9 January 1980. The television studio was blue, the suit, shirt and tie were all shades of blue. The mood was blue. He told the nation that he had discovered that the nation's finances were in bad shape, and that something would have to be done. He wanted to reduce the budget deficit and public sector borrowing. There were other problems: public debt was growing at a rate that was out of control; unemployment was rising.[17] The origin of the decision to address the nation is unclear. It was certainly the message that the assistant secretary of the department, Dermot Nally, wanted the public and political system to hear, and it was probably suggested by him. It was probably also something Haughey believed in.[18] Undoubtedly Haughey was anxious to be seen to take control, to be in charge, and to put a clear line between his government and the Lynch government.

While Haughey had been in cabinet for the previous two and a half years, he had been a semi-detached member of that government, refusing to publicly support various government positions.[19] He worked on his own brief in Health and Social Welfare, built up his public profile and reputation, developed links within the party and ignored everything else. The people at the top of Fianna Fáil were openly worried about his leadership, and his demand of personal loyalty caused even more resistance. Having seen Haughey deliver the message on the state of the nation's finances, O'Malley spoke to Colley, suggesting that maybe Haughey would do the right thing. Colley dismissed this. He knew Haughey well, he said, and did not trust him.[20] This was a problem for Haughey. He had a huge majority but no power if his own ministers would not support him. Haughey needed to establish Fianna Fáil as his party. For that he needed his own majority. With an eye on an early election, Haughey's government did not do what he had promised in that televised address.

Some of Haughey's behaviour was impressive. When a strike of petrol tanker drivers escalated in September 1980 Haughey showed his decisiveness. Attempts to resolve the dispute in the Labour Court had failed, as had ministerial interventions. There were queues at petrol stations in Dublin, and flying pickets at oil depots around the country extended the queues to other parts of Ireland. Industry complained that some businesses would have to close, and the fuel shortages restricted the postal service. The public was increasingly angry, and blamed the striking drivers rather than the government. Clearly impatient with the failure to resolve the dispute, Haughey called an emergency cabinet meeting for 30 September 1980. He proposed using the army to deliver petrol and offered that the Labour Court be invited to make a pay recommendation. That evening Haughey addressed the nation on TV and radio, outlining the government decision. Within days it had worked. The army successfully took delivery of petrol, allowing petrol stations to reopen, and the striking drivers eventually accepted a Labour Court recommendation.[21]

Still, this was not his government. And Haughey was less effective in this period than he hoped. He complained to Terry Keane that he was 'overwhelmed by a feeling of powerlessness'.[22] Despite Fine

Gael's growing popularity under Garret FitzGerald, offering a distinctive opposition for the first time, Haughey's most significant opposition was from within his own party. While the party grassroots was enthusiastically in favour of him, the parliamentary party was still split, with senior colleagues highly antagonistic to him. Given that Haughey, rather than any deep ideological differences, was the basis of the split, he may have felt there was not a lot he could do to assuage their fears. While Haughey made no attempt to placate his colleagues, it is questionable whether some could be placated. He had kept many in place, even though he only ever regarded at most a third of his cabinet as competent.[23] For Haughey, he wanted to get things done. His civil servant, Pádraig Ó hUiginn, recalled that in the aftermath of the second oil crisis, prime ministers in Europe such as Haughey understood that cabinet government might work in ordinary times, but it was too slow in an emergency: 'We have to take charge, we've to run this like a business – we can't be waiting for memos to go around.'[24]

Where Haughey's supporters wanted loyalty to the leader, just as they felt Lynch had been afforded loyalty by Haughey, his opponents could point out that Lynch moved slowly, never demanding too much, and was willing to compromise. While Haughey created an image of himself as leader, he failed to actually deliver leadership, in the sense that he failed to bring others with him. The more he tried, the more suspicious his opponents became. Haughey was paying the price of his taking power. He had to win his own majority.

At his first Árd Fheis in February 1980 he was welcomed in by the band of the Irish Transport and General Workers' Union (ITGWU) playing 'A Nation Once Again', an emotive nationalist rallying song.[25] If the symbols were nationalistic, he was less emotive in what he said. Speaking to the largest ever indoor political gathering in Ireland, he set out his priorities, naming 'Northern Ireland as the major national issue, and its peaceful solution as our first political priority.' He declared that 'Northern Ireland as a political entity has failed,' and promised to seek a new beginning, to make peace with his fellow countrymen of the Protestant faith, claiming somewhat implausibly that he had lived among them in his boyhood days.[26]

On the economy, Haughey reiterated his earlier warnings about the state of the public finances, and sought to find a 'partnership between workers, employers and Government'. He issued a warning to people that the Irish economy would have to modernise.[27] Haughey would commission the Telesis Report, an evaluation of Ireland's industrial policy. The consultants he hired recalled that Haughey had a vision: 'Out there is a new technology coming, and I want you to help Ireland be number one in that technology,' he told them.[28] Haughey told the Árd Fheis of his vision of the arts in Ireland. Critics (and some friends) assumed his interest in the arts was affected or a 'veneer' as he tried to 'better himself', but it appears to have been deep and sincere.[29] Kevin Rafter lists many of Haughey's connections with the arts and artists that went well beyond his retirement.[30] Haughey was still defensive about his past, and refused to do the traditional RTÉ Árd Fheis interview because the interviewer proposed to ask questions on the Arms Crisis. That issue would come up again that summer as a current affairs magazine, *Magill*, published 'Peter Berry's diaries', and over multiple issues raised questions for all the protagonists in the Arms Crisis.

The years 1980 and 1981 were spent in preparation for elections rather than governing. Garret FitzGerald had shown in those two Cork by-elections in November 1979 that he had made Fine Gael electable. It was different from 1948 and 1973, when a jaded public had alighted on Fine Gael as a default option after 16 years of continuous Fianna Fáil rule. Now Fine Gael stood for something. Under FitzGerald Fine Gael seemed modern and progressive, appealing especially to young people and women.[31]

Haughey was conscious that he was not universally popular. Fine Gael had decided to target Haughey, who its research showed was a polarising figure and one regarded with suspicion by many. Haughey's satisfaction rating at the start of his term was 54 per cent, marginally lower than that for Jack Lynch at the end of his term. The public reserved judgement, with a quarter of voters in one poll delivering a 'don't know' on Haughey. FitzGerald, by contrast, was generally more popular and widely seen as someone of great integrity. As time passed, however, those Haughey 'don't knows' were becoming dissatisfied.[32] If leadership changes are meant to boost a party's support, it had not worked for Fianna Fáil.

Haughey needed to fix that. He engaged Tim Bell, an English public relations and advertising executive who had influenced the Conservative Party victory in 1979, and told him, 'I want a new image.' When Bell explained that political communications was more sophisticated than 'image making', Haughey responded, 'OK, then. Do you know anyone who does new images?'[33] Haughey needed to win an election.

✻ ✻ ✻

Though Haughey had indicated in his January 1980 broadcast to the nation that he would reel in public spending, the election preparations meant spending was not curtailed at all. While he managed to end some long-running strikes and potential disputes, he did so at a significant cost to the exchequer. A long-drawn-out dispute in the Talbot Motor Assembly plant in Santry, north Dublin was settled on the eve of the 1981 election. This was a dispute about the redundancy of 90 workers who had rejected an offer well in excess of the statutory redundancy package. The Taoiseach's department took control of this, with Ó hUiginn coming up with an unorthodox plan at a weekend in Kinsealy.[34] Des O'Malley, the Minister for Industry and Commerce, and therefore the responsible minister, who had been helicoptered up to Dublin, refused to agree to it.[35] Haughey did it anyway. It offered the workers indefinite payments as long as they were unemployed. Many later received jobs in the civil service. The Talbot deal would cost the state about IR£475,000 (€2.1m in 2023 terms) in 1982 alone, with Barry Desmond, the Labour TD, estimating that it could cost IR£20 million (€70m in 2023) over the lifetime of the deal.[36] Haughey pursued popular but uneconomic ideas such as a plan to build an airport at Knock, which might have been part of an overall plan to develop the west of Ireland, but on its own an airport unconnected to any infrastructure would do little for the region.

In the late 1960s, as Minister for Finance, Haughey had tried to introduce a form of state-assisted pay bargaining. It was an idea he never gave up on. Haughey met with the ICTU in January 1980, just weeks after his appointment as Taoiseach, with the purpose of agreeing a 'national understanding',[37] a pay limit agreed between employers and unions. It was eventually agreed in October 1980, only with Haughey's direct intervention. It sought to limit pay rises, but these were, Haughey admitted, at the limit of what was affordable. There was a plan to stimulate growth through infrastructural investment. More generally inflation-chasing pay increases were conceded, as were social welfare payment increases, and necessarily taxes were also increased leading a contemporary observer to comment that Haughey 'has been running scared of the public sector since assuming office'. It was later revealed that his government underprovided for what it was scheduled to spend in 1981, essentially frontloading most of the spending in the early part of the year. Civil servants were deeply concerned at the way the government was misrepresenting the public finances. This was not decisive action. Haughey was buying time.[38]

FitzGerald was also thinking about elections. He had been so busy touring the constituencies that he had devoted less time to policy formulation than he should have.[39] He was also anxious to centralise power in himself. In mid-1980 he put to his party that he was leader and should have control over policy-making functions.[40] He and his economic adviser, Brendan Dowling, worked on new tax proposals, independently of Peter Barry, the finance spokesman.[41] These proposed a large reduction in income tax, to be paid for by an increase in VAT, and integration of the tax and social welfare systems.

The economy was worsening. Inflation was at 18 per cent, and unemployment was rising, and in particular the public finances were getting out of control. Despite this Fianna Fáil was planning to spend more. Oddly however, FitzGerald lacked credible policy alternatives in many areas. He had cowed his front bench, and tried to make all the running himself.[42] FitzGerald was able to stress the differences between the two parties when it came to Northern Ireland, but with the H-Block hunger strikes[43] support for the IRA was increasing. And Haughey had had a successful summit with Margaret Thatcher, the UK prime minister, so the accusations that he was a 'closet Provo' seemed less plausible.

Fianna Fáil won the by-election in Donegal in November 1980 by more than it had polled in the 1977 election. The party's polling numbers were also strong.[44] Haughey planned to call an election in early 1981, hoping to focus the campaign on 'the grave and tragic situation in Northern Ireland'. It was due to be called after the Fianna Fáil Árd Fheis in mid-February 1981, but that Árd Fheis was postponed due to the Stardust disaster in which 48 young people were killed in a fire at a night club in Haughey's own constituency. His control of election timing was limited.

The second hunger strikes started on 1 March 1981, the fifth anniversary of the ending of political prisoner status. These hunger strikes were more bitter and more emotive than an earlier set of hunger strikes, which had started in October 1980 and ended with the suggestion of a compromise by Margaret Thatcher. That compromise collapsed, with a sense of British betrayal among IRA prisoners. With many in the South sympathising with the hunger strikers, attitudes hardened on all sides.[45] Thatcher adopted a hard-line position, determined not to give in. Some prisoners and their families wanted to negotiate, but the Sinn Féin/IRA leadership under Gerry Adams was also determined not to give in.[46] The H-Block prisoners entered the electoral arena in April 1981 in what was to become the 'ballot box and Armalite' strategy, as Bobby Sands, one of the hunger strikers, contested and won a seat for Fermanagh and South Tyrone in the UK House of Commons. They would also contest the Irish elections. Bobby Sands was the first hunger striker to die, on 5 May 1981. Haughey was anxious not to be too critical of the

British, while not alienating republicans. He secretly opened a communication channel with Adams through Pádraig Ó hAnnracháin, breaking the norm that 'you don't talk to terrorists', a taboo continually broken by the British. It was something of a risk for Haughey though, given that if it were made public it might have confirmed in his opponents' minds that he was an IRA sympathiser.[47]

While the British were appreciative of Haughey's calm reaction, he failed to influence Thatcher's approach in any meaningful way, and republicans in the North and his own party were critical of his approach.[48] Haughey could have delayed calling an election for another year; he had a majority in the Dáil, and the ongoing hunger strikes would have given him a reason to. He seems to have believed that he could use the hunger strikes to his advantage.[49] Placing Northern Ireland at the top of his electoral agenda was a tactical error. On 21 May 1981, the day he called the election, two more hunger strikers died. It was impossible to avoid the hunger strikes as an issue, but it was one that split his party. It was a wedge issue for Fianna Fáil rather than Fine Gael, and so rather than weaponise it, Haughey should have tried to defuse it.

Haughey set a short three-week campaign, with polling day on 11 June 1981. Polls suggested economic issues were more important for voters than Northern Ireland, which was unsurprising given the depth of the recession. Fine Gael and Fianna Fáil and the media focused coverage on the leaders to a greater extent than ever before.[50] These were the two rivals for the office of Taoiseach.[51] Fine Gael emphasised FitzGerald's face on the poster. But FitzGerald was far from a natural campaigner. While he was physically imposing, he could be a poor public speaker, speaking too quickly, mumbling and using language that was suitable in a university setting, but not in public halls.[52] The party struggled to convey how his weekly payment to stay-at-home wives of IR£9.60 (€40 in 2023), which was essentially a tax credit, would be paid for. Haughey thought the payment was a good idea – 'I should have thought of that.'[53] That was the thing he respected most about FitzGerald – his ideas.[54] Haughey then went on to attack the proposal. That is what he did; he would vigorously oppose anything he hadn't come up with.

FitzGerald displayed a detachment from ordinary Irish people, which might have been fatal, but cohered with his self-image as a distracted genius. He was rarely interested in the people themselves; on one canvass in Limerick he could be heard surveying an elderly voter about whether Irish was spoken in her area when she was younger – he was doing research on the decline of the Irish language.[55] A headline at the time suggested he was not a natural: 'Garret tries hard to be a man of the people'.[56] A British reporter observed, 'Haughey kisses babies, and even more enthusiastically, their mothers. FitzGerald shakes babies by the hand.'[57]

Haughey toured the country, though support for the national campaign from within the party was lacking. Many of his senior ministers concentrated on their own seats, and canvassed for some other supporters – they were starting to learn the lessons of politics that Haughey's leadership had demonstrated. Despite the questions about Haughey's leadership from within his cabinet, Fianna Fáil was going all in on its focus on Haughey the leader. It released a campaign song that emphasised the leader. 'Charlie's Song', better known as 'Arise and Follow Charlie', sought to create an image in Haughey of a nationalist leader:

> From Southern glens to Western shores
> The ancient cry of freedom roars
> From Northern hills to Leinster's doors
> We'll Rise and Follow Charlie.
> Hail the leader, hail the man
> With Freedom's cause it all began
> With Irish Pride in every man
> We'll Rise and Follow Charlie.

But Ireland was still divided in its opinion on Haughey. Better than that, Fine Gael had a leader that it knew the people liked. In the context of a party system where to most outside observers the parties look and sound the same, Fine Gaelers often distinguished themselves from Fianna Fáil on the basis that Fine Gaelers are honest and decent, whereas Fianna Fáilers are not. Being led by 'Garret the Good'[58] against Haughey, who was often portrayed in much of the media almost as a cartoon villain, the leaders underscored those differences. Haughey refused an offer to do a head-to-head TV debate with FitzGerald. He insisted that Frank Cluskey, the Labour leader, should also be involved. This was done in the hope that Haughey could emphasise the differences between Fine Gael and Labour, and drive home the idea that coalition government was inherently unstable. Fine Gael claimed that Haughey feared a debate that placed him and FitzGerald in a clear contest for the electorate to choose from.[59]

The campaign was bitter, not least because of the distrust between Haughey and FitzGerald, but also because of the hunger strikes. There was rioting in Dublin in protest at the British government. At many election rallies Haughey received abuse from supporters of the hunger strikers. The hero of the arms trials who had taken the leadership of Fianna Fáil in part by using nationalist rhetoric now found himself not sufficiently republican for a growing section of the population and far too nationalist in his politics for many others. The worsening economy also helped Fine Gael, even if its policies were unclear to even its own TDs. Garret understood them – that was enough.

FitzGerald had the advantage of a broadly united party behind him, albeit one that had to accommodate very divergent opinions, with old-style conservatives such as Alice Glenn and liberal feminists such as Nuala Fennell in it. Haughey tried to emphasise the inherent dangers of coalition, emphasising differences between Fine Gael and Labour, and the credibility of Fine Gael's promises. Garret emphasised honesty, trying to target what he described as Fianna Fáil's 'six big lies'. But since these 'lies' were claims about Fine Gael's proposals, this merely drew attention to Fianna Fáil's criticism of Fine Gael. Still, polls showed the 'coalition' gaining on and overtaking Fianna Fáil.[60]

The results of the election in June 1981 were indecisive, but Fine Gael, at 36 per cent, had its highest vote share since 1927. That was not as impressive as how it converted these votes into seats, winning 65 out of the 166 seats. This was FitzGerald's victory. Fianna Fáil lost over five percentage points in support (to 45 per cent) from its 1977 high, and at 78 seats Haughey was five short of an overall majority. He was put in place to save backbench TDs' seats, but ended up calling the election at the wrong time and on the wrong issue. Haughey, it turned out, was not an electoral mastermind.

Never had Fine Gael been so competitive, coming to within 13 seats of Fianna Fáil. After the debacle in 1977 – when it went into the election ill-prepared – Fine Gael was a party transformed. But FitzGerald was not quite there yet. Even with Labour's 15 seats, and allowing that two seats taken by the Anti H-Block[61] campaign would not be occupied, FitzGerald was still two seats short for a bare majority. Frank Cluskey had been quite intransigent in advance of the election, demanding a referendum on divorce, the reintroduction of a wealth tax, and public control of financial institutions, all issues on which Fine Gael would struggle to agree.[62] Cluskey lost his seat, however, and was replaced as leader by the more moderate, if less stable Michael O'Leary, who was in favour of coalition. FitzGerald and O'Leary found it easy to strike a coalition deal, despite vocal opposition from the party chairman, Michael D. Higgins, and others on the left of Labour. Divisive issues such a wealth tax were fudged, and the parties were happy to agree to socially reforming measures in family law.[63] The new Dáil met on 30 June 1981. Fine Gael proposed an independent TD as Ceann Comhairle, and when FitzGerald was nominated for Taoiseach, Jim Kemmy, a socialist TD who shared FitzGerald's views on Northern Ireland and on Charles Haughey, voted for the Fine Gael leader, admitting it was a very difficult stance to take. Four other deputies abstained, giving FitzGerald a bare majority.

Garret FitzGerald was Taoiseach, and a lifetime ambition was achieved. But like Haughey, he was not there just to be an office holder. He had a vision for the country. FitzGerald predicted his new minority government would go the full term. He was experienced enough to know that was unlikely, but optimism was in his nature, and what else could he say? On the way to Áras an Uachtaráin to receive his seal of office from President Hillery, Dermot Nally, the monkish secretary to the government, told him that the financial situation was much worse than was publicly known. Later that evening, when introducing his cabinet, FitzGerald told the Dáil of the problem with the public finances.

It was precarious from the start.

8.

REVOLVING DOORS

On taking power in June 1981 FitzGerald had to build his minority government. To send out a signal of change and dynamism, he sought to emphasise youth in his ministerial choices. Like Haughey, he sought to centralise his control of key policy areas. In doing so FitzGerald made a few mistakes. Many in Fine Gael were unhappy that he had given so many cabinet places to Labour, though it is normal to give small parties in government a bonus in cabinet seats. In his decision to appoint young TDs to cabinet and remove some of the older conservative voices, he showed some steel that Haughey had lacked. But he forgot how this would be felt within his parliamentary party. That steel might have been political naivety.

FitzGerald failed to prepare Richie Ryan and Dick Burke – former ministers who had a reasonable expectation of reappointment – for their inevitable disappointment. Nor did he find any room for a Fine Gael woman in his cabinet even though he had said how much he wanted to advance the interests of women. He appointed Alan Dukes, a bright and capable economist, to Agriculture on his first day in the Dáil. That annoyed some of those who had felt they had done their time in the parliamentary party. On his wife Joan's suggestion, he appointed their friend Professor Jim Dooge to Foreign Affairs, even though he was not a TD. FitzGerald was looking for someone he trusted and who shared his political views.[1]

There is a rarely used right for a Taoiseach to appoint up to two government ministers from the Seanad. It is rarely used for a reason, as FitzGerald would find out. If a Taoiseach considered the impact it would have on the parliamentary party, they would discount it. Some in the Fine Gael backbenchers asked themselves, 'What's wrong with us?' Nor was it ideal that it would take months before Dooge could assume the office because of the normal delay in electing the Seanad, to which Dooge would be nominated. The Dáil was in recess when this happened, so Dooge was unable to take office until the end of October. In the meantime, John Kelly, himself a novice minister, formally undertook Dooge's ministerial duties.

FitzGerald's allocation of junior ministries was cack-handed, insensitive and showed impatience: 'In his first couple of hours at the top, Garret FitzGerald was rushing about breathlessly, leaving bruised egos in his wake.'[2] One of his supporters said FitzGerald's decisions had the effect of ending people's careers within the party.[3] It had an immediate impact; the government lost a vote on the appointment of Leas-Ceann Comhairle (deputy speaker) because one of those who felt rejected missed a vote.

FitzGerald was too busy for these common courtesies. He had a country to run. He made no attempt to mend fences or build relationships within his parliamentary party. Nor did he use all of the officials in his department. Pádraig Ó hUiginn, who FitzGerald did not trust, was pushed aside. FitzGerald was comfortable working directly with other departments, and so bypassed the Department of the Taoiseach, and came to rely on a small group of advisers.[4] FitzGerald did not have many friends in Leinster House, and appointed a close friend, Alexis FitzGerald, an experienced lawyer, as a special adviser who would sit at cabinet, which was highly unusual. Alexis FitzGerald would try to keep Garret's focus on a decision. He did not always succeed. Alexis would get impatient, especially at Garret's focus on Northern Ireland to the exclusion of other problems.[5] Garret FitzGerald created a personal *cabinet* of advisers in his various governments, including a former economics student of his, Patrick Honohan, and Michael Lillis, a diplomat from Foreign Affairs with whom he was friendly. Anxious to have youth in his cabinet, he also appointed a smart young barrister, Peter Sutherland, as Attorney General.

According to FitzGerald's son Mark, it was also because while FitzGerald was full of policy ideas, Sutherland was pragmatic enough to know what could be done and how.[6]

FitzGerald made John Bruton, a former student, his Minister for Finance. Though still in his early 30s, Bruton was an experienced, serious and strong-willed politician.[7] FitzGerald had found getting accurate information from Finance quite difficult, so in another example of the Taoiseach expanding his empire, he temporarily placed an adviser, Brendan Dowling, in the department.[8] Although FitzGerald appointed three Fine Gael members of the 1973 cabinet, the Fine Gael side of the cabinet gave an impression of youth – four Fine Gael cabinet ministers were still in their 30s. An advantage of all this youth was that FitzGerald, at 55, was the senior member of the government in terms of experience, age and status. Like Haughey, he was across all his ministers' briefs, and often knew more than they did. He contrasted with Haughey in one way. While both were prone to direct their ministers, at this stage in their careers FitzGerald was more willing than Haughey to appoint people who might stand up to him.

Bruton's immediate task in the summer of 1981 was to introduce a supplementary budget. The Haughey government's budget for 1981 had been built on sand. The full annual allocation was almost spent before half the year was out. FitzGerald blamed Haughey for the large deficit facing his government. Haughey claimed that FitzGerald was acting as a 'national bogey man' trying to frighten the nation into accepting his 'monetarist policies'.[9] The election manifesto that Fine Gael had run on was not viable. Three weeks after taking over, Bruton's emergency budget cut spending on capital programmes, and despite increased taxes – taking IR£336 million (about €1.5 billion in 2023 prices) out of the economy – he still had to increase the borrowing requirement. It was a deflationary budget, something the programme for government had said it would avoid. But it would also cause inflation by adding to the costs of post, electricity, telephones, public transport, as well as the VAT rate. It was only because the government was so new that the 21 July budget was passed. But it severely limited the policy options open to the FitzGerald government.

If FitzGerald seemed less interested in the economy than one might have expected, it was because of the worsening security situation in Northern Ireland. While Northern Ireland would by choice take much of his time, the ongoing H-Block hunger strikes meant that he was forced to devote a great deal of time to Northern fire-fighting. Hunger strikers continued to die, and a march on the British Embassy in Dublin on 18 July 1981 turned into a full-scale riot. He made numerous contacts with the British authorities to seek a solution, though at all times he publicly supported the UK position of not granting political status to the IRA prisoners.[10] The Provisional IRA and Sinn Féin were in secret talks with the British, but both sides seemed to harden positions when a settlement looked possible. FitzGerald was in a difficult position as Taoiseach, with little control of events. Public sympathy for the hunger strikers was growing, though he felt unable to be directly critical of the British government.[11] In opposition FitzGerald had criticised Haughey for not putting more pressure on the British prime minister, Margaret Thatcher, but now he was in a position that any such public pressure would contradict his policy of wooing unionists. Haughey tried to put pressure on FitzGerald, but he was much more restrained than might have been expected. After his month-long retreat to his island of the coast of Kerry in August, on 1 September 1981 Haughey met with Owen Carron, a recently elected Sinn Féin MP running under the Anti H-Block banner. FitzGerald refused to meet him. Haughey said that it was a private meeting and to emphasise that it took place at Haughey's home in Kinsealy with no advisers present.[12]

When the hunger strikes ended at the start of October due to pressure from the prisoners' families, both FitzGerald and Haughey urged Thatcher to be generous in her response and to go some way to meeting the prisoners' demands.[13] Rather than react to the problems in the North, FitzGerald was determined to make some of the running. He felt a real determination to deal with what he saw as the unfinished business of 1916, in which his parents were involved. He was not so naïve as to believe he could finish it, but he could help move things towards a conclusion.[14] He tried to continue Haughey's courting of Thatcher. Haughey had earlier secured the agreement to issue Anglo-Irish 'joint studies' to search for solutions and increased co-operation on Northern Ireland. These joint studies were really an opening of dialogue between the Irish and British governments, which had the effect of limiting public criticism of the other government.

The Fine Gael–Labour government agreed with FitzGerald's proposal – and long-held view – that the state should appeal to win over unionists by reviewing the constitution to making it less sectarian. This would include a review of Articles 2 and 3 of the constitution, which staked a claim to sovereignty of the whole island of Ireland, and a removal of the constitutional ban on divorce. In a radio interview in September 1981, FitzGerald declared, 'I want to lead a crusade, a republican crusade, to make this a genuine republic,' which, he said, was the only way to bring about national unity. He described the Irish state as 'sectarian ... our laws and our constitution, our practices and our attitudes reflect those of a majority ethos and are not acceptable to Protestants in Northern Ireland.'[15] Radical constitutional reforms normally require careful planning and the co-operation of the main parties. FitzGerald knew he would not get that from Haughey, so he tried to go over the heads of politicians – including many in his own party who would have been wary of what he was proposing – to appeal to the public. He referenced Éamon de Valera and Seán Lemass, and the 1967 Committee on the Constitution. Haughey was immediately critical of the proposed changes, suggesting it would 'sabotage' the policy of national unity.[16] Opinion polls did not help much either. While one poll in the *Irish Independent* suggested that almost half of voters would be willing to consider unspecified changes affecting the relationship with the North, another poll in the *Sunday Tribune* showed just 35 per cent in favour of dropping the claim in Article 3, but 46 per cent opposed a change.[17] At a summit meeting in November 1981, FitzGerald apprised Thatcher of his crusade, which he felt was well received, and tried to persuade her of the existence of Irish co-operation on security matters.[18] The Irish side tried very hard to get language into the text of a communiqué that the Taoiseach and UK prime minister were somehow joint authorities of Northern Ireland, something the UK regarded as too 'green'.[19]

In the end FitzGerald's constitutional crusade was 'stillborn'.[20] FitzGerald introduced one bill in the Seanad to end the death penalty, but this ran out of time. Haughey could reasonably object that he himself had effectively banned capital punishment in the 1960s. Even the more moderate politicians in Fianna Fáil rejected the premise for constitutional change. Some, such as Senator Eoin Ryan, a friend of FitzGerald's, was vehemently anti-Haughey and had been on the 1967 Committee, chose to repudiate 'the Taoiseach's deplorable and unfounded allegations of sectarianism in our laws and in the administration of our affairs.'[21] Ryan did not explain why he felt those changes were welcome in 1967 but not in 1981. Perhaps because he was never a deeply partisan Fine Gaeler, Garret could not understand the pull of party loyalty. Haughey's opposition was not purely cynical. He had a point. Unionism had a guarantee from the British government on the position of Northern Ireland. While that guarantee existed, unionism had no incentive to budge.

However, Haughey had not settled well into opposition in June 1981. What might have been a career-ending electoral disaster for him was mitigated by the fact that the number of TDs in Dáil Éireann had risen from 148 to 166 following a report from the constituency commission chaired by Supreme Court judge Brian Walsh, which was enacted in July 1980. This meant that although the Fianna Fáil vote had fallen substantially, the loss was just six seats on the 1977 total.

It took Haughey until November 1981 to appoint a front bench team. For some observers Haughey was 'arthritic', sullen without power.[22] He took to referring to the Fine Gael–Labour government as 'the present government' and any minister as 'the present minister'.[23] There was a febrile atmosphere in the party, as the anti-Haughey group led by Des O'Malley and George Colley flexed its muscles. PJ Mara, who Haughey had appointed to the Seanad in 1981, toured Leinster House keeping an eye on things for 'the Boss', reporting to him anything that might be interpreted as disloyalty. Haughey critiqued the FitzGerald government, claiming that it was dictated by 'harsh monetarism', whereas he preferred investment.[24] The appointment of Martin O'Donoghue – the architect of the 1977 manifesto – as spokesperson on Finance suggested that he still lacked control of his appointments. Though this may have been an attempt to split his rivals by bringing one into his fold, if anything, Haughey seemed to be losing control. It was not just Colley and O'Malley who were unhappy with the budgetary approach Haughey took in 1980–81. Some of his supporters, Ray MacSharry and Albert Reynolds included, were known to be unhappy.[25] Charlie McCreevy, one of Haughey's early supporters who had become disillusioned with his unwillingness to tackle the issues he said he would, was highly critical of Haughey in a newspaper interview in December 1981,[26] for which he lost his place in the parliamentary party.[27]

The Taoiseach, Garret FitzGerald, did not have the luxury of enjoying Haughey's travails in opposition. None of FitzGerald's other initiatives seemed to get anywhere. FitzGerald later blamed some of this inactivity on civil service inertia, which he felt was resistant to change. Some of his ministers, he thought, had 'gone native' – were too quick to accept their civil service advice.[28] Fine Gael had ambitious tax reform proposals, which entailed integrating the tax and social welfare systems. Brendan Dowling, the plan's architect, was outside the government structures, but felt that the proposals were being blocked by the Department of Finance, and the scheme had to be abandoned.[29] The FitzGerald government had committed to eliminating the budget deficit in four years. Getting a first normal budget through was made more difficult for John Bruton by Labour's opposition to some of his cost-saving measures, in particular the abolition of food subsidies. If the government split, Fianna Fáil would be able to say it had been right to claim that coalition government was inherently unstable. Budget items were shifted around, with subsidies cut rather than removed. John Bruton was determined to reduce the budget deficit, and initially had the support of his Taoiseach in this. They had to find savings somewhere. But there was resistance; that autumn backbench Fine Gael TDs sought to have certain programmes protected. While FitzGerald seemed to enjoy being immersed in detail, the cabinet was getting weary. The Tánaiste, Michael O'Leary, who had a low boredom threshold, left the cabinet discussions before the budget was finalised to get something to eat.[30] Managing coalition with O'Leary was difficult not because he wasn't committed to the government or even its tough measures – he was – but because he would go missing, and extraordinarily was studying for his bar exams at the time. Within Labour he was not seen as one who would defend the party's interests.

In late January 1982, the coalition parties signed off on the budgetary plans, but the minority government still needed the support of other TDs. FitzGerald approached Jim Kemmy and Joe Sherlock, both left-wing TDs who had supported FitzGerald over Haughey for Taoiseach. Both had made it clear that they were likely to oppose the budget, even though FitzGerald thought Kemmy's language was ambiguous, and he later said, 'on an optimistic linguistic interpretation of [Kemmy's] reference to food subsidies he had not seemed to require that they be maintained in full.'[31] In any case, FitzGerald speculated he could rely on the vote of other TDs. This was wishful thinking. Jim Kemmy was the most consistent in supporting the government, and had saved it from defeat on several occasions. Michael Noonan, a young Fine Gael TD from Limerick, was dispatched to talk to Kemmy, his constituency colleague. It was clear enough to Noonan that the budget would be lost, so he rang his constituency party to tell it to prepare for an election.[32] Kemmy had hardly made a secret of his views, airing them in a range of media outlets, but FitzGerald chose not to listen.

When the budget was announced on 27 January 1982 there was a litany of spending cuts and price rises. In the Dáil debate Haughey criticised the budget as 'savage and anti-social'.[33] On *Today Tonight*, the flagship current affairs programme, this list of budget measures made for miserable viewing. In particular, the imposition of VAT on clothes and footwear was causing problems, and was seized upon in the chamber and on the budget analysis programme on RTÉ. In the chamber FitzGerald was seen pleading with Kemmy. But the Limerick TD filed into the Níl lobby and it was clear the government had lost, 82 votes to 81. FitzGerald claimed to be quite 'happy and exhilarated', because he could go to the country on its budgetary strategy.[34] He went to Áras an Uachtaráin to seek a dissolution of the Dáil. The election date was set for 18 February 1982, but this was no election budget.

The budget episode exposed FitzGerald's political ineptitude. Though it was certainly a difficult budget delivered in challenging political circumstances, he failed to listen even when told in advance that the VAT issue would be a problem. Others wondered why they could not have exempted children's clothes and shoes, but FitzGerald explained that this would have led to anomalies because some women have small feet and could avail of the VAT exemption. FitzGerald later claimed this was an ill-advised joke, but in fact it was the reason given by Bruton in the budget speech.[35] It was an approach that was 'recommended in trenchant terms' by the Department of Finance.[36] FitzGerald said he did not believe the children's shoes issue was the reason for the collapse of the budget.[37] While those who opposed the budget did so on the basis of the whole budgetary approach, it is hardly plausible to say it was a myth that the VAT on children's shoes brought down the government, given that it had been immediately seized upon by those who voted against it and was the subject of intense discussions in the hours before the vote.[38]

If FitzGerald was to go to the country on his budgetary plan, to have a realistic chance of retaining the office of Taoiseach he needed

Labour support. Almost immediately the two parties agreed a voting pact, but only after having made changes to budgetary proposals announced a few days earlier. These included the removal of the proposed VAT on children's clothes and shoes. Having effectively called an election on the issue, FitzGerald dropped them at the start of the campaign.

Haughey had tried to avoid the need for an election entirely. Under the Irish constitution a president can refuse to dissolve the Dáil if the Taoiseach has lost its confidence, as FitzGerald had. If there was some potential for a new government being formed without an election, an election could be avoided. He needed to convince President Hillery to refuse FitzGerald's request. Fianna Fáil was surprised by the government's defeat and was not ready for an election just seven months after the last one. Haughey got President Hillery's old constituency colleague, Sylvester Barrett, and perhaps Brian Lenihan, to phone the Áras on the night of 27 January 1982. Hillery, sensing what it was about, refused to take the call or to see them. While refusing to dissolve the Dáil might have been appropriate – why else is the power given to the president? – Hillery felt it would have been inappropriate for a president to be seen to act on political pressure. These were communications that would have ramifications for Haughey's later career.[39]

In the February 1982 election campaign Haughey refused to give details of what budgetary strategy he would follow. On O'Donoghue's, O'Malley's and Colley's insistence Fianna Fáil accepted the outgoing Fine Gael–Labour government's broad fiscal limits. Haughey did so, but in the campaign decided to ignore that commitment. He thought the FitzGerald government was 'hypnotised by their own propaganda about public borrowing', suggesting Fianna Fáil would borrow more, to avoid a 'savage and anti-social' budget.[40] He vaguely offered that his budget would be 'fairer' without detailing what measures he would introduce.[41] Under pressure he then publicly accepted the fiscal limits again, but the divisions within the party, rarely far from the surface, were laid bare in a campaign where senior members of the party refused to publicly endorse its leader.[42]

If the economy dominated the campaign in the February election, it was also more presidential than any before. Haughey's suitability for office became a feature of the electoral campaign. In polls he was much less popular than FitzGerald for the position of Taoiseach.[43]

FitzGerald agreed to a leaders' debate, the first in Irish electoral history. He calculated that as he was much more popular than Haughey, the more often voters saw the two together, the more likely they would be to vote for Fine Gael. In that debate FitzGerald was clearly more nervous than Haughey. FitzGerald rattled off statistics, but rather than engage with the numbers, Haughey dismissed them. Haughey continued his oppositional approach, being critical of the government without being specific about his proposed alternatives. He emphasised employment as a key objective without really saying how he would go about delivering it. Haughey's key argument was that the coalition was inherently unstable, something that seemed patently true given its collapse. The Labour Party could not even agree on whether or not its voters should transfer their lower preferences to Fine Gael, with the party leader Michael O'Leary saying yes, but the party chair, Michael D. Higgins, saying that no electoral pact existed.[44]

Fine Gael might have become a professional campaigning party, but Garret FitzGerald was still no natural campaigner. He did not 'get' Ireland. While canvassing in Cork he was handed a large teddy bear dressed in red and white, and speculated that it was in support of the Polish Solidarity movement.

'They're the Cork colours', his handler groaned, not quite incredulous.

'They're the Cork colours . . . Really?' FitzGerald responded.

It was not a mistake that Charles J. Haughey would have made.

❖ ❖ ❖

In the end the election changed little. Fianna Fáil gained three seats to bring it to 81, including the two seats that had been lost to Anti H-Block candidates in 1981. Fine Gael lost two seats to 63 seats, while Labour was unchanged on 15. Sinn Féin The Workers' Party (SFWP), which was linked to the Official IRA, now had three seats. There were four independent TDs. Fianna Fáil had more seats than Fine Gael and Labour combined, and while FitzGerald would attempt to form a government, Haughey was closer to the 83-seat total required. FitzGerald was unlikely to sell his harsh budget to the left-wing SFWP. He tried to deal with Tony Gregory, a newly elected independent TD representing a deprived area of inner-city Dublin, but Gregory found it hard to warm to FitzGerald, who, he said, came to the meeting with an 'interpreter' to talk to the young working-class TD.[45] While FitzGerald had some sympathy for Gregory's case, he knew the state could not afford what Gregory was looking for. Haughey had no such compunction. Haughey sought Gregory's support on 23 February, with Gregory looking for a generous deal of investment in his constituency, as well as other commitments. Gregory was 'pushing an open door', and he felt that Haughey had a genuine understanding and concern for the problems in the area.[46] Haughey was criticised that he was buying Dáil votes, but he could reasonably defend his action on the grounds that it provided support for one of the most deprived areas of the capital.[47]

FitzGerald met with the Workers' Party deputies and completely conceded on the budget he had gone to the country on. The Labour Party, while not rejecting coalition, indicated that it would seek to renegotiate. It was then rejected by the Administrative Council of the Labour Party, whose chair, Michael D. Higgins, used his casting vote against coalition.[48] FitzGerald had been roundly rejected, despite his concessions, and he soon regretted having ever tried.[49]

Haughey, meanwhile, was having his own troubles. In what was normally a formal ratification of the leader to be the party's nominee for Taoiseach, the first Fianna Fáil parliamentary party meeting after the election was used for a leadership challenge. The interregnum between the general election and election of Taoiseach was an odd time to challenge for the party leadership, which lent credibility to the charges by Haughey supporters that his opponents were not acting in the party's best interests. Haughey brought forward the vote to the Thursday 25 February in order to starve Des O'Malley of the chance to get his campaign going. O'Malley had taken over from George Colley as the unofficial leader of the anti-Haughey faction. But O'Malley did not really want the job – he just wanted to stop Haughey, whom he regarded as a 'malignant' force.[50] His side assembled a list of likely supporters. O'Malley hoped Haughey would be shocked by the number of votes already amassed and then give up, but he was naive. Haughey was confident. His supporters, Ray MacSharry, Albert Reynolds and Seán Doherty, were busy canvassing TDs.

When Haughey arrived at the meeting in the Fianna Fáil party room on the third floor of Leinster House, a little after 11.30 a.m. on 25 February, he was greeted with rapturous applause. Haughey took control. The only real item on the agenda was to choose a name to go forward for nomination as Taoiseach. TDs spoke in turn, some for O'Malley, more for Haughey, but a lot simply appealing for party unity. Some were cagey, unwilling to declare who they'd vote for because they did not want to be on the losing side.[51]

The speakers continued. Up rose Pádraig Faulkner, the Louth TD, former minister, and an opponent of Haughey. He appealed for unity. O'Malley sat impassively, pulling hard on a cigarette. He knew it was gone. But when O'Donoghue rose to appeal for unity and for O'Malley to withdraw his challenge, O'Malley was done. O'Malley spoke, bowing to the inevitable, and the meeting agreed to a proposal from MacSharry that Haughey would be the party's nominee. There was no vote.

Having secured his leadership, Haughey then began the process of forming a government. He knew he had the support of one independent, Neil Blaney. Gregory also looked on track to accept a deal. The Árd Comhairle of Sinn Féin The Workers' Party that had initially said their three TDs would oppose Haughey then made a tactical decision to support him. The party, which had evolved from the electoral organ of the Official IRA, had moved so far from traditional Irish nationalism that some felt it occupied an outlook on Northern Ireland closer to Ulster unionism.[52] Haughey also ensured that John O'Connell, the Ceann Comhairle, was re-elected to that office, taking out another potential vote against his government. On 9 March 1982 Haughey was comfortably elected Taoiseach, by 86 votes to 79, but it was hardly secure. There was no commitment to lasting support. Any accidents and that parliamentary support could fall away.

9.

The Survivor

Those accidents happened in spades throughout 1982. One of the most extraordinary years in Irish political history confirmed for Haughey's opponents why they wanted him out, and the events of that year almost saw the end of Haughey's political career. Haughey lurched from controversy to controversy, displaying none of the self-assuredness so evident in the February election campaign. He was keen to secure control of the party. He was helped in that his opponents were hopelessly divided. George Colley declined a ministerial position when Haughey refused to make him Tánaiste or allow him a veto over appointments to Justice and Defence. Des O'Malley and Martin O'Donoghue were appointed to government, but these were the only two of the diminishing group of Fianna Fáil TDs who were explicitly against Haughey. Many of the others who had supported Colley in 1979 had accepted that power had shifted to Haughey. Haughey was gaining control of the party by attrition.

Haughey had used Colley's part in the abortive post-election heave to remove Colley's informal veto. It was hardly unreasonable, but the real reason was power. Haughey had lacked the nerve to sack Colley in 1980 when Colley made a speech in Baldoyle offering only conditional loyalty to Haughey. The logic in 1980 was that to do so would risk splitting the party. By 1982 the party was openly split, so that logic was removed. Haughey knew that Colley no longer held sway over a significant number of TDs. Colley had earlier exercised that veto in blocking Paddy Power, who was seen as too green a nationalist to take the Defence portfolio when Haughey took power in 1979. As if to emphasise his increased control, Haughey placed Power in Defence.

Haughey brought more of his own supporters into cabinet, including Pádraig Flynn, Seán Doherty and Ray Burke. There was particular shock at his choice of Doherty in Justice. A former garda, Doherty was regarded as unsuitable because he did not seem temperamentally able to deal with sensitive issues. Haughey's opponents' suspicions were heightened when Haughey removed Des Hanafin as the secretary of Fianna Fáil's fundraising committee, taking direct control of the party's finances.[1] It was revealed that the accounts for Haughey's constituency spending at the previous two elections had been withheld from the party.[2] Haughey took the unusual step of refusing a debate on the party's accounts at the Árd Fheis and sought and secured the expulsion of his constituency auditor, Paul Mackay, after he publicly asked questions about irregularities in the party's accounts.[3]

Many of the year's events were just bad luck or political miscalculation, but others showed a willingness to abuse power or disregard norms that were to have a long-term impact on the Irish state. It started off with something minor, almost comical. It was revealed during the February 1982 campaign that Pat O'Connor, Haughey's close friend, solicitor and election agent, and O'Connor's daughter Niamh had been charged with voting twice – they applied for a ballot paper at a polling station having already voted at an earlier polling station at which O'Connor was registered. They were acquitted on a point of law. It was embarrassing (and unnecessary) for Haughey, but confirmed in his opponents' eyes that Haughey was willing to break any rules. A solicitor risking losing his career showed what Haughey's supporters would willingly do for him. It earned O'Connor the nickname Pat O'Connor/Pat O'Connor.

Haughey had no Dáil majority. In order to secure his parliamentary position, he proposed to nominate a Fine Gael TD to the European Commission, thus causing a by-election, which Fianna Fáil could be expected to win. A couple of names were considered, but Dick Burke was chosen. This might have been seen as an act of treachery by Burke, but Garret FitzGerald had sidelined him, leaving him out of cabinet, and he owed nothing to FitzGerald. Burke still wanted FitzGerald's blessing and Burke took some persuading because of pressure from his party to refuse, with Pádraig Ó hAnnracháin, who had worked for Burke when Burke was a minister, trying to convince him to take the role. The plan backfired when Fine Gael won the ensuing by-election, further damaging Haughey's reputation for political skill. What seemed like a stroke of genius ended up just looking like a stroke.

Haughey's preference for loyalists over competent ministers also backfired. As well as being controversial, his appointment of Seán Doherty to Justice was ill-judged. He wanted a loyalist in Justice, it was suspected so that he could take control of files there. There were few more loyal than Doherty. Rumours of political interference in the Garda Síochána became rife under him. The Dowra affair involved the suggestion that Doherty had organised for a witness due to give evidence against Doherty's brother-in-law, a serving garda who was accused of assault, to be detained by the RUC to prevent the witness appearing in court. The witness was detained and the case was dismissed when he failed to appear. An investigation found no evidence of communication, though the RUC chief constable was critical of that investigation, and security co-operation between the Gardaí and the RUC deteriorated.[4] Another affair involved his attempts to 'transfer' a garda who tried to bring charges against a group of men found drinking in a bar after hours. There was other evidence that the department was being misused under Doherty. Frank Dunlop, a Fianna Fáil press adviser, later reported that Doherty gave him a copy of a file to give to Ray Burke of Garda investigations into possible corruption by Burke when serving on Dublin County Council.[5]

A further controversy was discovered only after Fianna Fáil left office. Doherty ordered the tapping of two journalists' phones, ostensibly in order find the source of leaks from cabinet (an unusual reason to tap someone's phone), and because one of the journalists was 'anti-national in his outlook'. Bruce Arnold, who had earlier been the subject of Liam Cosgrave's 'blow-ins' outburst, and Geraldine Kennedy, both political journalists, had their phones monitored by gardaí under the guise of 'national security'. Doherty wanted to find the 'politicians, power interests and financial interests' already plotting to bring down Charles Haughey.[6] Doherty was acting against strong departmental advice.[7] There were constant stories of suspicions that leaks from cabinet were coming from O'Malley and his supporters, though there was no evidence of any actual leaks, never mind their source. Had there been evidence it would have surely been used for Haughey to fire O'Malley. In October 1982 O'Malley received a note from Garret FitzGerald to say that he had had information that O'Malley's phone was being tapped, confirming what O'Malley already suspected. This represented a massive breach of trust in a cabinet colleague. Both sides were guilty of hypocrisy, as Haughey had been thought a source of leaks in Lynch's 1977 government, and O'Malley had frequently complained about Haughey's disloyalty to Lynch, while he was actively plotting against Haughey.

The suspicion was that the phone tapping was concerned not with cabinet leaks, but with possible intelligence on plots to oust Haughey. A later inquiry found that those who were monitoring the calls transcribed excerpts that were 'exclusively concerned with party political matters'.[8] Whether Haughey ordered it or not is debatable, but he was certainly aware of it. Though Doherty initially denied it, he later revealed he was acting with Haughey's knowledge and Haughey was shown materials from the transcripts. The whole episode showed Haughey's willingness to use state resources for his own partisan ends.

A more unfortunate event was to lend the second Haughey government a name it kept – GUBU. A series of brutal murders took place in quick succession in late July 1982: first a nurse, Bridie Gargan, who was sunbathing in the Phoenix Park, Dublin; and some days later a young farmer, Donal Dunne, in County Offaly. Murders were highly unusual in Ireland in the 1980s, especially when there was no connection to the Troubles. The ensuing manhunt quickly focused on a man with an unusual appearance. The Gardaí soon identified the suspect. On 13 August Malcolm Macarthur was arrested while hiding out in the flat of his friend, the Attorney General Patrick Connolly. A gun belonging to the murdered farmer was found in Connolly's flat.

Connolly made the mistake of flying to the US for a prearranged holiday just days after the arrest. Haughey spoke to him as Connolly was transiting through London and suggested – without success – that he should return to Dublin. By the time Connolly arrived in New York there was a large media pool to meet him. Garret FitzGerald tried to put more pressure on Haughey by cutting short his holiday in France. Haughey then insisted Connolly return, and in Abbeville Haughey fired him. At a press conference in Leinster House on 17 August Haughey described the situation as 'unbelievable' and 'bizarre': 'This was, as I say, a grotesque situation, one that none of us has ever experienced before. I don't think there's anyone in this room who has ever had such an experience of such an unprecedented situation.'[9] Conor Cruise O'Brien, a fierce critic of Haughey, reordered the words grotesque, unprecedented, bizarre and unbelievable to construct the acronym GUBU – a word that has entered the Irish political lexicon. The Attorney General was innocent of any wrongdoing, except misjudgement. Haughey too misjudged the situation by allowing the Attorney General to leave the state for a personal holiday while the story consumed the media. Haughey was unlucky in this bizarre occurrence, which allowed opponents to point out that trouble seemed to follow him around.

There were other less dramatic but more consequential issues for that Haughey government. Northern Ireland remained a key policy theme. Haughey opposed the UK Secretary of State's Prior initiative,[10] which sought to set up a regional assembly in Northern Ireland. Since Haughey returned to power in March 1982 little had been done to reactivate relations with Margaret Thatcher. Haughey wanted to organise a summit, but she was reluctant because of the Falklands War. When the war broke out Haughey condemned the Argentinian invasion and supported European Community (EC) imposition of sanctions against Argentina, though privately he was reported to have been thrilled by the invasion.[11] After the sinking of the *General Belgrano*, an Argentinian navy cruiser, outside the Falklands' maritime exclusionary zone, Paddy Power, Haughey's Minister for Defence, caused much comment when at a constituency meeting he called the British the aggressors in the conflict. Haughey disowned this and tried to get Power to withdraw the remarks, which Power (bravely and directly) refused.[12] As the leader of a minority government Haughey was conscious of the likely proximity of an election and might, having realised the popularity of his defence minister's position, adopted it himself.[13] This position was privately criticised by Brian Lenihan, who thought it irresponsible to deviate from the EC line.[14] It also indicated Haughey's declining control within the party. On 4 May Haughey released a statement reading:

> The Irish Government will seek an immediate meeting of the [UN] Security Council in order to prepare a new resolution calling for:
> 1. An immediate cessation of hostilities by both British and Argentinian forces, and
> 2. The negotiation of a diplomatic settlement under the auspices of the United Nations.
>
> The Irish Government regard the application of economic sanctions as no longer appropriate and will therefore be seeking the withdrawal of these sanctions by the Community.[15]

This was ostensibly a reaction to the sinking of the *Belgrano* and the ensuing loss of life. As Haughey told RTÉ Radio that day, Ireland was reasserting its traditional neutrality 'as a peace-loving nation'.[16] The intervention was taken without consultation with the Department of Foreign Affairs. The minister, Gerry Collins, admitted to the

UK ambassador that Haughey had taken control of foreign policy.[17] A stronger minister might have resigned. For Haughey's private secretary, Seán Aylward, Haughey's handling of the dispute was not his finest hour.[18] But anti-British feeling was still high in Ireland, and if it was not good policy, it was good politics.

Diplomatically, however, it was a failure as by the time it reached the UN Security Council the Irish resolution had been so watered down by amendments that even the British could support it.[19] The Falklands War caused a serious deterioration in relations between Ireland and the UK, and made any progress on the North unlikely. Haughey continued to make 'unhelpful' remarks about the Prior initiative, though Jim Prior's own remarks were hardly designed to encourage Irish nationalist participation. At the annual Wolfe Tone commemoration in Bodenstown on 26 September 1982 Haughey was critical of the British proposal, quoting Prior: 'Today we face a renewed political struggle in Ireland, arising from the present attempt "to tie Northern Ireland into the United Kingdom" forever.'[20] The overall effect was to freeze British–Irish relations, except for ongoing informal talks between Dermot Nally, the Irish government secretary and Robert Armstrong, the UK cabinet secretary.

The political upheaval in 1982 impacted Haughey's position within Fianna Fáil. From July there was 'a downward spiral in the popularity of the Fianna Fáil government'.[21] Within Fianna Fáil there was deep unease about Haughey's leadership, contributing to a tense atmosphere around Leinster House. The dissidents in the party were actively plotting against Haughey. Charlie McCreevy, who was annoyed at Des O'Malley's handling of the 'heave' against Haughey in February 1982, decided to prevent what he regarded as prevarication.[22] McCreevy put down a vote of no confidence in Haughey on 1 October. O'Malley was livid. He was away on government business and had not been warned of the McCreevy challenge, which pre-empted a planned challenge McCreevy already knew about.[23]

Haughey had time to seize the initiative. He first tried to get the party National Executive to issue a directive to the parliamentary party. It did not go that far, but it did pass a resolution in support of him.[24] It also changed the rules that would allow members to be expelled for up to six months by a simple majority of the constituency organisation. They would then not be eligible to run for election. Given that Haughey had more support among the grassroots, this was a way of putting extra pressure on any wavering TDs.[25] Haughey sought public declarations of support from his cabinet. O'Malley and Martin O'Donoghue refused, saying they reserved the right to vote against him in the motion. Haughey said that they would then have to resign. And so O'Malley and O'Donoghue resigned on 6 October, to which Haughey responded, 'Well fuck you anyway. I didn't think you'd have the guts to do it.'[26] It was probably a mistake by the two ministers not to force Haughey to sack them; that would have yielded the ministers more sympathy and emphasise that Haughey was someone who could not tolerate dissent. Some time later O'Donoghue received a package from Haughey's driver. It was two dead ducks, with a note: 'Shot over Kinsealy'.

The no-confidence motion was still on. Pressure was brought to bear on TDs in any way it could to support Haughey in the motion. David Andrews, who had a significant legal practice based on just one client, received a call from the company's owner, a close associate of Haughey, urging him to 'do the right thing'. Andrews saw this as a thinly veiled threat.[27] Many other opponents of Haughey received threatening calls.[28] Haughey proposed that the vote of confidence by the parliamentary party should be an open roll call vote, which was against the normal procedures, but Haughey had control of all the key offices in Fianna Fáil. Haughey won that motion, and then the outcome of his leadership motion was a fait accompli. On the night of 6 October Haughey won the roll call vote by 58 to 22. Though the media dubbed his opponents the 'Club of 22', it was in no way a club. There was no unity in it. Those loyal to Haughey were angry at his opponents. Some even thought Haughey was the victim of a British secret service plot.[29] Afterwards the tense atmosphere boiled over as some prominent anti-Haughey TDs were jostled and kicked by over-zealous Haughey supporters. Jim Gibbons was attacked and wrestled to the ground outside Leinster House. He never really recovered from those injuries.

Haughey had pulled through with a combination of luck, skill and venom.

✼ ✼ ✼

Haughey might have survived in the party, but his government did not. Fianna Fáil's parliamentary arithmetic was already challenging. It had relied on the casting vote of the Ceann Comhairle on a number of occasions. In some ways Haughey was unlucky. The Fianna Fáil TD, and loyal Haughey supporter, Dr Bill Loughnane died suddenly on 18 October 1982; and Haughey's old adversary Jim Gibbons was, because of his injuries, unable to attend the Dáil. Haughey's carefully constructed Dáil majority had vanished.

In other ways, Haughey was in an impossible position. The economy was in a mess, with public spending still at a level that was unsustainable for the economic activity in the country, and there was 'an imperative need for investment and that made a high rate of borrowing inevitable.'[30] The Haughey government's budget in 1982 more or less held the line of the defeated Bruton budget, but was more politically savvy.[31] It kept food subsidies, dropped taxes on clothes, but promised to reduce the deficit. It was hardly seen as a solution, but was thought a holding budget for an early election. Haughey's choice of Ray MacSharry as Minister for Finance was a good one, and in *The Way Forward* document, written by Pádraig Ó hUiginn, he had a plan to regenerate the economy while getting public spending under control. *The Way Forward* was Haughey's equivalent of Lemass's *Programme for Economic Expansion*. It was a serious document, but not one that was taken seriously at the time. Haughey's opponents in the party did not trust him to do anything but spend his way to electoral victory – a view that was hardly without merit.

Garret FitzGerald also used the distrust of Haughey to oppose any measure proposed. While not under pressure for his own leadership, FitzGerald took some criticism within Fine Gael for his management of his first government. His courting of the Workers' Party, as it had become known, was a misjudgement, and one former minister, Professor John Kelly, declined to serve on his front bench.[32] In June 1982 Bruton led the charge against Fianna Fáil's Finance Bill 'on the grounds of social justice and economic responsibility', even voting for amendments with which it disagreed.[33]

The industrial relations climate was still fractious, with most in the union movement still opposed to national pay agreements. Haughey wanted an agreement, but he had a reputation as being soft on unions.[34] The Department of Finance thought *The Way Forward* was too optimistic.[35] In late July, Haughey's government had agreed to put an embargo on public sector pay increases, but rowed back on this by early October.[36] Because Haughey was reliant on Tony Gregory and the Workers' Party for parliamentary support he knew an election was never far away.[37] The Workers' Party indicated it would not support *The Way Forward* plan. The party saw it as an opportune time for an election as the Labour leader, Michael O'Leary, had just quit his party to join Fine Gael. In late October O'Leary had lost an internal party motion to allow Labour to go into coalition without the need to refer to a special conference.

Fine Gael now had an advantage; Fianna Fáil splits were in the open and Haughey was damaged by his turbulent short period in office. Labour had just appointed a new leader, the young and inexperienced Dick Spring, about whom little was known. On 2 November Fine Gael put down a motion of no confidence in the government in the Dáil, and with Haughey's majority gone, on 4 November the Dáil was dissolved and Ireland headed to the polls on 24 November for the country's third election in 18 months.

In the election campaign Fianna Fáil used 'wedge' issues to stop the flow of support from it to Fine Gael. Haughey tried to make abortion an election issue, claiming that Fine Gael could not be trusted on it.[38] FitzGerald had defused the issue by agreeing to accept a constitutional referendum that would explicitly ban abortion.

Solving an immediate political problem would later cause him a much greater one.

A FitzGerald speech on Northern Ireland about the possibility of a joint policing authority led Fianna Fáil to suggest that he was a recruiting sergeant for the RUC. The attempt to paint FitzGerald as a British collaborator was seen by the media as either a joke or a measure of Haughey's desperation.[39] Fine Gael was in better shape. It had candidates in place, and morale was boosted by an opinion poll that showed the party level with Fianna Fáil at 42 per cent. FitzGerald was clearly preferred for the office of Taoiseach.[40] The campaign was short, and neither party differed significantly on the economic issues. John Bruton had worked on an economic plan that sought to generate jobs through attracting foreign direct investment. It wasn't full of promises of electoral 'goodies'; in fact some economists though it was too deflationary, and would prevent economic growth.[41] FitzGerald performed well in the leaders' debate, avoiding jargon and sticking to a couple of pre-prepared points. He focused on trust, in an attempt to emphasise the significant gap in public trust between himself and Haughey.[42]

This time the result was more decisive. Fine Gael got over 39 per cent of the vote and won 70 seats. Though Fianna Fáil won 45 per cent of first preference votes, it led Fine Gael by just five seats, on 75. Labour picked up a seat, that of Jim Kemmy. Between them Fine Gael and Labour had 86 seats, a clear majority. Spring and FitzGerald got on with each other, and respected one another. It was clear during the campaign that they wanted to work together.

The government negotiations took place in a convent in Donnybrook, a place suggested by John Rogers, a close confidant of Dick Spring and later the Attorney General, in order to prevent media intrusions.[43] The location was misinterpreted by Fergus Finlay, who later became one of Dick Spring's most trusted advisers, as an attempt 'to ensure that the inexperienced Labour leader was isolated from whatever back-up and support he could count on'.[44] This was to set the tone for the government over the next four years. The already prickly Spring would have anything that did not go his way interpreted as a slight by Finlay. Labour was a different party in the 1980s from the one that FitzGerald had worked with in the 1970s. The party had become even more ideological and split. There was a more vocal minority, led by Michael D. Higgins, resistant to coalition. Higgins was regarded as having 'a negative destructive role' in the Labour Party and would cause Spring more anxiety in government as he would continually have to second guess what the Labour left, the trade unions and the party's administrative council might accept.[45]

FitzGerald was conscious of this and conscious too that Spring was much younger – younger than his elder son. They did, however, share the same social democratic principles and they respected each other. In the programme for government negotiations Labour leaked that there were significant tensions, when the tensions were not that great.[46] Having secured the electoral result FitzGerald was strong within his party, which meant that he was willing and able to offer far more concessions to Labour than his colleagues would have liked. There was an acceptance that some Labour demands, such as a residential property tax, might be too much for Fine Gael, though FitzGerald himself had no problem with it. He worked on an alternative proposal – income related residential property tax – with his daughter-in-law Eithne FitzGerald, a Labour councillor.

Labour committed to eliminating the budget deficit, although in five years rather than four, and gave the government some wriggle room by giving 'due regard to prevailing economic conditions'.[47] Many of the most difficult decisions were fudged, and left for government. The Fine Gael–Labour programme for government was debated at a Labour Party special delegate conference in Limerick on 12 December 1982. Spring did not know the Labour Party that well, and used Frank Cluskey to sell the deal. Despite determined opposition from Michael D. Higgins, and a former General Secretary, Brendan Halligan, the party gave its new leader a chance, passing the agreement by 846 votes to 522.[48] The Fine Gael parliamentary party, though expressing some misgivings about the proposed property tax, gave the programme its almost unanimous approval – only John Kelly objected. On 14 December 1982, at the end of an extraordinary political year, Garret FitzGerald was elected Taoiseach by 85 votes to 79.[49]

✳ ✳ ✳

Having led Fianna Fáil to a third election without delivering an overall majority, Haughey faced yet another leadership challenge. FitzGerald was now in a position to help those opponents of Haughey in Fianna Fáil. One of the goals FitzGerald set himself on returning to office in 1982 was to restore the non-political character of the Garda Siochána.[50] FitzGerald had appointed Michael Noonan as Minister for Justice to investigate the rumours around phone tapping under the Haughey government. Noonan's departmental secretary, Andy Ward, was equally anxious about what had gone on and had kept records.[51] On 20 January 1983 Noonan revealed the details of the previous minister's phone taps of journalists. The Deputy Garda Commissioner, Joe Ainsworth, had agreed to do this, and the Garda Commissioner, Patrick McLaughlin, was also aware of it. The investigation found that there was no justification for these taps. It also revealed that the Tánaiste in that government, Ray MacSharry, had covertly recorded a conversation he had with another minister, Martin O'Donoghue, because he suspected he was going to be offered a bribe to support a challenge to Haughey's leadership (he was not). The Garda Commissioner and Deputy Garda Commissioner both resigned, having been asked by Noonan to reflect on their positions. The details of all this were released to a bewildered public, and it caused further difficulties for Haughey in opposition, and gave a temporary fillip to the government.[52] However, no long-term structures were then put in place to deal with the problem, as FitzGerald saw it, of political control of the Gardaí.

Haughey denied any knowledge of the phone tapping, and Seán Doherty loyally took the blame, telling an RTÉ radio programme that Haughey did not know of it.[53] But on top of another electoral defeat it was not just 'the usual suspects' calling for Haughey to go. Most media outlets reported that Haughey was on the brink of resignation.[54] Bertie Ahern, the party's chief whip, called to Haughey in Kinsealy on 26 January 1983 to tell him, 'If there was a vote today, you would lose' and that 'Michael O'Kennedy would probably win.' Haughey told him that he would not be quitting.[55] Haughey was once again fighting for his political life. Many assumed it was over.

The next day, 27 January, the *Irish Press* published Haughey's political obituary under the title 'Man of controversy'.[56] Haughey had a key weakness compared to the heave a year earlier. In February 1982 he was still likely to become Taoiseach, and TDs were aware that coming out against him could end their chances of promotion to cabinet. In early 1983, however, when Fianna Fáil faced the prospect of five years in opposition, Haughey had fewer obvious threats he could use against TDs.

There was an air of inevitability to Haughey's departure, and canvassing for support for his replacement was actively under way. That expectation that his career was over may have helped Haughey as few felt the need to seal the lid of Haughey's political coffin shut. At a parliamentary party meeting suggestions were made by Ray Burke that Haughey would go, but should not be subject to the indignity of being seen to be pushed.[57] PJ Mara went out to get the grassroots to canvass their TDs. With a bit of encouragement the members started to put pressure on those middle-ground TDs who wanted Haughey removed as leader.[58] This would be crucial.

Haughey also got lucky. A Fianna Fáil TD from Donegal, Clem Coughlan, was killed in a car accident on the way to Dublin on Tuesday 1 February. The vote on Haughey's leadership had been due to take place the following day, but the meeting was postponed for a week, against the objections of Haughey's opponents. Haughey still controlled the agenda because one of his loyalists, Jim Tunney, was party chairman. In fact his placement of Jim Tunney, Bertie Ahern and Brian Lenihan in three key party roles – party chair, chief whip, and director of policy and planning – was vital. It meant that

Haughey had control of key institutions when it mattered. A petition organised by Ray Burke, Ben Briscoe and Ber Cowan to bring the meeting forward to Friday 4 February was signed by 41 TDs, but the bombastic Tunney passed it on to Bertie Ahern, who passed it back. They just ignored it. The TDs were furious.

Another weekend in their constituencies meant that TDs were subject to more pressure from the grassroots to support Haughey. TDs received late-night telephone calls urging them to support Haughey, sometimes in threatening tones. There were reports of cars sitting outside TDs' homes. One TD claimed to be 'frightened beyond being frightened anymore'.[59] The ongoing tensions within Fianna Fáil had a lasting impact on TDs, many of whom were under severe strain. One young Fianna Fáil TD, Seamus Kirk, was hospitalised when he collapsed from exhaustion after a Comhairle Dáil Ceanntair meeting in his Louth constituency that was called to discuss the leadership.

Haughey told PJ Mara, 'We need confusion.'[60] Haughey's side added names to the possible contenders for the leadership. If TDs did not know who they would get – Gerry Collins, Michael O'Kennedy or Des O'Malley – they might be more likely to opt for what they had. Haughey issued a statement on 3 February that he was going to fight on 'in the best interests of the Party I have devoted all my political life to'. He implied that his opponents were puppets for more nefarious forces: 'The issue that faces Fianna Fáil today goes to the very heart of its existence. Are its policies and its leader in future to be decided for it by the media, by alien influences, by political opponents or worst of all by business interests pursuing their own ends?'[61] It was a bizarre statement that hardly did anything to help him, but his team kept up the pressure on TDs that weekend.

On Monday evening, 7 February 1983, crowds outside Leinster House held placards reading 'We support Charlie' and 'We back Charlie all the way'. John Wilson, who had been pitched as a leadership contender, said that Haughey would win. Haughey took control of the meeting, dealing first with a report into the phone tapping scandal, which he had commissioned from the party chairman, Jim Tunney. The Tunney Report unsurprisingly exonerated Haughey. David Andrews issued a minority report, which did not question his exoneration, but suggested Haughey should have known about the tapping. It failed to land a blow on Haughey. Haughey proposed that the meeting first consider whether Seán Doherty and Martin O'Donoghue be reprimanded (for their involvement in a separate taped conversation), but the decision was deferred until the leadership vote took place. It was a further attempt by Haughey to muddy the waters.

That motion to remove Haughey was proposed by Ben Briscoe, a middle-ground TD who had previously been seen as a Haughey supporter, but one who lacked any stature in the parliamentary party. Neither he nor any of the other middle-ground TDs made powerful speeches. Some, sensing the room going against them, equivocated. O'Kennedy indicated that he would support Haughey. Haughey eventually won the vote by 40 to 33. Haughey showed considerable skill and determination in coming through this third, and most serious, challenge to his leadership. He was lucky in that his opponents were never a united group. There was no consensus as to who might win if Haughey were removed, and O'Malley could not build a coalition behind him. O'Malley remained unpopular with many backbench TDs, having made no concerted effort to court them, something he acknowledged he was not very good at.[62] Back out on Kildare Street the crowd had grown, now cheering 'Charlie, Charlie, Charlie'. Asked if the leadership problem in Fianna Fáil was now over, John Wilson said 'I suppose it is.'[63]

Haughey had come close to quitting.[64] Terry Keane claimed that at an earlier heave against him he had written his resignation letter, saying he would give it all up and run off to the south of France.[65] That might have been wishful thinking on her part. Again, his finances, which had been raised as an issue in the challenge to his leadership, were such that he probably could not. On becoming Taoiseach in 1979 Haughey managed to get friends or supporters to gift him IR£780,622 (about €5 million in 2023) to clear his overdraft, while Allied Irish Banks, which had spent much of the previous five years pursuing Haughey for the money, wrote off the remainder, nearly IR£400,000 (€2.4m).[66] Haughey's lifestyle remained luxurious. He had started to borrow money again, IR£400,000 (€1.6m) in 1982, paid back from unknown sources only after he later returned to power. Other money went into Haughey's offshore accounts.

Had Haughey's premiership ended in 1983, he would have been reasonably judged as a Taoiseach who failed to deal with any of the problems Ireland faced; one that was consumed by a struggle for political and financial survival, but little else. Although he was in opposition to his rival, Garret FitzGerald, he had survived. This time FitzGerald had what appeared to be a stable majority. Haughey was determined to make FitzGerald's life as uncomfortable as he could.

10.

Garret the Good, the Bad and the Ugly

Garret FitzGerald should have learned from his mistakes in constructing his first cabinet, but he did not. The new Taoiseach offered to reappoint Jim Dooge, who had been acknowledged to be an effective minister, but Dooge had not been a candidate in either of the last two elections. He turned the offer down for health reasons. Alexis FitzGerald was also offered a return to the role of special adviser sitting at cabinet. While Garret found his presence very useful, for his advice and wisdom, Alexis had found the role somewhat frustrating and preferred to return to his legal practice. According to someone close to FitzGerald, he approached George Colley to see if he would serve in his government.[1] If FitzGerald did, it was refused, but it might be seen as an early attempt at bringing the moderate wings of Fianna Fáil and Fine Gael together.

In their absence, Peter Prendergast, the new government press secretary, was an important adviser. FitzGerald appointed Seán Barrett as chief whip, but after a time asked him to mediate between ministers. Later, in 1986, when Barrett was made Leader of the House, he became FitzGerald's 'chief of staff' and continued to sit at cabinet and in his role as mediator.[2] This would normally be a Taoiseach's job, and is indeed a source of power. It was a recognition that FitzGerald did not have the skill set, time or inclination to do this well. FitzGerald did not reappoint John Bruton to Finance, though he had been the author of the party's economic policy on which the programme for government was based. He did this, he said, to protect Bruton, and because Bruton would be more likely to bristle with Dick Spring.[3] He was probably right, but in failing to prepare Bruton, FitzGerald left him brooding for some months. As Minister for Industry and Commerce, Bruton was the minister who was most closely involved in the National Development Corporation – a Labour idea that would seek to put state investment into commercial enterprises. In not making Bruton Minister for Finance, FitzGerald did not avoid the inevitable disputes within government.

Given the instability of the previous two years and his distrust of Haughey, FitzGerald resolved that the government should last its full term. This had implications for how he would operate his government. He decided that in domestic affairs he would operate by majority vote in cabinet.[4] Votes are unusual in cabinet, and are a bad way to make cabinet decisions, except on minor issues. They give equal weight to each minister's opinion, regardless of how well informed or otherwise they might be. FitzGerald should have been able to use his political authority to deliver his preferred outcome, but he frequently found himself in the minority. The cabinet was in awe of him, and he often knew more about the ministers' briefs than they did themselves, so he could win at cabinet even when there was a consensus against him.[5]

The majority vote rule had two caveats. First, on Northern Ireland the cabinet accepted that FitzGerald would dictate government policy, a position which was normal and unproblematic, given that most shared FitzGerald's views. Second, cabinet votes could not split in such a way that would leave the Labour Party united in a minority. In coalition each party normally has a mutual veto, with the threat of collapsing the government giving it force. By his resolution not to allow the government fall he effectively removed Fine Gael's veto, and accepted that progress would be at the pace of the slowest party.[6]

Happily for FitzGerald, in Dick Spring he was dealing with a more pragmatic and stable leader of Labour than previous leaders since Corish. The programme for government had been written to maximise its chances of support from Labour. But it was immediately apparent that it would be difficult to stick to these commitments. Spring was young and prone to take offence easily. Happily for Spring, he had in Garret FitzGerald a leader of Fine Gael who shared his policy views. Unhappily for both, the parlous state of the economy meant the new government would not have the financial resources to engage in the sort of social democratic ideas both wanted. Almost immediately disputes arose as to where budget cuts should come.

Because of FitzGerald's determination that the parties would not split, he believed that everyone should get a say, and all sides should be allowed to contribute at cabinet. He preferred to have every argument and side argument explored. Cabinet meetings were tortuously long. But this was not the only problem. FitzGerald's own style and intellectual curiosity meant that he tended to see all sides of an argument. He tended to get bogged down in detail that should have been pre-agreed or dismissed as irrelevant. For some, FitzGerald was too easily swayed, often by intellectually attractive arguments.[7] Others felt he could have his mind changed, if your argument was well prepared, but if you were mistaken on a minor or tangential detail it could be hard to bring him back to the main point.[8]

His cabinet secretary, Dermot Nally, warned FitzGerald that he could not run government as he would a university seminar, that the purpose of the meetings was to take decisions.[9] But FitzGerald could not help himself. He loved meetings. His ministers soon got weary, and resented the time taken at cabinet. One suggested that without Alexis FitzGerald at the cabinet table to keep an eye on the Taoiseach, FitzGerald lost any sense of self-discipline.[10] One young minister, John Boland lost respect for FitzGerald. Another minister, Austin Deasy, ignored cabinet, and tried as much as possible not to take anything to cabinet.[11] In fact ministers in that government were unanimously of the view that the meetings went on too long, and were often pointless, not focused on a decision. If they were focused on a decision it would be on micro-level details, which FitzGerald enjoyed, rather than on the big picture. His civil servants found that he was an inefficient administrator, who had to deal with issues sequentially, unlike Haughey who could have a number of projects or ideas worked on at any one time.[12]

Cabinet meetings could last 12 or 14 hours, and continue into the next day. They rarely started on time, because there was usually some crisis to be averted first. Some ministers would phone the official manning the door to the cabinet room sometime after the cabinet was due to start to see if there was any point in coming over.[13] Gemma Hussey, describing one cabinet meeting, could have been talking about any of the government's meetings: 'Cabinet today was one long nightmare.'[14] The apocryphal line attributed to FitzGerald by John Boland was his analysis of a proposal: 'That's all very good in practice, but will it work in theory?' It was plausible enough to gain currency. All the professionalism and drive that FitzGerald had shown in reorganising Fine Gael was absent from his organisation of government. Government was too big and complex to work with his preference to micro-manage. The main effect of Garret FitzGerald's style of government management was to allow problems to drift on without resolution. That made him less effective than he could have been in dealing with some social issues.

✼ ✼ ✼

In his new government FitzGerald was determined to restart his failed 'constitutional crusade'. The political climate was better for him. By 1983 he had an electoral mandate, a stable coalition that was supportive, and after successive elections that had brought in newer, younger TDs, the Fine Gael parliamentary party was now more liberal minded. There was a sense that the Irish people were ready for change. Social mores had changed significantly since the 1970s. Feminist groups challenged traditional values. There was a move away from the authoritarian power of the Catholic Church. While Mass attendance was still high – at near universal levels outside Dublin in the early 1980s – some signs were there that the Church's hold on the people was waning. Television, access to education, the move to Mass in English after Vatican II and returning emigrants all exposed Irish people to ideas that they previously did not have access to. The number of vocations – people becoming priests or nuns – had already fallen sharply in the 20 years up to the early 1980s.[15]

But it would be hard to overstate the conservative reflexes many Irish people still had and how institutionalised these were in Ireland in the 1980s. There was a taboo around extramarital sex that seeped into Irish people's behaviour. In the mid-1980s it was not uncommon for newborn babies to be found abandoned or dead. In February 1984 a baby was found abandoned in the working-class suburb of Ballymun in north Dublin. Not long after that an eight-day-old baby girl was found dead in a cattle trough on a farm. Pregnancies might also take the life of a young mother. In January 1984 15-year-old Ann Lovett died hours after having given birth on her own in the rain near a grotto in church grounds in Granard, County Longford, seemingly too ashamed to seek help.

Even more controversial was the case of the Kerry Babies. On the evening of 14 April 1984, a young woman, Joanne Hayes, from Abbeydorney, near Tralee in County Kerry, went out to a field on the farm where she lived with her mother, her aunt and her three siblings, gave birth to a baby boy, left him down and went back into her house. Sometime later she returned to find the infant dead. She wrapped him and buried him near a pool on the farm. At the same time a newborn baby boy was found wrapped in plastic on a beach near Cahersiveen, about fifty miles from Tralee. The baby on the beach had been stabbed multiple times. Gardaí searched for evidence of a single woman who had recently given birth, and after a few weeks discovered that Joanne Hayes, who was known to be having an affair with a married man with whom she worked and had a one-year-old baby by him, had been in hospital, presenting as having recently given birth. Hayes was now the prime suspect in the case of the stabbed Kerry baby, even though the body had been found a very long way from her home. Hayes revealed in questioning that she had given birth to a baby who had died and she had buried it on her farm. A search of the farm failed to find the baby; Gardaí did not allow her to show where she had buried the infant's body.

Gardaí brought in Hayes's family and extracted statements from each of them and a confession from Joanne Hayes to the murder of the baby found on the beach near Cahersiveen. Though there were significant inconsistencies in each of the statements, Hayes was charged with infanticide and remanded in custody. Later that day Joanne Hayes's siblings discovered the body of the baby on her farm. The Gardaí now had two dead babies, and inconsistent stories from each of the family members. But the Gardaí in the case were convinced that Hayes was a woman of 'loose morals', so they now worked on the assumption that Hayes had had twins. While medical evidence showed that the two babies had different blood types, the Gardaí were so convinced that they had the right woman that a new theory emerged: she had become pregnant with twins by two different men – superfecundation – something that was vanishingly unlikely. When the Gardaí wrote the report, they described it as 'this bizzare [sic], unprecedented case'; they were perhaps influenced by 'GUBU', which had become well known. The local state solicitor for Kerry, Dónal Browne, was unimpressed by the Gardaí's work. There were glaring inconsistencies between the witness statements; it was unclear how the body of the Cahersiveen baby could have ended up there and the theory of two fathers was far-fetched. The confessions were withdrawn, and allegations were made that they had been extracted with violence, threats and intimidation.[16]

Garret FitzGerald would have known this sort of Garda behaviour was possible. In the summer of 1976, following the murder of the British ambassador, the then Minister FitzGerald was concerned at reports of a 'heavy gang' in the Gardaí who would beat up suspects of serious crimes, in particular crimes associated with paramilitaries, in order to extract confessions. He was so concerned that he considered threatening to resign unless the government agreed to investigate the claims.[17] In the autumn of 1984 a *Sunday Independent* investigation published allegations that 'heavy gang' tactics had been used on Joanne Hayes and her family, who had committed no crime. Now FitzGerald was Taoiseach he could do something about it. But neither FitzGerald nor Haughey, as leader of the opposition, took leadership positions on the issue. The FitzGerald government set up a tribunal of inquiry into the Kerry babies case, but rather than investigating the flaws in the Garda investigation the tribunal chair, Mr Justice Kevin Lynch, effectively put Joanne Hayes and her morality on trial, causing great anger among some feminist groups and also locals from the Hayes's homeplace. Haughey felt that Hayes had been 'treated harshly' in the tribunal.[18] It was odd that FitzGerald did not respond. He did not even mention the events in his autobiography.

A little later, in the warm summer of 1985, in the village of Ballinaspittle in west Cork, a woman and her two children stopped at a grotto to say the rosary. They saw the statue of the Virgin Mary move. Within days news of the moving statues had spread and soon hundreds of people were descending on the village. A month later thousands were visiting the village to witness the moving statues, and across the country people reported seeing statues move in churches and shrines. The moving statues became an inexplicable phenomenon, which dominated TV and radio shows. Academics tried to explain it as a mass delusion or an optical illusion. The Catholic Church refused to give credence to the phenomenon, and after time people stopped going to the shrine and reports of moving statues fell away.

It was in this Ireland of moving statues and judgemental attitudes that the FitzGerald government tried to deal with some of the most divisive social issues, issues that would still divide the country thirty years after Haughey and FitzGerald left office. One such issue was what to do about Haughey and FitzGerald's commitments to hold a pro-life or anti-abortion amendment. A Pro-Life Amendment Campaign (PLAC) formed in 1981 had petitioned the party leaders to commit to a referendum guaranteeing that abortion could not be introduced in Ireland. It came about because of fears that the Irish courts might introduce abortion in the way it had happened in the US Supreme Court through *Roe v. Wade*. Ireland was also being used as a testing ground for an international anti-abortion campaign. Before the 1981 election both parties had promised to hold a referendum, but the commitment was in general terms, with no specific wording. But PLAC remained deeply suspicious of Fine Gael, and Haughey could see the potential benefits of the abortion issue to raise doubts about Fine Gael.[19] The following Dáil term was so short that nothing happened. PLAC kept up the pressure on the political parties, and in advance of the February 1982 election PLAC told Haughey that FitzGerald had agreed to a referendum, having asked his Attorney General to study a possible wording. FitzGerald was by now under pressure within his party because his constitutional crusade was open to being seen as soft on the issue of abortion since his interviews announcing the crusade had suggested he wanted to remove Catholic influence from the constitution. The vast majority of people in Fine Gael opposed abortion, and some of that opposition was deeply held and more important to them than the party.

As Taoiseach, Haughey invited PLAC to submit a proposed wording.[20] In autumn 1982, on the eve of the second 1982 election, the Fianna Fáil Attorney General published the proposed wording: 'The State acknowledges the right to life of the unborn and, with due regard to the equal right to life of the mother, guarantees in its laws to respect, and, as far as practicable, by its laws to defend and vindicate that right.' Exactly who wrote this wording is unclear. FitzGerald regretted his earlier commitment, as the proposed wording was problematic on several grounds. Fearful of the electoral impact of being labelled pro-abortion, FitzGerald accepted the new wording and committed to introducing the amendment. PLAC issued a statement to accept FitzGerald's commitment, defusing the issue as an immediate electoral threat.[21]

Dick Spring, wisely – and bravely, given the atmosphere at the time – refused to be drawn into giving a commitment in the election campaign. In the programme for government negotiations, Fine Gael had pushed for a commitment to produce legislation to give effect to a referendum based on the outgoing government's proposed wording. Having just been elected, FitzGerald had the opportunity to give a vaguer commitment, but instead even named the date. Having dug himself a hole, FitzGerald continued to dig. Spring had reserved the right for Labour to have a free vote on the issue. Labour largely absented itself from the debate; the Labour Minister for Health, Barry Desmond, refused to bring forward legislation, leaving it to Michael Noonan, the justice minister, to do so.

The Attorney General, Peter Sutherland, a committed Catholic with deep convictions, told FitzGerald that 'the wording is ambiguous and unsatisfactory. It will lead inevitably to confusion and uncertainty, not merely amongst the medical profession, to whom it has of course particular relevance, but also amongst lawyers and more specifically the judges who will have to interpret it.' He was scathing about the term 'unborn', which had no standard definition as a noun, never mind a legal one: 'Far from providing the protection and certainty which is sought by many of those who have advocated its adoption, it will have a contrary effect.'[22] Sutherland fought to use an alternative wording to ban abortion. He suggested: 'Nothing in this Constitution shall be invoked to invalidate, or to deprive of force or effect, any provision of a law on the ground that it prohibits abortion.'[23]

FitzGerald vacillated between accepting this advice (which he published) and concern about the politics of refusing to proceed with the PLAC/Fianna Fáil amendment. The cabinet rejected the PLAC/Fianna Fáil wording at one meeting, but then introduced something close to that wording to the Dáil the following week. FitzGerald thought there was no majority in the Oireachtas for Sutherland's wording, and was concerned that Haughey might introduce a bill to give effect to its wording, which would make plain the divisions within Fine Gael.[24] Within Fine Gael splits emerged anyway, with the liberal TD Monica Barnes indicating she would vote against the bill in defiance of any party whip.[25] Haughey stuck by what became the 'Fianna Fáil wording' – which PLAC regarded as preferable and watertight – and effectively silenced opposition to his position within Fianna Fáil. Haughey refused to accept criticisms of the wording, and doggedly pursued a defensive and indecisive FitzGerald on the issue. Gemma Hussey, the Minister for Education, noted in her diary in March that 'Garret has shown a lack of leadership ... [he is] alarming me by a lack of decisiveness.'[26]

It was particularly embarrassing because the Protestant Churches came out against the proposed wording. FitzGerald's 'constitutional crusade' was meant to be about appeasing those minority elements in society, but his efforts on abortion were doing the opposite. He then voted against the bill that his minister introduced, and that he had initially supported. FitzGerald had changed his mind, but he couldn't bring his party with him on his alternative wording. Haughey won a victory of sorts when the Fianna Fáil wording was accepted by the Dáil in April 1983. With the help of some Fine Gael and Labour votes the Amendment Bill was passed in the Dáil, and a referendum set for September. Fine Gael did not campaign on it, though FitzGerald made plain his opposition to the proposed amendment, writing in the *Irish Independent* 'As a Christian I must vote No.'[27] His party was split. The referendum campaign was one of the nastiest in Ireland's history. Fianna Fáil campaigned enthusiastically in favour.[28]

On a comparatively low turnout (53 per cent), a majority of voters supported the Eighth Amendment to the constitution, 67 per cent to 33 per cent. The referendum was to have lasting implications, and Sutherland's advice proved prescient, as the new constitutional provision effectively gave the courts the unenviable task of making decisions on the right to life, such as in the X case, which would lead to further referendums in 1992 and 2002, until the issue was perhaps finally resolved in 2018 with the Eighth Amendment being replaced with wording that explicitly allowed the Oireachtas to legislate to provide for abortion. The abortion referendum in 1983 dented FitzGerald's self-confidence at a very early stage of his term. For a conviction politician, FitzGerald showed a lack of conviction. For a politician,

FitzGerald showed a lack of political acumen. For Haughey, he succeeded in exposing some divisions within Fine Gael, and damaged FitzGerald's 'constitutional crusade'. Conor Cruise O'Brien observed at the time that the referendum had 'nothing to do with the right to life, except the right of politicians to political life.'[29]

More broadly, the show of force by the Roman Catholic hierarchy made the government wary of introducing some of its more reforming measures. FitzGerald had hoped to form some sort of concordance with the Catholic Church in several areas, but it was unwilling to concede much.[30] The constitutional crusade to secularise the Irish state was not without some successes. The concept of illegitimacy for children born outside marriage was removed. Even more significantly, the FitzGerald government would take on the still-fraught issue of contraception. This was a measure that would cause trouble in both main parties, though it damaged Haughey more. Haughey had been the minister to introduce an 'Irish solution to an Irish problem'; his 1979 bill brought in a regime where contraception would be available on medical prescription 'for the purpose, bona fide, of family planning or for adequate medical reasons and in appropriate circumstances'. This was asking the nation's doctors to be moral guardians of the people. It did, however, pass without any confrontation between Church and State and showed Haughey's ability to go as far as possible – but it was not a show of leadership. He had found the issue 'a more seriously politically acute battle' than he had had earlier encountered in the Succession Act.[31]

In 1985 Barry Desmond, the Minister for Health introduced a Family Planning Bill that would liberalise access to contraception, removing the need for a medical prescription for non-medical products such as condoms. They would still only be available in pharmacies to over-18s. Haughey saw the bill as a political opportunity to damage FitzGerald. In denying calls for a free vote, where any TD or senator could vote according to their conscience rather than a whip, he told a parliamentary party meeting that the bill should be opposed because of the embarrassment and dangers it posed to the FitzGerald government.[32] By this stage Haughey's position as Fianna Fáil leader was more secure than it had ever been. His party, if not united, was sick of scheming and plots. Most of his opponents were simply resigned to accept him. He appointed a number of his critics to the Fianna Fáil front bench, but this was not an exercise in bridge-building. He was seeking complete control of the party. Haughey was still in opposition, however, and his approach to any issue often depended on whether he was in government or opposition. In government he could be pragmatic and constructive, in opposition he would be truculent. One new TD said of the attitude in the party at the time was to 'not give a fucking inch to Garret'.[33]

Haughey's main rival for the leadership brooded on the issue. Ten years earlier Des O'Malley had made a speech in the Dáil opposing the National Coalition's legislation to allow the sale of contraceptives in which he had argued that 'in any ordered society the protection of morals through the deterrence of fornication and promiscuity is a legitimate legislative aim and a matter not of private but of public morality.'[34] By 1985 O'Malley had changed his mind and in an impassioned speech, regarded by some as the best they had heard delivered in the Dáil, he asked, 'Do some Deputies and people outside the House think that because the law says something, therefore that is the way things are?' His speech was about more than the contraceptive issue; it was about the relationship between Church and State: 'I do not believe that the interests of this State, or our Constitution and of this Republic, would be served by putting politics before conscience in regard to this.'[35]

In his 'I stand by the Republic' speech O'Malley took the FitzGerald line on the meaning of what it meant to be a republic. He had already lost the Fianna Fáil whip on Northern Ireland policy, and did not vote in favour of the bill – he abstained – but his speech might have swayed some votes on the government side to vote in favour of the bill, which was passed by 83 votes to 80. Had it been defeated the government would have been terminally damaged.[36] Haughey was furious; this was a lost opportunity to bring down the FitzGerald government.³⁷ Haughey organised O'Malley's expulsion from the Fianna Fáil organisation. Though O'Malley had abstained on the vote, and was already outside the parliamentary party, his reasonable claims that he could not have defied a whip he was not subject to were ignored. George Colley had died in September 1983. Now in early 1985 Des O'Malley was out. There was almost no one left to stand up to Haughey. He was in control of Fianna Fáil. But it came at a cost; Fianna Fáil became seen as a socially conservative force in Irish society, something that would cause long-term damage to the party.

Buoyed by the success in enacting the Family Planning Bill, FitzGerald decided to take on a more difficult issue, the proposal to remove the constitutional ban on divorce that had been introduced in the 1920s by a government of which FitzGerald's father was a member. Divorce was a measure that the Labour Party wanted to introduce, as did FitzGerald, who had made it Fine Gael party policy in 1978. It was certainly less divisive than abortion. In opinion polls there were consistent majorities in favour of some change to the restrictive laws on marriage.

In late 1985, Michael O'Leary, by now a Fine Gael backbencher, introduced a Private Members' Bill (PMB) to call a referendum to change the constitution in relation to divorce. The government parties decided to allow a free vote, but the bill failed to get a second reading. The O'Leary Bill brought the ban on divorce to the fore, and FitzGerald said he was in favour of removing the ban, but wanted to wait for a committee report. Paddy Cooney, once regarded as a liberal in Fine Gael, used a debate in December 1985 on that report of the Committee on Marriage Breakdown to make clear his opposition to any change in the constitution, and to say that he believed a majority of Fine Gael TDs also opposed it.³⁸ Labour's response was to introduce its own bill, which FitzGerald opposed. He voted against it on the grounds that the Churches should first be consulted.³⁹ He had already started to do that, but if he thought his appeal to the Roman Catholic Church would yield him anything other than opposition he was to be disappointed.

FitzGerald clearly enjoyed getting into the minute details of problems, and now he could exercise his brain on the concept of nullity by ecclesiastical tribunals and how these might cohere with a divorce law. Opinion polls suggested clear support for the removal of the ban – 52 per cent to 42 per cent, with 6 per cent undecided in February 1986.[40] In April 1986, when the bill was published, support for legalising divorce was overwhelming: 57 to 36 per cent.[41]

But there was no attempt to prepare the ground on the more substantive issues that would ultimately dominate the referendum campaign, principally property. The Catholic Church came out vigorously against the proposal. Haughey, though not especially religious, stayed true to the path of social conservatism on which he had set Fianna Fáil much earlier.[42] Fianna Fáil had taken the unusual step of boycotting an Oireachtas committee on marital breakdown in 1981 – instead Haughey set up a Fianna Fáil committee.[43] In 1984 the Divorce Action Group accused Haughey of 'gagging' Fianna Fáil TDs on an Oireachtas committee on marriage breakdown.[44] When the referendum took place in 1986 Fianna Fáil did not take a position, though Haughey indicated he was opposed to allowing divorce in Ireland, and many of its TDs were active opponents of the proposed change.[45] Haughey may have been genuine in his belief in the family, and his innate social conservatism, but it was certainly hypocritical given his own personal life, and most likely Haughey's position was determined by politics – his need to gut Garret.

During the campaign divorce was framed as something that would be damaging for women, who might be cast aside by their husbands and not looked after financially because of the ex-husband's obligation to care for his new family. Alice Glenn, a reactionary Fine Gael TD, campaigning for No, proclaimed that 'A Woman voting for Divorce is like a Turkey voting for Christmas.'[46] There were suggestions that the proposed law would be unrestricted. These were false claims, but the Yes campaign failed to pre-empt or satisfactorily remove doubts in people's minds. Even though one of the anti-divorce lawyers, William Binchy, had set out the No side's main arguments in book form, no one on the Yes side had bothered to read it.⁴⁷ Fine Gael ran a 'lazy campaign', thought by one minister to be 'lousy and half-hearted', seeing many of the pro side withdraw from active campaigning as polling day approached.⁴⁸

In a remarkable reversal of public opinion the referendum was lost by 63 per cent to 37, and was another severe blow to FitzGerald's credibility. FitzGerald claimed that even if he lost some referendums, he put the issues on the agenda, which were then subject to later success, but that assumes that these setbacks were inevitable.⁴⁹ It fails to appreciate that the divorce referendum, while controversial, could have been successful if it had been introduced properly; and that the abortion amendment was a debacle that could have been avoided if FitzGerald had exercised better political judgement. If his crusade had failed, it was not because he was ahead of his time. It was because he did not exercise political leadership, skill or good judgement during these episodes.

His poor judgement on these issues may have been because his mind was elsewhere. He was thinking about the North.

11.

THE NORTHERN LINE

Northern Ireland was an issue on which Garret FitzGerald and Charles Haughey had strong and contrasting opinions. They differed on the approach to Northern Ireland – it was not that one was sensitive to unionism and the other a gut republican, though that was undoubtedly true. More than any issue Northern Ireland was central to Garret FitzGerald's political formation. His family background, he felt, gave him a special insight into the complexities of the issue. He had a very deep concern about Northern Ireland, which was unusual for Irish politicians. While the North – FitzGerald was also somewhat unusual in referring to it as 'Northern Ireland' – was often a subject of political debate, it was rarely given deep thought. FitzGerald saw it as a 'problem that must be solved between Irish people . . . north and south, nationalist and unionist' and that any solution would be internal, that the aim of British withdrawal could only come with unionist consent.[1]

Haughey, by contrast, argued that 'As long as Britain is [in Northern Ireland] it has to be solved between the Irish and British government'.[2] He too felt that his family background in Swatragh, County Derry gave him a special insight into the position of northern nationalists. Though he had not shown much evidence of strong republican beliefs growing up, there was some evidence of a 'gut republicanism'. If Haughey's republicanism, as evidenced in his behaviour during the Arms Crisis, came as a surprise to contemporaries, he exploited that reputation to enable him to take the leadership of his party in December 1979. Whereas Jack Lynch had been content to allow the issue drift, on coming to power Haughey was anxious to plan for reunification.[3]

Haughey was aware that time was one of his problems. He told a departing UK ambassador, 'I haven't got any time.'[4] He wanted to take significant initiative on Northern Ireland, but the proximity of elections meant he needed to deliver results more quickly than they were likely to be achievable. The problem for Taoisigh is that Northern Ireland is outside their ambit of control. Haughey walked a tightrope between doing what was expected of him by his more republican supporters and a desire to make progress on the North, which depended on co-operation with the British. No one was certain what Haughey's approach might be. Within the Department of the Taoiseach there was 'anxiety' that a carefully constructed strategy of shifting US support towards a constitutional nationalist position and isolating the Provisional IRA in Irish America would be cast aside.[5] But it became clear to his secretary, Dermot Nally that Haughey wanted to present himself 'as a moderate'.[6]

The more violently nationalist parts of Irish America welcomed Haughey's elevation in 1979, and Neil Blaney, who was in the US at the time visiting the pro-IRA lobby group, the Irish National Caucus (INC), made a statement calling on Haughey to engage with the INC. Irish government policy had been to engage with senior Irish-American political leaders to promote a moderate nationalist position, and to persuade them to use their influence with Britain to support the Irish government approach. Ireland had cultivated senior Irish American politicians, the so-called Four Horsemen, Speaker Tip O'Neill, senators Ted Kennedy and Patrick Moynihan, and Governor Hugh Carey, who had convinced President Jimmy Carter to make a statement in support of talks in Northern Ireland.

Haughey sought to reassure the Four Horsemen and Seán Donlon, the Irish ambassador to Washington, that he had no connection with the INC and that his approach was as set out in the Dáil on 13 December 1979.[7] In Haughey's speech to the Dáil he stated: 'it will be the constant endeavour of this Government, as it has been of their predecessor, to achieve the unity of the people of Ireland by peaceful means, by agreement, independence and in a harmonious relationship with our neighbour, Britain. We totally reject the use of force as a means of achieving that end.'[8] However, his Minister for Foreign Affairs, Brian Lenihan, later met with the Mario Biaggi, the head of the INC. Haughey came under pressure to clarify the government's position, and in Cork in July 1980 he sought to end any perceived ambiguity with strong denunciation of Noraid, a fundraising organisation for the Provisional IRA, and the INC.[9] Haughey suggested continuity in approach, and was clear in his commitment to the security of the state.

Government policy to date had been largely set in Derry. John Hume was hugely influential on Irish policy, with Jack Lynch, Liam Cosgrave and later Garret FitzGerald all looking to him for ideas and guidance. Hume's approach was that a solution would be very much internal to Northern Ireland, that the problem was one of relations between unionists and nationalists. Efforts were made to entice unionism to the table. Though he was not very hopeful of a solution, Haughey was determined not to be reactive. He was inclined to the view that any solution would have an all-island nature and would only be achieved if driven by the two governments working in concert. Haughey's objective was 'to get the British to declare their interest in the unification of Ireland'; that is, unionism would only move under pressure from the British.[10] On this Haughey was ultimately proved right.

Margaret Thatcher was too busy to think about Northern Ireland in the early days of her premiership, from May 1979. She was an instinctive English nationalist and saw Northern Ireland as a security problem. It was the dual Provisional IRA actions on 27 August 1979, the assassination of Lord Mountbatten in a boat off the County Sligo coast and the killing of 18 British soldiers in Warrenpoint, County Down that made her take interest. She felt the Irish government knowingly harboured terrorists and was not doing enough on security. Efforts on the Irish government's side for her to see their own domestic difficulties, and that a severe response would potentially only increase support for Provisional IRA activity, only served to increase Thatcher's anger. The aim to change British policy from seeing Northern Ireland primarily as a security problem was an ambitious one. Thatcher's 'own instincts [were] profoundly unionist'; she was personally affected by Irish nationalist violence when her friend and colleague Airey Neave was murdered in 1979.[11]

On coming to power in December 1979 a first step for Haughey was to establish a good relationship with Britain. Haughey put some pressure on the British to arrange a summit in London for May 1980, and at this he gave Thatcher a Georgian silver teapot with the words 'where there is discord, may we bring harmony' engraved on it, referencing her speech at the steps of 10 Downing Street on coming to power. According to Dermot Nally, 'there was a chemistry between them'.[12] Haughey emerged from a private meeting 'full of enthusiasm', certain that a relationship had been established.[13] Haughey believed that the approach of 'decolonisation' taken by Lord Carrington to Rhodesia/ Zimbabwe might be used for Northern Ireland.[14] This had seen Zimbabwe formed as an independent state under majority rule. The analogy was rejected by Thatcher, who argued that Northern Ireland was 'totally different'.[15] The text of the joint communiqué said that any change in the constitutional status of Northern Ireland 'would only come about with the consent of the majority of the people in Northern Ireland', but the leaders were committed 'to hold regular meetings on a continued basis' to facilitate development in the 'unique relationship'.

Between this summit and the next summit meeting, scheduled for Dublin in December 1980, the first hunger strikes started in Northern Ireland. These were a reaction to the 1976 decision by Harold Wilson's Labour government to end 'special category' status for paramilitary prisoners. They were no longer treated as political prisoners, and they refused to wear the prison clothes they were given. From 28 October 1980 seven of the Provisional IRA prisoners refused food. The hunger strikes put massive pressure on Haughey to deliver some concessions from the British. Síle de Valera made a speech in Donegal, in front of Haughey, excoriating Mrs Thatcher, which Haughey was quickly forced to disown. At a second summit, on 8 December, Haughey urged Thatcher to intervene, which she did, and the hunger strikes ended soon after.[16] At that summit in Dublin Castle, Haughey secured a commitment to issue 'joint studies' into areas for potential mutual co-operation that could improve relations and ultimately achieve peace.

Haughey looked to the 'totality of relationships', a phrase used in the summit communiqué, to suggest that the British were open to wide-ranging negotiations. While the British government appreciated Haughey's diplomacy, it was concerned with 'presentational issues', not least in the press reaction.[17] Brian Lenihan's 'gaffe' in saying that 'everything is on the table', including constitutional issues, led Thatcher to believe that the summit was being oversold, and led to her vitriolic criticism of Haughey at their next meeting.[18]

This led many critics to claim that Haughey had destroyed the good relationship he had established with Thatcher. But the description of the complete breakdown in relations seems to be overblown. The joint studies process continued. Haughey's governments co-operated fully with the British, and the relationship was good. Politically Haughey was unable to be too closely aligned with Thatcher, at least publicly. In one telling passage in a letter from Robert Armstrong,[19] relaying a conversation he had had with Dermot Nally, Armstrong observed that 'although practical co-operation between our respective police forces was excellent, the unwillingness of Irish ministers to take credit for their efforts in public speeches allowed the myth of Irish uncooperativeness to flourish in the North.'[20] Haughey effectively had to suspend official UK–Irish relations, but he had put in place a forum for dialogue between the British and Irish governments that would later bear fruit. He also offered an alternative approach to Northern Ireland than previous governments had used, one where a British–Irish dimension came to the fore. The renewed hunger strikes would get in the way of open dialogue, as would the June 1981 election that saw Garret FitzGerald take power.

On taking office FitzGerald agreed that 'Nothing in this State can take precedence over trying to resolve the tragedy of Northern

Ireland.' But he signalled a change in direction. He would 'endeavour to strengthen our links with the [Catholic] minority who have suffered so deeply in the last 12 years and re-establish the link with as wide as possible a spectrum of the [Protestant] majority section of the community.'[21] These priorities would consume FitzGerald over the next six years, during his two terms as Taoiseach. He would make progress on one aspect of Northern Ireland policy, to strengthen the links with the nationalist population, and ensure that the Irish government had an input into Northern Irish affairs through the mechanisms set up in the 1985 Anglo-Irish Agreement. Arguably that came at the cost of relations with the unionist community in Northern Ireland that had been his original priority.

During the hunger strikes anti-British sentiment was high in Ireland, and that would have even included supporters of Fine Gael. Rioting occurred in the summer of 1981, including an attack on the British Embassy. It was common to see black flags hanging from people's houses in solidarity with the hunger strikers. In an *Irish Times* poll almost 40 per cent of the respondents said they 'admired the idealism of the IRA but . . .'[22]

Nor did the quick succession of governments help with establishing relationships with the British government, but progress was being made at the level of officials. Dermot Nally had struck up a 'mutual respect and friendship' with Robert Armstrong.[23] Though Thatcher was reluctant, Armstrong was keen to look for some way forward, and he pushed her, probably beyond where she wished to go. In particular he knew that Thatcher, whose knowledge and interest in Irish affairs was minimal, could only be persuaded to proceed by appealing to security concerns.

Coming back into government in late 1982 FitzGerald found that:

> [E]verything had changed. The IRA threat in Northern Ireland, support for it was growing so rapidly I had to change tactics, and concentrate on trying to change British policy in Northern Ireland, rather than concentrate on changing things

here. So changes in this state, on becoming more open, and our nationalism becoming one that could accommodate Unionists as well . . . all that came later.'[24]

FitzGerald's interpretation might have been designed to suit what actually happened, as when he set out on the path that was to lead to the Anglo-Irish Agreement, it was still hoped that unionists would be encouraged to join a forum on the future of Ireland. Indeed, encouraging unionism to be less fearful of a united Ireland was a core political belief.

It was a suggestion by John Hume that later became the New Ireland Forum. Hume had wanted it to be a Council for a New Ireland, comprising non-violent Irish nationalists on the island. Hume's proposed council was to be an alternative to the British Secretary for State Jim Prior's devolved Northern Ireland Assembly, which the SDLP chose to boycott because it lacked an all-Ireland dimension. FitzGerald thought that this name might 'remind Unionists too forcibly of the "Council of Ireland" proposal in the Sunningdale Agreement'.[25] In mid-February 1983 he announced to his government a plan to set up a New Ireland Forum, but most of the cabinet objected, fearing that he would lose focus on the serious economic problems in the state.[26] Labour had independently called for something akin to a New Ireland Forum, so the objections were not fundamental.[27] FitzGerald set about convincing each cabinet member individually to withdraw their objection. This he did fairly easily by suggesting that they were open to being politically outmanoeuvred by Haughey, who might announce just such an initiative.[28] FitzGerald convinced John Hume to work on Haughey to accept the idea of the New Ireland Forum.[29] Fianna Fáil supported the SDLP call for a Council for a New Ireland, though Haughey's focus was different. In his Árd Fheis speech in February 1983 Haughey called for 'a final withdrawal of Britain from Ireland within a stipulated period of time'.

Irish government policy traditionally had been to emphasise the importance of ending partition. In the 1960s FitzGerald was among a number of people to challenge that, and there was a gradual shift away from what was seen as a sterile anti-partitionist campaign, which led to the Irish government suggesting an internal solution to Northern Ireland via an assembly in the Sunningdale Agreement. This included an all-island dimension, which was abhorrent to unionists. The ability of unionism to block Sunningdale made the Irish side sceptical of solutions that were exclusively internal. FitzGerald hoped that the Forum would produce a set of principles that might be acceptable to the UK government, on which there could be a basis for negotiations. He was keen that there would be proposals other than just Irish unity, which he knew would be rejected by the British.[30] The Forum would also make it harder for the Provisional IRA/ Sinn Féin to claim to speak for Irish nationalism.

In March 1983 the New Ireland Forum was convened 'for consultations on the manner in which lasting peace and stability could be achieved in a new Ireland through the democratic process'.[31] Originally T.K. Whitaker was proposed to chair it, but his name was withdrawn because of an expectation that it would be vetoed by Haughey, so Colm Ó hEocha, the president of University College Galway, was invited.[32] Over the course of a year the Forum received over 300 submissions, met in public 13 times and in private 28 times. Unionists declined to attend, though some members of the unionist community accepted invitations to speak at the meetings. Haughey dominated Fianna Fáil's delegation at the Forum: 'it was essentially Mr Haughey's gig'.[33] Haughey was in no rush to produce a report as it would give FitzGerald the basis for negotiations with the British. At one stage Haughey was enraged when he was accused of leaking private deliberations to the press. FitzGerald felt he had to massage Haughey's ego throughout the process.[34]

Haughey had initially insisted on the unitary state being called the 'only' option the Forum should propose, but agreed to it being referred to as the ideal or best option. Fianna Fáil and some in the SDLP objected to FitzGerald's apparent desire not to include a unitary state solution in the Forum report. Seamus Mallon, the deputy leader of the SDLP, was scathing about FitzGerald on this, thinking him naive to believe that Irish nationalists could produce a report that did not recommend the core goal of Irish nationalism. He also felt, plausibly, that it would leave the Provisional IRA as the only group 'speaking and killing for unity'.[35]

The Forum Report offered three possible solutions – a unitary state, a federal/ confederal state and joint authority with the British. FitzGerald intended to open talks with Thatcher on the idea of 'joint authority'. Perhaps more significant than the 'solutions' was the language of the report, which recognised 'the validity of both nationalist and unionist identities' and that the principle of consent was agreed: 'the political arrangements for a new and sovereign Ireland would have to be freely negotiated and agreed to by the people of the North and by the people of the South.'[36]

At a press conference on 2 May 1984, hours after signing the Forum Report, Haughey claimed that there was only one viable option, the unitary state with a new constitution, and that the other two options were merely outlined because they had been presented to the Forum.[37] It was a deliberate misinterpretation of the Forum that allowed him to claim to support the report while rejecting what was in it. This was highlighted by one official central to press relations as the reason the report received an unfavourable reaction.[38] On the other side, Fine Gael TD Paddy Harte felt FitzGerald missed an opportunity to woo Protestants, and Gemma Hussey felt he was ceding too much to Fianna Fáil.[39]

There was political fall-out from the report within Fianna Fáil. Haughey had insisted that he was the sole spokesperson on Northern Ireland policy. Des O'Malley expressed concern at Haughey's interpretation of the report, and the lack of internal party debate on it. He said that Ray MacSharry had been free to speak on the report. Haughey sought and secured O'Malley's expulsion from the parliamentary party on this issue, and the party reaffirmed Haughey's position, rejecting the alternative proposals in the Forum.[40]

In the Forum report FitzGerald got what he wanted; a basis for negotiations. Both Thatcher and FitzGerald had time, as they had both won elections that should see each in power until 1987, and the report gave FitzGerald some room for manoeuvre.[41] FitzGerald's confidence that progress could be made with the Forum report was based on the secret talks between officials. Michael Lillis, FitzGerald's diplomatic adviser seconded from the Department of Foreign Affairs, had spent time in London also developing relationships, in particular with David Goodall. In March 1984 the UK side agreed to open negotiations on the basis of 'some form of political involvement [for the Irish government] in Northern Ireland in return for formal recognition of the Union', which probably meant amending Articles 2 and 3 of the constitution.[42] A memorandum came to cabinet in Dublin to authorise this a few days after the Forum report was published, which elicited some resistance because it abandoned two of the three proposals in the report.[43]

FitzGerald thought he had achieved an acceptable concession in framing his preferred solution as 'joint authority', rather than joint sovereignty, but Thatcher did not really see the distinction.[44] FitzGerald struggled when talking with Thatcher. FitzGerald's government secretary, Dermot Nally, would urge him to 'speak slowly, speak slowly' when talking to her. It was advice he would try to adhere to, until, as Nally put it, 'the ideas started to crowd in, and he'd speed up. He couldn't vocalise his thoughts quickly enough.'[45] The British took a long time to formally respond. British officials were sympathetic to FitzGerald's goals, and the Armstrong–Nally secret talks continued, with Armstrong suggesting to Thatcher that the Irish side would accept some form of 'institutionalised consultation' mechanism.[46] If there was some hardening of the UK position it might have been because of the Brighton bombing on 12 October 1984; the Provisional IRA bombed the hotel where the Conservative Party conference was being held, killing five people, in an attempt to assassinate Thatcher.

A summit between the two governments at Chequers in late November was 'quite substantive if combative'.[47] The record shows

Minister for Agriculture, Charles Haughey, travelling to London with Taoiseach Seán Lemass and Minister for Finance, Jack Lynch, 1965

New TD Dr Garret FitzGerald with Tom O'Higgins (left) and Jim Dooge at the Fine Gael Árd Fheis in 1970

Charles Haughey speaks to the press after his acquittal at the arms trial in October 1970. He calls for Jack Lynch to 'do the honourable thing', with his solicitor and friend Pat O'Connor

Foreign Minister Garret FitzGerald and President Éamon de Valera greet the incoming British ambassador Sir Arthur Galsworthy at Áras an Uachtaráin, 1973

The Fianna Fáil front bench, with Charles Haughey back in, but still at the edge, 1975. Back (L-R): John Wilson, Gene Fitzgerald, Michael O'Kennedy, Brian Lenihan, Padraig Faulkner, Ruairi Brugha, Jim Tunney, Liam Cunningham, Bobby Molloy, Sitting (L-R): Jim Gibbons, Paddy Lalor, George Colley, Joseph Brennan, Jack Lynch, Desmond O'Malley, Charles Haughey

On the world stage: Garret FitzGerald and Liam Cosgrave meet with US President Gerald Ford and Secretary of State Henry Kissinger at the White House on St Patrick's Day, 1976

'Happy and exhilarated': the night of the collapse of the first FitzGerald government with John Bruton, Garret FitzGerald, Peter Barry and Ted Nealon and government chief whip, Fergus O'Brien (behind), January 1982

Divorce was an issue that Garret FitzGerald wanted to address in the early 1980s, but Charles Haughey refused to co-operate

Never hostile: before the Leaders' Debate in the February 1982 election, with Brian Farrell chairing

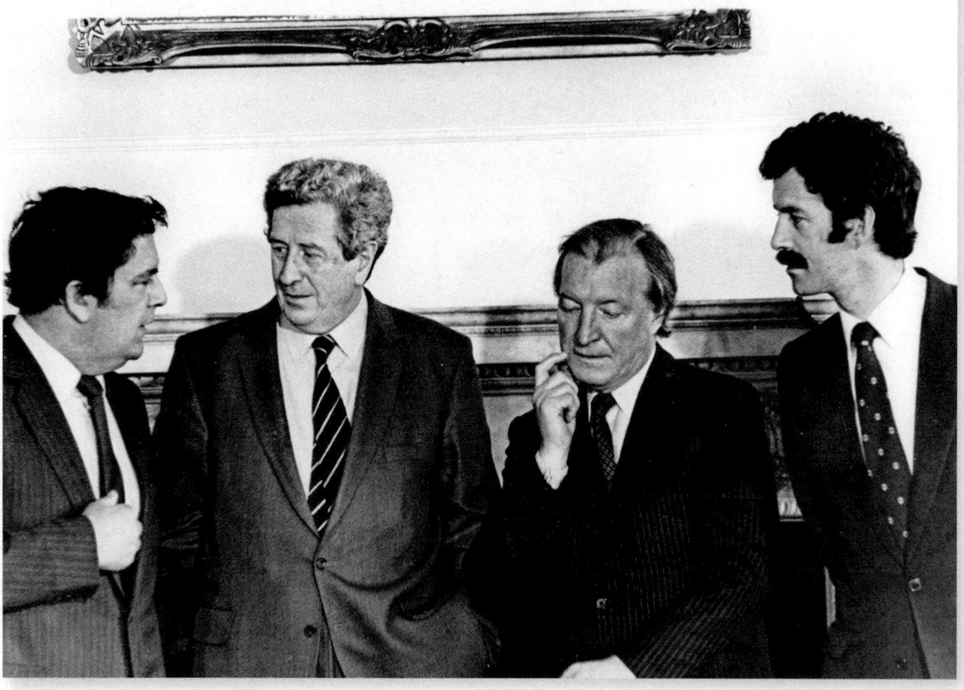

© Eamon Farrell, RollingNews.ie

The New Ireland Forum was somewhere that Garret FitzGerald tried to soothe Charles Haughey's ego. Also pictured are John Hume (left) and Dick Spring, 1983

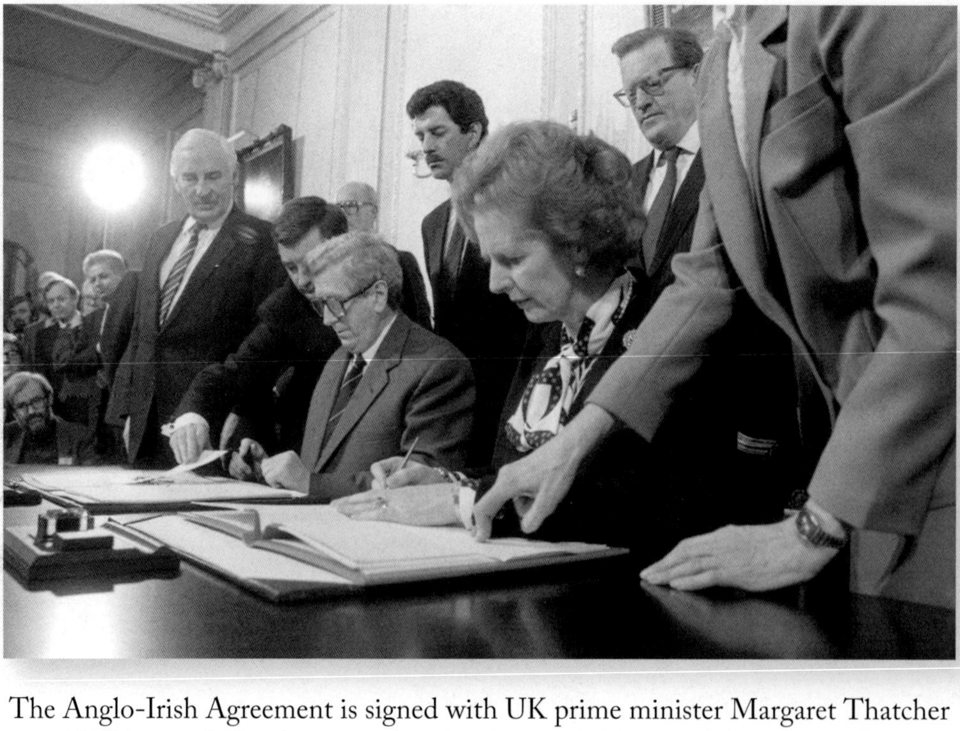

© Independent News and Media

The Anglo-Irish Agreement is signed with UK prime minister Margaret Thatcher at Hillsborough Castle, in 1985 under the watchful eyes of Peter Barry, Dick Spring and Tom King

Waving goodbye: Garret FitzGerald returning home on the day he resigned as Fine Gael leader, 1987

A new partnership: old enemies Charles Haughey and Des O'Malley outline their coalition agreement, 1989

Serving their leader: Albert Reynolds, Brian Lenihan and Michael Woods with Charles Haughey in 1990. By the end of 1991 Haughey had sacked Reynolds and Lenihan

Thatcher saying she did not like the way the conversation was going, and wondering aloud whether there was any point. She wanted a security focus, but the Fine Gael Minister for Foreign Affairs, Peter Barry observed that if that were the only outcome it would mean the end of the FitzGerald government.[48] If the summit was challenging, the press conferences afterwards were disastrous. The British wanted to issue a rather bland joint communiqué after the summit and have no press conference. FitzGerald insisted on a press conference in the Irish embassy. As a result Thatcher decided she should also give a press conference, something the Irish side would have no control over. Thatcher gave hers before FitzGerald's press conference, in which she went through the suggestions of the Forum report. She said, 'I have made it quite clear that a unified Ireland was one solution. That is out. A second solution was a confederation of the two States. That is out. A third solution was joint authority. That is out.'[49]

Thatcher's 'out, out, out' speech thrilled Ulster unionists, who claimed the Forum report 'lay in a burial plot somewhere in Chequers'.[50] In London FitzGerald, who had not heard Thatcher's comments, then gave 'the seven worst press interviews of my life'. The reaction in the press was wholly negative.[51] Newspapers' headlines the following morning led with 'OUT, OUT, OUT'. FitzGerald had to face a difficult parliamentary party meeting.[52] FitzGerald told that meeting that Thatcher was 'gratuitously offensive', which was leaked to the press. FitzGerald later claimed that the talks had moved on from those three solutions, though a watered-down version of 'joint authority' solution was still the basis for the negotiations.[53]

It also thrilled Haughey. FitzGerald was under constant attack from Haughey, who issued a personalised attack on FitzGerald, accusing him of 'abject capitulation' and 'craven desertion of the principles of the Forum Report'.[54] FitzGerald accused Haughey of 'continuing and deepening the misery of the people of Northern Ireland' by exploiting progress in negotiations with Britain for short-term political gain. 'That is a lie,' Haughey retorted.[55]

In fact the Chequers summit had clarified things for the government, and reduced public expectations. FitzGerald had been offering a referendum on Articles 2 and 3, but that was effectively taken off the table. The British were, in any case, sceptical that a referendum could be passed. Thatcher's view of FitzGerald was that 'he overestimated his own powers of persuasion over his own colleagues and countrymen.'[56] She was probably right, but in this period FitzGerald showed 'exceptional foresight and patience, [and] bore stoically' the attacks he received from all sides.[57]

The Armstrong–Nally talks were ongoing, though it was increasingly difficult for them to remain secret. Seeds planted much earlier were also beginning to bear fruit; the significant Congressional Irish lobby in the US put pressure on President Ronald Reagan – who had visited Ireland in the summer of 1984 – to try to persuade Thatcher to engage more positively with the negotiations. There is disagreement on the importance of the US involvement. Lillis and other Irish officials claim it was crucial, and Thatcher later said to one of her friends that the US had put pressure on her to engage with the idea of a formal Irish involvement in Northern Irish affairs, but Charles Moore thinks this overstates it.[58] However, it is fair to say US involvement helped FitzGerald at a time when momentum was flagging.

In early 1985 talks moved to the ministerial level, with Thatcher, Douglas Hurd and Geoffrey Howe on the UK side, and FitzGerald, Peter Barry and Dick Spring on the Irish side, though Armstrong and Nally were still central to the process. By April 1985 the basis for agreement was 'now discernible'.[59] The agreement would give the Irish government a consultative role in the running of Northern Ireland by way of a secretariat in Belfast, in exchange for improved security co-operation and SDLP participation in any future devolved assembly. FitzGerald became 'totally absorbed' in the talks at the expense of other issues facing the government.[60] Talks were rocky, and Thatcher was still not comfortable. Tom King, the hawkish and unionist Secretary of State for Northern Ireland, introduced fresh doubts when these were least needed.

FitzGerald and Thatcher signed the Anglo-Irish Agreement (AIA) in Hillsborough Castle, outside Belfast, on 15 November 1985. It gave the Irish government a formal say in the running of Northern Ireland, even if this was just consultative. It contained quite a bit of aspirational text about what the new Inter-Governmental Conference *might* do. Article One set out the principle of consent, now in an international treaty, and conceded that there was no majority in favour of a united Ireland at that time.[61] Articles Two, Three and Four set out the form of the Inter-Governmental Conference, and later articles dealt with the areas on which there would be consultation.

FitzGerald and Thatcher performed well in the subsequent press conference, and stuck to their well-practised scripts. Unionist reaction was predictable. In a show of unity the leaders of the two main unionist parties organised protests on the day the AIA was signed and others the following year; 'Ulster Says No' became their slogan at huge marches in opposition to the Agreement. Rather than weaken her resolve Thatcher seemed steeled by opposition, though she was upset when one of her close friends, Ian Gow, resigned from her government.[62] Unlike British backsliding over Sunningdale, Thatcher did not budge.

Haughey was categorical in his rejection of the Agreement, even sending Brian Lenihan to Washington to lobby US politicians against it, revealing Haughey's inability to collaborate or deal with dissent. Haughey had been close to Seamus Mallon, the more republican deputy leader of the SDLP, and had sought Mallon's opposition to the AIA, but when Mallon criticised Haughey for this, Haughey ended contact with him.[63] Haughey had a 'total overriding belief that you can pull everybody in with you because you believe you are right', but his problem was that he could not accept it when others disagreed.[64] There were divisions within Fianna Fáil; one TD, Mary Harney, was expelled from Fianna Fáil when she voted in favour of the Agreement.

While no one could or would claim that the Anglo-Irish Agreement was a final settlement, it did make the British acknowledge the Irish government's interest in affairs in the North. Haughey underestimated public and political support for the Agreement and the overall reaction in the press was positive. Opinion polls put support versus opposition to the Agreement at two to one, and Fine Gael party support also rose to 37 per cent, while FitzGerald overtook Haughey in leader satisfaction.[65] Privately Haughey told the UK ambassador in January 1986 that he thought the Agreement was 'working well so far'.[66] It was a mistake by Haughey to be publicly so opposed to the agreement, one which his adviser Martin Mansergh acknowledges cost him politically.[67] His ally and successor, Bertie Ahern, also agreed that Haughey went too far in his opposition to the Agreement.[68] It would damage Haughey's reputation with northern nationalists and confirm the impression that he was an oppositional politician who could not be constructive or collaborate with others.

In this period Haughey was constantly trying to cause difficulties for FitzGerald, and he frequently succeeded. He opposed an amendment to the Extradition Act, which would make it easier to extradite suspected IRA bombers, though it was eventually passed in early 1987 with the help of the ex-Fianna Fáil TDs Haughey had expelled or pushed out. But, for Ray MacSharry, too often it was 'opposition for its own sake, which ... had damaged the party's credibility'.[69]

Implementation of the AIA was disappointing for the British, who thought that Irish co-operation on security matters was lacking, a point conceded by Michael Lillis.[70] The Agreement increased the trust between the British and Irish governments that made possible the sorts of relationships that later Taoisigh would have with their British counterparts.[71] The team in Maryfield, where the Inter-Governmental Conference was based, had mechanisms for bringing concerns to each other. It also demonstrated to the unionist politicians that the UK government was prepared to proceed without them, which might have induced a reticence among them to allow other talks to proceed without them.[72] It was an important milestone in the path towards peace. This was the most important achievement of Garret FitzGerald's premiership. Domestically, however, the economy was what mattered to voters. Achievements there were harder to find.

12.

DRIFTERS

The Irish economy at the start of the 1980s was in abysmal shape. The annual inflation rate peaked at 23 per cent in 1982.[1] Prices had doubled between 1976 and 1981, mainly because of the oil crises. Unemployment was at 12 per cent in 1982, up from 7 per cent in 1973.[2] It would have been even worse had net emigration not risen again, after a decade of net inward migration. The size of the state had also increased dramatically since the early 1970s, from about 40 per cent of GNP to over 60 per cent in 1982.[3] Up to the 1970s there had been an unwritten rule that there should be no budget deficits for current spending, but this was breached in 1972, and the exchequer borrowing requirement increased during the 1970s, peaking at almost 16 per cent of GNP in 1982. The national debt also rose to over 70 per cent of GDP, and the cost of servicing that debt took almost all of the country's income tax take.[4] Growth was anaemic and Ireland was importing much more than it exported. A review of Ireland's post-independence performance written in 1982 said, 'Despondency seems to be on the increase, as though the intractability of our problems had at last sapped our will to solve them'. Another referred to the 'hastening drift of ungovernability'.[5] These were the challenges facing Garret FitzGerald in late 1982.

Many of FitzGerald's cabinet colleagues had been used to reading him or being lectured by him on economic matters. Many in his cabinet were in awe of him. Although he was not an academic economist, and had little knowledge of economic theory, he was a major figure in Irish life, someone who always seemed confident that he had the answers. But his political reputation had been damaged by the way he had allowed his first government to fall. He was also a social democrat in a party where many colleagues' instincts were more orthodox and conservative. Moreover, the Keynesian ideas he believed in were undergoing significant challenges at the time.[6] Added to this, he was in government with a divided Labour Party, which might agree a decision in a cabinet meeting on Tuesday only to have it reversed when the Administrative Council of the Labour Party met the following evening.

When it came to possible solutions to Ireland's economic impasse there was a paucity of ideas. Ireland had seen aggressive expansionary policies that relied on state investment. There was a scepticism that private industry would generate employment.[7] FitzGerald viewed the Department of Finance as 'unremittingly negative', and for FitzGerald's economic adviser, Patrick Honohan, the Department 'abdicated responsibility'.[8] The Department of Finance wanted to maximise the cuts to the deficit. It produced what became known as an 'Asgard List' of programmes that might be available to cut or sell. If it was designed to concentrate the minds of recalcitrant ministers, naming it the *Asgard*,[9] a symbolically important ship whose successor was used to train sailors, may have had the opposite of its intended effect. It might have hardened ministers' positions against politically damaging cuts. If the government had cut the *Asgard II* programme, however, it might have signalled that that it was taking the spending problems seriously.

FitzGerald knew that government spending was unsustainable, but he could not see what there was to cut. He sought to protect spending in education and he was sympathetic enough to most social programmes, which made it difficult for him to sanction cuts in them. FitzGerald felt that even if the economy had been brought under control he would not have gained any electoral benefit. So he saw no real benefit in front-loading cuts, which in any case could have been so deflationary that it would have stalled any chance of economic recovery.[10] He may well have been right in that.

The upshot of this was that the government had no coherent or agreed plan to deal with the country's economic situation. The policy was drift. Early on in that government the Minister for Finance, Alan Dukes, publicly announced that the government's borrowing requirement should remain within IR£750 million (€2.6 billion in 2023). The Tánaiste, Dick Spring, who was in hospital for an operation for an ongoing back problem, saw it as a 'pre-emptive strike'.[11] Spring called FitzGerald to point out that no such decision had been made, and FitzGerald readily agreed. FitzGerald had asked the former US diplomat, Henry Kissinger, who he knew and who ran an economic consultancy service, what the reaction of the markets might be if the Irish government had a current budget deficit of IR£900 million (€3.1 billion). Kissinger's reaction was that it would not matter much, and that markets would prefer a plan that could be delivered than one that would collapse.[12] The budget deficit of IR£900 million was agreed, though there was some controversy as to whether the final budget deficit was lower, which caused more tension within the government.[13] Even the higher budget deficit still meant that there would have to be painful cuts and tax rises.

The impact of Dukes's intervention was that it made Labour ministers more suspicious and resistant to cuts, and those ministers who proposed cuts, such as Fine Gael's Gemma Hussey, received heavy criticism for cuts to their budgets, in her case the school transport budget.[14] For many Labour ministers, their Fine Gael counterparts were a little too enthusiastic in their cuts. Not Garret FitzGerald, though. He found the cuts painful. He also appreciated the difficult position that Dick Spring was in.

The 1983 budget was described in *Irish Times* headline as the 'toughest budget for decades'[15] with the emphasis on tax rises rather than spending cuts. The top rate of tax went up five points to 65 per cent with an additional 1 per cent levy imposed on PAYE workers. VAT went up again, as did excise duties on alcohol and fuel. There were increases in motor tax, telephone charges and TV licences. FitzGerald's former economic adviser was publicly critical of the budget, mainly because it added to the burden on PAYE workers.[16] A Labour TD resigned the party's whip, and even Fine Gael TDs were unhappy with the severity of the budget. In March 1983 FitzGerald went on TV to address the nation, setting out the same issue that Haughey had set out three years earlier, that the country was spending more than it was earning.[17]

The issue of high taxes and unfair treatment of PAYE workers had been the subject of a series of large protests from 1979, and in April 1983 another big protest was organised by trade unions critical of the tax increases on PAYE workers.[18] Alan Dukes told a business gathering that tax reform would have to wait, which caused another crisis within the government. He was criticised by Spring, and FitzGerald offered his Minister for Finance no support.[19] This damaged the relationship between the Taoiseach and his Finance minister, a key one in any government. Dukes felt he was blocked from making necessary changes.[20] When Dukes discovered that his hair-shirt budget was not tough enough to stay within the agreed deficit he lacked the authority to demand further cuts. Barry Desmond successfully stood up to Dukes to protect his budget in Health and Social Welfare.[21] FitzGerald was intent on keeping the government in place, even if it would just drift on without direction. Spring felt there was no mechanism to manage the inevitable disputes in FitzGerald's government.[22]

The bigger issue for FitzGerald's government was that while it targeted balancing the books, it had no strategy for economic growth or for using the money the state spent more effectively. John Boland, the Minister for the Public Service, made some reforms to the civil service, but it remained structurally inefficient, and the public pay bill continued to grow. A National Planning Board that was designed to bring unions and employers together and introduce competitiveness was set up, but this possibly just delayed action. It was independent of government, when it might have benefited from more direct government involvement, and it did not come up with significant proposals. Another idea the government had was the National

Development Corporation (NDC), which was supposed to invest in commercially viable state enterprises, but when it was eventually formed it received few resources and was more like an advisory body, not the powerhouse that Labour had envisaged. The NDC was the subject of ideological disputes in cabinet, mainly between John Bruton and Dick Spring, which spilled over into personal animosities.

In these rows Garret FitzGerald seems to have lost the will for a fight. One such case was Irish Steel, a loss-making state-owned company, which was controlled by the Minister for Industry and Commerce, John Bruton. Bruton initially felt it needed to be given a chance,[23] but after time he concluded that it was 'soaking up money like a sponge' and that it should close.[24] This was a position Spring opposed, and 'Garret FitzGerald left it between them to decide'.[25] The state invested some more money, and in order to protect some jobs, secured some job losses, which might have been the worst of all worlds. Ten years later the state offloaded the company for IR£1, writing off IR£19 million of debts and agreeing to a further almost IR£20 million in state aid, but it later collapsed in 2001.

The problem was that no one really believed in Ireland. There were almost no entrepreneurs, and the government was expected to protect inefficient jobs rather than facilitate the creation of new jobs through economic growth. The government's new economic plan, launched in October 1984, Building on Reality, did anything but. After a glittering launch and tour of the country, it became clear that FitzGerald was selling snake oil. It was quietly shelved.

A significant ongoing issue was the cost of labour. FitzGerald was acutely aware of this and proposed that new entrants to the public sector should be given lower pay.[26] Emigration and Ireland's proximity to the UK put a high floor under which labour costs could not go. Ireland could not become competitive in the same way other 'catch-up' countries could.[27] Such a plan would require a pact with trade unions, but FitzGerald refused to engage in a social pact with trade unions and employers when the National Economic and Social

Council (NESC), which ostensibly worked out of his Department, produced a *Strategy for Development* document in 1986. It was supported by both employers and unions, and Pádraig Ó hUiginn told him, 'even Fianna Fáil will have to support you'. According to Ó hUiginn, FitzGerald instead set up a committee.[28] While FitzGerald was not averse to working with unions, he wasn't comfortable with them, and was suspicious of their power.[29] But given his position in government with Labour, this would have seemed an obvious way to deal with the issue of high pay.[30] And Ó hUiginn was right, because had Fianna Fáil proposed something similar, it would have neutralised the party's opposition.

Dukes's next budget was milder but still deflationary – further cuts were needed. Over a series of budgets public sector pay was never brought under control. Growing unemployment meant an increasing social welfare budget. FitzGerald was trying to accentuate the positive when, responding to Haughey, he said that 'the rate of increase [in unemployment] has slowed considerably'.[31] Unemployment was still going up, just not as fast as it had been – this was an admission of failure. Emigration had started to grow again. The national debt continued to grow, and by 1986 the PAYE tax take was almost wholly used to pay the interest on the national debt. Debt had grown to 120 per cent of GNP. While inflation came down to manageable levels, since it was largely imported this had more to do with moderating oil prices and weak economic growth than with sound economic management. The FitzGerald government's approach was to attempt to mitigate the effects of the recession, but in doing so it prolonged it. If in 1981 Ireland had to catch up with the rest of Europe, in the words of FitzGerald's economic adviser in that government, Patrick Honohan, 'the net result was that, by 1986, there was a lot more catching up to do.'[32]

FitzGerald had a way out of this, at least for himself. In late 1984 the European Commission was due for renewal. FitzGerald was thinking of appointing his old cabinet colleague and friend, Justin Keating, as Ireland's nominee to the Commission. There was not a lot of enthusiasm for Keating in cabinet. FitzGerald's confidante, Jim Dooge, suggested that FitzGerald take the job himself, but he rejected that outright: 'I came into politics to deal with the Northern Ireland problem and I can't turn my back on that'. Garret FitzGerald was afraid that Charlie Haughey would wreck it.[33] But his determination on getting the Anglo-Irish Agreement over the line meant that he had compromised on too many other things.

※ ※ ※

Other crises were to cause more problems for the government, even when the government dealt with them competently. PMPA, a car insurance company, Dublin Gas and the Insurance Corporation of Ireland all required bailouts during the government's tenure. In most cases the government acted swiftly to minimise the liability to taxpayers, but the series of crises damaged the government's reputation, in part because they were seen as bailing out private companies that had been mismanaged. In the case of Dublin Gas, the refusal of the government to nationalise the company under Bord Gáis caused one minister, Frank Cluskey, to resign in December 1983. His departure improved the cohesiveness of the government as there was a sense 'he didn't really want to be there'.[34]

Irish Shipping was a public company that had made poor commercial decisions and bore significant debts, some of which were state guaranteed. In order to avoid bearing even greater liabilities the government allowed Irish Shipping to collapse in November 1984, with a loss of almost 300 jobs. There were splits in cabinet on this, though not on party lines. The issue dragged on as the workers demanded compensation greater than the statutory redundancy, an issue that was to occupy too much cabinet time. The government was given legal advice that if it offered extra redundancy it could be challenged for other debts the liquidated company left behind. Having taken the decision against additional redundancy payments, the government records show that it continued to discuss the issue well after those discussions had anything useful to offer. FitzGerald really loved to talk.

In early 1985 Des O'Malley had been expelled from the Fianna Fáil organisation and was sitting as an independent TD. FitzGerald met with him and offered him a cabinet position on the assumption that he would join Fine Gael. For FitzGerald it was 'before I knew how right-wing [O'Malley] was!'[35] O'Malley turned down the offer. For O'Malley, tying himself to Fine Gael would be aligning himself with another large, ideologically indistinct party, but this time a party that was both hampered by its dependence on a split Labour Party and struggling to deal with the economy. The chair of Fine Gael's organisation in FitzGerald's own constituency, Michael McDowell, was by then so disillusioned with Fine Gael in government that he wrote to O'Malley to encourage him to set up his own party. That pressure also came from Mary Harney, recently expelled from the Fianna Fáil parliamentary party over her position on the Anglo-Irish Agreement.

When O'Malley formed the Progressive Democrats in December 1985 some Fine Gael deputies considered a move to the PDs, though just one TD finally did. It was to be a classical liberal party, socially liberal and in favour of private enterprise. The PDs initially soared in opinion polls and many thousands attended party rallies across the country. There was deep shock in Fianna Fáil when Bobby Molloy left the party to join the PDs; it led to speculation that others could follow, including Seamus Brennan, David Andrews and Charlie McCreevy. The new party effectively took over much of Fianna Fáil's organisation in Limerick and Galway. While the excitement tapered off, the polls showed that the party was at least as much an electoral threat to Fine Gael as it was to Fianna Fáil.

The Dáil term meant that an election was scheduled to take place by the end of 1987. In preparation for this, FitzGerald hoped to refresh his cabinet team with a reshuffle of ministers in February 1986. He had intended to do it earlier, but the Anglo-Irish Agreement negotiations led him to postpone it. In his autobiography he set out his rationale for each potential move. But it turned out to be another debacle. FitzGerald did not prepare the ground for the reshuffle, and there did not appear to be any purpose to it. One of the ministers he wanted to move, Labour's Minister for Health and Social Welfare Barry Desmond, flat out refused, and it was only after long pleadings by Dick Spring and the threat of a government collapse that FitzGerald secured from him an agreement that Desmond would drop the Social Welfare part of his portfolio, keeping Health. This had a knock-on effect for FitzGerald's other planned moves, for some of which he had already secured agreement from other ministers.[36]

Another problem was his plan to appoint a cabinet minister to co-ordinate European affairs, which was becoming increasingly important. He set out with this plan before consulting with the secretary to the government, Dermot Nally. Though someone of FitzGerald's experience should have known as much, Nally would have pointed out that a new cabinet position would have to have a department separate from Foreign Affairs, which FitzGerald had not envisaged. He had thought the ministers for Foreign and European Affairs would share a department. The alternative would be to create a minister without any department, which would also have weakened the proposed minister, Gemma Hussey.

The one significant move was to swap Alan Dukes with John Bruton, moving Dukes from Finance into Industry and Commerce. This was regarded as a move towards fiscal tightness and might have been done with an eye on the new political landscape. It was also because FitzGerald recognised that he had not backed Bruton when he should have, particularly in his first government. Bruton had been damaged by that and this move would be a chance for Bruton to redeem himself.[37] In spite of all this controversy, he did not promote any new ministers, so the government remained jaded, and those waiting for promotion were left increasingly dissatisfied. The overall effect was to cause anger and frustration in the government and the party.

Garret FitzGerald reacted to the electoral threat posed by the Progressive Democrats by almost casting off his social democracy. At the Fine Gael Árd Fheis in October 1986 FitzGerald set out a much tougher line on public sector pay and public spending, complaining about rigid pay structures. With an eye on the upcoming election, he told the audience that the government parties would not go into that election seeking re-election as a government. Rather Fine Gael would try to maximise its vote and hope for an overall majority to deliver the tough budgets that were now needed. He attempted to sound positive, but in doing so he emphasised a list of his government's failures. And he could hardly go to the country on the basis of rural electrification and running water, two of the things he outlined as achievements of the state.[38]

In that Árd Fheis speech FitzGerald made a clear attempt to frame the forthcoming election as a choice between himself and Charles Haughey as Taoiseach. But that framing might not have had the impact that he expected. FitzGerald's approval ratings had fallen significantly over the course of the government including a fall from 47 per cent to 33 per cent in just a month in 1984, and he was behind Haughey on 44 per cent.[39] Apart from a spike in support at the signing of the Anglo-Irish Agreement, Fine Gael support fell gradually while it was in office, bringing it back to the level it had been at before FitzGerald took over. In May 1986 Fianna Fáil had broken the 50 per cent barrier – this was no indication that the people were afraid of Haughey.[40] FitzGerald admitted himself that he did not expect that Fine Gael would win the election in 1987, and if it did, he had no intention of staying for long.[41] His main purpose in his last few months in office was to limit the chance that Haughey would get an overall majority and influence how Haughey would behave when, as was likely, he returned to power.

The 1987 budget was going to be another tough one. The government had already lost its majority due to resignations from both Labour and Fine Gael, those from Labour due to the significant cuts to which the party had agreed. In fact, by December 1986 it was clear the Fine Gael–Labour coalition had run its course. The government had relied on the PDs for the passage of the Single European Act, to enable the creation of the European single market, and an amendment to the Extradition Act. Only the casting vote of the Ceann Comhairle prevented the Dáil's dissolution before Christmas 1986. It says something of FitzGerald that in the middle of these difficult negotiations on the budget that collapsed the government he brought a memorandum to cabinet to change the electoral system.[42] His government just ignored him, but they were incredulous that he was thinking about electoral reform at a time his government was falling apart and the economy was in a state of collapse. It indicates a mind that was both continually active and completely ill-focused. The proposed budget caused considerable problems in the government and resulted in Fine Gael outvoting Labour in January 1987 – something FitzGerald had said he would not do. There was regret rather than anger on both sides, though a comment earlier attributed to Alan Dukes that Labour 'once bought, should stay bought' had left some animosity.

But there were no dramatic walkouts. The government petered out. In January it agreed that no agreement would be reached, and on 20 January 1987 the Labour ministers resigned their positions, but in polite, almost touching, terms in letters written to FitzGerald. The Bruton budget was not even put to the Dáil, which was a tactical error. It could have given the Fine Gael side a platform to set out its position and force other parties to indicate theirs, though perhaps FitzGerald thought that its position was not going to be electorally favourable. There was a sense that the FitzGerald era was over without even a fight.

Fine Gael went into the 1987 election admitting that the 'economic crisis overshadows all other considerations'.[43] The party's manifesto was hardly selling the outgoing government's successes. It was designed to shock voters into accepting the inevitable. FitzGerald called a long campaign, four weeks, in the hope to extract from Fianna Fáil commitments to follow the fiscal line FitzGerald saw as necessary. Fianna Fáil under Haughey did not play ball. While Fianna Fáil indicated that it would cut public expenditure and maintain spending at or below 1986 levels, it excoriated Fine Gael for where the government had chosen to place those cuts.

Fianna Fáil had a well-organised marketing campaign using the slogan 'There is a Better Way'. Haughey could point to the deep splits in the coalition on budgetary policy as the basis of the need for a strong majority Fianna Fáil government.[44] But the party made some basic errors; in some constituencies it ran either weak candidates or candidates from the wrong geographical areas. Fianna Fáil published a *Programme for National Recovery*, which was a series of policy goals rather than policies. It promised a prudent approach to the management of the public finances, but went into little detail. It also said it would not increase taxes. There were cynical messages that 'Health Cuts Hurt the Old, the Sick and the Handicapped' in a prominent billboard campaign. At this stage the Fine Gael party had little fight left in it, and Labour, exhausted from government, was simply trying to hold its own against a challenge from the Workers' Party. Haughey expected victory, but he was uninspiring during the long campaign. The relentless attacks on the government's record, which the electorate hardly needed to be reminded of, did not necessarily inspire confidence in Fianna Fáil. Fine Gael's position improved through the campaign, and Fianna Fáil's weakened – FitzGerald's strategy worked. In a live TV debate FitzGerald was seen to have won, and to have even rattled Haughey, forcing him to accept that he would not alter the Anglo-Irish Agreement.[45] FitzGerald could always raise his game for Haughey.

Voting took place on 17 February 1987. There would be no return to government for FitzGerald. While Fine Gael lost 20 seats and dropped 12 points in the vote share, the election could have been much worse for the party. Fine Gael had been trailing badly in opinion polls – at one stage in early 1986 the party was even behind the PDs. The results were another disappointment for Haughey. Fianna Fáil lost votes, from what had been seen as a low base in November 1982, and the six-seat gain – to 81 seats – was still three short of a majority. The PDs took more support from Fine Gael than Fianna Fáil, but they hurt both of the big parties.

Haughey had come remarkably close to his coveted majority, and there was not much evidence of a negative 'Haughey factor' in the electorate. Had he done less to facilitate the setting up of the PDs he might even have had a majority. While Haughey's election as Taoiseach was still not secure, there was no alternative government available, and no desire to return to a 1981–82-style series of elections. Despite this there was still a debate on the suitability of Haughey for the position of Taoiseach, just not within Fianna Fáil. Ray Burke told RTÉ's *This Week* programme, 'Nobody will decide on the leadership of Fianna Fáil except Fianna Fáil and our leader is Charles J. Haughey.'[46]

Garret FitzGerald had prepared two speeches for the first day of the new Dáil. One in the event of Haughey's election as Taoiseach, and one if no Taoiseach was elected. The president, Paddy Hillery, had said to FitzGerald that if no Taoiseach were elected he would refuse the dissolution of the Dáil – not that FitzGerald had any plans to seek such a dissolution – and that it would be up to Garret FitzGerald as caretaker Taoiseach to seek a resolution. For this FitzGerald would see his role as having 'to cajole the Dáil into electing Charles Haughey as Taoiseach!'[47]

Haughey did not need FitzGerald's help. He placed Seán Treacy, a former Labour TD who had split from the party on the contraception bill, as Ceann Comhairle. Haughey received the support of Neil Blaney (who got none of the reassurances he sought on the North), but it was only two-thirds the way through Tony Gregory's speech on the Taoiseach's nomination that it became clear Gregory would not oppose Haughey's nomination. The vote on Haughey's nomination was tied 82–82. On 10 March 1987, the Ceann Comhairle broke the tie to elect Charles Haughey as Taoiseach for the third time.

Once again Haughey's hold on power looked tenuous. Thanks to Garret FitzGerald, this time it would be different.

13.

TOP BOY

In 1987 a book by a schoolteacher in Kilbarrack, a working-class suburb on the northside of Dublin, was a surprise hit. *The Commitments* centred on a group of musicians trying to emulate the blues sound from Black American culture. The backdrop was unemployment, emigration and crime, albeit with comedic overtones. The message was that Ireland was a victim, the Irish were 'the Blacks of Europe' and within Ireland, northside Dubliners were the bottom dogs. This was the Ireland that Charles Haughey was to take charge of. It was a basket case.

Returning to government in 1987, Haughey 'was a different man'.[1] Despite failing to achieve a Dáil majority for the fourth time, his control of the Fianna Fáil party was absolute. Haughey had used the period in opposition to create an image of himself as the personification of Ireland. His adviser, Martin Mansergh, edited a 1,200-page volume of Haughey's speeches grandiloquently titled *The Spirit of the Nation*. He made a documentary called *Charles Haughey's Ireland* in a style that was part infomercial, part manifesto for himself. Earlier, when asked about the Celtic tradition, he had responded, only half-jokingly; 'What is the Celtic Tradition? Why, the Celtic Tradition is Croke Park, Fianna Fáil and myself.'[2] The personification of Ireland was going to save Ireland.

Returning to government, Haughey did not have to wait to see the country's accounts to know what needed to be done. Between the election and the meeting of the Dáil, Haughey had contacted Ray MacSharry to ask him to be his Minister for Finance. MacSharry was reluctant. He thought Fianna Fáil in opposition had engaged in a 'fast-and-loose approach to economic policy.'[3] But he agreed, with the implicit assumption that they would implement the necessary spending cuts that *The Way Forward* had envisaged four years earlier.[4] Haughey knew what he was getting with MacSharry; someone with an orthodox budget-balancing outlook, strong enough and independent enough to stand up to Haughey if it were needed. But it does not seem that Haughey was tempted to back down from what he knew had to be done.

Haughey told his ministers that it would be very difficult, but they would have to stay the course.[5] Many of those ministers who remembered his 1980 address to the nation were understandably sceptical. His other cabinet appointments did not generate confidence. His choices were once again conservative, giving jobs to those who had stuck with him rather than seeking out new talent. Some things had changed, however.

First, he was in complete control of his government, which, according to Dermot Nally, 'lived in fear of him.'[6] His ministers were impressed with his command of detail in a vast array of areas, and regarded him as exceptionally competent. Even if they disagreed with him, they were inclined to listen to his advice. They described him as methodical, decisive and in control, so they trusted him to lead.[7] They were also impressed by his work rate, and his ability to compartmentalise his work. He could keep a number of initiatives going at the same time, and if things were not going to plan in one area, his mood or determination in another was not affected. In cabinet he was tough on ministers. He would often challenge them, even if he agreed with their proposals, in part to test their command of the brief, but also to test their conviction.

Second, the economic situation was so dire that the unions and the public recognised the need for drastic action. The way in which UK unions had been sidelined by Thatcher in the 1980s made them more willing to engage with retrenchment proposals. Haughey had spent his career building links with the trade union movement, so he had a relationship with many of its leaders. Some of the new leaders, such as Peter Cassells, were more moderate, and so open to working with government.

Third, Haughey did not have to worry about being outflanked by the opposition. By adopting a similar approach to that advocated by Fine Gael and the PDs, Fianna Fáil was freed from electoral threats on the right, and there were few threats on the left, especially if he had the support of the union movement. Most importantly, Haughey was given political cover to act by Garret FitzGerald. Haughey was still in a minority and in the speech just after Haughey's nomination as Taoiseach, FitzGerald said Fine Gael would support the Haughey government:

> My party will not oppose such measures or legislative action required to implement the necessary budgetary provisions. It is important that the Dáil and public opinion generally understand that this is the situation. It is important that the narrowness of the margin by which Deputy Haughey was elected should give rise to no doubts as to the possibility of the new Government in this Dáil as at present constituted taking the steps that have become necessary in the national interest.[8]

Haughey and FitzGerald had had 'amicable' meetings between the election and Haughey's appointment to facilitate the handover. Haughey expressed his sympathy for FitzGerald in that his government was unlucky in facing so many crises.[9]

On 11 March 1987 FitzGerald surprised colleagues and commentators in announcing his resignation as Fine Gael leader. He had decided that Haughey had a chance to govern for four years and he lacked the 'physical and moral stamina' to continue in opposition. Three candidates contested the Fine Gael leadership, Peter Barry, John Bruton and Alan Dukes. FitzGerald did not express a preference, but because he was known to be more closely aligned with Dukes's outlook, some thought he campaigned for Dukes, who was elected leader on 21 March. In his 'Tallaght Strategy' speech in September 1987 the new Fine Gael leader endorsed the approach FitzGerald had earlier promised the minority Haughey government.[10] He said that Fine Gael would not bring down the government on issues of major government policy as long as Fianna Fáil stuck to planned spending limits. Dukes was also conscious of the need to avoid an election that Fine Gael was not prepared for.[11]

Haughey was also lucky in taking over at a time when the European and world economies were growing, and deregulation was making export-led growth a possibility. Indeed the 1987 first quarter results show the Irish economy had already started to grow. So the conditions were in place for Haughey to introduce an economic plan he had had in his back pocket for many years, one whose broad outline he had been developing for almost two decades. Haughey wrote to ministers setting out the cuts that would be needed, saying that a 'radical approach' should be adopted and that no expenditure should be thought 'sacrosanct and immune to elimination or reduction ... We do not want a series of justifications of the status quo or special pleadings.'[12] Given his track record there was some scepticism that he meant it, and given the depth of the depression, even more that the new approach would work.

Haughey says he 'formed the view in 1982 that the corrective action needed in the public finances was possible only in the context of a comprehensive and balanced economic and fiscal plan with the support of the main social partners.'[13] He claimed the idea had emerged from a meeting with the then German chancellor, Helmut Schmidt, at the edges of an EEC summit. Schmidt explained that he would be spending the weekend in talks with employers and unions to agree pay rates on the basis of the current economic climate. But social partnership, as it became known, was something Haughey had worked towards long before 1982. As Minister for Finance in the late 1960s he had pushed to create a dialogue between the Irish Congress of Trade Unions (ICTU) and the Federated Union of Employers (later IBEC).[14] He had maintained and developed links with trade unionists throughout the 1970s. In 1986, as leader of the opposition, Haughey had brought his front bench to ICTU's headquarters. He had earlier been impressed by the ICTU document *Confronting the Jobs Crisis*, seeing it as a serious attempt to engage in job creation rather than job protection.[15]

On his first day back in the Taoiseach's office Haughey met with MacSharry and Pádraig Ó hUiginn. Ó hUiginn had been moved out of the Department of the Taoiseach to the National Economic and Social Council (NESC) by Garret FitzGerald because of his closeness to Haughey. At the NESC Ó hUiginn developed a new plan, *Strategy for Development*, which envisioned a balanced budget based on wage restraints and incentives for industrial development.[16] FitzGerald had not engaged with it, but crucially both the unions and employers' organisations had signed up to this. Haughey was going to make it his own.

Haughey's economic plan was simple. In a way it was the opposite of the Fianna Fáil manifesto from ten years earlier. That one had promised to kick-start the economy by frontloading financial benefits and government spending. It was to drive a demand-led recovery. In 1987 government spending would be drastically curtailed, leading to state services being cut back. Income taxes reductions would be used to moderate pay demands. The state would look to develop export-led growth by identifying potential industries and companies that were most likely to succeed commercially. Haughey's would be a supply-led recovery. It also differed from the Fine Gael–Labour plan which only offered fiscal contraction and few incentives for growth.

MacSharry immediately announced cuts to public spending, and that continued through the year. The cutbacks were severe, leaving no one under any illusions about Haughey's seriousness. When Pádraig Flynn told a cabinet meeting that the people would not accept such harsh cuts, Haughey stood by his Minister for Finance. He told Flynn he could leave if he did not like it. Flynn stayed.[17] This was a different relationship between Taoiseach and Minister for Finance than had been seen for a decade – now they backed each other up. MacSharry stayed late in a cold Department of Finance with the departmental secretary identifying small amounts for savings.[18] At the same time an Expenditure Review Committee, given the nickname An Bord Snip, was set up to identify larger programmes or bodies that had outlived their usefulness and could be removed. Haughey backed MacSharry in all his efforts, with all government power centred here. Ó hUiginn, now back in the Department of the Taoiseach, reported to both Haughey and MacSharry.[19] The government papers from that time show a government that was obsessive. Small amounts of waste were uncovered and cut out. Though many of the decisions were unpopular and caused protests, the government stuck the course, and Haughey seemed in his element.

In order to drive forward a tripartite pay accord (farmers' organisations were also included, but were peripheral), Haughey centred it all from his department, which gave the process more authority. It was not limited to pay, as such agreements historically tended to be. Rather it would come to include all 'social partners' and set out policy in a number of areas, macro-economic, industrial, tax and social. In April 1987 Haughey met with the unions, but he wanted to get spending cuts introduced before proper negotiations began in the summer. The unions agreed to do this, and there was a phony war of the unions opposing spending cuts publicly, but without much vigour.[20]

The rewards were immediate and positive. The financial markets approved of the approach, and interest rates fell, easing the debt burden on the Irish state and mortgage holders. Though the impact on unemployment and emigration was not so swift, economic growth gave the country a cause for optimism for the first time in the decade.[21] Polls showed that Fianna Fáil support held up reasonably well after the tough budgetary measures were introduced.[22]

Negotiations opened with employers and the unions, with the government set to speak to each separately, at the request of the unions, who felt that to work with all three simultaneously would put unions in a minority. Employers' remaining scepticism might have been removed by the way the government stood up to a strike in the Electricity Supply Board (ESB) in May 1987 without conceding to pay demands. Haughey was central to 'delivering' the employers' groups, who cited 'the persuasiveness of Haughey'.[23]

Unions had been courted by Haughey for years, but they were also aware of the threat of failure. Thatcherism had damaged the labour movement in the UK, and though there was no such ideology in Ireland, it was the prevailing policy trend. Jack O'Connor saw the Tallaght Strategy as 'a licence to undertake a Thatcherite assault on organised labour'.[24] Though this was not true, it helped Haughey bring any recalcitrant trade unionists along. The unions agreed to below-inflation pay increases, with the promise that there would be no public sector redundancies, and tax decreases would be offered when they became feasible. The unions were keenly aware that being part of the decision-making process – even if it did mean signing up to austerity – was preferable to what had happened in the UK.[25] The Programme for National Recovery (PNR), signed in October 1987, was a major achievement for Haughey, though he had to work hard to hold it together in the following year, as groups sniped at aspects of the deal.[26] There was a central review committee, chaired by Ó hUiginn, but over which Haughey clearly had a constant eye, which allowed the social partners to monitor the PNR and raise issues as they emerged. It became a very powerful body that directed policy in a number of areas.[27] Haughey supported the UK's prime minister, John Major's decision to withdraw from the Social Chapter of the Maastricht Treaty, but perhaps with an eye on how the unions might perceive this, decided at the last minute that those countries with strong social laws were also the most competitive and so decided against an opt-out for Ireland.[28]

If Garret FitzGerald had gone into the 1987 election warning of a 'vicious circle', by the end of that year Haughey had created a virtuous cycle. The number of industrial disputes fell and the economy started to grow, easing the pressure on the government. The Industrial Development Agency (IDA) redoubled its efforts to attract foreign direct investment, and suddenly Ireland seemed a more serious option for international investors. The Single European Act (SEA), which created the EEC's single market, and which Haughey had cynically voted against in opposition, meant that Ireland now offered a stable, attractive and low-tax European base for companies to set up their operations. Haughey in opposition had suggested the Treaty would weaken Irish industry and cause problems for neutrality.[29] These concerns fell away as the Haughey government enthusiastically guided the SEA through the Oireachtas. Then, after *Crotty v. An Taoiseach*, a successful court challenge to the Treaty's constitutionality, Haughey led the campaign to ratify the Treaty by a referendum to change the constitution. This was comfortably passed on 26 May 1987. Haughey supported the Jacques Delors Commission's federalising plans. Ireland would later benefit from further economic integration, including from structural funds available to poorer regions, such as Ireland, for infrastructural development.

Haughey was hands-on in identifying jobs growth potential in indigenous industry. It was a question of 'picking winners'. In this spirit Haughey's government agreed to a plan to boost the Irish beef industry by supporting the largest Irish beef processor company, AIBP. In an extraordinary deal the Irish government agreed to give IR£25 million (€70 million in 2023) in IDA grants to fund the expansion of Goodman International. The company was owned by Larry Goodman, thought to be a 'good friend' of Haughey's.[30] There were reports of pressure on the IDA to approve the deal without the normal oversights, and cabinet was not allowed much time to vet the proposal, which would help make AIBP the largest beef processor in Europe, and Goodman one of Ireland's richest men.[31] Ray MacSharry was sceptical of the deal, fearing it would lead to over-capacity in the beef sector and that 'the project will increase substantially the dominant position held by Goodman. That would be detrimental to other processors and farmers.' He felt the cost for each new job was 'unprecedentedly and unacceptably high'.[32] However, Haughey and the Minister for Industry and Commerce, Albert Reynolds, won out.

In the end Ireland lost money on its financial supports for Goodman International, and even more on an export credit insurance scheme through which the state underwrote risks taken by Goodman, who was exporting beef to Iraq. It showed Haughey's impatience with bureaucracy, and his and Ó hUiginn's willingness to try bold ideas. Ó hUiginn might have reflected Haughey's outlook when he said that 'The cabinet system works OK in normal times, but not when you want speedy decisions.' Haughey said to Ó hUiginn, 'We have to take charge, we've to run it like a business.'[33] It was good business for Goodman; not so good for the Irish taxpayer.

A more successful venture was Haughey's sponsorship of the Irish Financial Service Centre (IFSC). The idea for an IFSC came from the financier Dermot Desmond. The plan was to make Dublin a centre for international investment in financial services by giving companies a series of financial incentives to locate in Dublin. The FitzGerald government had received a report from Desmond on how it might be done, but had shelved it. Haughey was interested, however. He asked Desmond to sit on an economic advisory committee, and then the idea appeared in the 1987 Fianna Fáil manifesto, though it did not make much of an impact. After the election Haughey set up an IFSC committee, chaired by Ó hUiginn, with representatives from Finance, the Central Bank, the IDA, Revenue, the banks and other financial institutions.

Dermot Desmond found the first committee meeting frustratingly slow, but Haughey took control of the following meeting.[34] According to Paddy Teahon, 'Haughey was very decisive. And uniquely once he made a decision, he could see it done. Resistance seemed to fall away.' The IFSC was included in the Finance Bill in March 1988.[35] Haughey invested significant time in selling the centre, including doing some international travel, something he tended to avoid because it disrupted his work schedule. The IFSC delivered some short-term growth, mainly in construction in Dublin's Docklands, but the real benefits accrued after Haughey had left office. It delivered many thousands of high-quality jobs, and over time the Docklands was transformed into Dublin's central business district.

The national debt was crippling the public finances at this time, as servicing it accounted for almost 80 per cent of income tax receipts. Dermot Desmond persuaded Haughey of the need to professionally and actively manage the debt, to reduce the costs of borrowing and servicing the debt. Haughey appointed a senior official at the Department of Finance, Michael Somers, as secretary of a debt management division within Finance. Somers pointed out that he had problems retaining staff. To address this the government introduced the National Treasury Management Agency Act in 1990 which provided for the establishment of the NTMA 'to borrow moneys for the Exchequer and to manage the National Debt on behalf of' the state. This meant that employees were outside the strict civil service rules on pay and promotion. The NTMA became very successful in reducing the Irish debt and reducing the cost of borrowing for the state.

Haughey showed similar vision, drive and success in several other initiatives. He saved Temple Bar, a run-down but historic area of Dublin, from demolition. The national transport company, Coras Iompair Éireann, owned the land and was renting it out to artists at low rents prior to a planned redevelopment. The artists approached Haughey with the idea of it becoming a cultural quarter, an idea Haughey liked. Temple Bar was probably more successful as a commercial attraction than an artistic setting. While it was saved from demolition, much of the artistic life in the area was driven out, to be replaced by tourist bars and hotels. His interest in the arts had earlier seen the foundation of Aosdána, a collective of prominent Irish artists and writers, designed to honour them, but also to provide financial support to enable them concentrate on their artistic work. This investment was one the state continued with, and much later one could link the success of Irish writers and artists internationally to have stemmed from Haughey's initiatives.[36]

Haughey's artistic adviser, Anthony Cronin,[37] was the source of another idea: the creation of a new art museum. Haughey's government gave state investment to create the Irish Museum of Modern Art, converting a seventeenth-century hospital in Kilmainham. While its collection never matched its surroundings, it has been quite successful. Haughey also wanted to upgrade state offices. The Department of the Taoiseach was housed in a cramped and grotty Government Buildings, with much of the central part of the complex occupied by the UCD School of Engineering. Haughey oversaw its move to Belfield and the upgrade of Government Buildings, making the space more appropriate for the expanding business of government. Haughey had a lift installed close to the Taoiseach's office that would allow someone enter the Taoiseach's quarters unobserved. This had the advantage of facilitating his affair with Terry Keane.[38]

Some see 1987 as the start of neo-liberalism in Ireland. It was not. Haughey's approach was very much a statist one, *dirigisme*, along French lines. He was attempting to improve the state's finances; he rejected the orthodox Department of Finance approach of book balancing, and engaged in quite significant capital investment in projects that might be expected to deliver returns. It forced the semi-state sector to work on commercial lines, but did not yet engage in privatisation. The state would also pick private industries and support them. This sometimes worked, but at times it led to massive transfers to private companies, and rumours of corruption followed.[39]

Allegations of crony capitalism were fair. Goodman sought a meeting with Haughey soon after Haughey took power in 1987.[40] The Goodman deal was hugely beneficial for Larry Goodman, but reduced competition in the beef processing market by giving one company extraordinary power. There was a financial connection between the two men. Haughey had received a IR£50,000 donation from Goodman in 1987 (€140,000 in 2023), and IR£75,000 in 1989 (€200,000 in 2023) to go to Fianna Fail's leader's account, a personal account Haughey used for his own expenses. Though Haughey denied ever doing any favours for Goodman, in 1988 Haughey responded to Goodman's lobbying to remove IDA performance clauses by having cabinet agree to their removal despite IDA objections.[41] Ó hUiginn claimed to have acted 'entirely on [his] own initiative' when he contacted the IDA the day after the Goodman group was refused the removal of the performance clause.[42] The FitzGerald government had withdrawn an export credit insurance scheme for beef exporters exporting to Iraq on the grounds that since Iraq was at war with Iran there was a good chance that the Iraqi regime would not pay. Only a government-underwritten insurance scheme enabled the trade to happen. Haughey's government reinstated export credit insurance for Goodman's company's beef exports to Iraq. When Iraq invaded Kuwait, that insurance was activated and the Irish taxpayer was to pick up the bill.

In the period after 1987 Haughey's personal income also grew. Subsequent tribunals discovered donations from many wealthy businesspeople, though the Beef Tribunal rejected allegations of undue influence by Goodman over Haughey's government. Haughey regarded these donations as unproblematic because 'there are many public-spirited people who subscribe to political parties and to individual politicians and have no anticipation of anything other than the political success of the individual ... because they are running the country well.'[43] While in cases it may have been true, it was an entirely self-serving explanation.

※ ※ ※

When Haughey first came to power in 1979 he outlined Northern Ireland as his 'first political priority'. He instigated ongoing summits with the British, which led to the signing of the Anglo-Irish Agreement by Garret FitzGerald and Margaret Thatcher in 1985. Though Haughey had opposed the Anglo-Irish Agreement, that was for tactical reasons, and the vanity of not liking to acknowledge another's success. In any case, he was duty bound to work with it since it was a formal international agreement. While he conceded he was not 'exactly in favour of the Anglo-Irish Agreement', back in office he sought to make it work, instructing an official to 'implement it to the hilt', and to 'keep the British to their promises.'[44] This was typical of Haughey. The rhetoric played to a domestic or party audience, but his actions were usually more reasoned.

In 1987 there was little chance of making much progress on the British–Irish relationship. While Haughey's return to government in 1987 increased Thatcher's suspicion, Thatcher had already if not quite lost interest in Northern Ireland, at least become disillusioned with it. She was disappointed with the AIA, which had disaffected many Ulster unionists but delivered no obvious benefits in increased security co-operation from the Irish state, and no meaningful concessions from SDLP leader John Hume.[45] Her pro-Irish cabinet secretary, Robert Armstrong, had retired and her main source of advice on Northern Ireland was now the experienced diplomat, Charles Powell. Her overriding goal, she told Haughey, was 'to beat the IRA'.[46] If she wasn't enthusiastically in favour of the AIA, she had given her word, and so was committed to the implementing it. But she was not going to engage in any new initiatives. She vehemently opposed a plan by her more orange Secretary of State for Northern Ireland, Tom King, to set up an Assembly. Thatcher was left 'both friendless and frustrated' by Northern Ireland.[47]

Haughey was under pressure to give more security co-operation to the UK. Haughey was aware that Jack Lynch had been forced out of office for offering security co-operation with the British, and so was anxious not to be seen as 'Thatcher's poodle'.[48] Extradition of IRA suspects for trial in the UK was a constant issue at the time, and Thatcher was dissatisfied with Haughey's response, especially in the wake of IRA atrocities such as the Enniskillen Remembrance Day bombing. Haughey agreed in principle to guide an extradition bill through the Oireachtas, which would fulfil the ratification of the European Convention for the Suppression of Terrorism, a requirement of the Anglo-Irish Agreement. This would remove the 'political offence exception', which was used by most people who sought to stop their extradition to the UK under the 1965 Extradition Act. Haughey faced considerable opposition from within Fianna Fáil. He met with members of the parliamentary party in an attempt to assuage their fears.[49] But it was only under the threat of an election and the promise to backbenchers that another amending bill would give the Attorney General the right to refuse to certify warrants for extradition that the bill was passed in late November 1987. Passing that amending bill angered Thatcher, but it was enough to satisfy his own parliamentary party, the Dáil – in which he had no majority – and to abide by the letter of the AIA.[50] Fianna Fáil members, however, continued to protest against extradition, which was a particularly divisive issue given the ongoing campaigns to overturn prominent miscarriages of justice in British courts, such as the Birmingham Six and the Guildford Four, and those highlighted in the Stalker Inquiry.

Relations between Haughey and Thatcher remained fraught as the Provisional IRA and the British security forces had some 'successes' against each other. It was a particularly active time for the IRA, and Thatcher's security concerns were reasonable given the IRA's earlier successful attempts to import heavy automatic weapons, rocket launchers and explosives from Libya. The route was stopped when the ship *Eksund* was intercepted in November 1987 by French authorities, and while the Gardaí and army were successful in seizing other IRA arms dumps in the Republic, some got through, which enabled the IRA's terrorist activity in the late 1980s.

In November 1988, when Fr Patrick Ryan, an Irish Catholic priest wanted for involvement in the Brighton bombing in 1984, was arrested in Belgium with bomb-making materials and deported to Ireland, the UK immediately sought his extradition. Thatcher and other UK politicians made statements in the House of Commons that Irish politicians found 'hysterical'.[51] The Irish government refused extradition on the basis that prejudicial statements in the British media meant it was unlikely Ryan would have a fair trial in the UK. Thatcher and Haughey clashed continually on this issue, which was probably personal for Thatcher, given that she had been the target of one of the bombings Ryan later admitted he had been involved in.⁵² A later attempt to try him in Ireland was rejected by the Director of Public Prosecutions on the basis of insufficient evidence, which also angered the British.⁵³ The British continued to lobby for amendments to strengthen the Extradition Act, which Haughey continued to resist.⁵⁴ In April 1990 delegates at the Fianna Fáil Árd Fheis voted in favour of a motion opposing extradition 'in present circumstances'.⁵⁵ The murder by the IRA of Ian Gow, a Conservative MP and close friend of Thatcher, in July 1990 would only increase her sense of isolation from Irish affairs.⁵⁶

While Haughey almost certainly did not wish to frustrate Thatcher's objective of defeating the IRA, he was sceptical that it could be achieved using her approach. He was perhaps more ambitious and imaginative in his approach to the problem. Haughey had engaged in what were to become the Hume–Adams talks. Fr Alec Reid had approached Haughey in 1986 with a view to opening a pan-nationalist dialogue with the SDLP and Sinn Féin/IRA. In May 1987 Haughey received a wordy memorandum from Gerry Adams outlining what they would want in return for an IRA ceasefire. It fell well short of the usual demand for British withdrawal, and said that the IRA would accept the outcome of negotiations between unionists and nationalists. The killing of eight IRA operatives in an attempted bombing of a police station in Loughgall, County Armagh that month might not have influenced the document, but it probably pushed the Sinn Féin/IRA leadership further along that road.

Haughey had to proceed with caution. There was an unwritten, and frequently broken rule that 'you don't talk to terrorists', although not one the British always obeyed. Haughey's reputation from the Arms Crisis was such that being publicly associated with Adams was not possible. And any chance of this was certainly removed in the aftermath of the Enniskillen Remembrance Day bombing. Haughey agreed with Reid's suggestion that John Hume be brought on board.⁵⁷ Hume's anti-IRA position meant that he could purify the talks. The Hume–Adams dialogue was public, but simultaneously there were indirect talks between Haughey and Sinn Féin/IRA.

Haughey authorised his adviser Martin Mansergh, Fianna Fáil TD Dermot Ahern and another member of the party's national executive to meet secretly with a delegation from Sinn Féin – Gerry Adams, Mitchel McLaughlin and Pat Doherty. Haughey made it a party initiative, not a government one. Crucially this offered Haughey deniability if the meetings were uncovered. Mansergh was Haughey's chief adviser on Northern Ireland, but despite his deep Irish nationalism, his Anglo-Irish background and academic approach made him distinct enough that he could not be realistically accused of collaborating with the IRA. Three meetings took place in 1988; these were exploratory, and without an agenda. They mainly involved Mansergh and Adams talking. The Fianna Fáil side tried to impress upon the Sinn Féin delegation that opinion in the Republic had moved considerably against the IRA.

One statement that Adams suggested would be helpful from the British was that it had no intrinsic interest in Northern Ireland and that it would be willing to leave if there were some form of agreement within Ireland. Mansergh could see that the talks were not really going anywhere and the cost of exposure was too great to run the continued risk to Haughey.[58] Reid maintained contact with all parties, but the talks ended. It was, however, one of the early threads in what would become the Northern Ireland peace process. Haughey, through Mansergh, had done enough to encourage Adams and others who were inclining away from the military strategy that a non-violent route would not be cut off before it started. In March 1989 Gerry Adams gave a clear indication that the IRA wanted to pursue a non-violent approach when he talked of leading a 'non-armed political movement to work for self-determination'.[59] The IRA was, however, still engaged in its horrific campaign, mainly targeting British soldiers, but also using 'human bombs'. In late 1990 a Catholic man, Patsy Gillespie, who worked in an army canteen, was chained to a van containing a bomb and ordered to drive to a British army base. The IRA detonated the bomb, killing Gillespie and five soldiers.

Peter Brooke, the new Northern Ireland Secretary, was appointed in 1989 with the expectation that he would not engage in any significant initiatives. However, Brooke was more interested in Ireland than Thatcher expected. He spent much of 1990 in an attempt to start inter-party talks aimed at restoring devolved power to Northern Ireland. By the end of the year that attempt was 'on hold', but Brooke made a significant speech on 9 November 1990, in which he said that Britain had 'no selfish or strategic interest in Northern Ireland', and that Sinn Féin would be welcome into a full political talks process if the IRA renounced violence.[60] Gerry Adams rejected this overture, but the IRA announced a three-day ceasefire over Christmas.

Brooke's speech was a significant staging post on the road to peace. While the Irish side may have had some input, Haughey could still do little. He was unfortunate that his time on the issue coincided with Thatcher's withdrawal from Northern Ireland as an active issue. The IRA was already thinking of a post-Thatcher scenario.[61] When Thatcher left the stage, Haughey engaged with John Major, who was more interested in Northern Ireland than perhaps anyone would have expected. Haughey was sceptical of the Brooke offer, fearing its de facto veto gave unionists no incentive to move their position, and he was still fearful of the electoral impact of being perceived as being too close to the British, while remaining of the opinion that it was only a British–Irish initiative that could deliver substantial progress.[62]

In December 1991 Haughey told Major that the IRA was ready to move. Major was naturally sceptical, and the text that Haughey supplied (from John Hume) was 'so heavily skewed towards the presumption of a united Ireland that [it] had no merit as a basis for negotiation'.[63] The IRA murder of eight Protestant workers in Teebane, County Tyrone in January 1992 made it hard for anyone to be optimistic. But Haughey persuaded Major to keep going. Haughey had too little time with Major to make much of a difference, but he did plant seeds in Major's mind that would later bear fruit.[64] Haughey made a contribution in at least showing a willingness to engage Adams and the leadership of Sinn Féin, though it seemed clear that Adams was intent on going slowly toward a route of non-violence that probably would have survived with or without Haughey's intervention. Few others, however, were likely to have taken the move to open dialogue with Sinn Féin.

These were times of exceptional activity and productivity from Haughey, similar to his work in the 1960s. Haughey was in control and Ireland was yielding the rewards of this productivity. Despite the severe austerity measures imposed, the economy was improving. Haughey was popular, with two-thirds of opinion poll respondents expressing satisfaction with Haughey and a net positive satisfaction with the government. Even better, the opposition was, if anything, losing support.[65] Fine Gael under Alan Dukes saw no reward for its mature decision to not block government measures. Also good for Haughey was that support for Des O'Malley's Progressive Democrats had collapsed. The PDs' *raison d'être* had been removed now that Haughey was doing what seemed to be the right thing.

The country felt optimistic for the first time in a decade. On the sporting field it rejoiced in the summer of 1988 when the Irish soccer team, managed by an Englishman, Jack Charlton, beat the English team in the Euros in West Germany. In 1987 Stephen Roche won the Tour de France, to be greeted by Haughey on the podium. The Irish rock group U2 was the biggest band in the world, even if its lead singer, Bono, was a Garret fan. If Ireland was in despair at the start of Haughey's government in 1987, by the end of the decade Haughey was at his peak. The only thing that could go against Haughey was his vanity.

14.

THE BONFIRE OF THE VANITIES

Haughey's 1987 minority government was remarkably successful in improving many of the headline economic figures, and despite the protests over health cuts, he and his party were popular. An opinion poll in February 1989 estimated Fianna Fáil support at 54 per cent, over twice that of Fine Gael.[1] Haughey enjoyed an image of 'strict but benign paternalism'.[2] He was able to govern effectively despite being in a minority in the Dáil. Haughey's government had lost a few votes on private members' motions, which had no real importance, and may have served to keep Fine Gael happy that their Tallaght Strategy was not a complete capitulation to Haughey.

But Haughey was determined to get his overall majority. On 26 April 1989, he returned from a trade mission in Japan to see his government at risk of losing a private members' motion proposing an extra IR£150,000 (€400,000 in 2023) to haemophiliacs who had been infected with HIV by contaminated blood products. The total cost was expected to be IR£9 million (€24 million in 2023). It was a not insignificant amount of money in the context of the cuts that had been pushed through in the previous two years. But given the improvement in the public finances, it was manageable.

Haughey was apoplectic when he arrived at Government Buildings and he told the chief whip, Vincent Brady, that he would call an election if the motion was passed, and to relay that message to the Fine Gael chief whip, Jim Higgins. Though Higgins initially regarded it as a joke, when he went to find the mild-mannered Brady the

Taoiseach was still forcibly expressing his anger and Higgins realised it was not. News of a possible election spread quickly through Leinster House.³ The opposition held its nerve and defeated the government, which made Haughey even angrier and more resolute. Bertie Ahern and Albert Reynolds tried to convince him to rethink the idea of dissolving the Dáil. Ray MacSharry might have been able to dissuade him; for Bertie Ahern, MacSharry 'was the only one to whom Haughey would have listened.'⁴ But MacSharry had become the Irish EC Commissioner in early 1989, so he was no longer involved in front-line Irish politics.

The decision to call an election might have been taken in a rush of blood, and Haughey had time to rethink. But a threat to call an election only has power if you go through with it. If he did not follow through, he could not credibly threaten it again. He might have genuinely thought, as he said to Ó hUiginn, 'Where will it stop?'⁵ The timing of the upcoming European Parliament elections to be held in June meant that unless he wanted to hold two national elections within two months, he would have to wait some time before dissolving the Dáil. While some were counselling him to avoid an election, others in cabinet, including Pádraig Flynn, were reported to be encouraging him: 'You'll sweep the land, Boss.'⁶ The country was then left wondering, but Haughey gave hints that an election was coming when many government bills were rushed through the Oireachtas. Haughey suggested that 'the main consideration is the capacity of the Government to govern effectively'.⁷

Despite the opposition of most of his cabinet, Haughey requested the dissolution of the Dáil on 25 May, and set the election date for 15 June 1989. The first opinion poll after the election was called showed Fianna Fáil's support falling slightly, though still at 50 per cent. However, it continued to slide throughout the campaign.⁸ Haughey's high positive popularity ratings in April that year slipped 30 points and into negative by June.⁹ Haughey had set out his inability to govern as the reason for the election, but the public reacted with suspicion. Some voters tend to apportion blame for early elections, and Haughey's fifth attempt to get an overall majority was easier to frame as a power play than as an attempt to improve Ireland's governability. Haughey had lost six inconsequential votes between 1987 and 1989, but was clearly able to govern effectively. There were rumours that Fine Gael would have rejected the government's health estimates in the autumn, and that Haughey was pre-empting that. PJ Mara was undoubtedly right in arguing that it would have been better to wait for that to happen and then to go to the country on that basis.[10]

Health became the main issue in the campaign.[11] Fine Gael was in a poor position to criticise the government, given that it had supported the government's approach, as had the Progressive Democrats. But Haughey's gamble backfired. It was an election that nobody wanted and an election that nobody won. For Charlie McCreevy, the Fianna Fáil backbencher, 'the whole campaign had been one long disaster ... I needed no one to tell me at any stage of the campaign that [Fianna Fáil] did not have a snowball's chance in hell of getting an overall majority.'[12] On a low turnout, the Fianna Fáil vote was steady at 44 per cent, but the party lost four seats. It was at 77 seats, now six seats short of a majority. Haughey blamed the health cuts as having taken a toll on the party's electoral performance, but he should have blamed his own naked ambition and political misjudgement.[13]

Haughey was damaged by the result, which once again showed his political judgement to be clouded by vanity and his need for complete control. The result left him further from an overall majority, but in his favour there was no clear alternative government. There was some talk of a grand coalition, something dismissed out of hand by Garret FitzGerald, a newly re-elected backbencher, speaking on RTÉ on 16 June, the night of the count. Haughey agreed, instructing his director of elections Seamus Brennan to put out the message that Fianna Fáil 'was not in the coalition business'.[14] The arithmetic was such that the PDs' six seats could give Haughey his majority. Then Mary Harney, a senior member of the PDs, gave a radio interview suggesting that the PDs might support a Fianna Fáil government in coalition. Haughey instructed Charlie McCreevy to contact Harney. Harney and McCreevy had become friendly in Fianna Fáil when they both opposed Haughey. They were both pragmatists; it might be the only way out of an impasse, an impasse that could be career-ending for Haughey or O'Malley, or both. Des O'Malley, who had taken a few days off after the election, was apoplectic when he heard Harney's suggestion.

Des O'Malley was invited to Haughey's office in Government Buildings on the evening of 20 June. Haughey was to make an offer to O'Malley. In the half-hour meeting Haughey proposed a confidence and supply arrangement for a fixed period of three or four years. There would be a policy basis for the deal, something along the lines of the Tallaght Strategy. He made a number of offers: to reduce the number of TDs needed to constitute a recognised Dáil party to six, to enable the PDs maintain their Dáil privileges; to consult O'Malley weeks in advance of any legislative proposals; and to give the PDs a chair or chairs of Oireachtas committees, then all in the gift of a Taoiseach. The deal would be based on a 'personal understanding' between the two men whose mutual suspicion went back twenty years. That was rejected by O'Malley, but there was a feeling that this was an opening gambit.[15] Neither the PDs nor the country would benefit from another election, which was the likely outcome of no deal with Haughey.

Haughey met Dukes two days later, essentially asking for a continuation of the Tallaght Strategy. Dukes, reasonably, rejected that, pointing out that the arrangement was working well, but that Haughey had called an election. Dukes proposed a grand coalition, something that neither man might have been able to deliver, but as he pointed out, Haughey was running out of options. 'It's either me or Dessie.'[16]

O'Malley and Dukes had agreed a pact before the election that the PDs would support Dukes as Taoiseach, and there was an expectation that they would stick to that, even if the numbers made it irrelevant. The Dáil met on 29 June, but failed to elect a Taoiseach. There was then pressure on Haughey to resign, which he eventually did, but only after a mini constitutional crisis. A Taoiseach's resignation in these circumstances is meaningless in real terms because he or she remains Taoiseach until another Taoiseach is elected, but Haughey's initial refusal to resign raised more suspicions of him among his already suspicious opponents.

Some in the PDs had already come to the conclusion that a coalition with Fianna Fáil was the least worst outcome, fearing a new election might annihilate the party.[17] It was frequently touted as a 'core value' of Fianna Fáil that it did not enter coalitions, but Haughey still perhaps hoped that a deal short of formal coalition agreement might be reached.

The next day, 30 June, Haughey and O'Malley exchanged letters – one of which was caught on camera, as Joe Walsh, the Fianna Fáil junior minister from Cork was seen sheepishly leaving the PDs' headquarters on South Frederick Street in Dublin. In that exchange, they agreed to set negotiating teams. The teams were Albert Reynolds and Bertie Ahern for Fianna Fáil, and Bobby Molloy and Pat Cox for the PDs. The meetings 'broke down almost as soon as they started'.[18] The PDs insisted on a coalition arrangement rather than one of confidence and supply. They wanted this agreed before policy was discussed, fearing that if policy were agreed first then refusing to support a government programme it had agreed to on the basis that it had no cabinet seats might look like 'a naked desire for Mercs and perks'.[19] Haughey publicly continued his 'no coalition' stance, but the alternatives of another election or his replacement as leader – something Ahern had pointed out was one of the few other options to end the impasse – were just as unappealing for Haughey.[20] Polls showed that the vast majority of people were opposed to what would be the sixth election in that decade.

On 3 July the Dáil met once again and once again failed to elect a Taoiseach. Haughey had changed his mind on coalition. On 4 July Haughey raised the possibility of a coalition with senior people in Fianna Fáil, but most were vehemently opposed. Pádraig Flynn issued a statement: 'All the members of the Cabinet are unanimous for no coalition . . . this is a core value that we must preserve.'[21] Haughey met O'Malley later that evening and privately conceded on a coalition. Haughey met with O'Malley and the PD negotiating team the following day, but without his own team. Reynolds was still publicly saying no coalition was on, and when the PD leader asked Haughey about that, he remarked, 'It's all right. I just haven't told them yet.'[22] The formal negotiations were on again. Haughey allowed Ahern and Reynolds to continue with the policy aspect, while he took control of the political side of the negotiations. On 6 July he told the Dáil that he was in coalition negotiations, though without using the word 'coalition'.[23]

Haughey met with Fianna Fáil TDs and ministers individually in an attempt to divide opposition to coalition. In a confusing few days – confusion mainly sown by Haughey – Fianna Fáil ministers and TDs believed that nothing had yet been conceded and that they would have the ultimate say.[24] In dealing with his party he deliberately avoided allowing any forum, cabinet, parliamentary party or national executive to set any red lines, giving them the impression there were still difficulties, but allowing him to continue with coalition negotiations. He asked for freedom to negotiate and agree a deal, which he achieved.[25] A meeting of the parliamentary party was vociferous in its opposition to coalition, claiming that grassroots activists would not accept it. Máire Geoghegan-Quinn, in particular, threatened not to vote for Haughey in the Dáil as Taoiseach, which would have meant no deal.[26] Haughey tried to contact her, but could not reach her.

While some policy items remained, much of the negotiations centred on whether the PDs would get two cabinet ministries. Haughey told O'Malley he could not deliver that, given the vocal opposition in his party. He may have been sincere in thinking that, but O'Malley thought Haughey was underestimating his ability to control his party. The PDs were adamant that two cabinet seats were necessary, feeling that a single minister would be too easily isolated in cabinet.[27] Still O'Malley himself was still not convinced. He met with the PD TDs and other senior party figures at his Dublin home in Rathmines on 11 July, the night before the Dáil was to meet again. They went backwards and forwards with arguments for and against. It seems a Hobson's choice – say no and there would be another election; say yes and the party might be devastated. Eventually the consensus in the room was that O'Malley should decide. He was by this stage quite emotional. Harney said to him, 'You've been fighting Haughey all your life, you know him.' And then O'Malley said 'OK – we'll do it.' There was not a lot of enthusiasm.[28]

Haughey still had some work to do on his own party. Ahern and Reynolds thought that two cabinet seats was too much and said so to Haughey: 'The party won't buy it', Ahern warned him.

'They'll do what they're feckin' told', Haughey replied.[29]

By this stage the pair were more annoyed at their treatment by Haughey than by the idea of coalition. Haughey had not been candid with them that he was effectively running the negotiation. On radio on the morning of 12 July – the day the Dáil was to meet – both Ahern and Reynolds reiterated the point about a single seat in cabinet. They were unaware that Haughey had already conceded two the night before.

Haughey told them he still had to finalise some details. He used the uncertainty to his advantage when he presented the programme for government to his cabinet and his parliamentary party. The party was given the impression that there would be another chance to raise objections. But there would not be any such opportunity. Later that day, all the Fianna Fáil TDs dutifully lined up and Haughey was elected Taoiseach for a fourth time by 84 votes to 79. As well as the 77 Fianna Fáil TDs and the six PD TDS, he got the support of Tom Foxe, an independent TD from Roscommon who ran on a campaign to protect his local hospital. Neil Blaney abstained, as did the newly elected Green Party TD, Roger Garland. Haughey got his way, mainly because he never gave his opponents within Fianna Fáil a chance to take a decision. The loyalty to the leader in Fianna Fáil was too strong for anyone not to vote for Haughey in the Dáil. As Haughey observed, 'Nobody but myself could have done it.'[30]

❖ ❖ ❖

Nobody but Haughey could have done it, but it had come at a cost. Albert Reynolds 'lost all faith and made up my mind – enough of Charlie Haughey!'[31] Reynolds privately stoked up Fianna Fáil supporters against the deal, which he refused to call a coalition, later referring to it as a 'temporary little arrangement'.[32] Pádraig Flynn told Haughey he thought it was a 'dirty little deal'.[33] They regarded it as an arrangement purely for Haughey's pursuit of power. It was pursuit of power, but what else was Haughey going to do? Coalition would have been demanded even if Fianna Fáil were under another leader, and another election would not have been helpful for Haughey, Fianna Fáil or the country.

There was another cost. By giving two seats at cabinet to the PDs, this denied two seats to Fianna Fáil people, although both O'Malley and Bobby Molloy had served in cabinet with Haughey previously. Some serving ministers had to be dropped. Haughey was usually conservative in his cabinet selection. This time he brought in just one new Fianna Fáil minister, Seamus Brennan, who was already an experienced TD. Many other TDs were now finding it hard to see a route to promotion under Haughey.

Haughey and O'Malley surprised most observers by working well together. While there was no warmness and the distrust remained, there was a respect and an acknowledgement of each other's position. As Bertie Ahern observed, 'Charlie never sprung anything on O'Malley in a meeting. He had always smoothed everything over beforehand.'[34] The government continued in its approach to the economy, and taxes were reduced as part of the next partnership deal, Programme for Economic and Social Progress. The PDs and Fianna Fáil agreed on reforming the tax system to abolish tax shelters and allowances in order to fund the reduction of tax rates. Ahern found 'there wasn't much we didn't agree about in practical terms'.[35] The economy continued to grow.

Haughey enjoyed his role as president of the European Council in 1990, which gave him access to European heads of government. Haughey wanted to ensure that Ireland did not do its presidency on the cheap, that Ireland looked the part, and spent considerable sums on the refurbishment of Dublin Castle, for instance. He bawled out an official when he saw a bottle of 'fucking Timotei' shampoo in one of the state apartments reserved for the leaders in Dublin Castle, ordering it to be replaced with something more upmarket and Irish.[36] This was typical Haughey; he did not see why Ireland had to accept mediocrity.

He had planned it as a 'green presidency', hoping to put an emphasis on the environment and environmental protection. His interest in environment was genuine – he had put in place a National Heritage Council, which later became a statutory body. But the fall of the Berlin Wall meant that international events would dominate Ireland's presidency. Haughey took on the role of world leader in helping to facilitate the reunification of Germany. Ireland and Haughey performed the role well, though it did stretch the resources of the civil service.[37] He worked extremely hard at every aspect of the presidency, and was well prepared for each meeting. His whole approach was about 'maintaining goodwill' for Ireland.[38] Supporting German reunification was easy for Haughey because it rhymed with the idea of Irish reunification. Helmut Kohl later thanked Haughey for his support at the time, but Haughey was by no means crucial. Kohl's power lay in his seniority within the European Community and because his support was needed for the project most desired by the French – economic and monetary union.[39] Haughey readily supported the closer political integration with Europe, despite a loss of sovereignty.

After the success of the EC presidency domestic troubles returned. There had not been a presidential election since 1973. Paddy Hillery had taken on the job without election, in part to restore some stability to the office. Well before his second term was up in late 1990, the political mood had changed and party fragmentation meant there would be a contest. At the suggestion of Ray Burke and PJ Mara, Haughey considered Brian Lenihan for the party's candidate for the presidency, an election that was to take place on 7 November 1990.

As a well-known senior statesman and popular across the political divide he seemed an obvious choice, and Fianna Fáil candidates had won every presidential election. But Lenihan was struggling with a severe illness; he had had a liver transplant in the US, and he was still on heavy medication. And it would mean a by-election in a constituency the party might lose. An alternative was to run John Wilson, who would have been as likely to get the Fianna Fáil core vote out and in a less risky constituency. Haughey decided that Lenihan could do better. Indeed, a year out from the election there was the sense that 'no one can beat Brian to the Park.'[40] Opinion polling confirmed this: in the summer of 1990 Lenihan was on 45 per cent, 20 points ahead of the nearest candidate.[41] Still Fianna Fáil allowed the parliamentary party to have a contest between Wilson and Lenihan, one that Haughey knew Lenihan would win with his imprimatur. But while Fianna Fáil could choose Lenihan, Garret FitzGerald had other ideas about enabling his election.

Garret FitzGerald remained active in the party within Dublin South-East. He ran again for the Dáil in 1989, delivering a remarkable result by winning two out of the four seats for Fine Gael on just 28 per cent of the vote. He was also central to the choice of his replacement as a constituency TD, Frances Fitzgerald (no relation), who was in the social democratic forum of Fine Gael and the chair of the Council for the Status of Women. Garret was determined that a social liberal would take the seat. It was a continuation of his belief from the 1960s that he could change the party from a conservative position to liberal social democracy.

In early 1990 Alan Dukes was looking for a candidate for the presidency. Fine Gael had never held the office, and it would be a major fillip for the party if it could. There was one obvious candidate – Garret FitzGerald. As someone who was widely respected and liked, FitzGerald had the qualities and a good chance to become president, thereby beating Fianna Fáil. But FitzGerald ruled out running early and frequently, pointing out that he would not be content to make anodyne statements from the Áras. Garret was too combative for such a role.

Dukes had earlier promised 'a candidate of vigour and stature', which most of the party's grassroots assumed meant FitzGerald.[42] There was an assumption that he would relent. As late as April 1990 Alan Dukes still harboured hopes that FitzGerald could be convinced to run. And if not Garret the Fine Gael grandee, Peter Barry might suit the role. Barry wanted FitzGerald to do it, and had no interest in the role for himself. Dukes, whose leadership was already under pressure, was getting desperate.

At the end of April 1990 Labour formally selected Mary Robinson as its candidate. When she launched her campaign in May a Robinson victory seemed unlikely. She was not well known outside political circles, and not very popular within those circles, even in what had been her party, Labour, from which she had resigned in opposition to the Anglo-Irish Agreement. However, Mary Robinson seemed to embody the changing times and social mores. As well as being a woman, she had been an activist lawyer for decades, championing socially progressive issues. Robinson promised a new vision for the presidency and quickly emerged as a threat to Lenihan's (and Haughey's) presidential ambitions. FitzGerald, who was an admirer of Robinson, suggested Austin Currie, a relatively unknown politician who had come down from Northern Ireland, where he had been a founder of the nationalist SDLP, to be elected to the Dáil in 1989. Currie was not ideal, and he knew that he might not have the full support of even his own party, but Dukes had run out of options.

Lenihan's problems lay elsewhere, however. Jim Duffy, a former Fine Gael activist and a UCD academic historian, was writing his thesis on the history of the Irish presidency. In particular he had worked on the 1982 period where Lenihan, among others, were trying to dissuade Hillery from dissolving the Dáil in order to allow Haughey a chance to form a government. Garret FitzGerald took an interest in Duffy's work and had earlier spoken to him about it. FitzGerald tried at times during the campaign to raise the issue of the 1982 phone calls to the Áras, but the media did not take an interest. There is disagreement as to whether FitzGerald actually hatched a plot to entrap Lenihan, but a series of events suggests, if not a conspiracy, there was at least some co-ordination within Fine Gael. Brian Murphy, a Young Fine Gael activist and much later an adviser to Leo Varadkar, was to ask a question on *Questions and Answers*, a flagship RTÉ current affairs programme, when Lenihan was on the panel. FitzGerald was offered as a last-minute guest, to replace the Fine Gael TD, Jim Mitchell, having returned from a trip to Italy for the purpose of the show on 22 October 1990, just two weeks from polling day.

FitzGerald was determined to raise the events of the night of his government's collapse in January 1982. Lenihan had told Duffy about his persistent attempts to contact President Hillery in Áras an Uachtaráin in 1982 to persuade him not to dissolve the Dáil. There was nothing legally or politically wrong with this, but Hillery thought the pressure he was put under was untoward.

On *Questions and Answers*, the presenter, John Bowman, asked FitzGerald a question about the role of the president. FitzGerald gave a typically lengthy answer, referring to the series of phone calls made to President Hillery on the night of 27 January 1982, the day FitzGerald's first government collapsed. Lenihan got involved, and said 'That's fictional, Garret.'

'It's not fictional, excuse me. I was in Áras an Uachtaráin when those phone calls came through and I know how many there were.'

Murphy's question related to this and so Bowman then pointed to Brian Murphy, 'the man in the second row'. He asked a pointed question.

'Mr Lenihan has said here this evening that we don't want a president meddling in party politics, but I want to ask Mr Lenihan directly about the events of 27 January 1982. He commented on it, but I want a straight answer. Did he make a phone call or phone calls to Áras an Uachtaráin in that period when Taoiseach Garret FitzGerald was seeking a dissolution of the Dáil?'

'No, I didn't at all. That never happened. I want to assure you that never happened.'[43]

FitzGerald had expected that Lenihan would be forced to admit the truth and be forced into an embarrassing climbdown. He was astounded by what appeared a barefaced lie.

Duffy was later in a phone box talking to Dick Walsh, the political editor of the *Irish Times*, about an article Duffy had written for the paper on the presidency when Walsh told him what Lenihan had said on *Questions and Answers*. Duffy was surprised and blurted out, 'That's not what he told me!' Duffy played the tape for the paper to show what Lenihan had said. The Fianna Fáil team was initially unconcerned. Lenihan doubled down on his position over the next few days.

Duffy was then put under pressure to release the tapes. On 24 October an *Irish Times* article said that it had seen evidence that Lenihan had contacted the president that night in 1982. Lenihan still denied it. Duffy's name was now in the public domain and he was put under intense pressure to release the recording publicly, which he initially resisted, but eventually succumbed. The following day those tapes were played. The Lenihan campaign knew it was a disaster, but Lenihan was oblivious. After talking to Haughey, Lenihan tried to involve President Hillery, which was either very naive or very smart. It would look as though Lenihan felt he had nothing to hide, but anyone would have known that Hillery was not going to get involved in the election campaign. Lenihan then went to RTÉ and on live TV claimed that he was on heavy medication for liver treatment when he spoke to Duffy, but that – and now he turned to face the camera – his 'mature recollection' was that he had not contacted the Áras. He would seek to contact President Hillery to confirm this. It was devastating. No one believed him.[44] 'Mature recollection' became a synonym for lying. Fine Gael immediately put down a motion of no confidence in the government to put pressure on the PDs.

The PDs had foolishly cast themselves, or allowed themselves to be cast, in the role of the watchdogs of Fianna Fáil, in part to assuage fears within the party that it would be just there to prop up Haughey. This naturally caused animosity in Fianna Fáil, and created expectations of the PDs that the party should not have always been so willing to fulfil. The PDs said that Lenihan's position caused difficulties for the party. There was a breakdown in communications; they had expected that Lenihan would just admit that he was mistaken and that he had tried to contact the president. It was a well-known story in political circles that Lenihan had been one of those who had tried to contact Hillery, and Lenihan had never before contested it. So when Lenihan continued to deny what everyone else could hear him saying on tape, it became a coalition issue.

It was a mistake of the PDs to get involved, but once they had, the PDs were now in a position where they were threatening to bring down the government if Lenihan did not resign. Haughey decided that Lenihan would have to go. But no one in Fianna Fáil expected that he could do this to his oldest political friend. Haughey publicly stated that he would not seek Lenihan's resignation, but privately he was putting pressure on Lenihan to resign. Lenihan refused, and then refused even to take a call from Haughey.[45] His subsequent sacking was at times farcical (including having a helicopter piloted by Haughey's son hovering over a house in Athlone where Lenihan was staying in an attempt to get a message to him to resign), but ultimately unseemly.

On 31 October 1990 Haughey formally wrote to Lenihan asking him to resign. Lenihan refused, and Haughey then wrote to President Hillery to ask him to dismiss Lenihan. Lenihan's campaign hoped that his sacking would yield him a sympathy vote. If it did, it was not enough. Comments by Pádraig Flynn about Mary Robinson probably evaporated some of that sympathy. He told a radio programme on 3 November that Mary Robinson 'has new clothes, a new look and new hairdo, and she has a new interest in family, being a mother and all that kind of thing. But none of us, none of us who remember Mary Robinson very well in previous incarnations ever heard her claiming to be the great ... [interruptions] Wait a moment. Mary Robinson reconstructs herself to fit the fashion of the time.'[46] The reaction to his comments was immediate as it seemed to reflect a sexism many thought endemic in Irish politics.

When voting took place Lenihan was ahead on first preference votes, but he lost to Robinson on the second count – Austin Currie's transfers – leaving him out of a job, and bitterness within the government. The presidency had been Fianna Fáil's. Now, the year after conceding on its 'core value' of one-party government, the party had lost another mainstay. Haughey's willingness to sack his oldest political friend cast off any illusions of remaining personal loyalties, though remarkably Haughey and Lenihan did not fall out over it. There was greater hostility within Fianna Fáil towards the PDs. This was one of the most prominent of demands that Haughey was forced to concede to the PDs, but the list was getting longer, including an agreement to set up a tribunal of investigation into practices in the beef industry. Haughey's list of loyalists was getting shorter.

Though she had been in Leinster House for twenty years, Mary Robinson had very few friends there. She was never very clubbable. Robinson was adept at political symbolism however, and became very popular, not least internationally. She received many invitations to speak at events and to the press. Her popularity irritated Haughey. Mara started to brief against her.[47] When Robinson received an invitation to give the BBC's Dimbleby Lecture in London, the government refused her permission to do so on the basis that it was 'not appropriate'. Normally the government would be merely asked to approve a script. Haughey approached Robinson with an interpretation of the constitution that would prevent Robinson from speaking to the press, which she interpreted as an attempt to 'muzzle' her.[48]

Robinson's victory showed that Haughey was somewhat out of step with emerging attitudes on social issues in Ireland. He remained very slow to liberalise laws on contraception and divorce, possibly for short-term political gain, but maybe also because he and his party were more conservative than the country on these attitudes.

✢ ✢ ✢

In the autumn of 1990 one government colleague said to Haughey that it was rare that a Taoiseach could choose his own time of leaving, and suggested he might think of going out on a high. Haughey laughed, responding, 'not in a million years'.[49] In the summer of 1991 he privately told a departing UK ambassador that when the time came he planned to try one last time for an overall majority.[50] But he must have known the end was nigh. If one minister was willing to say it to his face, many more must have been thinking it. They were. Many of his parliamentary party were unhappy at his judgement. The 1989 election decision, the coalition and the Lenihan sacking were too much for many on his backbenchers.

At the 1990 Árd Fheis – even before the Lenihan sacking – Haughey had failed to excite the crowd.[51] Haughey was getting older, more visibly frail and he was losing more work time to illness. When Haughey heard a rumour that Lenihan might be nominated for the presidency of Fianna Fáil (technically separate to but in practice always held by the party leader) at the 1991 Árd Fheis, he sent for Lenihan's constituency colleague, Liam Lawlor, to get him to talk Lenihan out of it. Lawlor refused, saying, 'I know nothing about it and I owe you nothing. I'll be here when you're gone.'[52] Fianna Fáilers were starting to look to life after Haughey. It would be his own side, not FitzGerald, that would deliver the final blow.

At the 1991 Árd Fheis Haughey was introduced by Máire Geoghegan-Quinn. She had come to the view that there needed to be a change at the top and so struggled with her warm-up speech. In the end she came up with a form of words that praised Haughey but seemed to look beyond him: 'There will never be a time like it again: never such excitement, never such achievement, never such heartache, never such happiness, as the time they will talk of as the Haughey era,' she roared. As she gave her speech, she felt his eyes burning into her. Haughey could see that she was talking about him as a historical figure.

Haughey had no intention of giving up without a fight. He relied on his old *modus operandi* within the parliamentary party. PJ Mara acted as his eyes and ears. Mara would make comments about people being 'out of sorts' or having 'trouble with the wife'. Albert Reynolds alleged that a white van was seen observing his apartment in what was thought an attempt to intimidate him.[53] Even if it were true, it was too late.

A series of scandals, some involving Haughey, others not, added to the whiff of corruption. The chief executive of Greencore, the recently privatised Irish Sugar Company, was forced to resign when it was revealed he had benefited from an unusual share buyback scheme. The chairman of Greencore was Bernie Cahill, a close associate and friend of Haughey, and the chairman of Haughey's son Conor's company Feltrim Mining. This placed Haughey close to a scandal that had nothing to do with him. When Haughey sought an expression of confidence in Cahill in a government statement, his cabinet refused.[54]

Another affair emerged, this time over the purchase of land by Telecom Éireann for IR£9.4m (€23.5 million). The land was initially passed through a property company, UPH, established by Dermot Desmond, which profited significantly in the transaction. UPH was part-owned by Michael Smurfit, a wealthy friend of Haughey's who was the chairman of Telecom Éireann. Haughey's response was uncharacteristically ham-fisted. On RTÉ Radio's *This Week* programme he suggested that Smurfit and Séamus Paircéir – who also had an interest in UPH and was chair of another state company – should 'step aside'. They had not been told of this in advance, and Paircéir, who had done nothing wrong, immediately resigned in anger. Smurfit did so two days later. It eventually transpired that Dermot Desmond was the main beneficiary of the property deal.[55] Other controversies that had been simmering came into focus, including the sale of Carysfort College to University College Dublin for almost IR£10m (€26 million). A friend of Haughey's made a profit of over IR£1.5m (€3.9 million) on the deal. Another involved Dermot Desmond's NCB stockbrokers sending confidential information about a competitor to Ciarán Haughey's Celtic Helicopters. It looked to many observers that there was a 'golden circle' in Irish business that Haughey was facilitating.

In the same interview as his reaction to the Telecom controversy, Haughey said, 'Some of these Chinese leaders stay on until 80 or 90 but I think that is probably a bit long. When the time comes I will know whether to stay or go.'[56] Ahern thinks that Haughey had made his mind up to retire in the spring of 1992.[57] Haughey was in some pain in the late 1980s and early 1990s from kidney stones, and had visibly lost strength. Haughey's comment was meant as a joke, but Fianna Fáil TDs did not find it funny. The accumulation of scandals was too much for some.

Four backbench Fianna Fáil TDs – Noel Dempsey, Liam Fitzgerald, M.J. Nolan and Seán Power – happened to be away together on a golf trip around this time. They knew each other well but they were still afraid of talking openly to each other about their doubts about Haughey. Dempsey brought up the Carysfort issue, and Paircéir's effective dismissal, and they agreed that they should issue a statement.[58] The statement contrasted Haughey's treatment of Cahill and Paircéir. Haughey reacted by bringing forward a party meeting, and successfully defused the situation, suggesting his departure would not be far off.[59] The controversies refused to go away; Dick Spring suggested that Haughey would not act against Bernie Cahill because Haughey had made representations to Cahill about getting Desmond's company and his friend's legal practice to act in the privatisation.[60] Haughey's denials – 'no such meeting ever took place' – appeared evasive.[61]

A Fianna Fáil motion of no confidence followed in early November 1991, which Pádraig Flynn, Albert Reynolds and three junior ministers indicated they would support. They were sacked, and Haughey easily won the vote, 55 to 22. It was remarkable how he was still able to hold sway. Gerry Collins was privately scathing of Haughey but went on RTÉ News to plaintively appeal to Reynolds not to 'burst the party open'. In replacing the ministers, Haughey had demonstrated his own political impotence. In a more wide-ranging reshuffle than he had ever done, Haughey proposed Jim McDaid as Minister for Defence. McDaid had been photographed a year earlier smiling when an attempt to extradite an escaped IRA member convicted of attempted murder was rejected by the Supreme Court.

McDaid was the man's local TD and no one suspected him of having IRA sympathies. Des O'Malley said to Haughey that his appointment to Defence was inappropriate. McDaid agreed to withdraw his name, but this time it was Haughey who took the blame, not the PDs. It mirrored Haughey's inability to choose his own ministers for Defence and Justice in his first government.

The final blow came when Seán Doherty went on an RTÉ light entertainment show, *Nighthawks*. On the show Doherty was asked about the phone-tapping scandal from almost ten years earlier. Doherty was unapologetic, and said he had a job to do, but that he 'was let down by the fact that people knew what I was doing'.[62] Haughey had previously denied any knowledge of the phone tapping. The show was pre-recorded, and Doherty had to nudge the interviewer, Shay Healy, that he had said something of significance. The presenter then played it to a political journalist, Bruce Arnold, one of the victims of the tapping, who confirmed it was a scoop. The press were tipped off. When the programme was broadcast on 15 January 1992 Haughey immediately denied any knowledge of the tapping. Doherty, who was still devoted to Haughey and harboured hopes of returning to the Dáil, now regretted saying anything. He went to Carr Communications, a firm well used to giving media training to politicians. After some prevaricating Doherty decided to make a statement.[63] On 21 January Doherty made a statement that began: 'I am confirming tonight that the Taoiseach, Mr Haughey, was fully aware in 1982 that two journalists' phones were being tapped, and that he at no stage expressed any reservations about this action.' He went on to detail how Haughey had asked Doherty to take the blame for something Haughey had in fact ordered, all done 'in loyalty to the leader'.[64]

Haughey initially came out fighting, questioning Doherty's reliability as a witness.[65] O'Malley claimed to be 'devastated' by the Doherty statement, though Doherty was only confirming what most had already known, or at least assumed to be the case. This was not the problem; it was that governing was becoming increasingly difficult. The imaginative leader and effective administrator was by now just fire-fighting. O'Malley told Haughey, 'This can't go on.' O'Malley's and Bertie Ahern's impression of Haughey was that 'all the fight had gone out of him.' Haughey told Ahern, 'I've had my nine lives.'[66] Haughey announced his intention to resign on 30 January and formally resigned the office of Taoiseach on 11 February 1992.

The Haughey–FitzGerald era was over. Their impact would last longer, though.

15.

LONG SHADOWS

From the early 1990s Ireland underwent a remarkable transformation. The economy grew at breakneck speed, with employment almost doubling in 15 years.[1] What had been a country of emigration became one of immigration. The physical appearance of Ireland too changed radically, as its roads infrastructure was improved, urban retail areas became more internationalised and parts of Dublin city saw the growth of urban quarters that looked much wealthier, more cosmopolitan, more European. The people on the streets were different too; where it was once unusual to see anyone who was not white Irish, the population became much more diverse. Ireland became less Catholic, as Mass attendance, which had still been at near universal levels in the early 1980s, fell markedly from the early 1990s. This was accompanied by equally remarkable changes in social attitudes, with a significant liberalisation of views on issues such as marriage, homosexuality and abortion. Ireland's election of Mary Robinson as president in 1990 was unusual not just for her sex but also her more liberal attitudes on these issues and engagement with topics that Ireland had tended to ignore.

One of the issues that Irish politics had often overlooked in practical terms was Northern Ireland. Despite the rhetoric about reunification of the island, little was ever done. This changed in the 1980s, culminating in the Belfast or Good Friday Agreement signed in 1998, which saw the formation of a newly devolved assembly in Belfast and later the formation of a government that included the DUP's Rev. Ian Paisley sharing power with Martin McGuiness, formerly a senior commander in the Provisional IRA. It represented a partial resolution of the conflict in Northern Ireland, which had claimed the lives of over three and a half thousand people.

Mary McAleese, Ireland's second woman president, and the first from Northern Ireland, said in 2003, 'if the men and women of Ireland's past could choose a time to live, there would be a long queue for this one. It is far from perfect but it is as good as it has ever been.'[2] This was not just a politician selling her country; several measures, for example *The Economist*'s 'quality of life' index, put Ireland at or near the top of places to live.

It is easy to put these changes down to structural factors over which politicians had limited control – the EU single market, increased productivity, increased external demand through globalisation and low and stable interest rates. Some economists see it as Ireland just catching up, but it does not explain why Ireland caught up from the 1990s and not earlier or later.[3] Some historians tend to see Ireland's changing fortunes as a function of luck, but many see Ireland's earlier poverty as a result of pathologies in the political class and the political system.[4] For many historians, when things go right, it was bound to happen; when things go wrong, it's the fault of bad people. But politicians took many of the decisions that enabled what the prominent historian Roy Foster describes as 'luck'. Ireland's decision to join the EEC, to open its economy, to invest in education were not inevitable decisions. They were taken by politicians with a vision for the country. They had long-term effects that would help those leaders in the 1980s. During the Haughey–FitzGerald years there were some bad decisions and non-decisions that postponed Ireland's growth. But there were also positive political decisions taken and enabled by both Haughey and FitzGerald that were important causal factors in the ensuing economic miracle. Without control of the public finances, a stable industrial relations regime and the decision to target foreign direct investment in new technologies, those other positive factors in Ireland's favour would not have been sufficient to see an Irish miracle. The same can be said of Northern Ireland. Without the normalisation of relations with Britain that the Anglo-Irish Agreement enabled and the risky move to engage with Sinn Féin, albeit covertly, when the 'responsible' thing to do was to eschew the overtures from the violent nationalist movement, the peace process could not have made the advances it did. On social issues FitzGerald at least pushed for the secularisation of the state, though Haughey probably acted as a brake on what FitzGerald could do.

※ ※ ※

To claim that the Haughey–FitzGerald axis would deliver some sort of golden age for Ireland did not seem likely in the immediate aftermath of each man's retirement. Haughey's initial retirement would be dignified. His famous speech, quoting Othello, of having done the state some service was well received and even his harshest critics had to concede that Haughey was an exceptional politician, who had indeed done the state some service. He withdrew to his home, Abbeville, and continued to partake in a small number of public functions, but he maintained a dignified silence even if privately he was scathing of the performance of his successors. He would not get into public debates. That was the plan, and to some extent that was how he behaved.

One problem for him was that his friend Ben Dunne would have a panic attack caused by drink, drugs and stress in a hotel suite in Florida nine days after Haughey retired. Dunne was arrested and found with enough cocaine to be charged with drug trafficking. It started a legal dispute within the Dunne family trust, during which Dunne revealed that he had paid over IR£1m (€3.5 million in 2023) to Haughey. When confronted with this, Haughey initially said that Dunne was unstable and not to be believed. The Dunne dispute revealed other payments to politicians and in 1997 the McCracken Tribunal was set up to investigate these payments. It reported very quickly and found that Haughey's finances were unorthodox, that he engaged in tax evasion, that his evidence was not credible and that he had obstructed the work of the Tribunal. It said that the receipt of payments was unacceptable for a senior politician because it left them open to charges of corruption, though it could find no link between Dunne's payments and any action by Haughey to benefit Dunne.[5]

The Moriarty Tribunal was established in 1997 to expand on the details of McCracken. It meant that Haughey had to endure more investigations into his financial affairs. He was the subject of a criminal investigation for obstructing the McCracken Tribunal, though the trial did not proceed because it was deemed he could not get a fair trial because of comments made by the then Tánaiste, Mary Harney.[6] Around this time he ended his relationship with Terry Keane, to which she responded by making details of their love affair public on *The Late Late Show*. There was genuine shock among some of the Irish public who had either never heard the rumours of his affair or decided that they were an attempt to slander Haughey.[7]

The Moriarty Tribunal evidence provided a drip feed of details about Haughey's private financial affairs to the public. Much of the coverage had the tone of celebrity gossip, as Ireland was given a glimpse into the lifestyles of the rich and famous. All along Haughey tried to obstruct the Tribunal's inquiries. He had to give evidence even when he was quite ill, and this may have made his final years quite melancholy.[8] The Tribunal reported in December 2006, a few months after Haughey's death on 13 June, but already the public had heard most of the allegations.

The Moriarty Tribunal report found that Haughey's lifestyle had been paid for through a bill-paying service operated by Haughey's accountant, Des Traynor. It rejected Haughey's claims that he had left all his financial affairs to Des Traynor and was unaware of how his lifestyle was being financed. He tried to blame others, and at no time took responsibility for his actions. It found that between 1979 and 1996 Haughey received over IR£9 million (about €27 million in 2023) from wealthy donors, from his party and from other sources. Those sources included the Fianna Fáil party's leader's allowance and a fund set up to pay for Brian Lenihan's medical treatment. Many of the business people who donated to Haughey were under the impression they were donating to Fianna Fáil, not supporting the party leader's lifestyle.⁹ Most payments 'were made in forms that were secretive, opaque and frequently involved offshore vehicles'.[10]

Haughey's defence, put out by friends, was that it was common for politicians to rely on personal donations, and they pointed to a number of historical figures such as Daniel O'Connell and Winston Churchill. Furthermore, Moriarty could not find any smoking guns. There were no clear links between payments and corruption. Indeed, none of the many investigations into Haughey's finances found clear links between Haughey the public figure's public actions and Haughey's private finances. The fact that many of his friends continued to finance him after his retirement suggests that they were not just in it for what Haughey could do for them. However, Moriarty did find that Haughey would intervene in ministerial decisions, often benefiting donors, for instance by granting passports.[11] He used his financial resources for political power, sometimes just to help out a constituent, sometimes to keep a TD from going bankrupt and so saving his government. His evasion of tax was clearly indefensible, but it was something his old friend Harry Boland noticed early on; when Haughey saw how much tax he had paid one year, he instructed Boland to 'get it back'.[12] In private, as in public, Haughey was impatient with rules and bureaucracy, which he felt should not apply to him.

For some supporters Haughey's private finances are just that – private. But his private finances had an impact on public life, and, again, one that went well beyond his time in office. The 'low standards in high places' that George Colley had referred to in the late 1960s continued after his departure. Even if there was not always overt corruption – though in the links between politics and the property industry there frequently was overt corruption – Haughey's behaviour normalised financial relationships between business and politics that were at the very least unhealthy for a democracy. Haughey was not just doing what everyone else was doing. His activities were anathema to the generation older than him in Fianna Fáil, as it was to many in his own generation, such as Colley. Haughey used his power to enhance his own financial position. Two days after becoming Taoiseach Haughey was canvassing property developers for help to clear a debt with AIB.[13] Michael Smurfit noted that money and power were 'very much intermingled' in Ireland in these years, and he later found that 'the culture has changed. The country has matured. It has been clearly decided that this form of crony capitalism doesn't work.'[14] Haughey, more than anyone else, normalised that crony capitalism. His acolytes who were later found to have received corrupt payments, people such as Ray Burke and Frank Dunlop. Other people who accepted money in questionable circumstances, such as Pádraig Flynn and Bertie Ahern, were only doing what they saw the Boss do. Haughey's cosiness with business was not all an altruistic attempt to encourage business in Ireland. He was skimming off the top.

The judgement of Haughey as a political leader in modern Ireland must be heavily influenced by those revelations that came after his retirement. His behaviour gave credence to a view that Ireland was somehow exceptionally corrupt. Though there is no evidence for Irish exceptionalism – except that the Irish state might in fact be unusually low in corruption – it became a common trope used to mobilise a certain anti-politics sentiment in the 2000s.[15]

Many have speculated about some deep personal insecurity that drove Haughey to accrue wealth and create the image of a lord of the manor. But it seems more likely that he was a *bon vivant* for whom money simply made it much easier to live life to the full.[16] His money and affairs show a man who simply enjoyed himself.

Haughey's willingness to do the politically expedient thing exposes a deep hypocrisy and base political calculus. Haughey was publicly conservative on social issues, despite his own 'continental' attitudes to marriage and fidelity. He possibly felt that his genius should free him from the social mores and financial woes of ordinary people. This caused Fianna Fáil to be a conservative party when as recently as the 1970s, and certainly in the 1960s, it had been seen as a reforming party. Perhaps Haughey was just pushing against FitzGerald's attempt to lead a liberal crusade.

Haughey's charisma – and he was possibly unique in that period in possessing a genuine charisma – meant that those around him would bend and break rules to please him. One source close to Seán Doherty observed, 'What tortured Doherty most was the prospect of being cut off from Haughey ... [Haughey] subsumed you into his personality and seldom needed, thereafter, to give specific instructions – you developed a "What would Charlie want done now?" reflex and acted upon it.'[17]

His ability to understand power politics was remarkable. He was able to outplay his opponents even when it appeared his career was over. He seemed to have an innate understanding of both the institutional and psychological bases for power. But he assumed power was a zero-sum game. He could not collaborate unless he was the top man. Haughey was frustratingly unwilling to accept honest dissent and said that 'loyalty' was the most important quality in a friend.[18] That loyalty was one-way, however, born of self-interest and a vanity that he was always right. Terry Keane observed that 'Charlie always had the uncomplicated belief that the greater good was served by him getting what he wanted.'[19]

While he was genius at power politics, tactically outplaying rivals, he could not build coalitions of equals or almost equals. If people did not display unconditional loyalty, they were seen as a threat that had to be destroyed. This caused him to make strategic errors, such as the expulsion of Des O'Malley. O'Malley was an irritant for Haughey, an independent-minded minister, but O'Malley was a more capable minister than he was a capable challenger. O'Malley or even Colley were only real threats to Haughey's leadership because Haughey's behaviour made them mistrust him. They were proved right to mistrust him. His attachment to money prevented him from being what he could have been, and wanted to be – another Seán Lemass.

✻ ✻ ✻

On retirement FitzGerald was able to devote more time to the care of his wife, Joan, who had been increasingly disabled by arthritis during his premiership. FitzGerald borrowed, invested and lost a lot of money in an aircraft leasing company, Guinness Peat Aviation, of which he was a director, before its collapse. He got a loan write-off worth about IR£200,000 (€500,000 in 2023). FitzGerald remained active in public life, particularly through a column in the *Irish Times* and in debates on the European Union, to which he remained a committed advocate. Joan FitzGerald died in 1999, and in his later years he moved into a modest house with his daughter. FitzGerald died in May 2011, aged 85. His death precipitated an outpouring of praise, and for many correspondents to the paper he wrote for FitzGerald was Ireland's greatest Taoiseach.

It is ironic that FitzGerald, who was no natural campaigner, was better at achieving power than using it. In an interview for his eightieth birthday FitzGerald almost seemed wistful when considering his terms as Taoiseach. He could point to the Anglo-Irish Agreement, but beyond that there was little else. He hoped his failed attempts at the divorce referendum had prepared the ground for future change.[20] For Michael Noonan, 'Garret changed how we thought about the North, divorce, Europe, those kinds of issues.'[21] This view is widely shared. On Northern Ireland and Europe, his views were already mainstream. And he was not pushing divorce on a reluctant Irish people; there had been a campaign on divorce for many years and polls showed that Irish people were prepared to vote for it. It was his government's ill-preparedness, not the Irish people's, that led to its defeat.

One critical commentator at the time he left office went much further in his criticism. Colm Tóibín wrote, 'Garret FitzGerald contributed nothing to Irish society since he became leader of Fine Gael ten years ago ... [he subsumed] all serious policy commitment into marketing and manipulation.'[22] That was an unfairly harsh assessment, possibly motivated by disappointment that FitzGerald failed to live up to his promise. FitzGerald governed in difficult times, inheriting rather than creating a crisis, but his circumstances were not uniformly negative. When coming to office he had a fairly united party behind him, goodwill from the public, a favourable media –

parts of which were obsequious – and, in Haughey, an opponent who suited FitzGerald's image of honesty. Part of his problem was that he was instinctively a technocrat who was convinced that solutions could be found by just getting smart people to debate enough. By the end they had run out of ideas and could not contemplate action.

Ministers in FitzGerald's governments were under enormous strain. The Labour ministers were certainly not alone in being in a 'state of physical and mental exhaustion ... on the point of collapse from tiredness'.[23] FitzGerald was able to go home for lunch most days. He could take solace in European summits, which were almost a retreat for him. But he added to his cabinet's exhaustion. His mismanagement of their time exhausted their energy levels. His unwillingness or inability to manage disagreements in cabinet made the experience worse. He bombarded them with notes and queries, and rarely just let them get on with their job. Quite early on in his government ministers were considering whether it would be better if he went.[24] It was probably only personal respect and the uncertainty of who might succeed him that prevented an active push to remove him. While he acted in the national interest, it did not seem to do the nation much good.

FitzGerald's name became a byword for failure. He failed to deal with the worsening public finances; Ireland continued to shed jobs and people through emigration. His major initiatives in social reform failed to come to fruition, and by mismanaging a referendum on abortion he caused significant suffering and more political upheaval. He would leave his party in a period of decline. Leo Varadkar, later to become Taoiseach himself, invoked FitzGerald to excoriate Brian Cowen for his performance in the office: 'The Taoiseach is no Seán Lemass, Jack Lynch or John Bruton. He is a Garret FitzGerald.'[25] FitzGerald and his governments would fail to take the sort of measures that would address the country's woeful economic performance, which were allowed to drift.

While it is true that FitzGerald's governments failed to deal with the economic crises, by 1987 many economic indicators, apart from unemployment, were already going in the right direction. John Bruton thought the government at least prevented worse from happening: 'We stopped Ireland from going down the plughole. We were heading for Argentine status.'[26] FitzGerald also invokes fierce loyalty among people who saw him as maintaining decency in Irish politics at a time when it came under strain.

In reforming Fine Gael, achieving office, surviving those three elections and holding his government together in difficult circumstances, FitzGerald proved his former cabinet colleague Conor Cruise O'Brien right: 'There is steel under all that pretty wool.'[27] When he chose Fine Gael in the early 1960s it was not the party he wanted it to be, but by the time he retired Fine Gael was 'a somewhat different party, performing a somewhat different role than what it was when I took over'.[28] He was fearless, and he ran a government that was free from scandal. He professionalised his party, and offered a clear alternative to Fianna Fáil, as a more modern, progressive party. Coming after the Haughey GUBU government this was welcome, but it was not enough. The assessment of him as an honest and decent Taoiseach who ran a scandal-free government sets the purpose of government a little too low.

FitzGerald was initially too ambitious, and guilty of overreach. He set himself too great a challenge in his constitutional crusade. This led to failure, which meant he did not enjoy being Taoiseach, but 'I felt there was a job to do and it was better that I should be there to do it than not ... The big thing was "don't leave Haughey in with an overall majority".'[29] His career would be guided by his opposition to his great rival, Charles J. Haughey. FitzGerald was obsessed with Haughey, convinced that Haughey was such a danger to Irish society that he must be kept out of office at any price. Though FitzGerald came to politics full of self-confidence and full of ideas, he became so fearful of a Haughey government that it made his own approach to governing uncharacteristically fitful and cautious. It was his opponent who defined FitzGerald. He ran his government to try to influence or prevent a Haughey one, not for a distinct FitzGerald agenda. One adviser thought FitzGerald was 'psyched out by Haughey', always left guessing what Haughey would do.[30] Haughey was the star around which FitzGerald rotated. This was FitzGerald's problem. He became an anti-Haughey Taoiseach, who drifted on in office just to keep Haughey out.

There is no shame in that. Any leader has to deal with the constraints facing them. The least successful politicians do not understand that and end up overreaching and achieving nothing. Haughey was one such constraint he faced, and FitzGerald had to adapt to manage him. FitzGerald was a success in that. If most political leaders try to accrete power, FitzGerald gave power away. His desire to do one thing on Northern Ireland and to corral Haughey meant he was constrained in exercising power himself beyond Northern Ireland. The Anglo-Irish Agreement was the apogee of FitzGerald's achievements. This was the culmination of a lifetime of FitzGerald's moving Irish nationalism on from its old irredentist nature. But in achieving the Anglo-Irish Agreement FitzGerald had excluded the one group, unionists, he had hoped to draw in. By then, as he told the British, his greater desire was the defeat and isolation of Sinn Féin and the Provisional IRA, and to prevent the subversion of the state.[31] But FitzGerald probably got as far as was likely possible at the time on Northern Ireland. And FitzGerald successfully corralled Haughey into doing the right thing. Haughey may have always wanted to, but he always struggled with the need to be popular and his desire to deliver the overall majority that eluded him right to the end.

More so than any other Taoiseach, Haughey's behaviour in politics would suggest that he was more ruthless than sentimental. For one senior civil servant, Paddy Teahon:

Charlie Haughey operated a good deal of the time by fear . . . It was extraordinary. There was just this aura about him. I remember walking down the corridor of government buildings one day, feeling a slight unease, you know that feeling when the hair is standing up on your neck? I thought "that's odd". And when I spun around, there he was, ten yards behind me.[32]

But the devotion he inspired cannot have been based on threats alone. Some could see that a move of Haughey's hand would move others into action. The basis of his power was obviously in part personal – if Haughey changed his mind, the party's and government's policy was changed – but it also lay in institutions that the office of Taoiseach bears; Haughey could sack a minister, and that was something he acknowledged as important, even if he did not have to use it that often.[33] He acted always to maintain control the institutions of the party which would allow him to rid himself of rivals. If FitzGerald achieved what he could by giving away power, Haughey achieved power through attrition.

His power also came from his political skill. He was methodical, efficient and sharp, with an exceptional work rate. Bertie Ahern noted his intuitive intelligence that allowed him to find a flaw in legislation: 'Haughey will smell something in a Bill and say that's the line to take ... He'll say, "Go for that."'[34] More than most, Haughey could compartmentalise the different aspects of his life. Stresses in one area did not cloud his thinking in others. He could switch on the charm when he needed to, as Bertie Ahern recalled: 'I might see him beforehand when he was furious about something or other. Then he would go into those big meetings smiling. He knew how to create a good atmosphere.'[35] When in January 1983 his career seemed to be caving in around him, he was able to regroup and successfully fight back against what seemed to be overwhelming odds.

If Haughey was immensely successful politically, his electoral return for his party is more questionable. Personally he found it easy to get elected, but Haughey never risked not topping the poll to get an extra Fianna Fáil seat in his own constituency. He failed to get an electoral majority, and he cannot be said to have put in place a clear strategy to deliver one in the way FitzGerald did. In his defence, if we observe a decline in the Fianna Fáil vote in the 1980s, it was coming off a historic high and the real fall in Fianna Fáil support came after he left office. Also, Ireland was undergoing significant social changes that unmoored voters from their historic party attachments.[36] Haughey was facing a resurgent Fine Gael, though some of that resurgence might have been due to an antipathy to Haughey among many in the country. Indeed it was Fianna Fáil's inability to pick up transfers, which might reflect the polarising effect of Haughey, that denied the party an overall majority in 1987.[37]

Neil Blaney felt that Haughey 'was simply power-crazed with an ambition to be powerful for the power of position'.[38] His use of the North as an issue frustrated and appalled Blaney. Haughey used power to build more power, and his *modus operandi* 'included elements of fear and domination engendered by him in individuals in both private and public sectors'.[39] One critic found that Haughey 'exercised his authority for the pleasure of that exercise, rather than to achieve an integrated national set of objectives'.[40] He felt there was no evidence of boldness in Haughey, no preparedness to risk power for breakthroughs.

Yet neither FitzGerald nor Haughey was interested in power for power's sake. Both had visions for Ireland that they set out to achieve. Haughey was bolder in his actions that most other political leaders in modern Ireland. He took chances, but apart from the Arms Crisis he was generally cautious, careful not to risk his career. This might be a criticism, but it is also reasonable. Bold leadership need not be reckless. Haughey saw himself as a visionary, and he was better than any other Taoiseach in the modern era at taking ideas and bringing them to fruition. Again, we can see impatience with anything that might stop him. As he observed, 'It takes vision and courage to spend money for posterity. You make up your mind, then you just go ahead and go it.'[41] In Northern Ireland, Haughey took risks, first in possibly sowing the seeds for the civil war through his support for the nationalist defenders who became the Provisional IRA, but later to bring the IRA along a non-violent path. For the journalist Ed Moloney, 'one of the great ironies of the peace process [is] that no single Irish politician did more to start the Provos on the path that eventually resulted in the ceasefires.'[42] This is an exaggeration, but Haughey made a significant contribution through calculated risks, not reckless gambles.

It was his transformation of the Irish economy at a time when Ireland was at a nadir in its economic history that best showed his political skill at work. Haughey introduced severe austerity measures, but unlike ideologues in the UK or US he did so with the blessing, if not the support, of the unions. And in contrast to the UK and the US, spending was actually cut. While unemployment remained high in the immediate aftermath, it did not grow, as had happened in the UK. He put in place a new economic governance structure which survived well after his departure and was never really challenged politically. He did this against the policy orthodoxy of the time, which was to exclude trade unions. While one might be cynical of his claim that his party was not 'of the right or the left', he was no ideologue, and instead used political skill to achieve a political vision. This vision was of an economically and culturally vibrant country, comfortable in its own skin.

Haughey was enormously self-confident and quite proud of his background. His lifestyle, a deliberate rejection of the ascetic lives favoured by the founders of Fianna Fáil, displayed a sense that financial success was not something to be ashamed of, but an ambition for which Ireland should aim. For him the nation should no longer celebrate its poverty but strive for excellence. He would not accept Ireland as a follower or an also-ran. Haughey was an elitist who rejected the idea that Ireland was condemned to being for ever a second-rate nation. On that promise he largely delivered. In doing so he was helped by another elitist, Garret FitzGerald.

In his autobiography Garret rather sweetly says that Joan and he 'lived happily ever after'. Ireland did not live happily ever after. New problems emerged, as they will in any country, no matter how lucky or well run it is. The Ireland we see at an almost four-decade remove is in large part a result of Charlie and Garret and how they interacted. Their last interaction was in October 2005, when FitzGerald went to visit a very ill Charlie Haughey in Kinsealy. Charlie and Garret reminisced about old times – 'We didn't talk politics, there was no point in that.'

Acknowledgements

It takes a village. As with any venture, this work owes a debt of gratitude to many people who have helped along the way.

I have benefited greatly from teachers throughout my life, some of whom may not remember me – it has been a while. A lot is written negatively about Catholic education in Ireland in the 1970s and 1980s, but my experience was largely positive. I benefited greatly from the space and guidance afforded me by, among others, Seán Ahern, Bruce Bradley SJ, John Daly, Seán Hanley, John Kennedy, Leonard Moloney SJ, Jody O'Connor, and especially Jim Maher SJ, who never let me away with a lazy argument.

In Trinity I was helped enormously by the three Michaels, Gallagher, Laver and Marsh – for which I am forever grateful.

I have benefited from speaking with a large number of people at various stages for what is a lifelong study of cabinet government and politics in Ireland. Many of the people that I spoke did not want their name anywhere near the book, and so they aren't – but thank you.

These have included both Garret FitzGerald and Charles Haughey, but among others Bertie Ahern, Dermot Ahern, David Andrews, Seán Barrett, Peter Barry, John Bruton, John Bowman, Stephen Collins, Liam Cosgrave, Brian Cowen, Noel Dempsey, Barry Desmond, Seán Donlon, Alan Dukes, Máire Geoghegan-Quinn, Seán Haughey, Mary Harney, Paddy Hillery, Patrick Honohan, Jerry Kelliher, Wally Kirwin, Muiris MacCongail, Ray MacSharry, Colm McCarthy, Charlie McCreevy, Maurice Manning, Martin Mansergh,

Micheál Martin, Katherine Meehan, Donagh Morgan, Frank Murray, Brian Murphy, Michael Noonan, Stephen O'Byrnes, Martin O'Donoghue, Rory O'Hanlon, Michael O'Kennedy, Michael O'Leary, Mary O'Rourke, Ruairi Quinn, Peter Ryan, Albert Reynolds, Dick Spring, Paddy Teahon, John Wilson and Michael Woods.

When he was dying I asked my father about many of the people he shared a cabinet table with, which were fascinating portraits. Another, perhaps less biased source is the *Dictionary of Irish Biography*, which is a fantastic free resource for anyone interested in Irish history.

David Farrell gave me access to his father's, Brian Farrell, interviews with senior politicians and public servants from the 1980s held in the UCD archives.

In Cádiz, where this work was largely written, I am thankful to Sofía Pérez de Guzmán Padrón for providing me a place to write.

It was written with the support of my university, Dublin City University. There I am grateful for the support of some past Heads of School – and the current one, Tanya Ní Mhuirthile – my Dean Derek Hand and the big bossman, Daire Keogh.

My editors at Independent Newspapers have helped me along with writing especially Cormac Bourke, Jody Corcoran, Alan English, Madeleine Keane, Liz Kearney and Jon Smith.

Various iterations of this work were read and commented on along the way by Kevin Rafter, Catherine Lynch, Joseph O'Malley and Gary Murphy. Their comments have helped enormously to improve the book. I have also benefitted from discussions of the politics of the time with other friends and colleagues such as Sarah Carey, Maura Conway, Jonathan Arlow, Ken Carty, John Coakley, Jody Corcoran, Michael Gallagher, John Garry, Seán McGraw, Theresa Reidy Gëzim Visoka, Tom Hickey, Jonathan Lynn, Iain McMenamin, Deiric Ó Broin, Ian O'Hora, but most especially Gary Murphy and Kevin Rafter.

I was fortunate to run this idea by my literary agent, Conor Nagle, who connected me with Deirdre Nolan of Bonnier Books. Deirdre was enthusiastic about the project the whole way and

Lisa Gilmour was incredibly helpful, positive and super-efficient throughout the whole production process.

Some colleagues I've been working with on other projects took up the slack as I was not able to devote the time needed. Thanks and apologies to Alex Baturo, Francesco Cavatorta, Michael Gallagher, Alex Marland, Theresa Reidy, Gala Palavicini.

My children, Martha, Pepe and Donogh, who I hope enjoy reading about the time that their grandfather was a big noise. Thanks and love to you for all the craic, head wreck and house wreck along the way.

My wife, Catherine Lynch, read an entire early draft and suggested many improvements. She practically wrote it herself! I am grateful for her love and support and for having married a top-of-the-range bird.

My parents Des and Pat O'Malley were great in their own different ways. I am very grateful to them both for all they have given me, and I dedicate this book to their memory.

ENDNOTES

1. Flawed Pedigree

1. Dick Hogan, 'Only apathy would worry FF in Cork', *Irish Times*, 5 November 1979.
2. William K. Roche, 'The Development of Industrial Relations', in J.H. Goldthorpe and C.T. Whelan (eds), *The Development of Industrial Society in Ireland*, Oxford University Press, 1992, p. 314.
3. Ronan Fanning, 'Jack Lynch', *Dictionary of Irish Biography*, Cambridge University Press, 2010.
4. Stephen O'Byrnes, 'The inside view of Room 560', *Irish Press*, 8 December 1979.
5. Stephen O'Byrnes, 'We voted "to save our seats"', *Irish Press*, 8 December 1979.
6. Dick Walsh, *The Party: Inside Fianna Fáil*, Gill & Macmillan, 1986, p. 141.
7. David Andrews, *Kingstown Republican: A memoir*, New Island, 2007, p. 77.
8. Desmond O'Malley, *Conduct Unbecoming: A memoir*, Gill & Macmillan, 2014, p. 125.
9. Dick Walsh, 'Colley: I did not promise loyalty to the Taoiseach', *Irish Times*, 21 December 1979.
10. Garret FitzGerald, *All in a Life*, Macmillan, 1991, p. 339.
11. Dáil Éireann debate, 11 December 1979, Vol. 317 No. 7.
12. Ibid.
13. 'Garret at 80', RTÉ interview with John Bowman, broadcast in September 2006.
14. Garret FitzGerald, *Just Garret*, Liberties Press, 2010, p. 288.
15. Dáil Éireann debate, 11 December 1979, Vol. 317 No. 7.
16. Leaders' Debate, *Today Tonight*, RTÉ, broadcast 16 February 1983.
17. Raymond Smith, *Garret: The enigma*, Aherlow Press, 1985, pp. 12,16.

18. David Davin-Power, 'Encounters with Charlie Haughey', RTÉ blog, 6 January 2015.
19. Willie O'Brien, 'Garret FitzGerald and the Fine Gael Party' in James Dooge (ed.), *Ireland in the Contemporary World: Essays in honour of Garret FitzGerald*, Gill & Macmillan, 1986, pp. 40–41.
20. Paddy Harte, *Young Tigers and Mongrel Foxes*, O'Brien Press, 2005, p. 238.
21. Frank Litton, 'Preface', *Unequal Achievement*, Institute for Public Administration, 1982, p. ix.

2. Children of Men

1. Interview with Garret FitzGerald, Ranelagh, 24 January 2005. He deposited 450 boxes to the UCD archives.
2. Desmond FitzGerald, *The Memoirs of Desmond FitzGerald*, Routledge & Kegan Paul, 1968, p. 17.
3. 'Garret at 80', RTÉ interview with John Bowman, broadcast in September 2006; Fergus FitzGerald, 'Editor's Introduction' in *The Memoirs of Desmond FitzGerald*, Routledge & Kegan Paul, 1968, pp. xii–xiii.
4. William Murphy, 'Desmond FitzGerald', *Dictionary of Irish Biography*, 2009, https://doi.org/10.3318/dib.003136.v1.
5. Garret FitzGerald, *All in a Life*, Gill & Macmillan, 1991, pp. 27–28.
6. Gary Murphy, *Haughey*, Gill Books, 2021, pp. 2–10; Martin Mansergh (ed.), *The Spirit of the Nation: The speeches of Charles J. Haughey*, Mercier Press, 1986, p. xxxi.
7. 'Commandant Seán Haughey', *Irish Independent*, 6 January 1947.
8. Vincent Browne, 'The Charlie Haughey story, Part I', *Sunday Independent*, 3 September 1978.
9. 'Talking to Charles Haughey', *Irish Times*, 17 December 1960; Terry Clavin, 'Harry Boland', *Dictionary of Irish Biography*, 2019.
10. Stephen Kelly, 'Fresh evidence from the archives: The genesis of Charles J. Haughey's attitude to Northern Ireland', *Irish Studies in International Affairs*, Vol. 23, 2012, p. 159.
11. FitzGerald, *All in a Life*, pp. 29–30.
12. 'Charles James Haughey: An Irish Times profile', *Irish Times*, 6 June 1969.
13. Ronan McGreevy, 'VE Day 75: Haughey, FitzGerald and that *Irish Times* front page', *Irish Times*, 8 May 2020.
14. Charles Haughey, 'Battles long ago', *Irish Times*, 11 May 1962.

15. Patrick Maume, 'Kevin Boland', *Dictionary of Irish Biography*, October 2009.
16. By 1948 Fianna Fáil had been in power for 16 years, and Ireland was beginning to look like a one-party state. After the 1948 election, which was Fine Gael's worst ever result, an inter-party government was formed, a coalition of all parties in the Dáil except Fianna Fáil. It was an ideologically diverse mix under the leadership of Taoiseach John A. Costello. A second inter-party government was formed in 1954, again under Costello.
17. Jim Farrelly, 'The heads will roll – Mrs Lemass', *Irish Independent*, 8 December 1979.
18. 'Commandant Seán Haughey.' *Irish Independent* 7 January 1947.
19. John Horgan, *Seán Lemass: The Enigmatic Patriot*, Gill & Macmillan, 1997, p. 160.
20. Patrick Maume, 'Haughey, Charles James (C.J.).', in James McGuire, James Quinn (eds), *Dictionary of Irish Biography*. Cambridge University Press, 2016.
21. 'Co-opted on to FF National Executive', *Irish Press*, 13 December 1955.
22. 'Quiet by-election', *Cork Examiner*, 1 May 1956.
23. His younger brother, Pádraig.
24. RTÉ, *Haughey*, Episode 1: *The Outsider*, 2006.
25. Colm Keena, *Charlie's Millions*, Gill & Macmillan, 2006, pp. 26–27; 'Talking to Charles Haughey', *Irish Times*, 16 December 1960; *Haughey* Part I: 'The Outsider', RTÉ, 2006.
26. RTÉ, *Haughey*, Episode 1: *The Outsider*.
27. 'The front runners', *Irish Press*, 1 July 1977.
28. FitzGerald, *All in a Life*, p. 49.
29. FitzGerald, *Just Garret*, chapter 4.
30. Lars Mjøset, *The Irish Economy in a Comparative Institutional Perspective*, Report No. 93, National Economic and Social Council (NESC), 1992, p. 9.
31. 'Garret at 80', interview with John Bowman.
32. FitzGerald, *All in a Life*, p. 64
33. 'Garret at 80', interview with John Bowman.
34. Patrick Lynch, 'Garret FitzGerald: A personal memoir' in James Dooge (ed.), *Ireland in the Contemporary World: Essays in honour of Garret FitzGerald*, Gill & Macmillan, 1986, p. 33.
35. Garret FitzGerald, 'Seeking a national purpose', *Studies: An Irish Quarterly Review*, Vol. 53, No. 212 (Winter, 1964): pp. 337–351.
36. Patrick Lindsay, *Memories*, Blackwater Press, 1992, pp. 190–191.

37. Stephen Collins and Ciara Meehan, *Saving the State: Fine Gael from Collins to Varadkar*, Gill Books, 2020, p. 107.
38. Ciara Meehan, *A Just Society for Ireland? 1964–1987*, Palgrave Macmillan, 2013.
39. Murphy, *Haughey*, p. 142.

3. Young Turks

1. Stephen Collins, *The Power Game: Ireland under Fianna Fáil*, O'Brien Press, 2000, p. 41.
2. Murphy, *Haughey*, p. 49.
3. Dáil Éireann debate, 14 May 1957, Vol. 161 No. 9.
4. 'Deputy suspended amid scenes', *Irish Times*, 23 April 1959; 'Another parliamentary secretary appointed', *Irish Times*, 7 May 1960.
5. 'Talking to Charles Haughey', *Irish Times*, 17 December 1960.
6. 'The Peter Berry diaries' *Magill*, June 1980; Brian Farrell, *Seán Lemass*, Gill & Macmillan, 1991, p. 103.
7. Deaglán de Breadún 'C. J. Haughey's golden days', *Irish Times*, 28 March 1984.
8. Fine Gael had continued with a dual leadership since 1948, when Mulcahy was the leader of the party, but Costello was the party's nominee for Taoiseach.
9. John Horgan, *Seán Lemass*, Gill & Macmillan, 1997, p. 197.
10. Cited in Horgan, *Seán Lemass*, p. 202.
11. 'The Peter Berry diaries', *Magill*, June 1980.
12. Maurice O'Connell, *No Complaints: A memoir of life in rural Ireland and in the Irish public service* (ed. J. Anthony Gaughan), Kingdom Books, 2020, p. 74.
13. Murphy, *Haughey*, p. 112.
14. Seán O'Rourke, 'In Finance every budget was balanced', *Irish Press*, 16 May 1986.
15. Declan Costello, 'Lashing critics of Fine Gael policy', *Irish Times*, 25 March 1965; Finola Kennedy, *Cottage to Crèche: Family change in Ireland*, IPA, 2001, pp. 226–227.
16. 'Radical departure in scheme of free legal aid', *Irish Times*, 16 February 1962.
17. 'Good value for tax money? Justice Minister's belief', *Irish Times* 28 November 1962.

18. 'Man before Special Criminal Court: Nine more to appear today', *Irish Times*, 28 November 1961.
19. John Bowman, 'Letter tells of Haughey role in "breaking" IRA', *Irish Times*, 1 January 2001.
20. Conor Brady, *Guardians of the Peace*, Gill & Macmillan, 1974, pp. 242–243.
21. Murphy, *Haughey*, p. 130; Dáil Éireann debate, 26 October 1966, Vol. 224 No. 14.
22. 'Cattlemen query subsidy for meat factories', *Irish Independent* 17 February 1965.
23. 'Farm crux deadlock broken' *Irish Independent*, 9 November 1966; John Horgan, *Seán Lemass: The Enigmatic Patriot*, Gill & Macmillan, 1997, p. 337.
24. Garret FitzGerald, 'Towards an equitable society', *Irish Times*, 21 January 1969.
25. Said to party meetings in Dublin and Drogheda on 10 and 12 June 1969; see Martin Mansergh (ed.), *The Spirit of the Nations: The speeches of Charles J. Haughey*, Mercier Press, 1986, pp. 112–113.
26. John Healy, 'The wild one', *Magill*, March 1988, pp. 46–50.
27. Brian Farrell, *Chairman or Chief? The role of Taoiseach in Irish government*, Gill & Macmillan, 1970, pp. 69–70.
28. Thomas F. O'Higgins, *A Double Life*, Town House, 1996, p. 189; Collins and Meehan, *Saving the State*, p. 105.
29. Dick Walsh, *The Party: Inside Fianna Fáil*, Gill & Macmillan, 1986, pp. 88–89.
30. Tom Garvin, *Judging Lemass: The measure of the man*, Royal Irish Academy, 2009, p. 222.
31. 'Supporters cheer Mr Haughey on his return', *Irish Independent*, 1 November 1966; O'Higgins, *A Double Life*, p. 209.
32. Murphy, *Haughey*, p. 169.
33. Backbencher, 'Haughey, the golden outsider', *Irish Times*, 27 August 1966.
34. Conor Lenihan, *Haughey: Prince of Power*, Blackwater Press, 2015, p. 47.
35. 'Cabinet may be told of new leader today', *Irish Independent*, 1 November 1966.
36. 'A compromise on new taoiseach? Two main contestants', *Irish Times*, 10 October 1966.
37. Paul M. Sacks, *The Donegal Mafia: An Irish Political Machine*, Yale University Press, 1976.

38. Horgan, *Seán Lemass*, p. 333.
39. Jack Lynch, 'My life and times', *Magill*, November 1979, p. 42.
40. 'Decision deferred: Inside politics', *Irish Times* 5 November 1966.
41. 'Lynch: Reluctant Taoiseach' *Irish Times* 4 November 1966
42. Dick Walsh, *The Party: Inside Fianna Fáil*, Gill & Macmillan, 1986, p. 91.
43. Terry Keane, 'Charlie's girl', *Sunday Times*, 16 May 1999.
44. Paddy Terry, *Rambling Recollections*, unpublished memoir, pp. 176–177.
45. Ibid., p. 181.
46. Kevin Boland said, 'We were all organised by Haughey', in Stephen Collins, *The Power Game*, p. 40.
47. Frank McDonald, *The Destruction of Dublin*, Gill & Macmillan, 1995, p. 29.
48. Frank McDonald and Kathy Sheridan, *The Builders: How a Small Group of Property Developers Fuelled the Building Boom*, Penguin, 2008, p. 25.
49. Ibid., p. 28.
50. 'Colley asks youth for commitment', *Irish Times*, 22 April 1967.
51. Murphy, *Haughey*, p. 203.
52. In April 1970 he was the subject of a *Hello!*-style interview with photos of his family and his 'rambling' mansion in what was an otherwise serious current affairs magazine: Liam MacGabhann, 'What is Haughey's next move?', *This Week*, April 1970.
53. 'Mr Haughey's House', *Irish Times*, 30 May 1969, 13 June 1969 and 14 June 1969; 'Haughey explains sale of house', *Irish Times*, 4 June 1969.
54. Haughey sale not liable for tax', *Irish Times*, 18 June 1969.
55. 'Haughey becomes finance minister', *Irish Times*, 11 November 1966.
56. An analysis of the number of times articles in the *Irish Times* mentioned the names of the leading politicians in the years 1966 to 1969 shows that 'Mr Lynch' appeared in 4,981 articles, 'Mr Haughey' in 2,116, 'Mr Blaney' in 1,747 and 'Mr Colley' in 1,551.
57. 'Mr Haughey's house', *Irish Times*, 30 May 1969; Paddy Hillery interview, 26 August 2006.
58. Anne Chambers, *TK Whitaker: Portrait of a Patriot*, pp. 180–181.
59. Charles J. Haughey interview, Kinsealy, 23 October 2004.
60. 'Minister for Industry at inauguration', *Irish Times*, 11 May 1937.
61. Paddy Hillery interview, 2006
62. Seán O'Rourke, 'In Finance', *Irish Press*, 16 May 1986.
63. Murphy, *Haughey*, pp. 216–217.

64. Philip O'Connor, 'A Very Political Project: Charles Haughey, Social Partnership and the pursuit of an "Irish economic miracle", 1969–92', PhD thesis, Dublin City University, 2019.
65. Paddy Hillery interview, 2006.
66. O'Connor, *A Very Political Project*, p. 55.
67. FitzGerald, *All in a Life*, p. 78; Stephen Collins and Ciara Meehan, *Saving the State*, pp. 118–119.
68. 'Questions to be answered', *Irish Press*, 13 June 1969.
69. Niamh Puirséil, *The Irish Labour Party 1922–73*, UCD Press, 2007, p. 268; Charles Haughey, Radio Éireann broadcast, 1969, available under 'Haughey, Ryan and Dunne Address Voters', RTÉ Archives, AA6185.
70. Dick Walsh, 'FF will field 121 candidates', *Irish Times*, 4 June 1969.
71. Michael Gallagher (ed.), *Irish Elections 1948–77: Results and Analysis*, Routledge, 2009, p.243.
72. Paddy Hillery interview with Brian Farrell, 15 April 1988, UCD archives.

4. Arms and the Man

1. Paddy Harte, *Young Tigers and Mongrel Foxes*, O'Brien Press, 2005, p. 140.
2. 'Broadcast by An Taoiseach', RTÉ Television, 13 August 1969.
3. 'Army takes up position', *Irish Independent*, 15 August 1969.
4. Garret FitzGerald, 'Seeking a national purpose', *Studies: An Irish Quarterly Review*, Vol. 212 (Winter, 1964), p. 350.
5. Seán Lemass, 'One Nation', a pamphlet issued by Fianna Fáil of a speech delivered by Lemass at a meeting of the Oxford Union Society on 15 October 1959.
6. Mary Daly, *Sixties Ireland: Reshaping the economy, state and society, 1957–1973*, Cambridge University Press, 2016, p. 329.
7. Brian Girvin, '"Lemass's Brainchild": The 1966 Informal Committee on the Constitution and change in Ireland, 1965–73', *Irish Historical Studies*, Vol. 38: 151 (2013), pp. 408–409.
8. Girvin, 'Lemass's Brainchild', pp. 412, 415.
9. Roy Foster, *Modern Ireland 1600–1972*, Penguin, 1999, p. 555.
10. O'Higgins, *A Double Life*, pp. 210–11.
11. Jack Lynch, 'The situation in the six counties of North-East Ireland', speech, Tralee, 20 September 1969.
12. See John Walsh, *Patrick Hillery: The Official Biography*, New Island, 2008, p. 197.

13. O'Malley, *Conduct Unbecoming*, p. 56.
14. 'Mr Haughey has Northern Minister as dinner guest', *Irish Independent*, 13 February 1965.
15. '"Minorities nothing to fear" – Haughey', *Irish Times*, 13 November 1962.
16. Quoted in Keogh, *Jack Lynch: A biography*, Gill & Macmillan, 2009, p. 206.
17. Stephen Kelly, 'Fresh evidence from the archives' p. 158.
18. Cited in Anne Chambers, *T.K. Whitaker: Portrait of a patriot*, Doubleday, 2014, p. 272.
19. O'Malley, *Conduct Unbecoming*, p. 56; Kelly, 'Fresh evidence'.
20. NAI DT 2000/6/658 Cabinet minute, 16 August 1969.
21. Martin Mansergh, *Spirit of the Nation*, p. 139.
22. 'Other moves in crisis', *Sunday Independent*, 17 August 1969.
23. Pádraig Faulkner, *As I Saw It*, Wolfhound Press, 2005, pp. 92–95.
24. Peter Berry, 'The Peter Berry diaries', *Magill*, June 1980, pp. 51–52; Faulkner, *As I Saw It*, p. 94; Patrick Maume, Pádraic 'Jock' Haughey, *Dictionary of Irish Biography*, December 2012.
25. Quoted in John Bowman, 'Letter tells of Haughey role in "breaking" IRA', *Irish Times*, 1 January 2001.
26. Captain James Kelly to the Committee of Public Accounts, 10 February 1971, para. 6828.
27. Michael Heney, *The Arms Crisis of 1970: The Plot that Never Was*, Head of Zeus, pp. 35, 39–40.
28. Berry, 'The Peter Berry diaries', pp. 53–4.
29. Ibid., p. 55.
30. Ibid., pp. 55–56.
31. Paddy Hillery, September 1969, quoted in Walsh, *Patrick Hillery*, p. 192.
32. 'Force against NI not ruled out by Government – Blaney', *Irish Times*, 9 December 1969.
33. Horgan, *Seán Lemass*, p. 356.
34. 'Youth leads new executive', *Irish Press*, 19 January 1970.
35. They were John Kelly, a Belfast republican and a founder of the Provisional IRA and Albert Luykx, hotelier and businessman.
36. Vincent Browne, 'The Arms Crisis 1970', *Magill*, May 1980, p. 45.
37. Private interviews.
38. Heney, *The Arms Crisis of 1970*, pp. 346, 349, 363.
39. Murphy, *Haughey*, pp. 282–3, 284–5.
40. Dáil Éireann debate, 25 November 1980, Vol. 324 No. 7.

41. Browne, 'The Arms Crisis of 1970', p. 50.
42. Berry, 'The Peter Berry diaries', p. 60.
43. Transcript of arms trial; see MacIntyre, *Through the Bridewell Gate*, pp. 71–2.
44. Browne, 'The Arms Crisis of 1970', p. 53.
45. Heney, *The Arms Crisis of 1970*, pp. 192–3.
46. Private interview.
47. James Kelly, *Orders for the Captain?*, Kelly, 1971, pp. 27–8.
48. Private interview; Des O'Malley, 'The truth matters – except when it comes to RTÉ and the Arms Crisis', *Sunday Independent*, 13 June 2021.
49. Faulkner, *As I Saw It*, p. 96.
50. Walsh, *Patrick J. Hillery*, pp. 218–225.
51. Kelly, *Orders for the Captain?*, pp. 38, 40.
52. Dáil Éireann debate, 5 May 1970, Vol. 246 No. 4.
53. Justin O'Brien, *The Modern Prince: Charles J. Haughey and the quest for power*, Merlin, 2002, p. 43.
54. Michael Mills, *Hurler on the Ditch*, Currach Press, 2005, p. 55.
55. 'Four are remanded on bail for week: Charges of conspiracy', *Irish Times*, 29 May 1970.
56. Daniel McConnell, 'High Court judge hid upstairs as gardaí arrested Haughey', *Irish Examiner*, 5 May 2020.
57. Private interview.
58. 'Blaney freed – evidence insufficient: Haughey and three others for trial', *Irish Times*, 3 July 1970.
59. 'Judge withdraws from arms trial: Jury discharged after remarks by defence counsel – new hearing date known today?', *Irish Times*, 30 September 1970.
60. 'Phone conversation with Mr Berry', *Irish Press*, 20 October 1970.
61. 'Aid fund operation', *Irish Press*, 20 October 1970.
62. '"Stop it altogether": Gibbons to Haughey: Alleged plea about arms "operation"', *Irish Times*, 24 September 1970.
63. The observation of John Peck, the UK ambassador to Ireland, cited in O'Brien, *The Modern Prince*, p. 49.
64. Conor Cruise O'Brien, *States of Ireland*, Hutchinson, 1972, p. 349.
65. *Later with O'Leary* broadcast on RTÉ One, 3 May 2001.
66. Vincent Browne, 'Foreword' in Stephen Kelly, *A Failed Political Entity: Charles Haughey and the Northern Ireland question, 1945–1992*, Merrion Press, 2016, p. xviii.
67. Justin O'Brien, *The Arms Trial*, Gill & Macmillan, 2000, p. 192.

68. 'Judge addresses arms trial jury', *Irish Press*, 24 October 1970.
69. Heney, *The Arms Crisis of 1970*, pp. 317–318.
70. 'Haughey challenge to Lynch', *Irish Press*, 24 October 1970; 'Fianna Fáil part of my life – Haughey', *Irish Times*, 7 June 1971.
71. 'Dissidents will await reaction', *Irish Press*, 24 October 1970.
72. Pádraig Flynn in RTÉ, *Haughey*, Episode 2. Some others of the 1977 intake indicated they followed the trial closely and were impressed by Haughey, for instance Albert Reynolds and Charlie McCreevy.
73. Tom MacIntyre, *Through the Bridewell Gate: A diary of the Dublin arms trials*, Faber & Faber, 1971, p. 18.
74. 'Dissidents will await reaction', *Irish Press*, 24 October, 1970.
75. Stephen Collins, *The Power Game: Ireland under Fianna Fáil*, O'Brien Press, 2000, p. 64.
76. Heney, *The Arms Crisis of 1970*.
77. MacIntyre, *Through the Bridewell Gate*, p. 17; Vincent Browne, 'Lynch partly responsible for the 1970 Arms Crisis', *Irish Times*, 27 October 1999.
78. O'Malley, *Conduct Unbecoming*, p. 67.
79. Kelly, in *A Failed Political Entity*, offers this argument, and Martin Mansergh, in an interview in December 2019, agreed with this characterisation.
80. Shane Kenny, *Go Dance on Somebody Else's Grave*, Kildanore Press, 1990, p. 9.
81. Collins and Meehan, *Saving the State*, pp. 127–128.

5. Trading Places

1. Dáil Éireann debate, 2 July 1969, Vol. 241 No. 1.
2. FitzGerald, *Just Garret*, p. 125.
3. Arthur Noonan, 'A new look front bench for Fine Gael', *Irish Times*, 17 July 1969.
4. Backbencher, 'The FitzCosgrave blueprint', *Irish Times*, 17 December 1966.
5. Paddy Harte, *Young Tigers and Mongrel Foxes*, O'Brien Press, 2005, p. 105.
6. Quoted in Stephen Collins and Ciara Meehan, *Saving the State: Fine Gael from Cosgrave to Varadkar*, Gill Books, 2020, pp. 127–128.
7. O'Higgins, *A Double Life*, pp. 238–40; FitzGerald, *All in a Life*, pp. 92–3.

8. Collins and Meehan, *Saving the State*, pp. 127–128.
9. June Levine, 'The Irish Women's movement in the Republic of Ireland, 1968–80' in *The Field Day Anthology of Irish Writing*, Vol. 5, Cork University Press, 2002, pp. 180–181.
10. Quoted in Geoffrey Stern, *Leaders and Leadership*, LSE, 1993, p. 81.
11. John Peck, *Dublin from Downing Street*, Gill & Macmillan, p. 122.
12. Michael McInerney, 'Cosgrave launches attack on critics in Fine Gael', *Irish Times*, 22 May 1972; Collins and Meehan, *Saving the State*, pp. 129–130.
13. Harte, *Young Tigers*, p. 110
14. Olivia O'Leary, 'Neil Blaney: Past and future', *Magill*, 2 May 1985.
15. 'Aid fund operation', *Irish Press*, 20 October 1970.
16. In Re. Haughey [1971] IR 217. His statement is available at: http://archive.oireachtas.ie/1971/EVIDENCE_17021971_0.html.
17. John Healy, 'Journey to country stopped in tracks', *Irish Times*, 2 December 1972.
18. Dáil Éireann debate, 29 November 1972, Vol. 264 No. 2.
19. Houses of the Oireachtas, *Report of the Independent Commission of Inquiry into the Bombings in Dublin 1972–73* (the Barron Report), 29 June 2004, pp. 92–93, 95.
20. FitzGerald, *All in a Life*, pp. 108–109.
21. Vincent Browne, 'Garret FitzGerald: Profile of expectation', *Magill*, January 1978, p. 13.
22. Jack Lynch, 'My life and times', *Magill*, November 1979, p. 46.
23. Quoted in Ciara Meehan, 'Towards a "Modern Progressive Society": The National Coalition and Social Reform, 1973–7.' *Irish Historical Studies* 38, no. 151, 2013, p. 462.
24. Quoted in Ted Nealon, *Ireland: A Parliamentary Directory 1973–74*, Institute of Public Administration, 1974, pp. 68–69.
25. Colm Rapple, 'North not big issue for voters here', *Irish Independent*, 26 February 1973.
26. Chris Glennon, 'Fianna Fáil to begin big, final push tomorrow', *Irish Independent*, 27 February 1973.
27. Colm Rapple 'Prices incomes now a top priority', *Irish Independent*, 5 March 1973.
28. Liam Cosgrave interview, 2 November 2004.
29. James Downey, 'FitzGerald: Better not to be too nice', *Irish Times*, 26 May 1981.

30. FitzGerald, *All in a Life*, p. 195.
31. Interview with Seán Donlon, Dublin, 19 November 2019.
32. Secretary of State for Northern Ireland, *Northern Ireland Constitutional Proposals*, HMSO, March 1973, para. 110.
33. FitzGerald, *All in a Life*, p. 197.
34. 'Quotes of the week', *Sunday Independent*, 4 January 2004.
35. Garret FitzGerald, quoted in John Coakley and Jennifer Todd, *Negotiating a Settlement in Northern Ireland, 1969–2019*, Oxford University Press, p. 60.
36. Graham Spencer (ed.), *Inside Accounts*, Vol. 1, *The Irish Government and Peace in Northern Ireland, from Sunningdale to the Good Friday Agreement*, Manchester University Press, 2019, interview with Seán Donlon, p. 23.
37. Conor Cruise O'Brien, *Memoir: My Life and Times*, Poolbeg Press, pp. 350–352.
38. David McKittrick and David McVea, *Making Sense of the Troubles*, revised edn, Viking, 2012, pp. 114–117.
39. Dermot Nally interview for TV3, *Taoiseach*, Episode 4, 2011.
40. 'Doomsday', *Document*, BBC Radio 4, broadcast 11 September 2008.
41. Seán Donlon in Spencer (ed.), *Inside Accounts*, Vol. 1, p. 29.
42. FitzGerald, *All in a Life*, p. 182.
43. Ted Nealon, 'Garret at Large 1975', *7 Days*, 1975, available at https://www.youtube.com/watch?v=FSKbeTGO8rQ.
44. FitzGerald, *Just Garret*, pp. 160–161.
45. O'Brien, *My Life and Themes*, p. 343. O'Brien might not have been the most objective observer of FitzGerald, but others have made this allegation.
46. RTÉ Television, 'Taoiseach addresses the nation', 10 December 1975.
47. John O'Hagan, 'The Irish economy 1973 to 2016' in Thomas Bartlett (ed.), *The Cambridge History of Ireland*, Vol. IV, Cambridge University Press, 2018, p. 502.
48. Justin Keating, 'Garret: His quest for truth', *Irish Independent*, 26 November 1982.
49. On Michael D. Higgins's part in Labour in-fighting, see Barry Desmond, *Finally and In Conclusion*, New Island Books, 2000, and John Horgan, *Labour: The price of power*, Gill & Macmillan, 1986.
50. Maurice Manning, 'The political parties' in Howard Penniman (ed.), *Ireland at the Polls: The Dáil Elections of 1977*, American Enterprise Institute, p. 87.

51. Quoted in Joseph O'Malley, 'Cosgrave hits news media' *Sunday Independent*, 22 May 1977.
52. Brian Farrell and Maurice Manning, 'The election', in Penniman (ed.) *Ireland at the Polls*, p. 140–42; Collins and Meehan, *Saving the State*, p. 166.
53. Dick Walsh. 'Lynch preferred as Taoiseach but Cabinet scores in survey', *Irish Times*, 13 June 1977.
54. Browne, 'A profile in expectation', *Magill*; Willie O'Brien, 'Garret FitzGerald and the Fine Gael Party' in Dooge, *Ireland in the Contemporary World*, p. 37; quoted in Diarmuid Ferriter, 'Garret's humanity always shone through the torrent of words and statistics', *Sunday Independent*, 22 May 2011.

6. Let's Sack Jack

1. Dick Walsh, 'O'Brien and Haughey least favoured for leadership', *Irish Times*, 3 June 1977.
2. Conor Lenihan, *Haughey: Prince of Power*, Blackwater Press 2015, pp. 83–84.
3. Sir John Peck, quoted in Murphy, *Haughey*, p. 292.
4. Murphy, *Haughey*, p. 289.
5. Walsh, *Patrick Hillery*, p. 250.
6. Tim Ryan, *Mara PJ*, Blackwater Press, 1992, p. 27.
7. Walsh, *Patrick Hillery*, pp. 247–248.
8. Lenihan, *Haughey*, p. 82; Walsh, *The Party*, p. 137; Patrick Gallagher in RTÉ, *Haughey*, Episode 2: *Arise and Follow*.
9. Tim Ryan, *Mara PJ*, p. 27; Frank Dunlop, *Yes, Taoiseach*, Penguin, 2004, p. 38.
10. Michael McInerney, 'Haughey to get seat executive', *Irish Times*, 16 February 1972.
11. Ronan Fanning, 'Aiken, Francis Thomas' in James McGuire and James Quinn (eds), *Dictionary of Irish Biography*, Cambridge University Press, 2016.
12. John Maddock, 'Jeers, cheers and tears for Lynch on tour', *Irish Independent*, 23 February 1973.
13. E.B. Murphy, 'Charlie to go over the top if . . .', *Sunday Independent*, 4 March 1973.
14. Kevin O'Connor, *Sweetie: How Haughey spent the money*, KO Publications, 1999, chapters 13 and 14.

15. Gerry Ryan, *Would the Real Gerry Ryan Please Stand Up?*, Penguin, 2008, Chapter 7.
16. Keena, *Haughey's Millions*, p. 73.
17. Colm Keena, '"Unique" secrecy of Haughey's finances outlined: Moriarty tribunal', *Irish Times*, 7 April 2006.
18. Murphy, *Haughey*, p. 203.
19. 'I.T.G.W.U. presents book to Haughey', *Irish Times*, 7 October 1970.
20. Dáil Éireann debate, 5 April 1974, Vol. 271 No. 12.
21. Paul Tansey, 'New economic plan is advocated by Haughey', *Irish Times*, 6 November 1975.
22. Frank Dunlop, *Yes, Taoiseach*, pp. 43–45; Desmond O'Malley, *Conduct Unbecoming*, pp. 94–95, 106.
23. He emphasised the importance of cultivating the party's grassroots to Ken Carty, then a young Canadian doctoral student, in 1973.
24. 'FF sets out North line', *Irish Press*, 30 October 1975; 'Radical swing in policy by F.F.', *Irish Times*, 30 October 1975.
25. Joseph O'Malley, 'Lynch now Fianna Fáil captive', *Sunday Independent*, 2 November 1975.
26. 'SF welcomes FF withdrawal call', *Irish Press*, 15 October 1975.
27. Dick Walsh. 'O'Brien and Haughey Least Favoured for Leadership', *Irish Times*, 3 June 1977.
28. James Downey, *Lenihan: His Life and Loyalties*, New Island Books, 1998, p. 105. There is no contemporary evidence of Haughey speaking against it, or being in favour of it. Brian Lenihan (interview with Brian Farrell, 11 April 1988) said Haughey disapproved of 'the whole philosophy behind the package of goodies or with the commitments'.
29. Murphy, *Haughey*, p. 359.
30. Bertie Ahern, *The Autobiography*, Hutchinson, 2009, p. 43.
31. PJ Mara in RTÉ, *Haughey*, Episode 2, *Arise and Follow*.
32. Ryan, *Mara PJ*, pp. 29–30.
33. Walsh, *Patrick Hillery*, Chapter 20.
34. Vincent Browne, 'The making of a Taoiseach', *Magill*, January 1980.
35. Renagh Holohan, 'Fianna Fáil and Haughey are tops in opinion poll', *Irish Times*, 10 May 1979.
36. Gene Kerrigan, 'The war in Fine Gael', *Magill*, October 1983, p. 12.
37. Garret FitzGerald interview, 24 January 2005.
38. Stephen O'Byrnes, *Hiding behind a Face*, Gill & Macmillan, p. 19.
39. O'Byrnes, *Hiding behind a Face*, p. 25.

40. Quoted in Smith, *Garret: The Enigma*, p. 375.
41. O'Byrnes, *Hiding behind a Face*, pp. 43–44.
42. Ibid., pp. 37–38.
43. Stephen Collins, 'Haughey settled bill for 1979 postal strikers' food and drink', *Irish Times*, 8 November 2014; O'Malley, *Conduct Unbecoming*, p. 123.
44. Jack Lynch interview with Brian Farrell, 1989.
45. Séamus Brennan in RTÉ, *Haughey*, Episode 2, *Arise and Follow*.
46. Charlie McCreevy interview, 2019; Ray MacSharry interview, 2019.
47. Private interviews; Stephen O'Byrnes, 'We voted "to save our seats"', *Irish Press*, 8 December 1979.

7. Taking Control

1. Private interviews.
2. Dáil Éireann debate, 11 December 1979, Vol. 317 No. 7.
3. 'No pledge on loyalty – Colley', *Irish Press*, 21 December 1979.
4. Revealed in Brian Farrell interview with Pádraig Ó hUiginn, 29 May 1991.
5. Bertie Ahern interview, 2019.
6. Máire Geoghegan-Quinn interview, 2019.
7. IPA Yearbook and Diary 1980 (Supplement). Institute of Public Administration.
8. Donal Foley, 'The Saturday column', *Irish Times*, 2 February 1980.
9. O'Connell, *No Complaints*, p. 86; Desmond O'Malley interview, 2019.
10. James Downey, 'Haughey: fearful of unpopularity', *Irish Times*, 25 May 1981.
11. Jim Kirby, a mid-ranking civil servant in the Department of Justice during the phone-tapping period, in Joe Joyce and Geraldine Kennedy, 'The GUBU diary', *Irish Times*, 29 September 2012.
12. Michael Moriarty, *Report of the Tribunal of Inquiry into Payments to Politicians and Related Matters* Part I, 2006, p. 546.
13. Private interviews.
14. Martin Mansergh interview, December 2019.
15. Fionnuala O'Kelly (later Kenny) in Ryan, *Mara PJ*, pp. 80–81.
16. Ryan, *Mara PJ*, pp. 81–82.
17. Richard Breen et al., *Understanding Contemporary Ireland*, Macmillan, 1990, p. 218.

18. Paddy Teahon interview, December 2019.
19. Brian Farrell, 'The context of three elections' in Howard Penniman and Brian Farrell (eds), *Ireland at the Polls 1981, 1982 and 1987*, Duke University Press, 1987, pp. 3–4.
20. O'Malley, *Conduct Unbecoming*, p. 128.
21. James Morrissey, 'Inside cabinet on army decision', *Sunday Independent*, 5 October 1980; Frank Byrne, 'Six weeks of panic and confusion . . .', *Sunday Independent*, 5 October 1980.
22. Terry Keane, 'Temptation', *Sunday Times*, 23 May 1999.
23. Charles Haughey interview, 2004.
24. Ian Hyland, 'In conversation with Pádraig Ó hUiginn', originally published in Ian Hyland (ed.), *Ireland Inc: A History of Irish Business*, reproduced in *Business and Finance*, 5 April 2019.
25. 'Rousing welcome for Haughey', *Irish Press*, 16 February 1980.
26. 'Economy calls for hard decisions, says Taoiseach', *Irish Times*, 18 February 1980.
27. Ibid.
28. Erik S. Reinert, *How Rich Countries got Rich . . . and Why Poor Countries stay Poor*, Public Affairs, 2007, p. 98.
29. In RTÉ's *Haughey* documentary, Episode 1, *The Outsider*, his friend Harry Boland suggested he learned to talk about the arts because that would be expected of him in the circles in which he was now moving. See also Downey, *Lenihan*, p. viii.
30. Kevin Rafter, *Taoisigh and the Arts*, Martello, 2022.
31. Richard Sinnott, 'The Voters, the Issues and the Party System', in Howard Penniman and Brian Farrell (eds) *Ireland at the Polls, 1981, 1982 and 1987*, Duke University Press, 1997, pp. 94–8.
32. Ibid., pp. 82–84.
33. Tim Bell, *Right or Wrong: the Memoirs of Lord Bell*, Bloomsbury, 2014, pp. 73–77.
34. Des O'Malley interview, 2019.
35. Ibid.
36. Denis Coghlan, '88 jobless share £½m a year', *Irish Times*, 18 June 1982; John Kielty, 'The motor trade's last stand', *Business and Finance*, 15 November 1981.
37. Dick Walsh, 'Haughey holds first meeting with ICTU', *Irish Times*, 22 January 1980.
38. 'Pay rises in pact are limit, says Haughey', *Irish Times*, 24 November 1980; Eugene McEldowney, 'National pay deals at a crossroads', *Irish*

Times, 25 May 1981; Vincent Browne, 'How Haughey cooked the books in 1981', *Magill*, February 1982.
39. Vincent Browne 'How the coalition blew it in '82', *Magill*, February 1982, pp. 19–20.
40. FitzGerald, *Just Garret*, p. 290.
41. O'Byrnes, *Hiding behind a Face*, p. 53.
42. Ibid.
43. In a dispute with the UK government about the removal of 'special category' status for prisoners the IRA termed political prisoners, and whom the UK government saw as terrorists, IRA prisoners refused to wear prison clothes and later refused food.
44. An *Irish Times*/IMS poll gave the party 49 per cent in October 1980 (published 9 October), and 52 per cent in November 1980; 'Poll shows FF would win a general election', *Irish Times*, 28 November 1980.
45. David McKittrick, 'More favour NI troops—poll', *Irish Times* 24 September 1981.
46. Richard O'Rawe, *Blanketmen: An Untold Story of the H-Block Hunger Strike*, New Island Books, 2005.
47. Ed Moloney, *A Secret History of the IRA*, Allen Lane, 2002, pp. 261–262.
48. Stephen Kelly, '"Mr Haughey's silence condemns him": Charles J. Haughey and the second Republican hunger strike 1981', *Irish Political Studies*, 2017, 32(3): 454–478.
49. Paul Bew, *Ireland: The Politics of Enmity, 1789–2006*, Oxford University Press, 2007, p. 529.
50. Michael Breen et al., *Resilient Reporting: Media coverage of Irish elections since 1969*, Manchester University Press, 2019, pp. 101–102.
51. Labour, under Frank Cluskey, had refused to enter a pre-election pact with Fine Gael, but it was known to favour FitzGerald over Haughey. The party was committed to putting a programme for government to a party conference for approval. However, the media covered the election as 'Fianna Fáil versus the coalition'.
52. Charles Moore, *Margaret Thatcher: The Authorised Biography*, Volume 2: *Everything She Wants*, Allen Lane, 2015, p. 300.
53. O'Byrnes, *Hiding behind a Face*, p. 90; Dunlop, *Yes, Taoiseach*, pp. 224–225.
54. Bertie Ahern interview, 2025.
55. Rodney Rice, 'Different styles of Haughey and FitzGerald on the campaign trail', *Day-by-Day* programme, RTÉ Radio 1, 8 June 1981.

56. Olivia O'Leary, 'Garret tries hard to be a man of the people', *Irish Times*, 30 May 1981.
57. Peter Dunn, 'The other fella', *Sunday Times*, 7 June 1981.
58. In fact this epithet was ironic, coined by John Healy, an *Irish Times* columnist and acolyte of Charles Haughey.
59. Dick Walsh, 'RTÉ says TV debate now definitely off', *Irish Times*, 6 June 1981.
60. James Downey, 'Fine Gael's tax policy and question of coalition were the central issues', *Irish Times*, 11 June 1981.
61. The Anti H-Block TDs were elected on a platform of support for those on hunger strike in Northern Ireland.
62. 'Cluskey outlines coalition terms', *Irish Times*, 13 May 1980.
63. Farrell, 'The context of three elections', p. 9.

8. Revolving Doors

1. Garret FitzGerald interview, 2005.
2. O'Byrnes, *Hiding behind a Face*, p. 108.
3. Harte, *Mongrel Foxes*, p. 241
4. Wally Kirwan interview, 9 December 2019.
5. Garret FitzGerald, 'The Anglo-Irish Agreement' in Patrick Lynch and James Meenan (eds) *Essays in Memory of Alexis FitzGerald*, Incorporated Law Society, 1987, p. 225.
6. Quoted in John Walsh, *The Globalist: Peter Sutherland, his life and legacy*, 2019, pp. 43–44.
7. FitzGerald, *All in a Life*, p. 362.
8. Garret FitzGerald interview, 2005.
9. 'Haughey calls FitzGerald a "bogey man"', *Irish Times*, 6 July 1981.
10. Interview on *Today Tonight*, RTÉ One, broadcast 14 August 1981.
11. FitzGerald, *All in a Life*, p. 371.
12. Frank McDonald, 'Haughey says RTÉ should interview Carron despite ban', *Irish Times*, 1 September 1981.
13. 'Taoiseach urges prison changes', *Irish Times*, 5 October 1981.
14. Private interview.
15. RTÉ Radio 1, *This Week*, broadcast on 27 September 1981. Full text available from 'FitzGerald wants crusade against "sectarian Republic"', *Irish Times*, 28 September 1981.
16. Maurice Hickey, 'Garret killing unity – Haughey', *Irish Independent*, 29 September 1981.

17. John Wallace, 'New "crusade" bid likely despite adverse polls', *Irish Press*, 19 October 1981.
18. Margaret Thatcher papers PREM19/1070 f358.
19. Ibid., PREM19/509 f113.
20. FitzGerald, *All in a Life*, p. 380.
21. Seanad Éireann debate, 8 October 1981, Vol. 96 No. 1.
22. Olivia O'Leary, 'Charles Haughey: Waiting, watching and waiting', *Magill*, December 1981.
23. 'Haughey still rules – in his head', *Irish Times*, 3 December 1981.
24. Charles Haughey speech to Conference of Fianna Fáil Constituency Directors of Election, 19 September 1981, in Mansergh (ed.) *Spirit of the Nation*, p. 521.
25. Noel Whelan, *Fianna Fáil: A Biography of the Party*, Gill & Macmillan, 2011, p. 208.
26. *Sunday Tribune*, 27 December 1981.
27. It is common for a TD to 'lose the whip' for what might be seen as acts of disloyalty to the party, such as voting against the party's instruction. This is usually a temporary punishment, which means losing the right to attend parliamentary party meetings, but may include losing positions on parliamentary committees.
28. Interview with Garret FitzGerald, 2006; *All in a Life*, pp. 385–386.
29. O'Byrnes, *Hiding behind a Face*, pp. 120–121.
30. Patrick Maume, 'O'Leary, Michael.' In James McGuire, James Quinn (ed.), *Dictionary of Irish Biography*, Cambridge University Press, 2011, and private interview with official from Department of Finance.
31. FitzGerald, *All in a Life*, p. 395.
32. Interview with Michael Noonan, September 2019.
33. Dáil Éireann debate, 27 January 1982, Vol. 332 No. 2.
34. Frank McDonald, 'Non-aligned deputies bring down coalition', *Irish Times*, 28 January 1982.
35. Dáil Éireann debate, 27 January 1982, Vol. 332 No. 2.
36. O'Connell, *No Complaints*, 2020, p. 87.
37. FitzGerald *All in a Life*, p. 398.
38. Denis Coghlan, 'FG tried a deal on clothing VAT', *Irish Times*, 28 January 1982.
39. 'Catherine Butler's memories of Charlie', *Magill*, 22 June 2006; Walshe, *Paddy Hillery*, p. 478.
40. Dáil Éireann debate, 18 December 1981, Vol. 332 No. 13.

41. Denis Coghlan, 'Fairer budget promised as Haughey costs alternatives', *Irish Times*, 9 February 1982.
42. T. Ryle Dwyer, *Haughey's Thirty Years of Controversy*, Mercier Press, 1992, pp. 82–83.
43. Dick Walsh, 'Fianna Fáil takes lead in poll but Haughey still trails', *Irish Times*, 16 February 1982.
44. Michael Finlan, 'Higgins denies election pact with Fine Gael', *Irish Times*, 5 February 1982.
45. RTÉ, *Haughey*, Episode 3, *The Survivor*, broadcast June/July 2005.
46. Gene Kerrigan, 'Pushing on the open door: How Haughey came to terms with the Gregory deal', *Magill*, March 1982; Tony Gregory in RTÉ, *Haughey*, Episode 3, *The Survivor*.
47. Dáil Éireann debate, 9 March 1982, Vol. 333 No. 1.
48. O'Byrnes, *Hiding behind a Face*, pp. 153–4.
49. FitzGerald, *All in a Life*, p. 403–404.
50. O'Malley, *Conduct Unbecoming*, p. 131.
51. Ibid., p. 132.
52. Kevin Kelley, *The Longest War: Northern Ireland and the IRA*, Zed Books, 1988, p. 270.

9. The Survivor

1. Dick Walsh, 'Hanafin removal opposed', *Irish Times*, 31 March 1982.
2. Denis Coghlan, 'Haughey election fund data withheld – auditor', *Irish Times*, 27 September 1982.
3. Denis Coghlan, 'FF dissident faces expulsion', *Irish Times*, 18 May 1983.
4. 'Dowra affair papers show huge rift between RUC and Garda over 1982 arrest of Fermanagh man', *Impartial Reporter*, 1 January 2015.
5. Dunlop, *Yes, Taoiseach*, p. 265.
6. Raymond Smith, *Garret: The Enigma*, Aherlow, 1985, p. 18.
7. Bruce Arnold, *Haughey: His Life and Unlucky Deeds*, HarperCollins, 1993, pp. 209–210.
8. Michael Noonan's report published 20 January 1983, reproduced in Joe Joyce and Peter Murtagh, *The Boss*, Poolbeg Press, 1983, p. 394.
9. 'Haughey "did not know on Friday"', *Irish Press*, 18 August 1982.
10. The proposal was made by Jim Prior, Secretary of State for Northern Ireland for three years from September 1981.

11. Haughey message to Thatcher, 16 April 1982, Thatcher MSS (Churchill Archive Centre): THCR 3/1/20 f86 (T75A/82); Terry Keane, 'Charlie's Girl', *Sunday Times*, 16 May 1999.
12. Dunlop, *Yes, Taoiseach*, p. 268.
13. J.J. Power, 'Sinking of the "Belgrano"', *Irish Times*, 31 January 2012.
14. James Downey, *Lenihan*, p. 127.
15. Dáil Éireann debate, 4 May 1982, Vol. 334 No. 1.
16. Department of the Taoiseach Papers, National Archive 2012/90/868.
17. 'The Falklands crisis and Anglo-Irish relations' HE Ambassador at Dublin to the Secretary of State for Foreign and Commonwealth Affairs, 22 June 1982, Thatcher MSS (Churchill Archive Centre): THCR 1/20/3/19 f18.
18. Charles Moore, *Margaret Thatcher: The authorised biography, Volume 1: Not for Turning*, Allen Lane, 2013, p. 621.
19. Michael Lillis, 'Mr Haughey's Dud Exocet' *Dublin Review of Books*, Issue 21, Spring 2012.
20. 'Haughey asserts role on north', *Irish Times*, 27 September 1982.
21. Richard Sinnott, 'Voters, Issues, and the Party System' in Penniman and Farrell (eds.) *Ireland at the Polls*, p. 85.
22. Charlie McCreevy interview.
23. O'Malley, *Conduct Unbecoming*, pp. 134–135.
24. Joyce and Murtagh, *The Boss*, pp. 257–258.
25. Denis Coghlan, 'Fianna Fáil may expel nine TDs for six months', *Irish Times*, 8 October 1982.
26. O'Malley, *Conduct Unbecoming*, p. 135.
27. Andrews, *Kingstown Republican*, pp. 94–95.
28. Joyce and Murtagh, *The Boss*, p. 257.
29. John M. Feehan, *Operation Brogue: A study of the vilification of Charles Haughey*, Mercier Press, 1984. Feehan later retracted this book for what he saw as Haughey's insincerity.
30. Haughey comment to Margaret Thatcher, 30 March 1982, PREM19/749 f45.
31. Ken O'Brien, 'Crocks of gold hold budget together', *Irish Times*, 26 March 1982; 'A political budget', *Irish Times*, 26 March 1982.
32. Farrell, 'The context of three elections', pp. 20–21.
33. Dáil Éireann debate, Wednesday 9 June 1982, Vol. 335 No. 6; O'Byrnes, *Hiding behind a Face*, p. 182.
34. Hastings, Brian Sheehan and Pádraig Yeates, *Saving the Future: How social partnership shaped Ireland's economic success*, Blackhall Publishing, 2007, p. 55.

35. Stephen Collins, 'Senior civil servant urged Haughey's government to drop "highly optimistic" projections', *Irish Times*, 27 December 2013.
36. Eugene McEldowney, 'Government and ICTU close to pay agreement', *Irish Times*, 4 October 1982.
37. Haughey comment to Margaret Thatcher, 30 March 1982, PREM19/749 f45.
38. Olivia O'Leary, 'Abortion poll is a major issue – Haughey', *Irish Times*, 6 November 1982.
39. O'Byrnes, *Hiding behind a Face*, pp. 207–208; Dick Walsh, 'Haughey accuses FG of helping British on North', *Irish Times*, 18 November 1982; David McKittrick, 'Collusion allegations ridiculous says Dukes', *Irish Times*, 23 November 1982.
40. Jack Jones, 'Fianna Fáil and Fine Gael now tying for support of voters', *Irish Times*, 27 October 1982.
41. Paul Tansey, 'Garret keeps cards close to his chest', *Irish Times*, 9 November 1982.
42. Maev Kennedy, 'Trust is the issue, says FitzGerald', *Irish Times*, 13 November 1982.
43. O'Byrnes, *Hiding behind a Face*, p. 218.
44. Fergus Finlay, *Snakes and Ladders*, New Island Books, 1998, p. 2.
45. Various private interviews; Barry Desmond, quoted in Denis Coghlan, 'Destructive role played by Higgins – Desmond', *Irish Times*, 10 March 1982; see also Horgan, *Labour*, p. 79 and Finlay, *Snakes and Ladders*, pp. 57–58.
46. Dick Spring interview, 2006.
47. Fine Gael–Labour Programme for Government 1982, published in full in the *Irish Times*, 13 December 1982.
48. Farrell, 'The context of three elections', pp. 25–26.
49. One Fine Gael TD was elected Ceann Comhairle and so did not cast a vote. Fianna Fáil and the Workers' Party TDs, and two independents, Neil Blaney and Tony Gregory, opposed him.
50. FitzGerald, *All in a Life*, p. 424.
51. Fitzgerald, *All in a Life*, p. 437.
52. See Joyce and Murtagh, *The Boss*.
53. *This Week* RTÉ Radio 1 broadcast on 23 January 1983.
54. Dick Walsh, 'Haughey resignation thought imminent as support crumbles', *Irish Times*, 27 January 1983.
55. Ahern, *The Autobiography*, pp. 72–73.
56. 'CJ Haughey – man of controversy', *Irish Press*, 27 January 1983.

57. Michael Mills 'Haughey will pick his time', *Irish Press*, 28 January 1983.
58. 'How Haughey won the fight to stay on as party leader', *Irish Press*, 8 February 1983.
59. James Downey, *Lenihan*, New Island Books, p. 130.
60. Murphy, *Haughey*, p. 478.
61. 'The Haughey statement', *Irish Press*, 4 February 1983.
62. Vincent Browne, 'O'Malley's prospectives', *Magill*, December 1979; Des O'Malley interview, 2019.
63. 'Victory greeted with cheers', *Irish Times*, 8 February 1983.
64. Seán Haughey in RTÉ, *Haughey*, Episode 3, *The Survivor*. Neil Blaney says he was asked to convince Haughey to fight on, in Olivia O'Leary, 'Neil Blaney: Past and future', *Magill*, 2 May 1985.
65. Keane, 'Charlie's girl', *Sunday Times*, 16 May 1999.
66. Keena, *Haughey's Millions*, p. 95.

10. Garret the Good, the Bad and the Ugly

1. Private interview.
2. Garret FitzGerald interview, 2006.
3. FitzGerald, *All in a Life*, p. 425.
4. Garret FitzGerald interview, 2006.
5. Katherine Meenan interview, 2019.
6. FitzGerald, *All in a Life*, p. 425.
7. Gemma Hussey in John Walsh, *The Internationalist*, p. 36.
8. Patrick Honohan, interview.
9. Dermot Nally, interview in *Taoiseach*, TV3.
10. John Bruton interview, 2019
11. Austin Deasy interview with Brian Farrell, 24 May 1989.
12. Private interviews.
13. Private interviews with civil servants, 2019.
14. Gemma Hussey, *At the Cutting Edge, Cabinet Diaries 1982–1987*. Gill & Macmillan, 1990, p. 207.
15. Daithí Ó Corráin, 'Catholicism in Ireland, 1880–2016: Rise, ascendancy and retreat' in Tom Bartlett (ed.), *The Cambridge History of Ireland, Part IV: The Long View, Ireland 1880–2016*, Cambridge University Press, 2018, pp. 729–732.
16. This description is summarised from Tom Inglis, *Truth, Power and Lies: Irish society and the case of the Kerry babies*, UCD Press, 2003.

17. FitzGerald, *All in a Life*, p. 313.
18. 'Joanne Hayes "treated harshly"', *Irish Times*, 28 January 1985.
19. Emily O'Reilly, *Masterminds of the Right*, Attic Press, 1992, pp. 74–75, 77.
20. Farrell, 'The context of three elections', p. 23.
21. Ibid., p. 24.
22. Peter Sutherland, 'Advice to An Taoiseach', *Irish Times*, 16 February 1983.
23. Peter Sutherland's 1983 advice on the Eighth Amendment, published in the *Irish Times*, 16 February 1983.
24. Fitzgerald, *All in a Life*, p. 446.
25. Renagh Holohan, 'Barnes to defy FG party whip', *Irish Times*, 8 February 1983.
26. Hussey, *At the Cutting Edge*, pp. 37, 40.
27. Garret FitzGerald, 'As a Christian, I must vote No', *Irish Independent*, 6 September 1983.
28. Dick Walsh, 'Taoiseach and Haughey at odds on vote', *Irish Times*, 5 September 1983.
29. Quoted in O'Reilly, *Masterminds*, p. 79.
30. Katherine Meenan interview, 18 December 2019.
31. Kennedy, *Cottage to Crèche*, pp. 232–233; Dáil Éireann debate, 28 February 1979, Vol. 312 No. 3.
32. Denis Coghlan, 'Haughey sees Bill as political opportunity', *Irish Times*, 14 February 1985.
33. Private interview 2025.
34. Dáil Éireann debate, 4 July 1974, Vol. 274 No. 3.
35. Desmond, *Finally and In Conclusion*, p. 246; Dáil Éireann debate, 20 February 1985, Vol. 356 No. 2.
36. Desmond, *Finally and In Conclusion*, pp. 246, 250.
37. Private interview.
38. Dáil Éireann debate, 6 December 1985, Vol. 362 No. 8.
39. Dáil Éireann debate, 26 February 1986, Vol. 364 No. 2.
40. John Cooney, '52% seen as favouring end to divorce ban', *Irish Times*, 10 February 1986.
41. MRBI survey report 3340/86.
42. He told Thatcher this: Moore, *Not for Turning*, p. 595; also Terry Keane, 'Temptation', *Sunday Times*, 23 May 1999.
43. 'Labour challenge to FF on divorce issue', *Irish Times*, 4 December 1981.

44. 'Marital committee members "gagged" by Haughey', *Irish Times*, 29 September 1984.
45. 'Haughey believes divorce would create problems', *Irish Times*, 21 May 1986.
46. In her election literature, available at https://irishelectionliterature.com/2009/09/10/the-alice-glenn-report-may-1986/.
47. Finlay, *Snakes and Ladders*, p. 33.
48 John Cooney, 'Divorce defeat blamed on FG's "lazy campaign"', *Irish Times*, 2 July 1986; Hussey, *At the Cutting Edge*, p. 222; R. Darcy and Michael Laver, 'Referendum dynamics and the Irish divorce amendment', *Public Opinion Quarterly*, 1990, 54(1): 1–20.
49. 'Garret at 80', interview with John Bowman.

11. The Northern Line

1. 'Leaders' Debate', *Today Tonight*, broadcast on RTÉ, 16 February 1982.
2. Ibid.
3. Dermot Keogh, *Jack Lynch*, pp. 206–207.
4. UKE Dublin telegram to FCO ('Farewell calls'), conversation between UK Ambassador and Taoiseach, PREM19/0283 f11
5. Seán Donlon, 'NI Policy with Haughey in power', *Irish Times*, 28 July 2009.
6. Stephen Kelly, *A Failed Political Entity*, p. 116.
7. Seán Donlon, 'Haughey bid to tighten grip on Northern policy derailed', *Irish Times*, 28 July 2009.
8. Dáil Éireann debate, 13 December 1979, Vol. 317 No. 9.
9. 'Haughey seeks end to US aid for illegal groups', *Irish Times*, 28 July 1980.
10. Seán Donlon 'Haughey bid to tighten grip on Northern policy derailed', *Irish Times*, 28 July 2009.
11. Margaret Thatcher, *The Downing Street Years*, HarperCollins, 1993, p. 385.
12. Dermot Nally in RTÉ, *Haughey*, Episode 2, *Arise and Follow*.
13. Noel Dorr, 'The Years Before Good Friday: Some personal memories', in Mary Daly (ed.), *Brokering the Good Friday Agreement: The Untold Story*, Royal Irish Academy, 2019, p. 53.
14. Martin Mansergh interview, December 2019.
15. Moore, *Not for Turning*, p. 596.

16. Peter Taylor, 'Bobby Sands: The hunger strike that changed the course of N Ireland's conflict', *BBC News*, 1 May 2021.
17. FCO letter to No. 10, 10 December 1980, PREM19/507 f138.
18. Moore, *Not for Turning*, p. 603.
19. The UK cabinet secretary.
20. Armstrong minute to Kenneth Stowe, 4 February 1981, PREM19/507 f26.
21. Dáil Éireann debate, 30 June 1981, Vol. 329 No. 1.
22. '75% in South favours reunification, says poll', *Irish Times*, 22 August 1984.
23. Moore, *Everything She Wants*, p. 302.
24. 'Garret at 80', interview with John Bowman.
25. FitzGerald, *All in a Life*, p. 464.
26. Ibid., pp. 464–465.
27. Ruairí Quinn, *Straight Left: A Journey in Politics*, Hodder Headline, 2005, pp. 194–195.
28. FitzGerald, *All in a Life*, p. 465
29. Ted Smyth 'New Ireland Forum helped begin process of changing hearts and minds', *Irish Times*, 14 November 2015.
30. FitzGerald, *Just Garret*, p. 356.
31. *New Ireland Forum Report*, Stationery Office, May 1984, Chapter 1, preface.
32. Chambers, *T.K. Whitaker*, p. 327; Ted Smyth, 'The New Ireland Forum: Redefining Irish nationalism and setting the agenda for the Anglo-Irish Agreement' in Daly (ed.), *Brokering the Good Friday Agreement*, p. 36.
33. Andrews, Kingstown Republican, p. 97.
34. FitzGerald, *All in a Life*, p. 479–80.
35. Seamus Mallon, *A Shared Home Place*, Lilliput, 2019, p. 69.
36. *New Ireland Forum Report*, Chapter 5.2 (3) and (4).
37. Dick Walsh. 'Party leaders clash over unitary state', *Irish Times*, 3 May 1984.
38. Smyth, 'The New Ireland Forum', p. 43.
39. Harte, *Mongrel Foxes*, p. 244; Hussey, *At the Cutting Edge*, p. 99.
40. Dick Walsh. 'Fianna Fáil backs Haughey position on Forum Report', *Irish Times*, 28 June 1984.
41. Robert Armstrong, 'Ethnicity, the English and Northern Ireland: Comments and reflections', in Dermot Keogh and Michael H. Haltzell (eds), *Northern Ireland and the Politics of Reconciliation*, Cambridge University Press, 1994, pp. 205–206.

42. Moore, *Everything She Wants*, p. 304.
43. Hussey, *At the Cutting Edge*, p. 105.
44. FitzGerald, *All in a Life*, p. 478; 'What Thatcher said at press briefing', *Irish Times*, 23 November 1984.
45. Moore, Everything She Wants, p. 300.
46. Armstrong minute to Thatcher, 1 November 1984, PREM19/1289 f141.
47. Michael Lillis, 'The Anglo-Irish Agreement of 1985', in Daly (ed.), *Brokering the Good Friday Agreement*, p. 62.
48. No. 10 record of conversation 19 November, Chequers (MT–Taoiseach Fitzgerald), PREM19/1408 f344 and PREM19/1408 f337.
49. 'What Thatcher said at press briefing', *Irish Times*, 23 November 1984.
50. Jim Cusack, 'Forum Report "in a burial plot in Chequers"', *Irish Times*, 21 November 1984.
51. TV3, *Taoiseach*, Episode 5.
52. FitzGerald, *All in a Life*, p. 523.
53. TV3, *Taoiseach*, Episode 5.
54. Denis Coghlan, 'Haughey accuses FitzGerald of talks capitulation', *Irish Times*, 21 November 1984.
55. Dáil Éireann debate, 14 December 1984, Vol. 354 No. 13.
56. Thatcher, *The Downing Street Years*, p. 393.
57. Michael Lillis, 'Anglo-Irish Agreement: How the deal was done', *Irish Times,* 6 November 2015.
58. Michael Lillis interview in Spencer (ed.), *Inside Accounts*, Vol 1, pp. 87–89; Alistair McAlpine, *Once a Jolly Bagman*, 1997, p. 272; Moore, *Everything She Wants*, pp. 341–342.
59. Moore, *Everything She Wants*, p. 326.
60. Hussey, *At the Cutting Edge*, p. 179.
61. The text of the Agreement is available at https://cain.ulster.ac.uk/events/aia/aiadoc.htm.
62. Moore, *Everything She Wants*, pp. 333–334.
63. Mallon, *A Shared Home Place*, pp. 68–69.
64. Terry Keane, 'Temptation', *Sunday Times*, 23 May 1999.
65. John Cooney, 'Anglo-Irish pact is backed by 59%', *Irish Times*, 23 November 1985; Jack Jones, 'Fianna Fáil lead cut back to 8%', *Irish Times*, 25 November 1985.
66. Thatcher Archives, PREM19/1810 f94.
67. Martin Mansergh interview, December 2019.

68. Bertie Ahern interview, April 2025.
69. Ray MacSharry and Pádraic White, *The Making of the Celtic Tiger: The inside story of Ireland's boom economy*, Mercier Press, 2000, p. 43.
70. Moore, *Everything She Wants*, p. 339.
71. Interview with Daithí Ó Ceallaigh in Spencer (ed.), *Inside Accounts* Vol. 1.
72. Michael Lillis, 'The Anglo-Irish Agreement of 1985', in Daly (ed.), *Brokering the Good Friday Agreement*, p. 65.

12. Drifters

1. Central Statistics Office data.
2. Stefan Gerlach, Réamonn Lydon and Rebecca Stuart, (2016), 'Unemployment and inflation in Ireland: 1926–2012', *Cliometrica* 10(3): 345–364.
3. Richard Breen et al., *Understanding Contemporary Ireland: State Class and Development in the Republic of Ireland*, St Martin's Press, 1990, p. 45.
4. Frank Barry, 'Irish economic development over three decades of EU membership', *Czech Journal of Economics and Finance* (2003), 53(9–10): 394–412.
5. Frank Litton (ed.), *Unequal Achievement: The Irish experience: 1957–1982*, Institute of Public Administration, 1982, Preface; Thomas J. Barrington, 'Whatever happened to Irish Government?' in the same volume, p. 104.
6. Patrick Honohan, 'The Role of the Adviser and the Evolution of the Public Service', in M. Hederman (ed.), *The Clash of Ideas: Essays in Honour of Patrick Lynch*, Gill & Macmillan, 1988.
7. Patrick Honohan and Brendan Walsh, 'Catching up with the leaders: The Irish hare', *Brookings Papers on Economic Activity* (2002), 33(1): 1–78.
8. Honohan interview, 2019.
9. The *Asgard* was the yacht used by Erskine Childers, the father of the president of the same name, to import guns into Howth in 1914 for the Irish Volunteers. The *Asgard II* was commissioned in 1981 as a national training vessel. It sank in 2008.
10. FitzGerald, *All in a Life*, p. 426.
11. Finlay, *Snakes and Ladders*, p. 13.
12. FitzGerald, *All in a Life*, p. 435.

13. Ken O'Brien, 'Dukes rejects attacks on budget figures', *Irish Times*, 12 February 1983.
14. See early 1983 in Hussey, *At the Cutting Edge*.
15. *Irish Times*, 10 February 1983.
16. Ken O'Brien 'Dukes did not have time for proper job on public spending', *Irish Times*, 14 February 1983.
17. 'Tough year for us all, says Taoiseach', *Irish Times*, 19 March 1983.
18. Eugene McEldowney, 'How Mr Dukes taxed his way into trouble', *Irish Times*, 6 April 1983.
19. O'Byrnes, *Hiding Behind a Face*, p. 239.
20. Alan Dukes interview 2019
21. Finlay, *Snakes and Ladders*, p. 34.
22. Dick Spring interview, 2006.
23. Seán McCárthaigh, 'Bruton pushed cabinet to save Irish Steel', *Irish Examiner*, 27 December 2013.
24. Hussey, *At the Cutting Edge*, p. 166.
25. Finlay, *Snakes and Ladders*, pp. 22–23.
26. Árd Fheis speech, 1986; 'Taoiseach says unemployment must be priority', *Irish Times*, 20 October 1986.
27. Frank Barry (ed.), *Understanding Ireland's Economic Growth*, London: Macmillan, 1999.
28. Interview in Hyland, *Ireland Inc.*
29. Philip O'Connor, 'A Very Political Project: Charles Haughey, Social Partnership and the pursuit of an "Irish economic miracle", 1969–92', unpublished PhD thesis, Dublin City University, 2019.
30. Gary Murphy, *Electoral Competition in Ireland since 1987*, Manchester: Manchester University Press, p. 18.
31. Dáil Éireann debate, 13 November 1985, Vol. 361 No. 9.
32. 'Taoiseach says unemployment must be priority', *Irish Times*, 20 October 1986; Patrick Honohan, 'Fiscal adjustment in Ireland in the 1980s', *Economic and Social Review* (1992), 23(3): 285–314; Honohan and Walsh, 'Catching up with the leaders', p. 6.
33. Jim Dooge interview with Brian Farrell, 24 May 1989.
34. FitzGerald interview, 2006.
35. Ibid.
36. FitzGerald, *All in a Life*, pp. 624–626; Desmond, *Finally and in Conclusion*, pp. 312–314.
37. FitzGerald interview, 2006.

38. 'Taoiseach says unemployment must be priority', *Irish Times*, 20 October 1986.
39. Denis Coghlan, 'Opinion Poll puts Haughey ahead of FitzGerald', *Irish Times*, 8 May 1984.
40. Geraldine Kennedy, 'Fianna Fáil breaks the 50pc barrier', *Sunday Press*, 11 May 1986.
41. FitzGerald, *All in a Life*, pp. 640–641.
42. Desmond, *Finally and in Conclusion*, p. 201.
43. Fine Gael, *Breaking Out of the Vicious Circle*, election manifesto, 1987.
44. 'Haughey appeal to electorate on hung Dáil', *Irish Times*, 16 February 1987.
45. Seamus Martin, 'Low-key debate lacks animosity', *Irish Times* 13 February 1987.
46. *This Week*, RTÉ Radio 1, 15 February 1987.
47. FitzGerald, *All in a Life*, pp. 644–645.

13. Top Boy

1. Dermot Nally in RTÉ, *Haughey*, Episode 4, *Disclosure*.
2. Olivia O'Leary, 'Haughey at the Forum', *Magill*, May 1984.
3. MacSharry and White, *The Making of the Celtic Tiger*, p. 43.
4. Ibid., p. 44.
5. Mary O'Rourke, *Just Mary: A Memoir*, Gill & Macmillan, 2013, p. 43.
6. Dermot Nally in RTÉ, *Haughey*, Episode 4, *Disclosure*.
7. Mary O'Rourke, *Just Mary*, pp. 50–51; Bertie Ahern, *The Autobiography*, p. 102; various interviews with ministers in that government.
8. Dáil Éireann debate, 10 March 1987, Vol. 371 No. 1.
9. FitzGerald, *All in a Life*, p. 645.
10. 'Dukes sets out conditions for budget support', *Irish Times*, 3 September 1987.
11. Brian Girvin, 'The Campaign', in Michael Gallagher and Richard Sinnott (eds), *How Ireland Voted 1989*, PSAI Press, 1990, p. 11.
12. MacSharry and White, *The Making of the Celtic Tiger*, pp. 68–69.
13. Charles J. Haughey, 'Social Partnership: Its origins and achievements', no date, available from www.charlesjhaughey.ie.
14. O'Connor, 'A Very Political Project', pp. 53–55.
15. Murphy, *Haughey*, pp. 520–521.

16. Haughey, 'Social Partnership'.
17. Murphy, *Haughey*, pp. 527–528.
18. Ray MacSharry interview, December 2019.
19. Charles J Haughey, 'Social Partnership'.
20. O'Connor, 'A Very Political Project', pp. 144–146.
21. Maev-Ann Wren, 'Breaking the debt mould', *Irish Times*, 31 December 1987.
22. Denis Coghlan. 'Poll shows support for FF at 43%', *Irish Times*, 6 July 1987.
23. Hastings et al., *Saving the Future*, p. 39.
24. Jack O'Connor in Hastings et al., *Saving the Future*, p. 176.
25. Hastings et al., *Saving the Future*, p. 9
26. O'Connor, *A Very Political Project*, pp. 190–194.
27. Ibid.
28. Katherine Butler, 'Haughey pursued a reputation on the Euro-stage', *Cork Examiner*, 31 January 1992.
29. 'Haughey calls for debate on European act', *Irish Times*, 1 November 1986.
30. Albert Reynolds, *My Autobiography*, Transworld, 2009, p. 138.
31. Alan Byrne, '£250m beef deal sealed', *Irish Press*, 15 June 1987.
32. Seán MacCárthaigh, 'State papers 1987: Larry Goodman sought bigger state grants for private company', *Irish Examiner*, 30 December 2017.
33. Pádraig Ó hUiginn interview in Ian Hyland, *Ireland Inc.*
34. 'Dermot Desmond on the IFSC past and future', *Finance Dublin*, June 2003.
35. Paddy Teahon interview, November 2019.
36. A Booker Prize judge in 2023 claimed the success of Irish authors was due to the country's investment in the arts.
37. Anthony Cronin (1928–2016), poet and arts adviser. Well known in the Dublin literary scene, Cronin was more prominent as Haughey's arts adviser than as a poet.
38. Private interviews.
39. 'Quinn fears corruption over Temple Bar', *Irish Times*, 3 July 1990.
40. 'O hUiginn says he was just a messenger', *Irish Times*, 7 October 1992.
41. Matt Cooper, *Who Really Runs Ireland?* Penguin, 2009, p. 389.
42. Marie O'Halloran, 'O hUiginn says he acted entirely on own initiative', *Irish Times*, 20 March 1992.

43. Christine Newman, 'Personal funds valid if motives "disinterested"', *Irish Times*, 23 September 2000.
44. Reported instructions from Haughey to Declan O'Donovan on his appointment to the Anglo-Irish Secretariat in 1989, quoted in Catherine Day, 'Panel 3 Overview', in Daly (ed.), *Brokering the Good Friday Agreement*, pp. 137–138.
45. Charles Moore, *Margaret Thatcher: The authorised biography*, Vol. 3: *Herself Alone*, Allen Lane, p. 279.
46. Moore, *Herself Alone*, p. 278.
47. Ibid., pp. 265–266.
48. Martin Mansergh interview, 2019.
49. Denis Coghlan, 'Haughey defers announcement on extradition', *Irish Times*, 18 November 1987.
50. Denis Coghlan and James Downey, 'Extradition Bill passes after FG changes accepted', *Irish Times*, 4 December 1987.
51. Dáil Éireann debate, 6 December 1988, Vol. 385 No. 2.
52. Julian O'Neill, 'IRA Brighton bomb: Patrick Ryan admits link to 1984 attack', *BBC News*, 24 September 2019, https://www.bbc.com/news/uk-northern-ireland-49797327.
53. Jim Cusack and Denis Coghlan, 'DPP finds evidence against Fr Ryan insufficient', *Irish Times*, 13 October 1989.
54. PREM19/3404.
55. 'Motion against extradition is supported by delegates', *Irish Times*, 9 April 1990.
56. Moore, *Herself Alone*, p. 597.
57. Ed Moloney, 'Haughey risked his career in daring search for peace', *Irish Times*, 19 June 2006.
58. Martin Mansergh, 'The Early Phase of the Irish Peace Process', in Daly, *Brokering the Good Friday Agreement*, pp. 106–107.
59. Tim Pat Coogan, *The Troubles: Ireland's Ordeal 1966–1995 and the Search for Peace*, p. 337.
60. Peter Brooke, 'Brooke suggests full SF political role if violence renounced', *Irish Times*, 10 November 1990.
61. Moore, *Herself Alone*, p. 596.
62. Mansergh interview, 2019.
63. John Major, *The Autobiography*, HarperCollins, p. 447.
64. Finlay, *Snakes and Ladders*, pp. 110–111; Mansergh, 'The Early Phase of the Irish Peace Process', pp. 107–108.
65. Girvin, 'The Campaign', pp. 10–11.

14. The Bonfire of the Vanities

1. Jack Jones, 'Significant boost for government', *Irish Times*, 6 February 1989.
2. Denis Coghlan, 'A time to bask in the sun for Fianna Fáil', *Irish Times*, 24 February 1989.
3. Garret FitzGerald, 'Charles Haughey: portrait of an enigma', *Irish Times*, 8 May 1993.
4. Bertie Ahern, *The Autobiography*, p. 105.
5. Murphy, *Haughey*, p. 537.
6. Ibid., p. 542.
7. Denis Coghlan, 'Opposition "not the key" in poll decision', *Irish Times*, 12 May 1989.
8. Denis Coghlan, 'Support for FF slides further in latest poll', *Irish Times*, 12 June 1989.
9. Michael Marsh and Richard Sinnott, 'How the voters decided', in Gallagher and Sinnott (eds), *How Ireland Voted 1989*, pp. 104–105.
10. Ryan, *Mara PJ*, p. 94.
11. Marsh and Sinnott, 'How the voters decided', pp. 111–12.
12. Charlie McCreevy, 'On the campaign trail', in Gallagher and Sinnott (eds), *How Ireland Voted 1989*, p. 44.
13. No.10 record of conversation (MT, Haughey), 26 June 1989, PREM19/2666 f247.
14. Denis Coghlan, 'Haughey rules out deals in bid to form Government', *Irish Times*, 19 June 1989.
15. O'Malley's private papers; Stephen Collins, 'Will Charlie, PDs now make it up?', *Sunday Press*, 25 June 1989.
16. Alan Dukes interview, 2019.
17. O'Malley, *Conduct Unbecoming*, pp. 182–183.
18. Ahern, *The Autobiography*, p. 106.
19. Collins, *The Power Game*, p. 196.
20. Shane Kenny, *Go Dance on Somebody Else's Grave*, pp. 87–88.
21. Denis Coghlan, 'Coalition remains a stumbling block to FF–PD deal', *Irish Times*, 5 July 1989.
22. Collins, *The Power Game*, p. 197.
23. Dáil Éireann debate, 6 July 1989, Vol. 391 No. 3.
24. Collins, *The Power Game*, p. 199.
25. Kenny, *Go Dance on Somebody Else's Grave*, p. 147.
26. Mark Brennock, 'Haughey wins endorsement for coalition with PDs', *Irish Times*, 12 July 1989.

27. O'Malley, *Conduct Unbecoming*, pp. 183–184.
28. I was in the room at the time.
29. Ahern, *The Autobiography*.
30. Collins, *The Power Game*, p. 200.
31. Reynolds, *My Autobiography*, p. 132.
32. O'Rourke, *Just Mary*, p. 65; John Cooney. 'Reynolds belittles pact with PDs', *Irish Times*, 19 February 1990.
33. Interview in RTÉ, *Haughey*, Episode 4, *Disclosure*.
34. Ahern, *The Autobiography*, p. 140.
35. Ibid., pp. 127–128.
36. This is a story told to me independently by a number of officials.
37. UK Ambassador Nicholas Fenn note to FCO, April 1990, PREM19/3404.
38. Katherine Butler, 'Haughey pursued a reputation on the Euro-stage', *Cork Examiner*, 31 January 1992.
39. N. Piers Ludlow, 'The European Institutions and German Reunification', in Leopoldo Nuti et al. (eds), *Europe and the End of the Cold War: A reappraisal*, Routledge, 2008, pp. 165–166.
40. Maol Muire Tynan, 'No one can beat Brian to the Park', *Irish Times*, 21 October 1989.
41. Emily O'Reilly, *Candidate: The truth behind the presidential campaign*, Attic Press, 1991, pp. 72–73.
42. O'Reilly, *Candidate*, pp. 18–19.
43. Ibid., p. 115.
44. Ibid., pp. 130–132.
45. T. Ryle Dwyer, *Short Fellow: A biography of Charles J. Haughey*, Marino, pp. 381–384.
46. 'Saturday View', RTÉ Radio 1, broadcast on 3 November 1990.
47. Private interview with civil servant, December 2019.
48. Mary Robinson, *Everybody Matters: A memoir*, Hodder, 2013, p. 161.
49. Máire Geoghegan-Quinn interview, October 2019.
50. Fenn to FCO, 25 July 1991, PREM 19–3403.
51. Joe Carroll, 'No encores as Charlie scales the European heights', *Irish Times*, 9 April 1990.
52. Downey, *Lenihan*, p. 191.
53. Deaglán de Breadúin, 'A "can-do" politician who rarely strayed outside his brief', *Irish Times*, 7 February 1992.
54. Arnold, *Haughey*, pp. 264–265.
55. John McManus, 'Desmond named as main mover and beneficiary', *Irish Times*, 9 July 1993.

56. RTÉ Radio, *This Week*, 22 September 1991.
57. Ahern, *The Autobiography*, p. 129.
58. Noel Dempsey interview, 10 December 2019.
59. Maol Muire Tynan, 'Haughey acts to head off likely challenge', *Irish Times*, 29 September 1991; Denis Coghlan, 'Haughey placates dissidents', *Irish Times*, 3 October 1991.
60. Dáil Éireann debate, 30 October 1991, Vol. 411 No. 7.
61. Ibid.
62. On RTÉ *Nighthawks*, broadcast on 15 January 1992.
63. Joyce and Murtagh, *The Boss*, pp. xiv–xvi.
64. 'Taoiseach given transcripts, says Doherty', *Irish Times*, 22 January 1992.
65. 'Allegation absolutely false – Haughey', *Irish Times*, 23 January 1992.
66. O'Malley, *Conduct Unbecoming*, p. 189; Ahern, *The Autobiography*, p. 132.

15. Long Shadows

1. Eoin O'Malley, *Ireland's Long Economic Boom: The Celtic Tiger Economy, 1986–2007*, Palgrave, 2024, p. 7.
2. Mary McAleese, speech delivered to the Re-imagining Ireland Conference, Charlottesville, Virginia, 7 May 2003.
3. See O'Malley, *Ireland's Long Economic Boom*, chapter 3 for a discussion of potential explanations.
4. See, for instance, J.J. Lee, *Ireland 1912–1985: Politics and Society*, Cambridge University Press, 1989; R.F. Foster, *Luck and the Irish: A Brief History of Change, 1970–2000*, Penguin, 2007; and Tom Garvin, *Preventing the Future: Why was Ireland so poor for so long?*, Gill & Macmillan, 2005.
5. Brian McCracken, *Report of the Tribunal of Inquiry (Dunnes Payments)*, Stationery Office, 1997, pp. 70–73.
6. Tom Brady, 'Haughey on charge of hindering tribunal', *Irish Independent*, 23 July 1998; 'Judge rules fair trial for Haughey is not possible', *Irish Times*, 27 June 2000.
7. Broadcast on 16 May 1999.
8. Vincent Browne, 'Haughey: The final years', *Magill*, 14 June 2006.
9. See, for instance, 'Smurfit contradicts Haughey's evidence', *Irish Examiner*, 24 May 2001.
10. Moriarty, *Report of the Tribunal of Inquiry*, p. 545.
11. Ibid., p. 422.

12. RTÉ, *Haughey*, Episode 1, *The Outsider*.
13. McDonald and Sheridan, *The Builders*, p. 33.
14. Tom Lyons, 'Smurfit never spoke to Haughey again after Telecom affair', *Irish Times*, 3 April 2014.
15. According to Transparency International, in 2024 Ireland was in joint tenth place in the list of the least corrupt places in the world.
16. John Downing, 'It's time to do a complete review of the Arms Crisis and reveal all the facts', *Irish Independent*, 27 October 2020.
17. Joyce and Murtagh, *The Boss*, 1997, p. xvi.
18. *Hot Press*, Vol. 8, No. 24, 14 December 1984.
19. Terry Keane, 'Charlie's Girl', *Sunday Times*, 16 May 1999.
20. 'Garret at 80' interview, TV3.
21. Michael Noonan interview, 2019.
22. Colm Toibín, 'So farewell then, Garret FitzGabble', *In Dublin*, February 1987.
23. Ray Kavanagh, *Spring, Summer and Fall: The Rise and Fall of the Labour Party, 1986–1999*, Blackwater Press, 2001, p. 20.
24. Hussey, *At the Cutting Edge*, p. 95.
25. Dáil debates, 9 March 2010 Vol. 704, No. 3.
26. Interview with Lionel Barber, 'Diplomatic mission for a heavy hitter', *Financial Times*, 30 December 2004.
27. Conor Cruise O'Brien, 'Babies, wild dogs and coalition', *Magill*, June 1981.
28. Garret FitzGerald in RTÉ, *Fine Gael: A Family at War*, Episode 1, 2003.
29. Katie Hannon, *The Naked Politician*, Gill & Macmillan, 2004, p. 245.
30. Katherine Meenan interview, December 2019.
31. Moore, *Everything She Wants*, p. 328.
32. Niamh Horan, '"Wind energy could be IFSC of the West", claims Teahon', *Irish Independent*, 11 November 2018.
33. Charles Haughey interview, 2004.
34. Alan Murdoch, 'FF's genial horse-trader-in-chief', *Irish Times*, 12 July 1984.
35. Ahern, *The Autobiography*, p. 102.
36. Eoin O'Malley and R. Kenneth Carty, 'A Conservative Revolution? The disequilibrium of Irish politics', in Michael Marsh, David M. Farrell, and Gail McElroy (eds), *A Conservative Revolution? Electoral change in twenty-first century Ireland*, Oxford University Press, 2017.

37. Michael Gallagher, 'The Outcome', in Laver, Mair and Sinnott (eds), *How Ireland Voted 1987*, p. 83.
38. Kevin Rafter, *Neil Blaney: A soldier of destiny*, Blackwater Press, 1993, pp. 110–111.
39. Moriarty, *Report of the Tribunal of Inquiry*, p. 546.
40. O'Brien, *The Modern Prince*, p. 128.
41. Seán Duignan, *One Spin on the Merry-go-Round*, Dublin, Blackwater Press, 1995, p. 10.
42. Ed Moloney, *A Secret History of the IRA*, Penguin, 2002, p. 263.

Glossary

Alliance Party of Northern Ireland (APNI) a cross-community moderate party in Northen Ireland aimed at finding a settlement acceptable to both traditions in the North

Apprentice Boys of Derry: A Protestant fraternal society founded to commemorate the closing of the city's gates during a siege of Derry city in 1688 by forces loyal to Catholic King James II. Like the Orange Order marches, which are common in Northern Ireland in the summer months, these tend to be divisive and are seen by some Irish nationalists as triumphalist

Áras an Uachtaráin (the Áras) residence of the President of Ireland

árd comhairle national executive (of a political party)

Árd Fheis national conference (of a political party) (plural árd fheiseanna)

B-Specials or Ulster Special Constabulary a quasi-military police reserve, predominantly Protestant and later disbanded

Cathaoirleach speaker (chairperson) of Seanad Éireann

Ceann Comhairle speaker (chairperson) of Dáil Éireann

Comhairle Dáil Ceantair constituency branch of a party. Comhairle Ceanntair is the district unit amalgamating a number of cumainn covering a local authority electoral area, the party organisational unit at the constituency level

Cumann local party branch (plural cumainn)

Cumann na nGaedheal a political party formed out of the split in Sinn Féin. It was pro-Treaty. It disbanded in 1933 when it merged with other parties to create Fine Gael

Dáil Éireann directly elected lower house of parliament to which the Irish government is answerable

Democratic Unionist Party (DUP) a radical and uncompromising loyalist party that challenged UUP dominance in Northern Ireland by opposing any and all efforts at settlement with the nationalist community

European Economic Community (EEC) later the European Community (EC) and European Union (EU) transnational community of states in Europe with an increasingly state-like role

Federated Union of Employers: Founded in 1942 as a trade body and lobby group to represent the interests of employers in Ireland. It later became the Federation of Irish Employers until it merged with the Confederation of Irish Industry in 1993 to form the **Irish Business and Employers Confederation** (Ibec)

Fianna Fáil the largest political party in Ireland from 1932 until 2011, formed out of the split in Sinn Féin in the 1920s as to whether to take seats in the Dáil. It had earlier rejected the Treaty with the UK that partitioned Ireland and gave it a form of limited sovereignty

Fine Gael second largest party in Ireland from 1932 to 2011, formed out of a merger with a number of smaller parties and Cumann na nGaedheal

Gaeltacht an Irish-speaking area, now most common on the western seaboard

Garda, Gardaí, Garda Siochána the Irish civilian police force

H-Blocks, HM Prison Maze, Long Kesh a prison and internment camp for paramilitary prisoners and suspects

Irish Congress of Trade Unions (ICTU): The umbrella body for trade unions in Ireland. Formed in 1959, it comprises about 50 individual unions. It enjoyed unprecedented power during the social partnership era up to 2009, but, perhaps as a result of its success, it lost members, as workers no longer felt it necessary to belong to a union

Irish National Caucus (INC): A lobby group founded by Fr Seán McManus that sought to encourage US support for British withdrawal from Northern Ireland, and had alleged links to the IRA and INLA

Irish National Liberation Army (INLA): Founded in 1974 from a split with the Official IRA, it was a left-wing paramilitary organisation that opposed the Official IRA ceasefire. It had a political wing founded at the same time, the Irish Republican Socialist Party

Irish Republican Army (IRA) a military organisation aimed at achieving Irish independence. This can refer to any of a long number of groups, and is usually prefaced with a word to indicate which. For instance, the Provisional IRA was an offshoot of the Official IRA, formed in January 1970, that was devoted to getting Britain to leave Ireland and ending partition. The Provisionals were more violent and more sectarian than the Officials, which had shifted to the left in the 1960s

Leinster House seat of the houses of parliament in Dublin

Oireachtas parliament (it has two houses: the Dáil and the Seanad)

Phoenix Park, the Park a large public park in Dublin city, where Áras an Uachtaráin is located

Progressive Democrats (PDs) small liberal political party founded in 1985 as a breakaway from Fianna Fáil

Radio Telifís Éireann (RTÉ) the national broadcasting service located in Donnybrook, Dublin

Royal Ulster Constabulary (RUC) the predominantly Protestant civilian police force set up when Northern Ireland was formed after partition

Seanad Éireann indirectly elected upper house of parliament

Sinn Féin a series of nationalist parties associated with violent republicanism. The current iteration was formed in 1970, sometimes called the Provos because of the association with the Provisional IRA

Social Democratic and Labour Party (SDLP) nationalist party in Northern Ireland founded in 1970 to represent the interests of Catholics in the North

Tánaiste deputy prime minister of Ireland

Taoiseach prime minister of Ireland

Teachta Dála (TD) Dáil deputy, a member of the Irish parliament

Ulster Unionist Party (UUP) Official Unionists the once-monolithic party representing unionism in Northern Ireland

Vatican II (the Second Ecumenical Council of the Vatican): Called by Pope John XXIII in 1962 and met for three years. It signalled a modernisation of some aspects of Catholic dogma and practice. It was most notable for changes to mass, which was now said in local vernacular languages rather than Latin

Workers' Party, The (WP and formerly SFWP) radical left party that was formed from a split in Sinn Féin in 1970

X case: Miss X was a 14-year-old girl who became pregnant as a result of rape. Her family, who were bringing her to the UK to procure a termination, contacted gardaí regarding the protection of DNA evidence. The Gardaí contacted the Attorney General's office, and he sought and received an injunction in the High Court, delivered by Declan Costello, preventing Miss X from travelling abroad. This decision was overturned in the Supreme Court on the basis that Miss X was threatening to take her own life

Biographies

Adams, Gerry (1948–), Irish nationalist politician. Adams was an early leader of the Provisional IRA in Belfast, something he continues to deny, and became leader of Sinn Féin in 1983, moving the party and the IRA to adopt an electoral strategy. He was elected MP in the House of Commons, but in line with party policy refused to take his seat. He accepted overtures from John Hume to start talks about an IRA ceasefire, which culminated in the Belfast/Good Friday Agreement of 1998. He did not serve in any governments, and concentrated on growing Sinn Féin in the Republic of Ireland.

Ahern, Bertie (1951–), Fianna Fáil politician, minister and Taoiseach. From Dublin, Ahern was first elected to the Dáil in 1977. He rose quickly, and was chief whip and a key adviser to Haughey in 1982. He was made Minister for Labour in 1987 and promoted to Finance in 1991. He became party leader in 1994 and was Taoiseach from 1997 to 2008.

Ahern, Dermot (1950–), Fianna Fáil politician. A solicitor by training, Ahern was elected to Dáil Éireann in 1987 and held his seat in subsequent elections. He became Haughey's chief whip in 1991, and then appointed to cabinet in 1997, serving in positions such as Justice and Foreign Affairs, until his retirement in 2011.

Aiken, Frank (1898–1983), revolutionary and government minister. A member of the IRA, he opposed the Treaty but also tried to avert the civil war. He was a founding member of Fianna Fáil, and was very close to Éamon de Valera. He was a government minister in all Fianna Fáil governments until 1969.

Andrews, David (1935–), barrister, politician and government minister. Andrews was first elected for Fianna Fáil in 1965 for Dún Laoghaire, which he represented until his retirement in 2002. He held a variety of junior ministerial posts under Jack Lynch, but as a vocal opponent of Haughey he remained on the back benches. Albert Reynolds and Bertie Ahern both appointed him to senior ministerial posts, including Foreign Affairs.

Armstrong, Robert, later Lord Armstrong of Ilminster (1927–2020), British civil servant. He was private secretary to Roy Jenkins in the Home Office, and then to prime ministers Edward Heath and Harold Wilson between 1970 and 1977. He became permanent secretary in the Home Office, and then secretary to the Cabinet Office in 1979, a position he held until 1987. He was more positive about dialogue with Ireland than other civil servants.

Arnold, Bruce (1936–2024), journalist and cultural commentator. Originally from London, Arnold moved to Dublin to study at Trinity College Dublin. He became an art and theatre correspondent for the *Irish Times*, and later wrote for the *Sunday Independent* and *Irish Independent*. Arnold wrote many books on Ireland, art and Irish politics. He became an increasingly conservative commentator.

Barry, Peter (1928–2016), businessman and politician. The son of a Fine Gael TD and a tea merchant, Peter Barry developed the business into Barry's Tea, now one of the main tea companies in Ireland. He was elected to the Dáil in 1969 and became Minister for Transport and Power in 1973. As deputy leader of Fine Gael he held senior ministerial positions in all of FitzGerald's cabinets. He was seen as a more green nationalist, but always moderate in his politics and his nature.

Berry, Peter (1909–1978), civil servant, Secretary at the Department of Justice from 1961 to 1971. The son of a policeman, he was educated in Charleville CBS. He worked in the Department of Justice from 1927, and was the head of security and intelligence section from 1941. He was a stickler for protocol and regarded as a security hawk, who frequently clashed with ministers. He later gave evidence against Haughey in the arms trial.

Blaney, Neil T. (1922–1995), Fianna Fáil politician and minister. Representing a Donegal constituency, he was more militant nationalist than most in cabinet, sometimes known as 'the South's Ian Paisley', and was critical of the Fianna Fáil leadership at the outbreak of the Troubles. He was implicated, with Haughey, in the Arms Crisis, but his case was struck out. He left Fianna Fáil, continuing to serve as an independent TD until his death.

Boland, Henry (Harry) (1887–1922) was involved in the 1916 Rising, having joined the IRB and GAA much earlier. He was instrumental in Sinn Féin's success in the 1918 election, and sided with de Valera against the Treaty, ending a friendship with Michael Collins. He was killed in the Civil War.

Boland, John (1944–2000), Fine Gael politician. Educated at CBS Synge Street in Dublin, he was an unsuccessful Fine Gael candidate for the Dáil in 1969 but was elected to the Seanad that year. He was elected to the Dáil in 1977 and impressed when he shadowed Haughey in Social Welfare. Even though he was on the right of the party, Boland was promoted to cabinet in 1981 and appointed Minister for the Public Service in 1982. He lost his seat in 1989 and retired from politics.

Brennan, Séamus (1948–2008), Fianna Fáil politician and minister. Brennan was appointed, by Lynch, General Secretary of Fianna Fáil in 1973 and seen as responsible for the 1977 majority. He was elected to the Dáil in 1981, and though he was part of the anti-Haughey faction, constituency work and organisation meant he maintained good relations across the party. He was promoted to cabinet in 1989 and held various posts up to his retirement in 2008 on medical grounds.

Briscoe, Ben (1934–2023), Fianna Fáil politician. He was elected to the Dáil for Dublin South Central in 1965 and retained his seat until 2002. Briscoe, who was Jewish, was the son of Bob Briscoe, a revolutionary in the Irish War of Independence.

Brooke, Peter (1934–), Conservative Party politician. Elected to the House of Commons in 1977, he became chair of the party in 1987, and was appointed Secretary of State in 1989, which he held until 1992. He stood down from the Commons in 2001.

Browne, Noël (1915–1997), doctor and politician. His parents and several siblings died of tuberculosis when he was very young and he was brought up in England and educated at Jesuit public schools. He returned to Ireland to study medicine at Trinity College, later becoming a TD for the newly formed Clann na Poblachta and was made Minister for Health in 1948. The Mother and Child scheme, which he introduced, contributed to the collapse of the first inter-party government. He later switched political allegiance, but remained an outsider in Irish political life and a hero for many on the left.

Burke, Raphael (Ray) (1943–) auctioneer, Fianna Fáil politician and cabinet minister. He was first elected to the Dáil in 1973, retaining the seat held by his father Paddy, or the Bishop. He was a minister for state in Lynch's 1977 government, and retained by Haughey, to whom he became very close. Haughey brought him into the cabinet in late 1980. He served in all of Haughey's cabinets in various positions, and later was briefly Minister for Foreign Affairs in Bertie Ahern's first government. He was jailed for tax evasion, and was found by the Flood Tribunal to be 'corrupt' in his awarding of a radio licence.

Cahill, Bernie (1930–2001), businessman. Cahill studied dairy science, and worked in the dairy business for many years, building up a business in Ireland for the UK company Express Dairies. He was chairman of Irish Sugar when it was privatised as Greencore, and became chairman of Aer Lingus, where he was credited with successfully restructuring the loss-making airline.

Cassells, Peter (1949–), trade unionist. Cassells was a civil servant who later joined the Irish Congress of Trade Unions, an umbrella body for unions, first as a policy officer, and rising to become the general secretary in 1989. He served on a variety of government bodies after his retirement.

Childers, Erskine (1905–1974), politician and fourth president of Ireland. The English-educated Fianna Fáil politician was the son of an English civil servant who became prominent in the Irish revolution. Respected but regarded as a bit naive in Fianna Fáil, he was elected a TD in 1938, becoming a government minister in 1951. He was elected president in 1973, but died a year later.

Cluskey, Frank (1930–1989), politician and trade unionist. He came from a family of strong trade unionists, left school early and became a butcher's apprentice, then worked for a union. He was elected to the Dáil for Labour in 1965, becoming a junior minister in 1973. He won the leadership in 1977, but on losing his seat, lost the leadership in 1981. He regained the seat and spent a short, unhappy spell in cabinet in FitzGerald's second government.

Colley, George (1925–1983), Fianna Fáil politician, government minister. A solicitor by training, Colley was elected in 1961 and was made parliamentary secretary in 1964 and Minister for Education in 1965. He was defeated in a leadership contest in 1966, but held positions in Fianna Fáil governments until 1982. He died in 1983 following a heart attack. He was generally seen as a man of great integrity, if lacking flair.

Colley, Harry (1891–1972) was a revolutionary and Fianna Fáil politician who fought in the GPO in 1916, and later was a founder member of Fianna Fáil, active in its national executive, and a TD from 1944 to 1957.

Collins, Gerard (Gerry) (1938–), Fianna Fáil politician. Collins was the son of a Fianna Fáil TD and old IRA fighter. He was an assistant secretary general for Fianna Fáil in 1965 and was elected to the Dáil in the by-election that followed the death of his father. He was made Minister for Posts and Telegraphs in the aftermath of the Arms Crisis, and served in all Fianna Fáil governments until 1992. He was elected an MEP in 1994.

Connolly, Patrick (1927–2016), barrister and Attorney General March–August 1982. Best known for the GUBU affair, he was one of Haughey's legal team in the arms trials.

Cooney, Patrick (Paddy) M. (1931–), politician and government minister. He failed at three attempts at election to the Dáil for Fine Gael before winning a by-election in 1970 for Longford-Westmeath. He rose quickly and was appointed to the front bench and then made Minister for Justice in 1973. He held posts in both of FitzGerald's governments. Initially seen as a liberal, he became more conservative as his career progressed.

Corish, Brendan (1918–1990), trade unionist and politician. The son of a Labour TD for Wexford, he was educated at the local CBS. He worked as a clerical officer in local government, taking on his late father's seat in 1945. He was appointed Minister for Social Welfare in the second inter-party government, but opposed re-election of that government. In 1973, as Labour leader, he worked well with Liam Cosgrave in government, and retired from politics in 1982.

Cosgrave, Liam (1920–2017), TD, minister and Taoiseach, was the son of W.T. Cosgrave, the first President of the Executive Council (later to be known as Taoiseach). He was educated at CBS Synge Street, Castleknock College and King's Inns. He was elected to the Dáil in 1943 and rose through the ranks of Fine Gael, serving as chief whip and Minister for External Affairs. Regarded as a conservative, he was more a pragmatist, later winning the leadership of Fine Gael. He was Taoiseach from 1973 to 1977, heading the so-called National Coalition.

Costello, Declan (1926–2011), Irish politician, Attorney General and High Court judge. He was the son of **John A. Costello (1891–1976)**, who was Taoiseach during the two inter-party governments. Costello Jnr. was a barrister and Attorney General from 1926 to 1932. He was then elected to the Dáil. He was chosen as Taoiseach as a compromise, to keep out the party leader, Richard Mulcahy. Declan Costello was elected to the Dáil for Fine Gael in 1951 and was instrumental in pushing a social democratic agenda in the party. He was made Attorney General in 1973, serving in that capacity until 1977, at which time he left politics, having been appointed to the High Court.

Currie, Austin (1939–2021), activist and politician. From County Tyrone, Currie became active in the civil rights movement in the 1960s. He was elected as an MP to the Northern Ireland parliament in 1964 and later assemblies. He was a founder of the SDLP in 1970. He moved to the South in 1989 when he was elected a TD in Dublin West, and served as minister for state from 1994 to 1997. He was Fine Gael's candidate for the presidency in 1990. He lost his seat in 2002 and retired from electoral politics.

de Valera, Síle (1954–), politician and government minister. Born and educated in Dublin, she was elected TD for Fianna Fáil, the party her grandfather Éamon had founded, in Dublin Mid-County in 1977, becoming the youngest TD in that Dáil. A noted supporter of anti-H-Block protests, she lost her seat in 1981. After a number of failed attempts, she regained a seat in Clare in 1987, and was a cabinet minister from 1997 to 2002, and later a minister for state. She retired from politics in 2007.

Desmond, Barry (1935–), Labour politician. From Cork and a graduate of UCC, Desmond started his career in the trade union movement, and was later elected to the Dáil for Dún Laoghaire in 1969, a seat he held until 1989. He was a minister for state in FitzGerald's first government, and then elected deputy leader of the Labour Party, he was Minister for Health and Social Welfare from 1982 to 1987. He was seen as a moderate in the Labour Party. Desmond later served on the European Court of Auditors.

Desmond, Dermot (1950–), businessman and financier. Desmond founded a stockbroking firm, National City Brokers, which he later sold at significant profit. In 1995, he founded International Investment & Underwriting (IIU), a private equity firm that had interests in many businesses. He was an adviser to and a financial supporter of Haughey.

Dillon, James (1902–1986), politician and barrister. The son of the nationalist MP John Dillon, born in Wexford, James Dillon opposed the rise of Sinn Féin after 1916. He was first elected as an independent TD in 1932 and soon became vice-president of the newly formed Fine Gael, resigning over the party's support for neutrality. He was Minister for Agriculture in the two inter-party governments in the 1940s and 1950s, first as an independent and then back in Fine Gael. He became Fine Gael leader in 1959, resigning after the 1965 election.

Donlon, Seán (1940–), civil servant and executive. Donlon initially trained for the priesthood in Maynooth, where he was a contemporary of John Hume. He entered the Department of Finance in 1961 before moving to External Affairs (later Foreign Affairs). He set up the Anglo-Irish Division in 1973 and was posted to Washington as ambassador in 1978, returning to Dublin to head up the Department. He left for the private sector, returning to become chief of staff to Taoiseach John Bruton.

Dooge, James (Jim) (1922–2010), academic and politician. Born in Liverpool to Irish parents, he studied engineering at UCD and went on to work for the ESB's hydrology department. He was also a Fine Gael county councillor. He then moved into academia, where he specialised in hydrology, taking a post in UCD. He was elected to the Seanad in 1961 and remained there until 1977. Garret FitzGerald appointed him to cabinet as Minister for Foreign Affairs, where he was regarded as a success in that short-lived government.

Dukes, Alan (1945–), economist and politician. Dukes worked in Brussels for the Irish Farmers' Association, and was then appointed chief of staff to Dick Burke during his commissionership. He stood for Fine Gael in the European Parliament elections in 1979 and was elected to the Dáil for Kildare in 1981. Appointed to government in 1981, he then took the leadership in 1987, but was forced to stand down in 1990 because of poor election results. Dukes re-entered cabinet in the Rainbow coalition but lost his Dáil seat in 2002.

Dunne, Bernard (Ben) (1949–2023), businessman. In 1983 Dunne took over the management of the Dunnes Stores chain that had been founded by his father. It was one of Ireland's largest supermarkets. He had earlier been kidnapped by the IRA. A dispute about the financial management of the company in 1992 led to him being bought out of the family trust that controlled Dunnes Stores. He then became involved in a number of new businesses.

Faulkner, Brian (1921–1977), politician. Born to a well-established family of industrialists, Faulkner was educated at St Columba's College in Dublin, an Anglican secondary school. Initially on the liberal wing of unionism, he then appealed to Orange populism to rise within the party, serving in many ministerial roles in Stormont. He was seen as too much a hardliner in 1963 to take the leadership, and opposed many of Terence O'Neill's initiatives. He took over the leadership in March 1971 at perhaps the most difficult time for any unionist leader, and struggled to hold the party together. He was killed in a riding accident.

Faulkner, Pádraig (1918–2012), politician and minister. Born in County Louth, Faulkner became a national school teacher. He was elected to the Dáil for Fianna Fáil in 1957 and served as parliamentary secretary with responsibility for the Gaeltacht from 1965 to 1969. A Lynch loyalist, he held various cabinet positions in Fianna Fáil governments until he was elected Ceann Comhairle in 1980.

FitzGerald, Alexis (1916–1985), lawyer and political adviser. Educated at Waterpark College, Clongowes Wood College and UCD, Alexis FitzGerald then studied law, founding the law firm that would become McCann FitzGerald. He lectured in political economy in UCD for many years and was son-in-law to John A. Costello, to whom he acted as an adviser when he was Taoiseach. He was associated with the Just Society tradition in Fine Gael and was later an adviser sitting at cabinet in Garret FitzGerald's first government.

Fitzgerald, Gene (1932–2007) Fianna Fáil politician. Prominent in Cork GAA circles, Fitzgerald was elected to the Dáil in a by-election in Mid Cork constituency. Jack Lynch appointed him to cabinet in 1977, and he supported Colley in the leadership election of 1979, but in the subsequent heaves loyally backed Haughey, who regarded him with contempt. Jovial and friendly, Fitzgerald was a surprise choice for Minister for Finance. He chose to run for election to the European Parliament in 1984, retiring in 1994.

Flynn, Pádraig (1939–) Fianna Fáil politician, cabinet minister and EU Commissioner. Elected to the Mayo West constituency in 1977, he was brought into Haughey's cabinet in 1982, and again in 1987 and 1989, even though he was opposed to the Fianna Fáil–Progressive Democrat coalition. He resigned from that cabinet having voted to remove Haughey as leader, and was brought into Albert Reynolds's government. He was later appointed to the European Commission. In the Mahon Tribunal he was found to have corruptly sought money from a property developer.

Geoghegan-Quinn, Máire (1950–), politician and EC Commissioner. Elected to the Dáil in 1975 in a by-election caused by the death of her father, Johnny Geoghegan, she was a junior minister from 1977 and promoted to cabinet in 1979. She then held some junior roles, before resigning in protest at Haughey's leadership in 1991. Albert Reynolds promoted her and she was briefly considered a leadership contender when Reynolds resigned in 1994. She later held a number of posts at European level.

Gibbons, James (Jim) (1924–1997), Fianna Fáil politician and farmer. A well-read, socially conservative man, Gibbons was elected to Dáil Éireann in the 1957 election. He was parliamentary secretary to the Minister for Finance from 1965 to 1969. Though he supported Colley in the leadership campaign, Lynch promoted him to cabinet in 1969. While not close to Lynch, he served in his remaining cabinets, was dropped by Haughey in 1979 and lost his seat in 1982.

Goodall, Sir David (1931–2016), British diplomat. A Catholic with Irish roots, Goodall served in the British Army before joining the Foreign Office (FO) in 1956. He served in many countries before becoming head of the FO's Western European department in Bonn from 1979 to 1982. He was then seconded to the Cabinet Office. He worked with Michael Lillis to push for increased dialogue, and pushed Thatcher to engage in Northern Ireland, leading eventually to the Anglo-Irish Agreement. He later served as High Commissioner to India.

Goodman, Larry (1937–), businessman. Goodman was a meat trader who created one of the most successful Irish businesses. Goodman International started in meat processing, but expanded into dairy, becoming one of the largest agri-foods business in Europe. He benefited from state supports at key stages in the development of the business, which has made him a controversial figure.

Goulding, Cathal (1923–1998), socialist revolutionary. Goulding joined Fianna Éireann, the youth wing of the IRA, and later joined the IRA while still in his teens. He was interned for the duration of the Emergency (the Second World War) and then tried to revive the depleted IRA. He rose within the organisation, becoming chief of staff in 1962. He developed a Marxist analysis of Irish history, and moved Sinn Féin and the IRA sharply to the left, which caused a split and the formation of the Provisional IRA. He remained in the Official IRA, and was critical of what he saw as sectarianism in the Provisional movement.

Gregory, Tony (1947–2009), teacher, activist and politician. Originally involved in republican politics, he was a member of the IRA in the 1960s. He remained with Official Sinn Féin after the split with the Provisionals, but left because of frustrations with ideological in-fighting. Gregory was elected to the Dáil in 1982, holding his Dublin Central seat until his death.

Harney, Mary (1953–), politician and government minister. Harney was appointed to the Seanad by Taoiseach Jack Lynch in 1977, having stood unsuccessfully for the Dáil. She was elected to the Dáil in Dublin-South West and retained her seat until her retirement in 2011. She was expelled from the Fianna Fáil parliamentary party in 1985 and then was a founder of the Progressive Democrats. She served as a junior minister in the Haughey coalition, and later, as leader of the PDs, was Tánaiste and held various senior ministries.

Harte, Paddy (1931–2018), politician. Born in Lifford, County Donegal to a Fine Gael family, Harte was a shopkeeper. In 1961 he was elected to Dáil Éireann, and repeatedly re-elected until his defeat in 1997. He was appointed minister of state in 1981. Harte devoted much of his career to building bridges between the communities on the island.

Haughey, Pádraig (Paddy, later better known as Jock) (1932–2003), Charlie Haughey's younger brother, played Gaelic football for Dublin, winning an All-Ireland medal in 1958. He was later summonsed by the Public Accounts Committee, which called him as a witness in a committee hearing where he refused to answer questions. This led to the landmark *In re Haughey* judgment, which showed the willingness of the courts to interfere in the operation of the Oireachtas.

Hanafin, Des (1930–2017), Fianna Fáil politician and businessman. From Tipperary Hanafin was elected to the Seanad in 1969 and remained a senator, with one break, until 2002. He was the Fianna Fáil treasurer for the 1970s, but was independent-minded and critical of Charles Haughey. Hanafin was a social conservative, opposing any social liberalising measures.

Healy, John (1930–1991) was a political journalist who wrote a well-informed but biased political column in the *Irish Times*, sometimes under the pseudonym Backbencher. He was responsible for coining the ironic sobriquets 'Honest Jack', 'Garret the Good' and others about Haughey's political opponents. Born in Charlestown, County Mayo, he was the author of *No One Shouted Stop!* on the decline of his home town and rural Ireland.

Hefferon, Colonel Michael (1910–1985), army officer. He joined the Irish army in 1933 and was aide de camp to President Seán

T. O'Kelly from 1945 to 1959. In 1963 Hefferon was appointed Director of Military Intelligence. He retired in April 1970, after which he was a key witness in the arms trial.

Higgins, Michael D. (1941–) academic, Labour politician and President of Ireland. A sociologist based in University College Galway, at college Higgins initially joined Fianna Fáil but then moved to the Labour Party. After two failed attempts at election to Dáil Éireann, Higgins was nominated to the Seanad in 1973 and elected to the Dáil in 1981 for Galway West, a seat he would lose and gain again. Generally seen as on the left of Labour, he opposed coalition with Fine Gael. He became a minister in 1992 and was elected President of Ireland in 2011, a role in which he was noted for being outspoken against the governments of the day.

Hillery, Patrick J. (Paddy) (1923–2008), cabinet minister and president of Ireland, was a prominent Fianna Fáil politician, who was instrumental in devising the free education plan in Ireland. He became Ireland's first EEC Commissioner, and was elected President of Ireland unopposed in 1976, to fill the vacancy created by the resignation of Cearbhall Ó Dálaigh.

Honohan, Patrick (1949–), economist. Honohan is an economist who has worked in policy throughout his career. He started off at the International Monetary Fund (IMF), then worked in the Central Bank of Ireland as chief economist, before working for FitzGerald. He later worked in the World Bank and was the Governor of the Central Bank of Ireland between 2009 and 2015.

Hume, John (1937–2020), nationalist politician. Hume was born in Derry to a working-class family and began to train for the priesthood, but he did not complete his studies and became a teacher. In the 1960s, he was an advocate for civil rights, and in 1969 was elected as an independent nationalist in the Foyle constituency for the Stormont Assembly. In 1970, he was a founder of the Social Democratic and Labour Party (SDLP). A long-time opponent of the Provisional IRA and the use of violence, he held a leadership role in nationalism and was particularly influential in southern politics. Eventually he was one of the signatories of the Belfast or Good Friday Agreement, something he had fought for his entire life.

Hussey (née Moran), Gemma (1938–2024), Fine Gael politician. From Wicklow and educated at UCD, Hussey was elected to the Seanad for the NUI panel in 1977 as an independent. She then joined Fine Gael and was elected to the Dáil for Wicklow in February 1982. Considered on the liberal wing of Fine Gael, she was one of the people FitzGerald attracted into the party. He appointed her Minister for Education in November 1982 and later Minister for Social Welfare. She retired from electoral politics in 1989.

Keane, (née O'Donnell), Ann Teresa (Terry) (1939–2008) socialite and journalist, wrote gossip columns for many years for the *Sunday Independent* and later the *Sunday Times*. In these she would drop hints of her affair with 'Sweetie', which most people in media and politics knew was Haughey. When she revealed the affair on *The Late Late Show* in 1999, there was genuine surprise among many, some of whom had thought the rumours of the affair were British black propaganda.

Keating, Justin (1930–2009), academic, broadcaster and politician. Born in Dublin, the son of the artist Seán Keating, he was educated at Sandford Park, UCD and the University of London, where he gained a degree in biochemistry. He was a lecturer in veterinary anatomy at Trinity College and also became a broadcaster on RTÉ's agricultural programming. A lifelong Marxist and atheist, he was prominent in various organisations on the Irish left, and was elected for Labour in 1969. He opposed Ireland's EEC membership, and served in government as Minister for Industry and Commerce during the 1973–77

National Coalition government, during which he was friendly with Garret FitzGerald. He lost his Dáil seat, but became a senator until 1981, when he retired from frontline politics, though remained a commentator.

Kelly, Captain James (1929–2003), an army intelligence officer and republican from County Cavan, was deeply affected by witnessing the Battle of the Bogside in August 1969. Kelly retired from the army in 1970 and was later charged with conspiracy to import arms, but spent the rest of his life claiming he was acting on orders.

Kelly, John (1931–1991), academic and Fine Gael politician. Kelly was an accomplished legal scholar, who after practising at the bar, returned to UCD, where he rose to become dean of the Law School. He was elected to the Seanad in 1969 and the Dáil in 1973. He was chief whip in the National Coalition and its Attorney General for just a few weeks. A conservative, he did not enjoy serving in the short-lived 1981 government.

Kelly, John (1936–2007) a Belfast republican who had been involved in the border campaign in the 1950s and was a founder of the Provisional IRA. He was a key figure in the Arms Crisis, acquitted in the second arms trial.

Kemmy, Jim (1936–1997), trade unionist and politician. A stonemason by trade, Kemmy was a socialist from Limerick city who was unusual in being openly atheist and taking unpopular positions. He left Labour to run under the Democratic Socialist banner, his own micro-party, getting elected to the Dáil in 1981. He rejoined the Labour Party, becoming its chair, and remained a TD until his death in 1997.

Kennedy, Geraldine (1951–), journalist and politician. Kennedy was a political journalist writing for the *Irish Times*, *Sunday Tribune* and *Sunday Press*. She was one of two journalists known to have had their phones tapped by the Gardaí in 1982. Kennedy became a Progressive Democrat TD in 1987, but lost her seat in 1989, and returned to journalism, becoming the political editor and later the editor of the *Irish Times*.

Lawlor, Liam (1945–2005), Fianna Fáil politician. Lawlor was elected to the Dáil for Dublin County West in 1977, and won and lost his seat many times, but secured it from 1987 to 2002. Allegations of corruption were made against him in the Flood Tribunal and he was jailed three times for refusing to co-operate while a TD, and then expelled from Fianna Fáil.

Lenihan, Brian (1930–1995), Fianna Fáil politician, minister and Tánaiste, was closely associated with Haughey through his long career. He was an early reforming minister, who in 1990 was Fianna Fáil's candidate for the presidential election, during which he was sacked by Haughey.

Lillis, Michael (1946–), Irish diplomat. Born in Dublin, Lillis joined the Department of Foreign Affairs in 1969. He was assigned to the new Anglo-Irish Division in 1972 and was posted to the US in 1976, where he was tasked with persuading Irish-American politicians to take a more nuanced view of the conflict in Northern Ireland. Appointed as an adviser by Garret FitzGerald, he was tasked with opening up the discussions that would lead to the Anglo-Irish Agreement and was part of the secretariat that was set up under that agreement.

Loughnane, Bill (1915–1982), politician and medical doctor. He was first elected to the Dáil in 1969, and represented Clare in all Dáileanna until he died. He was a strong Irish nationalist, whose nationalism manifested itself mainly in being vehemently anti-British.

Luykx, Albert (1917–1978), hotelier and businessman, originally from Belgium, who became an Irish citizen and was an acquaintance of Neil T. Blaney. Luykx was a Flemish nationalist and a Nazi collaborator. He was a co-defendant of Haughey's in the arms trials.

Macarthur, Malcolm (1945–), socialite, criminal and murderer. Of Anglo-Irish stock, Macarthur lived a peripatetic life spending his inheritance. When it ran out, he returned to Ireland, turning to robbery, at which he was unsuccessful. He was convicted of murder in 1982 and released in 2012.

Mac Conghail, Muiris (1941–2019), broadcaster and journalist. The son of the artist Maurice MacGonigal, Mac Conghail was an editor of RTÉ's flagship *7 Days* current affairs programme and later head of the Government Information Service in the Cosgrave government – appointed on the recommendation of Joan FitzGerald. He was later the head of programming in RTÉ.

McCreevy, Charlie (1949–), Fianna Fáil politician, cabinet minister and EU Commissioner. McCreevy was elected to the Dáil for Kildare in 1977. Initially an enthusiastic supporter of Haughey, he then became one of his fiercest critics. Albert Reynolds brought him into cabinet in 1992, and he became a powerful Minister for Finance under Bertie Ahern. Ahern nominated him to the European Commission in 2004, where he held the Internal Market portfolio until 2010.

McDaid, James (Jim) (1949–), medical doctor and politician. McDaid was elected to Dáil Eireann for Donegal North-East in 1989, at his first attempt. He was nominated as Minister for Defence in 1991, but was never appointed. He later sat in cabinet from 1997 to 2002, and later held a variety of junior ministries. He resigned from the Dáil in 2010 in protest at Fianna Fáil's handling of the financial crisis.

MacEntee, Seán (1889–1984), revolutionary and government minister. Born in Belfast, he was attracted to radical politics in the revolutionary 1910s. He joined the Irish Volunteers in 1914 and was imprisoned during the War of Independence. While he opposed the Treaty, he maintained good relations with the pro-Treaty side. His wife, Margaret, was Garret FitzGerald's godmother. MacEntee was seen as an orthodox Minister for Finance. He remained in cabinet until 1965.

MacSharry, Ray (1938–), politician and EC Commissioner. MacSharry was elected to the Dáil in 1969 for the Sligo-Leitrim constituency. He was made a minister of state in 1977 and promoted to cabinet by Haughey in 1979. Seen as one of the most capable ministers, Haughey chose him for Finance in 1987, but he moved to the European Commission in 1988. He retired from politics in 1992 to pursue business interests.

Mansergh, Martin (1946–), civil servant, Fianna Fáil adviser and politician. Of Anglo-Irish heritage, the English-educated Mansergh worked in the Department of Foreign Affairs, from which he was seconded to write speeches for Haughey in 1981. He left the civil service to become head of research for Fianna Fáil. He was a trusted adviser on Northern Ireland and other issues to successive Fianna Fáil Taoisigh, and was a key player in the 1998 Belfast/Good Friday Agreement. He later represented Tipperary in the Dáil and was made minister of state.

Mara, PJ (1942–2016), businessman and public relations consultant. Originally a Fianna Fáil member in Haughey's constituency, he became a close adviser to Haughey. He was appointed Fianna Fáil press secretary in 1983 and government press secretary from 1987 to 1992. He later organised Fianna Fáil's electoral campaigns in 1997, 2002 and 2007.

Molloy, Bobby (1936–2016), politician and government minister. From Galway he was elected to Galway West in 1965 and held his seat until his retirement in 2002. He was made Minister for Local Government as a result of the Arms Crisis. He was dropped by Haughey when he formed his first cabinet in 1979, and left Fianna Fáil to join the PDs in 1986. He was again a minister in the 1989 coalition with Fianna Fáil.

Mulcahy, Richard (1886–1971) was a soldier, revolutionary and politician. Educated at Mount Sion in Waterford, he left school early to work in the Post Office. He joined the Gaelic League, the Irish Volunteers and the IRB, and was involved in 1916 Rising, later becoming chief of staff of the IRA. He supported the Treaty, on the grounds that the IRA could not last six months. He was both Minister for Defence and chief of the new national army, becoming a hate figure for the execution of his erstwhile republican colleagues. He became leader of Fine Gael in 1944, but when he seemed likely to become Taoiseach in 1948 the Clann na Poblachta leader, Seán McBride, objected, and he stepped aside for Costello, remaining as party leader.

Nally, Dermot (1927–2009), civil servant. The son of a senior civil servant, Mr Nally (as he was universally known) began his career in the Department of Local Government, where his intelligence and application was noticed in drafting the Planning Act in the early 1960s. He moved into the Department of the Taoiseach in January 1973 to advise the Taoiseach, Jack Lynch, and became secretary to the government in July 1980. From then on he was a constant presence with Taoisigh at all European summits and summits related to Northern Ireland. He retired in 1993.

Noonan, Michael (1943–), Fine Gael politician. A schoolteacher from Limerick, Noonan won a seat in the Dáil in 1981. He was appointed to Justice in December 1982 and served in all Fine Gael governments up to 2017. He was leader of Fine Gael after a heave against John Bruton in 2001, but the party performed disastrously. He seemed to be retired until a failed coup against Enda Kenny brought him back to the front bench, after which he served as Minister for Finance.

O'Brien, Conor Cruise (1917–2008), writer, journalist, diplomat, politician and academic, started his career in the Irish diplomatic service, running the Irish News Agency. He was seconded to the United Nations, where he was a UN special representative of a region in newly independent Congo (now the Democratic Republic of the Congo). He left the diplomatic service and became an academic in New York University, leaving that post to enter Irish politics. In 1969 he was elected to the Dáil as a Labour TD for Dublin North-Central, and was a fierce critic of Charles Haughey. O'Brien became Minister for Posts and Telegraphs in 1973, and was vehemently anti-IRA. He lost his seat and was later appointed editor of the *Observer* newspaper in London, a post he held until 1981. He continued to write in the Irish media, and in later life adopted a unionist position.

O'Connor, Jack (1957–) trade unionist. A full-time trade unionist from the 1980s, he worked for SIPTU, becoming General President from 2003 to 2017, and President of ICTU from 2009 to 2011. He later served as chairman of the Labour Party.

Ó Dálaigh, Cearbhall (1911–1978), judge and President of Ireland. An unsuccessful Fianna Fáil candidate for the Dáil, he was subsequently appointed Attorney General in 1946. Appointed to the Supreme Court in 1953, he became chief justice in 1961. His court was an ambitious one that expanded legal rights. He was an agreed presidential candidate in 1974, following the death of Erskine Childers, but his republican views and touchy nature meant he had a poor relationship with Liam Cosgrave. He resigned following criticism from a government minister over his decision to refer a piece of legislation to the Supreme Court to test its constitutionality.

O'Donnell, Brendan (1940–), civil servant. He joined the Department of Agriculture in 1959, worked for Charles Haughey there, and then was brought with him in various ministerial appointments. He was later appointed by Haughey as chief executive of An Bord Glas (the horticultural agency).

O'Donoghue, Martin (1933–2018), Fianna Fáil politician and academic. He worked as an associate professor of economics in Trinity College,

Dublin, and from 1970 was an adviser to Taoiseach Jack Lynch, to whom he became a very close confidant. He was elected TD in 1977 and was made Minister for Economic Planning, until that post was abolished in 1979. He was later appointed Minister for Education.

Ó hAnnracháin, Pádraig (1921–1988), journalist, civil servant and adviser. He was private secretary to Éamon de Valera in opposition. In government he became the Head of the Government Information Service under three Taoisigh, until Liam Cosgrave moved him to the Department of Education. There he privately advised Haughey, and remained a close confidant who then appointed him second secretary in the Department of the Taoiseach.

O'Higgins, Thomas F. (1916–2003), politician and judge. The son of a Fine Gael TD and minister, and the nephew of Kevin O'Higgins, he was elected to the Dáil in 1948 and became Minister for Health in 1954. He was seen as a moderniser, if not quite a social democratic. He ran for the presidency in 1966 and almost beat Éamon de Valera. He became deputy leader of Fine Gael in 1972, and ran again in 1973 for the presidency. He lost that and was appointed to the High Court, and then Chief Justice in 1974. O'Higgins was seen as a conservative judge, though this may have been a reaction to the more activist members of the bench at the time. O'Higgins's youngest daughter later married Mark FitzGerald, Garret's youngest son.

Ó hUiginn, Pádraig (1924–2019), civil servant. Born in Cork, he entered the civil service in 1941 in the Department of Local Government. After a secondment to the UN he returned in 1964 to head the national physical planning institute An Foras Forbartha. He transferred to the Department of Economic Planning in 1977 and joined the Department of the Taoiseach when that was abolished by Haughey. He was distrusted by FitzGerald, because he was seen as close to Haughey. Generally regarded as one of the most capable, if not the most rule-bound, civil servants of his generation.

O'Kennedy, Michael (1936–2022), lawyer and politician. From a republican family in Tipperary, he became a senator in 1965 and was elected a Fianna Fáil TD in 1969. He was promoted to cabinet in 1972, and was Minister for Foreign Affairs from 1977. Briefly considered a leadership contender, he was the only cabinet minister to publicly support Haughey for the leadership. In 1981 he briefly became an EC commissioner before returning to Irish politics.

O'Malley, Desmond (1939–2021), politician and government minister. He was first elected for Fianna Fáil in a by-election in 1968 caused by the death of his uncle. He became chief whip in 1969, and was made Minister for Justice in 1970 during the Arms Crisis. He served in various Haughey governments, but resigned in 1982, and was expelled from Fianna Fail in 1985, founding a new party, the Progressive Democrats, later that year. He was in government again with Haughey as part of a coalition with Fianna Fáil in 1989, and with Albert Reynolds in 1991, until he took the PDs out of government in 1992.

O'Malley, Donogh (1921–1968), Fianna Fáil politician and government minister. From Limerick and trained as an engineer, O'Malley is best known for his introduction of free secondary education in Ireland. He developed a deserved reputation as a wild man, and was close to Haughey and Brian Lenihan. His death at aged just 47 was deeply felt by Haughey.

O'Neill, Terence (1914–1990) politician, prime minister of Northern Ireland. Born in London to an Anglo-Irish aristocratic family, his father was an MP killed in action during the First World War. O'Neill was educated at Eton and joined the army at the outbreak of the Second World War. He was elected to the Northern Irish parliament in Stormont for the Ulster Unionist Party in 1946 and served in various ministerial roles before becoming prime minister in 1963. He was a modernising and more innovative unionist leader, who was conscious of slights to the nationalist population, but struggled to hold his party together when there were demonstrations for increasing civil rights for Catholics. An election called to hold his party together was only partially successful and in April 1969 he resigned under pressure from hardline unionists within the party.

Paircéir, Séamus (1929– 2011), public servant and businessman. He was appointed to the board of the Revenue Commissioners in 1980, and became chairman in 1984. His investigation of Charles Haughey's tax affairs was controversial, and he was later found to have made a decision beneficial to Dunnes Stores following a representation made by Haughey.

Paisley, Ian (1926–2014), Protestant preacher and unionist politician. The son of a Baptist preacher from County Tyrone, Paisley was ordained a Protestant minister in 1946. He was an evangelical who took a very strong anti-Catholic line, founding the Free Presbyterian Church of Ulster in 1951. He was alienated from official unionism and attacked any attempts at rapprochement with Catholics or Irish politics. He organised counter-demonstrations to the civil rights marches in 1968 and was seen to encourage anti-Catholic violence, becoming increasingly political. He founded the Democratic Unionist Party in 1971 and was elected to the British House of Commons in 1970 for North Antrim, a seat he would hold for 40 years. He became a leading voice of intransigent unionism, opposing the Sunningdale Agreement, Anglo-Irish Agreement and the Good Friday Agreement. Eventually, in 2007, Paisley entered the new Northern Ireland Executive, working with Martin McGuinness of Sinn Féin, who had been a leading member of the Provisional IRA.

Power, Paddy (1928–2013), politician and government minister. Elected to the Dáil for Kildare in 1969. A strong supporter of Haughey, he was promoted to cabinet when Charles Haughey became Taoiseach in 1979. He retired from politics in 1989.

Prendergast, Peter (1939–), political operative. Prendergast was a marketing specialist for a range of food companies and an unsuccessful Fine Gael candidate in Dublin South-East in 1973 and 1977. He was appointed general secretary of the party in 1977, and later became the head of the Government Information Service (GIS).

Prior, Jim (1927–2016), UK Conservative politician. Elected to the House of Commons in 1959, he remained an MP until 1987. Prior held a number of posts, including Leader of the House, and was an unsuccessful candidate for the Tory leadership in 1975. He was a cabinet minister in several Thatcher governments, including Secretary of State for Northern Ireland for three years from September 1981.

Reid, Fr Alec (1931–2013), Catholic priest. A priest in the Redemptorist order, Reid was based in the Clonard monastery in west Belfast for much of the Troubles. He was trusted by most sides in the conflict as an honest broker, and pushed for an opening of dialogue with the IRA and Sinn Féin.

Reynolds, Albert (1932–2014), businessman and Taoiseach. Originally from Roscommon, Reynolds made money in the 1960s as a nightclub owner. He was elected to the Dáil in 1977, and was promoted to cabinet by Haughey, always holding economic ministries. Seen as an effective minister, he opposed the coalition with the PDs, and moved against Haughey, eventually winning and becoming Taoiseach in 1992. That government fell, as did his second government, a coalition with Labour, forcing his resignation in 1994. In 1997 he tried for the Fianna Fáil nomination for the presidency, but was passed over.

Robinson (née Bourke), Mary (1944–), lawyer, activist, President of Ireland. Born to a wealthy Catholic family in Mayo, she was educated at Trinity College Dublin, where she studied law. She took up a career in academia and was elected to the Seanad in 1969. Robinson took on many liberal causes, including pushing for the decriminalisation of homosexual acts. She unsuccessfully ran for election to the Dáil for the Labour Party. She left Labour in opposition to the Anglo-Irish Agreement in 1985. Robinson was then approached by Labour to run for the presidency, which she won in 1990, pushing the boundaries to create a more active office. She resigned the presidency to take up a position in the UN.

Ryan, Eoin (1920–2001), lawyer and Fianna Fáil politician. The son of James Ryan, one of the volunteers in the GPO in 1916, he served in the Irish army during the Emergency and then was appointed to the national executive of Fianna Fáil. A successful commercial lawyer he was a part-time politician, serving in the Seanad from 1957 to 1987. He was friendly with Garret FitzGerald and firmly in the anti-Haughey camp in Fianna Fáil.

Ryan, Fr Patrick (1930–2025), Catholic priest. Ordained in the Pallottine Order in 1954, he was a known IRA sympathiser, who later admitted his involvement in the IRA. He ran unsuccessfully as an independent candidate in the 1989 European elections in the Munster constituency.

Ryan, Richard (Richie) (1929–2019), Fine Gael politician and government minister. A solicitor by training and a formidable debater, Ryan was first elected to the Dáil in 1959, and was appointed Minister for Finance in 1973. Generally seen as a centrist in Fine Gael, he was an orthodox finance minister. He became an MEP in 1979, and was later appointed to the European Court of Auditors.

Sherlock, Joe (1935–2007), trade unionist and politician. A trade union official who worked at Irish Sugar, he joined Sinn Féin The Workers' Party, formerly Official Sinn Féin. He was elected in 1981, but lost his seat and regained it on a number of occasions. He moved to Democratic Left when the Workers' Party split, and later joined Labour on its merger. He retired due to ill health at the 2007 election.

Smith, Paddy (1901–1982), IRA volunteer and politician, was elected to the fourth Dáil and served in government from 1947. He was seen as truculent, and a frequent dissenter in Lemass's government.

Smurfit, Michael (1936–), businessman. Smurfit entered his father's packaging business at a young age, and quickly rose to senior positions in the company. As CEO he expanded the business, making it one of the largest in Europe. Smurfit also has interests in Ballymore, a large property company. He gave evidence to the Moriarty Tribunal that Haughey had solicited money from him.

Spring, Dick (1950–), Labour politician and Tánaiste. A former rugby international from Kerry, Spring was the son of a veteran Labour TD, Dan Spring. Seen as a moderate within Labour, he showed great maturity in holding the party together, and delivered a remarkable electoral triumph in 1992. He served in the second Reynolds government and Bruton government as Tánaiste and Minister for Foreign Affairs.

Sweetman, Gerard (1908–1970), politician. Educated at Downside School in England, which left him with a distinctive Anglo-Irish accent, and later at Trinity College, Dublin, Sweetman was elected to the Seanad for Fine Gael in 1943 and to the Dáil in 1948 for Kildare. He was appointed Minister for Finance in 1954, but his orthodox approach led to divisions within the government and unpopularity within Fine Gael. Sweetman was killed in a car accident in 1970.

Teahon, Paddy (1945–), civil servant. Teahon joined the civil service after leaving school in Killarney, Co. Kerry. He started in Posts & Telegraphs, then moved to Finance, and on to the Department of the Taoiseach when Economic Planning and Development was folded into it. He rose to be secretary of the department in 1993, and was a key figure in the Good Friday Agreement negotiations. He retired in 2000, and was made chairperson of Campus and Stadium Ireland

Development Ltd, also taking on a number of other private appointments, including with Treasury Holdings.

Traynor, Des (1931–1994), accountant, banker and financier, was the first clerk in Haughey Boland, becoming a partner in 1961. He was on the board of many companies, and through Guinness Mahon Bank, he facilitated a widespread tax evasion scheme for wealthy Irish people. Traynor managed Haughey's finances up to Traynor's death.

Traynor, Oscar (1886–1963) was a revolutionary and Fianna Fáil politician, who was a member of the IRB and Irish Volunteers, taking part in the 1916 Rising, and later an IRA organiser. He opposed the Treaty, and was initially opposed to de Valera's founding of Fianna Fáil, though he later joined the party, becoming a government minister. He was electorally very popular, usually polling over the quota.

Tunney, James (Jim) (1923–2002), Fianna Fáil politician. He was elected to the Dáil in 1969 for Dublin North-West. He was a Haughey loyalist, who served as party chairman for ten years. Tunney was known as 'The Yellow Rose of Finglas', because of his habit of wearing a yellow flower in his buttonhole.

Ward, Andrew (Andy) (1925–1999), civil servant. Born in County Cork, he joined the civil service in 1944 and moved to the Department of Justice in 1950. He rose to become one of the youngest secretaries in 1970, succeeding Peter Berry. He was well regarded as a thorough and impartial civil servant, who later helped with drafting the Anglo-Irish Agreement.

Whitaker, T. Kenneth (Ken) (1916–2017), civil servant and economist. Born in County Down and raised in Drogheda, he joined the civil service on leaving school. Seen as exceptionally bright, he was made Secretary of the Department of Finance in 1956 and was associated with the document *Economic Development* and the subsequent opening up of the Irish economy. In 1969 he became Governor of the Central Bank and was appointed a senator in 1977 by Jack Lynch and reappointed by Garret FitzGerald.

Wilson, John (1923–2007), Fianna Fáil politician. Wilson taught classics in schools and later at UCD before being elected to the Dáil in 1973. He was appointed to cabinet in 1977 as Minister for Education and then served in every Fianna Fáil cabinet until his retirement in 1993. In 1997 he sought the Fianna Fáil nomination for the presidency. He was generally seen as a moderate in the party.

Index

A
abortion 142–3, 157–61
Adams, Gerry 113, 114, 209–10, 211–12
Aer Lingus 25, 68
Argentina 138
Ahern, Bertie 11–12, 95, 146–7, 180, 214, 217, 219, 220, 232
Ahern, Dermot 210
AIBP 202
Aiken, Frank 33, 77, 91
Ainsworth, Joe 145
airspace, British access to 100
alcohol consumption and alcoholism 61
All-Party Oireachtas committee on the constitution 51
Alliance Party 80
Allied Irish Banks 149
An Fórsa Cosanta Áitiúil (FCA) 20
Andrews, David 148, 188
Anglo-Irish Agreement (1985) 172, 173, 179–80, 192, 206–7, 234–5, 240, 243
Anglo-Irish Treaty (1921) 19
  anti-Treaty supporters 17, 82
  pro-Treaty supporters 17, 20
  see also loyalists; nationalists; Northern Ireland; unionists
Aosdána 204
Apprentice Boys 49
'Arise and Follow Charlie' 115
arms amnesty, IRA 35
Arms Crisis 5, 55–8, 103, 110, 245
  trials 64–6, 74

Armstrong, Robert 171, 172, 176, 178, 207
Arnold, Bruce 136, 231
Articles 2 and 3, Irish constitution 51, 53, 80, 123, 176, 178
arts funding 44, 110, 204
assassination attempt against Margaret Thatch 176
'Asgard List' 182
Aylward, Seán 139

B
B-Specials 49
babies, abandoned 155–7
Barnes, Monica 159
Barrett, Seán 151
Barry, Peter 87–8, 112, 177, 178, 197, 223
Battle of the Bogside (1969) 49
beef processing and export 202–3, 205–6
Behan, Brendan 21
Bell, Tim 111
Belvedere College, Dublin 16
Berry, Peter 33, 35, 56–7, 59–60, 61, 64, 65, 110
Biaggi, Mario 169
Blair, Tony 11–12, 49
Blaney, Neil 40–1, 52, 54, 55–66, 67, 68, 74, 90, 132, 193, 219, 245
Boland, Harry 20, 23, 24, 237
Boland, John 153, 154, 184
Boland, Kevin 22, 52, 63, 64, 90
Bowman, John 224
Brady, Vincent 213–14
Brennan, Paudge 63

Brennan, Seamus 95, 188, 215, 220
Brighton bombing (1984) 176, 208–9
Briscoe, Ben 147, 148
British government 11–12, 49, 51, 52, 54, 79, 167
  access to Irish airspace 100
  Falklands War 138–9
  freeze in British—Irish relation 139
  general election (1974) 82
  H-Block hunger strikes 113–14, 116, 122
  invites talks with Sinn Féin 211–12, 235
  Irish extradition bill 207–9
  Margaret Thatcher and Northern Ireland 113–14, 122, 137–8, 169–71, 175
  ministerial talks and the Anglo-Irish Agreement (1985) 178–80, 207, 234–5
  New Ireland Forum Report 176–7, 178
  Prior initiative 137–8, 139
  Sunningdale Agreement 79–83
  withdrawal from Northern Ireland 82, 94, 173–4
  withdrawal from the Maastricht Treaty 201
British soldiers 2, 50, 210
Brooke, Peter 211
Brosnan, Seán 1
Browne, Dónal 156
Browne, Noël 25, 28, 46–7
Bruton, John 121, 125–6, 127, 142, 143, 151–2, 185, 189, 197, 241–2
Burke, Dick 72, 119, 135
Burke, Ray 134, 146, 147, 193, 221, 238
Burke-Savage SJ, Ronnie 16
by-elections
  1956 24
  1982 134–5
  Cork (1979) 3–4, 100, 110
  Donegal (1980) 10, 113
Byrne, Alfie 24
Byrne, John 42, 43

C
Cahill, Bernie 229, 230
Carey, Hugh 168
Carron, Owen 122
Carter, Jimmy 168
Casey, Bishop Eamonn 11
Cassells, Peter 197
Catholic Church 3, 11, 25, 72, 96, 154–5, 157, 158, 161, 163, 164, 233
'Celtic Tiger' 11, 14
Charles Haughey's Ireland TV documentary 195
Charles, Prince 2
Childers, Erskine 91
Christian Brothers Schools 15, 19
Citizens' Defence Committees 55–6, 65, 74
Cleary, Father Michael 11
Cluskey, Frank 103, 116, 117, 144, 187
coalition governments 12
  Fianna Fáil and Progressive Democrats (PDs) 215–20, 225–6
  Labour Party and Fine Gael 1, 32, 47, 70, 74, 94, 96
    under Garret FitzGerald 117–18, 119–21, 129, 143–5, 151–5, 157–65, 182, 190, 191
    1981 campaign and general election 114–17
    1982 (November) campaign and general election 142–3, 158–9
    Irish economy 118, 121–2, 125–8, 182, 183–8
    Northern Ireland policy 122–4 (*see also* Anglo-Irish Agreement (1985)
  under Liam Cosgrave
    1973 campaign and general election 76–7
    1977 campaign and general election 85–6
    Irish economy 84–5
    Northern Ireland policy 76, 78, 79–83
Colley, George 4–6, 7, 23–4, 26, 33, 40, 41, 43, 77, 91, 95, 97, 101, 104, 108, 125, 128, 131, 133, 151, 163, 239
Colley, Harry 23–4, 33
Collins, Gerry 138–9, 147, 230
Collins, Michael 19, 20, 23
Committee on the Constitution 51, 123, 124
Commonwealth 22

Connolly, Patrick 137
contraception 72–3, 85, 96, 99, 161–3
Cooney, Paddy 75, 87, 163
Coras Iompair Éireann 204
Corish, Brendan 32, 45, 52, 70, 76, 78
Cosgrave, Liam 38–9, 46, 47, 48, 52, 62–3, 82, 136
   and FitzGerald 72, 73, 74, 76, 77–8, 84
   Labour and Fine Gael coalition 76, 77–8, 82, 84, 85–6
   Offences Against the State Bill (1972) 75–6
Costello, Declan 27–8, 34, 38, 39, 87
Costello, John A. 28, 32, 47
Coughlan, Clem 146
Council of Ireland proposal 80–2
Cowen, Ber 147
Cox, Pat 217
Craig, Sir James 16
Criminal Justice Act 34
Cronin, Anthony 205
Cuban Socialism 46
Cumann na mBan 19
Cumann na nGaedheal 20
Currie, Austin 223, 227

D
the Dáil 8, 9, 12, 24, 38, 87, 193, 197
   abortion referendum 157–61
   Arms Crisis 59, 63–4
   civil servants' amendments to records 42
   Fianna Fáil and Progressive Democrat coalition 216–20
   Fianna Fáil lack of majority 141, 208, 213
   Fine Gael motion of no confidence in government (1982) 142
   GF's maiden speech 71
   GF's first speech as Taoiseach 118
   GF's request to dissolve 127, 128
   Haughey rebuilding career 93–4
   January 1982 budget debate 127
   Offences Against the State Bill (1972) 75–6
   opposition to Haughey as Taoiseach 103–4
   presidency contest 221–7

de Valera, Éamon 17, 20, 22, 23, 26, 51, 60, 123
de Valera, Síle 3, 100, 170
Deasy, Austin 153
death penalty 34, 124
Delaney, Colonel P.J. 61
Democratic Left 12
Democratic Unionist Party (DUP) 80
Dempsey, Noel 230
Department of Agriculture 35–6, 41, 43, 53, 119
Department of Defence 54, 55, 56, 134, 138, 230–1
Department of Education 37–8
Department of Finance 41, 43–4, 45, 46–7, 48, 77–8, 84–5, 87, 97, 105, 121, 127, 141, 151–2, 182, 183, 184, 189, 195–6, 199–200, 204
Department of Foreign Affairs 78, 105, 106, 119, 138–9, 176, 189
Department of Health and Social Welfare 5, 95, 96, 100, 159, 161, 184, 189
Department of Industry and Commerce 111, 185, 189, 202
Department of Justice 32–5, 53, 59, 63, 134, 135, 145
Department of Posts and Telegraphs 2
Department of Transport 59, 68
Desmond, Barry 111, 159, 161, 184, 189
Desmond, Dermot 203–4, 229, 230
Dillon, James 22, 27, 28, 32, 38
divorce 51, 99, 163–5
Divorce Action Group 164
Doherty, Seán 6–7, 99, 131, 134, 135–6, 145, 148, 231
Donegan, Paddy 98
Donlon, Seán 79, 83
Dooge, Jim 26, 119–20, 151, 187
Dowling, Brendan 112, 121
Downing Street Declaration 11–12
Doyle, P.V. 42
Dublin
   bombings (1974) 83
   city centre bombing (1972) 75–6
   H-Block hunger strike riots (1981) 116, 122, 172
   redevelopment 203–4, 220, 233
Dublin Castle refurbishment 220

Dublin Corporation 24
Dublin Corporation Scholarship 20
Dublin Gas 187
Dublin North-East constituency 31, 77
Duffy, Jim 223–5
Dukes, Alan 119, 183, 184, 189, 197–8, 212, 216, 222–3
Dunlop, Frank 106, 238
Dunne, Ben 235–6
Dunne, Donal 136–7

E
Easter Rising 17
The Economist 26, 234
economy, Irish 2, 6, 10, 11, 14, 24, 26, 31, 32, 77, 84–5, 86, 107–8, 110, 111–12, 118, 121–2, 125–8, 141, 143, 144–5, 151–2, 153, 184–8, 190, 191–2, 195–6, 198, 220, 234
education, free secondary 37–8
electoral system, Irish 46, 51–2, 191
Electricity Supply Board (ESB) strikes 201
Elizabeth II, Queen 2
the Emergency 18
emigration 26, 181, 185, 186, 200
Enniskillen Remembrance Day bombing 207, 209
European Commission 134–5, 186–7
European Convention for the Suppression of Terrorism 207
European Economic Community (EEC) 26, 33, 76, 78, 105, 138, 202, 220–2, 234
European Movement 26
European Parliament 99, 214
European Union (EU) 240
Extradition Act 180, 191, 207–8, 209

F
Fagan, Anthony 59
Fahey, Jackie 99
Falklands War 138–9
Fallon, Garda Richard 'Dick' 59–60
Family Planning Bill 161–2, 163
the Famine 34
farmers/agricultural industry 2, 36, 84, 97

fascism 17
Faulkner, Brian 81–2
Faulkner, Pádraig 54
Federated Union of Employers 45, 198
female cabinet minister, first 105
feminism/feminist groups 73, 96, 116, 154, 157
Fennell, Nuala 116
Fianna Fáil xiv, 1, 2–4, 12, 20, 213, 230, 242, 244–5, 246
   1961 general election 32–3
   1965 general election 38, 40
   1969 campaign and general election 43, 46–8
   1973 campaign and general election 77, 91
   1977 campaign and general election 86–6, 94–5
   1981 campaign and general election 114–17
   1982 (February) campaign and general election 9, 128–9, 130
   1982 (November) campaign and general election 142–3
   1987 campaign and general election 191–2
   1989 campaign and general 214–16
   Árd Fheis (1970) 57
   Árd Fheis (1980) 109–10
   Árd Fheis (1990) 209, 228
   Árd Fheis (1991) 228
   Arms Crisis 55–70
   candidate to run for Dáil presidency 221–7
   CH asks GF to work for him 26–7
   CH choses first government 104–6
   CH choses second government 131–2, 133–4
   CH elected as leader 4–10, 101, 103–4
   CH elected to the National Executive 24, 90–1
   CH joins committee on party reorganisation 24
   CH manoeuvres Lynch out of leadership 99–101
   CH rebuilds career in the 1970s 89–91, 93–7

CH runs in 1951 and 1954 general
elections 23–4
coalition with Progressive Democrats (PDs) 10, 12, 215–20,
225–6
defections to the Progressive
Democrats (PDs) 188
GF votes for party 26, 27
Lemass retirement and replacement
39–41
and Northern Ireland policy 50–4,
66, 94, 109–10, 173, 174–5, 179
(*see also above* Arms Crisis)
Offences Against the State Bill
(1972) 75
party leadership challenges 130–1,
146–8
Programme for Economic Expansion 26, 31, 32
Programme for National Recovery
(PNR) 192, 201
property development 42–3
rejection of extradition bill 208, 209
the TACA 42
vote of no confidence against CH
139–41
The Way Forward programme 141,
142
see also Haughey, Charles (Cathal)
J., Lemass, Seán; Lynch, Jack
Fine Gael 3–4, 9, 10, 12, 21, 22, 26,
27–8, 212, 242, 245
1969 campaign and general election
47, 48
1977 campaign and general election
85–6, 98
1981 campaign and general election
114–17
1982 (February) campaign and
general election 129, 130
1982 (November) campaign and
general election 142–3, 158–9
1987 campaign and general election
188, 191, 192
1989 campaign and general election
215–16
amateurism 27, 85, 97
Anglo-Irish Agreement (1985) 180
Árd Fheis (1977) 85

Árd Fheis (1978) 98
Árd Fheis (1986) 189–90
Arms Crisis 62–3
candidate to run for Dáil presidency
222–3
coalition with Labour Party 1, 47,
70, 74, 76–7, 80–1, 84–6, 94,
117–18, 117–18, 119–24, 125–8,
129, 143–5, 151–5, 157–65, 182,
183–8, 190–1
Cosgrave replaces Dillon 38–9
fiftieth Árd Fheis 74
general election (1961) 32–3
general election (1965) 28, 38
GF elected Taoiseach (1981) 117–18
GF reforms 98–9, 110
GF resignation and new leadership
contest 197–8
GF voted in as leader 87
IRA murder party senator 83
Irish electoral system 46
move towards social democracy
27–8
Offences Against the State Bill
(1972) 75
'quota squatting' 98
on the Succession Act 34
support for Fianna Fáil 197
Tallaght Strategy 198, 201, 213, 216
Towards a Just Society paper 39, 47
see also Cosgrave, Liam; Dukes,
Alan; FitzGerald, Garret
Finlay, Fergus 143–4
FitzGerald, Alexis 28, 120, 151, 153
FitzGerald, Desmond (Tommy) 16–18,
23
FitzGerald, Eithne 144
FitzGerald, Garret xiii–xv, 12, 240–3,
245, 246
1981 campaign and general election
114–17
1982 (February) campaign and
general election 129, 130
1982 (November) campaign and
general election 142–3
1987 campaign and general election
188, 191, 193
7 Days TV show 84
Árd Fheis speech (1986) 189–90

FitzGerald, Garret (cont.)
  Arms Crisis 59, 103
  on British unilateral withdrawal from Northern Ireland 82
  as candidate for the Dáil presidency 222–5
  canvasses for Liam Cosgrave's removal as leader of Fine Gael 72, 74, 76, 84
  Catholicism 72
  character xv, 3, 8, 21, 71, 73
  childhood 15–16, 17
  choses first government 119–21
  choses second government 151–2
  collapsed companies and government bailouts 187–8
  contraception 161–2
  death of 14, 240
  distrust of Charles Haughey 8–9, 74, 103–4
  divorce policy 163–5
  Donegal by-election (1980) 10
  early ambitions to lead Fine Gael 72
  early support of Fine Gael 22, 27–8
  education 16, 21
  elected Taoiseach (1981) 117–18
  elected to the Dáil (1969) 48
  election campaign (1969) 47
  family background 8, 15–18
  free education policy 37–8
  on the front bench of Fine Gael 71–2, 73
  Garda 'heavy gang' allegations 156–7
  general election (1961) 32
  Irish economy 76, 84–5, 112, 118, 121–2, 125–8, 144–5, 151–2, 153, 181–3, 186–8, 190, 191, 199, 203, 234, 241–2
  1983 budget 183–4
  1984 budget 186
  lack of plans for growth 184–6
  leaders debate against CH 129
  maiden Dáil speech 71
  marriage 23
  and the media 9, 47, 53, 72, 73, 84, 215, 240
  membership of the EEC 78
  as Minister of Foreign Affairs 78–80, 81, 83, 87
  minister reshuffle plans (1986) 188–9
  move away from social democracy 189–90
  move towards the left/social democracy 26, 28, 36–7, 39, 222
  non-political career 25–6, 28–9
  Northern Ireland policy 11, 27, 50, 52–3, 71, 74, 78, 79–80, 81, 83–4, 99, 122–4, 143, 152, 167, 171–4
  ministerial talks and the Anglo-Irish Agreement (1985) 178–9, 192, 234–5, 240, 243
  New Ireland Forum and Forum Report 173, 174–8
  Offences Against the State Bill (1972) 75
  over-long and detailed government meetings 153–4
  personal finances 92–3, 240
  Pro-life and abortion referendum 157–61
  Public Accounts Committee (PAC) inquiry into Haughey controlled relief funds 74–5
  reforms Fine Gael 98–100, 110
  relationship with Charles Haughey 7–8, 12, 26–7, 29, 242–3, 246
  resignation as Fine Gael leader 197–8
  retirement 239–41
  runs for the Seanad (1965) 28–9
  the SDLP and John Hume 79–80, 81, 83
  speaks out on Haughey's election 7–8
  as spokesperson for Finance 73–4, 76, 77
  on the Succession Act 34
  support for Allies, WWII 22
  supports Haughey's government 197
  at UCD 18, 21, 23, 26, 28
  US attitude to Northern Ireland conflict 83–4
  voted in as Fine Gael leader 87–8
  wealth tax 76, 84–5
  women's rights 73

Fitzgerald, Gene 105–6
FitzGerald (née O'Farrell), Joan 23, 84, 119, 239, 246
Fitzgerald, Liam 230
FitzGerald (née McConnell), Mabel 16–18, 50
FitzGerald, Mark 121
FitzGerald, Patrick 16
Flynn, Pádraig 134, 199, 214, 217–18, 220, 226, 230
Foxe, Tom 219
France 17
Free State Army 19, 53
free travel 13, 44

G
Gaelic League 16
Gallagher, Matt 25, 42, 43
Garda Síochána 35, 59, 135
   Arms Crisis 61
   'Heavy Gang' allegations 85, 156–7
   IRA arms seizures 208
   the Kerry Babies 155–6
   murder of Richard Fallon 59–60
   Offences Against the State Bill (1972) 75
   phone tapping controversy 145
   Special Branch intelligence 54, 55
Gargan, Bridie 137
Garland, Roger 219
General Belgrano, sinking of the 138
general elections, Irish
   1951 23–4
   1961 26, 32–3
   1965 28, 38, 40
   1973 76–7
   1977 85–6
   1981 114–17
   1987 192–3
   1989 214–16
   February 1982 9, 128–30
   November 1982 142–3
Geoghegan-Quinn, Máire 105, 218, 228
German reunification 221
Gibbons, Jim 54, 55, 56, 58, 60, 61, 63, 64–6, 68, 96, 141
Gillespie, Patsy 210
Glenn, Alice 116, 164

Good Friday/Belfast Agreement 12, 79, 233
Goodall, David 176
Goodman International 202–3
Goodman, Larry 202, 205–6
Goulding, Cathal 54
Gow, Ian 179, 209
GPO 17, 26
Gray, Tony 31
Green Party 12
Greencore scandal 229
Gregory, Tony 130, 142, 193
GUBU acronym coined 137
Guinness Mahon merchant bank 92
Guinness Peat Aviation 240

H
Halligan, Brendan 144
Hall's Pictorial Weekly 84
Hanafin, Des 134
Harney, Mary 179, 188, 215–16, 236
Harte, Paddy 49, 175
Haughey Boland accountants 23, 24–5, 92
Haughey, Charles (Cathal) J. xiii–xv, 243–6
   1973 campaign and general election 77, 91
   1977 campaign and general election 86, 89, 94–5
   1981 campaign and general election 114–17
   1982 (February) campaign and general election 9, 128–9, 130
   1982 (November) campaign and general election 142–3
   1987 campaign and general election 192–3
   1989 campaign and general election 214–16
   affair with Terry Keane 91–2, 236
   Arms Crisis and trial 5, 7, 8, 55–70, 103, 110, 245
   asks GH to work for Fianna Fáil 26–7
   Attorney General's involvement in murder 136–7
   Ben Dunne payments scandal 235–6

Haughey, Charles (Cathal) J. (cont.)
  building links with trade unions and employers 198–9, 200–1
  calls an election to block private members' motion 213–15
  calls for Lynch's resignation 66, 69, 89
  as candidate for Taoiseach on Lemass's retirement 39–40, 41
  character xv, 5, 7, 9–10, 14, 19–20, 21, 33, 41–2, 67, 107, 196, 239, 243–4, 246
  Charles Haughey's Ireland TV documentary 195
  choses first government 104–6
  choses second government 131–2, 133–4
  coalition with Progressive Democrats (PDs) 10, 12, 215–20
  contraception 96, 161–3
  daily operations as Fianna Fáil leader 106–7
  death 14
  death of Donogh O'Malley 44–5
  death penalty and Criminal Justice Act 34
  divorce policy 164
  Dublin Corporation seat 24
  Dublin North-East constituency 31, 77
  education 15, 18, 19–20
  elected as Fianna Fáil party leader 4–7, 10, 101
  elected to Fianna Fáil National Executive 24, 90–1
  election campaign (1969) 46–7
  environmental concerns 221
  extradition bill and the British government 207–9
  Falklands War 138–9
  family background 8, 15, 18–20
  father-in-law, Lemass resigns leadership 39–40
  final months in office 227
  financial support for pensioners 44
  financial support for sport and the arts 44, 110, 204–5
  first Árd Fheis (1980) 109–10
  first election to the Dáil 24
  free education policy 37–8
  free legal aid policy 34
  free travel policy 13, 44
  freeze in British—Irish relations 139
  funding for victims of the Troubles 54–5, 59, 74–5, 92 (*see also above* Arms Crisis and trial)
  general elections (1951 and 1954) 23–4
  government buildings upgraded 205
  GUBU acronym coined 137
  H-Block hunger strikes 113–14, 116, 122, 170–1
  hospitalised after a 'riding accident' 62
  and the IRA and Sinn Féin/Sinn Féin WP 54, 55, 93, 114, 122, 131–2, 142, 209–10
  Irish economy 6, 31, 107–8, 110, 111–12, 121, 127, 128–9, 141, 191–2, 234
    growing the 195–6, 198–206, 246
  Irish Financial Service Centre (IFSC) 203–4
  joins Fianna Fáil 22
  leaders debate against GF 129
  leadership challenges 131–2, 146–8
  Lenihan as candidate for the Dáil presidency 221–2, 223–6
  links to multiple scandals and decision to resign 229–32
  Macushla Revolt 35
  manoeuvres Lynch out of leadership 99–101
  marriage 23
  McCreevy vote of no confidence 139–40
  and the media 9–10, 14, 31, 39–40, 42, 43, 68, 107, 145, 195
  as Minister for Health and Social Welfare 5, 95, 96, 100, 108
  as Minister of Agriculture 35–8, 39, 43, 53
  as Minister of Finance 41, 42–4, 45, 46–7, 48, 54, 70, 74, 112
  as Minister of Justice 32–5
  National Industrial and Economic Council 45
  non-political career 23, 24

Northern Ireland policy 35, 52–4, 57, 83, 94, 109–10, 113–14, 137–8, 139, 167–71, 173, 245
Anglo-Irish Agreement (1985) 179–80, 192, 206–7
Hume—Adams talks 209–10
New Ireland Forum and Forum Report 174–5, 177
and talks with John Major 211–12
Offences Against the State Bill (1972) 75
Official Secrets Act 35
opposes amended Extradition Act 180
as opposition leader 124–5, 195
PAC inquiry 74–5, 89
party loses Dáil majority (1982) 141
peace in Northern Ireland 11–12
petrol tanker drivers strike 108
phone tapping controversy 135–6, 145, 147–8, 231
political mishaps and miscalculations after 1982 election to Taoiseach 133, 134–7
post-retirement scandals 235–8
pragmatic approach to politics 13
as president of the European Council (1990) 220–1
Pro-life and abortion referendum 157–61
Programme for National Recovery (PNR) 192, 201
property acquisitions 43, 92
property development and redevelopment 42–3, 204–5
public image overhaul 111
rebuilding career in the 1970s 89–91, 93–7, 107–8
relationship with Garret FitzGerald 7–8, 12, 26–7, 29, 246
resignation from office 232
restrictions on tobacco advertising 96
retirement speech 235
road accident 45
sacked by Lynch 5, 63
sacks Lenihan 226–7
Single European Act (SEA) 202
Special Criminal Court 35
The Spirit of the Nation book of speeches 195

as spokesman on Health and Social Welfare 93
state assisted pay bargaining 112
Succession Act 13, 34
suspect financial affairs and lavish lifestyle 5, 8, 14, 24–5, 41–2, 43, 91–2, 103, 148–9, 206, 235–8, 246
the TACA 42
televised address to the nation (1980) 107–8, 111
at UCD 20, 21, 22–3
The Way Forward programme 141, 142, 196
Haughey, Ciarán 229
Haughey, Conor 229
Haughey, Johnnie 18–19, 20, 23
Haughey (née Lemass), Maureen/Máirín 23, 40
Haughey, Patrick 'Jock' 24, 54–5, 56, 57, 67, 74
Haughey (née McWilliams), Sarah 18–19
'Haughey's Fusiliers' 20
Hayes, Joanne 155–7
Healy, John 9, 37–8, 42, 72
Healy, Shay 231
Heath, Ted 79, 82
Hefferon, Colonel Michael 55–6, 57, 58, 63, 65
Heney, Michael 68
Higgins, Jim 213–14
Higgins, Michael D. 85, 117, 130, 144
High Court 73
Hillery, Paddy 35, 37, 39, 45, 48, 52, 57, 62, 68, 90, 95–6, 118, 128, 193, 221–2, 223, 224–5, 226
Honohan, Patrick 120, 182, 186
horse breeding 44
Howe, Geoffrey 178
Hume, John 79–80, 81, 83, 169, 173, 207, 209–10, 211
Hume—Adams talks 209–10
hunger strikes, H-Block 113–14, 116, 122, 170–1, 172
Hurd, Douglas 178
Hussey, Gemma 154, 160, 175, 183, 189

I

industrial action *see* strikes
Industrial Development Agency (IDA) 201–2, 206
inflation rates 1–2, 121–2, 181, 186
Insurance Corporation of Ireland 187
Irish Army 49, 50, 52, 54, 55–6, 57–8, 61, 63, 108, 208
  see also Kelly, Captain James
Irish Civil War 19
Irish Congress of Trade Unions (ICTU) 45, 112, 198–9
Irish Financial Service Centre (IFSC) 203
Irish Free State 15
Irish Independent 123, 160
Irish Museum of Modern Art 205
Irish National Caucus (INC) 168–9
Irish Press 84, 100, 146
Irish Republican Army (IRA) 13, 18, 53, 81, 93, 168, 211
  arms amnesty 35
  Arms Crisis 54–70
  Border campaign 34–5
  Dublin and Monaghan bombings (1974) 83
  extradition of suspects 207–9, 230
  H-Block hunger strikes 113–14, 116, 122, 170–1, 172
  Hume–Adams talks 209–10
  kidnap of Dutch business man (1975) 83
  murder of Fine Gael senator 83
  murder of UK ambassador to Dublin (1976) 83
  split between Officials and Provisionals 56
  targeting British soldiers 210
  see also Provisional IRA; Sinn Féin/Sinn Féin the Workers' Party
Irish Republicans 8, 16–17
Irish Shipping 187–8
Irish Steel 185
Irish Times xiii, 9, 14, 22, 25, 31, 42, 43, 86, 172, 183–4, 225, 240
Irish Volunteers 17, 19

J

Jacques Delors Commission 202
John Paul II, Pope 3

K

Kavanagh, Patrick 21
Keane, Terry 91–2, 108, 148
Keating, Justin 45, 85, 186–7
Kelly, Captain James 55–6, 57–8, 59, 60, 61, 62, 65, 66
Kelly, John 120, 145
Kemmy, Jim 117, 126, 127, 143
Kenneally, Willie 5
Kennedy, Geraldine 95, 136
Kennedy, Ted 168
Kerrigan, Pat 1
Kerry Babies 155–7
Killilea, Mark 99
King, Tom 178, 207
Kirk, Seamus 147
Kissinger, Henry 183
Kohl, Helmut 221

L

Labour Court 108
Labour Party 1, 12, 27, 32, 45–7, 48, 70, 74, 76, 116, 117, 129, 130, 142, 143–5, 152, 163, 173, 182, 183, 190–1, 192, 223
  coalition with Fine Gael 47, 70, 74, 76–7, 80–1, 84–6, 117–18, 119–24, 125–8, 129, 143–5, 151–5, 157–65, 182, 183–8
Labour Party, British 82, 83
language, Irish 16, 18
Larkin, Jim 1
The Late Late Show TV show 73, 236
Lawlor, Liam 90, 228
Leahy, Pat xiii–xiv
legal aid, provision of free 34
Leinster House 4, 5–6
Lemass, Peggy 23
Lemass, Seán 23, 24, 25, 27, 31–2, 33, 35, 36, 37–8, 39, 40, 41, 42, 44, 50–1, 90, 107, 123

Lenihan, Brian 33, 35, 37, 40, 51, 89, 93, 101, 105, 106, 146–7, 169, 179, 221–2, 223–7, 236
Lillis, Michael 120, 176, 178
Linehan, Hugh xiii–xiv
Local Defence Force 18, 20
Loughnane, Dr Bill 100, 141
Lovett, Ann 155
loyalists 49, 65, 75, 82
Luykx, Albert 57–8
Lynch, Jack 1, 2–3, 4, 38, 39, 41, 43–4, 48, 49–50, 51–2, 55, 56, 71, 109
  Arms Crisis 56–7, 60–3, 66, 67–9
  bringing Haughey back in to the fold 93
  Offences Against the State Bill (1972) 75
  as Taoiseach (1966–1973) 41, 43–4, 48, 49–50, 51–2, 55, 56, 71
  as Taoiseach (1977–1979) 86, 95, 97, 99–101
Lynch, Mr Justice Kevin 157

M
Maastricht Treaty 201
Mac Conghail, Muiris 89–90
McAleese, Mary 234
Macarthur, Malcolm 137
McConnell, John 16, 50
McCracken Tribunal 235–6
McCreevy, Charlie 125, 139, 188, 215, 216
McDaid, Jim 230–1
McDowell, Michael 188
McEllistrim, Tom 99
McEntee, Seán 28, 33
MacEoin, Lieutenant General Seán 59, 68
McGee, Mary 73, 96
McGuinness, Martin 233–4
Mackay, Paul 134
McLaughlin, Mitchel 210
McLaughlin, Patrick 145
McMahon, Phil 63
MacSharry, Ray xiv, 5–6, 105, 125, 131, 141, 145, 175, 180, 195–6, 199–200, 214
Macushla Revolt 35
McWilliams, Pat 20

Magill 110
Major, John 11–12, 201, 211
Mallon, Seamus 175, 179
Mansergh, Martin 106, 195, 210
Mara, PJ 6, 90, 95, 106, 125, 146, 147, 215, 221, 228–9
media coverage
  Charles Haughey 9–10, 14, 31, 39–40, 42, 43, 107, 145, 195
  Garret FitzGerald 9, 47, 53, 72, 73, 84, 215, 240
milk and beef prices 36
Mills, Michael 84
Molly, Bobby 188, 217, 220
Moloney, Ed 245
Monaghan bombings (1974) 83
Moore, Charles 178
Moriarty Tribunal 236–7
Morning Ireland xiv–xv
Mother and Child Scheme 25
Mountbatten, Lord 2, 100, 169
Moynihan, Patrick 168
Mulcahy, Richard 32
Murphy, Brian 224
Murphy, Gary 68
music revival, Irish 3

N
Nally, Dermot 118, 153, 168, 170, 172, 176, 178, 189, 196
National Coalition of Fine Gael and Labour
  see under coalition governments
National Development Corporation (NDC) 152, 185
National Economic and Social Council (NESC) 105, 185–6, 199
National Farmers' Association (NFA) 36
National Industrial and Economic Council 45
National Planning Board 184
National Treasury Management Agency Act (1990) 204
nationalists/nationalism, Irish 11–12, 16, 49, 79, 80, 81, 169, 173, 175
  see also Irish Republican Army (IRA); Provisional IRA; Sinn Féin/Sinn Féin the Workers' Party

Nazi Germany 22
Nealon, Ted 84, 98
New Ireland Forum and Forum
    Report 173, 174–8
Nighthawks TV show 231
Nolan, M.J. 230
Noonan, Michael 126, 145, 159, 240
Noraid 169
Northern Ireland
    Anglo-Irish Agreement (1985) 178–80
    Arms Crisis 5, 55–70
    Fianna Fáil policy 2, 6, 8, 50–4, 66, 94, 109–10, 174–5, 179 (see also under Haughey, Charles (Cathal) J.)
    Fine Gael and the Fine Gael–Labour coalition policy 76, 78, 79–82, 122–4, 180 (see also under FitzGerald, Garret)
    Good Friday/Belfast Agreement 233–4
    government 51, 79–83, 169, 173, 178–80, 233–4
    Prior initiative 137–8, 139
    prospect of peace 11–12
    and Seán Lemass 50–1
    Stormont parliament suspended 79
    Sunningdale Agreement/power-sharing executive 79–83, 174
    the Troubles 2–3, 11, 49–54
    'unity by consent' policy 27, 50–2, 66
    see also Irish Republican Army (IRA); Provisional IRA; Sinn Féin/Sinn Féin the Workers' Party
Northern Ireland Assembly 173
Northern Ireland Constitutional Proposals, British government White Paper 79–82
Norton, William 32

O
Ó Dálaigh, Cearbhall 83, 98
Ó Faoláin, Seán 17
Ó hAnnracháin, Pádraig 106, 114, 135
Ó Móráin, Micheál 59, 60–1, 62–3

O'Brien, Conor Cruise 43, 45, 65, 80, 81, 82, 86, 137, 161, 242
O'Connell, John 132
O'Connor, Jack 201
O'Connor, Pat 134
O'Donnell, Brendan 95, 106
O'Donoghue, Martin 94–5, 125, 128, 133, 140, 145, 148
Offences Against the State Bill (1972) 75, 83
Official Secrets Act 35
Ó hEocha, Colm 174
O'Higgins, Thomas (Tom) 72, 76, 87, 129
Ó hUiginn, Pádraig 105, 106, 109, 111, 120, 141, 186, 199, 200, 201, 203, 206, 214
oil crises 1, 84, 97, 109, 181
O'Kennedy, Michael 94, 101, 105, 146, 147
O'Leary, Michael 126, 129, 142, 163
O'Malley, Desmond xiv, 10, 45, 63, 93, 101, 104, 108, 111, 125, 128, 131, 133, 136, 139, 140, 147, 162–3, 175, 188, 212, 216–20, 239, 231–2
O'Malley, Donogh 33, 35, 37–8, 40, 44–5
O'Neill, Captain Terence 51
O'Neill, Tip 168

P
Paircéir, Séamus 229, 230
Paisley, Rev. Ian 80, 233–4
Papal Mass, Dublin 3
Papal Mass, Galway 11
'paper branches' 98
Parnells GAA 21
PAYE workers 97, 183, 186
pensioners, financial support for 44
petrol tanker driver strikes 108
phone tapping controversy 135–6, 145, 147–8, 231
PMPA 187
postal strikes 2, 100
Powell, Charles 207
Power, Paddy 133–4, 138
Power, Seán 230
Prendergast, Peter 98, 151

Prior initiative 137–8, 139
Prior, Jim 139
Pro-Life Amendment Campaign (PLAC) 157–61
Programme for National Recovery (PNR) 192, 201
Progressive Democrats (PDs) 12, 188, 190–1, 192, 212, 215–20, 225–6
property development, Dublin 42–3
Protestant Church 160
Protestants 18, 71, 82, 110, 175, 211
  see also loyalists; unionists
Provisional IRA 2, 5, 6, 55–6, 66, 74, 75, 82, 122, 168, 169, 174, 175, 176, 245
Public Accounts Committee (PAC) inquiry into the Haughey-controlled relief funds 74–5, 89

Q
Questions and Answers TV show 224–5
'quota squatting' 98

R
Rafter, Kevin 110
Reagan, Ronald 178
Red Cross, Irish 54
Reid, Fr Alec 209, 210
revolution, Irish 15
Reynolds, Albert 11–12, 99–100, 105, 125, 131, 202, 214, 217, 218, 219, 220, 230
Robinson, Mary 12, 72, 223, 226–7, 233
rock bands, Irish 3
Rogers, John 143
RTÉ 9–10, 63, 73, 84, 110, 138, 145, 193, 224, 229, 231
RUC (Royal Ulster Constabulary) 49
Ryan, Eoin 26, 124
Ryan, Fr Patrick 208–9
Ryan, Richie 72, 74, 78, 84–5, 87, 119

S
Sands, Bobby 113–14
Saor Éire 59
Schlüter, Otto 59
Schmidt, Helmut 198

SDLP 79–80, 83, 173, 174–5, 178, 179, 207, 209, 223
Seanad 28, 38, 71, 119–20, 124
Second World War 20, 22
7 Days TV show 84
sex, extramarital 155
Shaw, George Bernard 16
Sherlock, Joe 126
Single European Act (SEA) 190–1, 202
Sinn Féin/Sinn Féin the Workers' Party 13, 17, 94, 113, 122, 130, 131–2, 142, 174, 192, 209–10, 211–12, 235
Smith, Paddy 35
Smurfit, Michael 229, 238
Social Partnership 13
social welfare system 27, 77, 100, 112, 186
Socialist International 45
Somers, Michael 204
Spanish Civil War 17
Special Criminal Court 35
The Spirit of the Nation (C. Haughey) 195
sports funding 44
Spring, Dick xiv, 10, 142, 143–5, 152–3, 158–9, 178, 183, 184, 185, 189, 230
St Joseph's CBS, Fairview 20
Stardust nightclub fire disaster 113
Stormont executive 79, 82
Strategy for Development (P. Ó hUiginn) 199
Studies 27
Succession Act 13, 34
Sunday Independent 85, 156–7
Sunday Tribune 123–4
Sunningdale Agreement 79–83, 174
Supreme Court 33, 64, 73
Sutherland, Peter 120–1, 159, 160
Sweetman, Gerard 47

T
TACA 42
Talbot Motor Assembly plant dispute 111
Tallaght Strategy 198, 201, 213, 216

tax
　avoidance 43, 235, 237
　cuts 2, 77, 199, 220
　exemptions 44
　income tax 97, 181, 183, 186, 204
　increases 112
　inequality protests (1979) 1
　shelters 220
Teahon, Paddy 244
Telecom Éireann 229
telecoms system, national 2
Telesis Report 110
Thatcher, Margaret 113, 122–3, 137–8, 169–71, 175, 176–80, 196, 207–8, 211
The Way Forward programme 141, 142, 196
This Week radio show 193
Thornley, David 45
tobacco advertising, restriction on 96
Today Tonight TV show xv, 127
Tóibín, Colm 240
Towards a Just Society paper, Fine Gael's 27–8, 39, 47
Traynor, Des 92, 236
Traynor, Oscar 23–4, 32–3
the Troubles 2–3, 11, 49–54
　Battle of the Bogside (1969) 49
　see also Irish Republican Army IRA; Provisional IRA
Tully, James 76
Tunney, Jim 146–7, 148
Tunney Report 148

U
Ulster Unionist Party (UUP) 80, 81–2
Ulster Volunteer Force 18
Ulster Workers' Council strike 82–3

unemployment 1–2, 11, 181, 186, 187
unionists 13, 18, 49, 53, 79, 80, 81, 82–3, 94, 124, 169, 172, 173, 174, 177, 179, 207
United Nations (UN) 50, 52, 139–40
United States of America (USA) 52, 73, 100, 158
　attitude to Northern Ireland conflict 83–4, 168, 179
　Congressional Irish lobby 178
　Four Horsemen 168
　Irish National Caucus (INC) 168
University College Dublin (UCD) 18, 20, 21, 22–3, 26, 28

V
Varadkar, Leo 241
VAT increases 127, 128, 183
Vatican II 51
VE Day 22

W
Walsh, Joe 217
Walsh, Mr Justice Brian 33, 64, 73, 124
War of Independence 18, 19
Ward, Andy 145
Whitaker, Ken 44, 52, 53, 174
William Binchy lawyers 164–5
Wilson, Harold 82–3
Wilson, John 147, 148, 222
women's rights 73, 96
　see also abortion; contraception; divorce
Woods, Michael 6
worker lock-out protests (1913) 1

Y
Yeats, W.B. 17